What Professionals are Saying . . .

Mike Lew's work must be read! The male sexual abuse victim has been denied, ignored, mistreated for far too long.   —Claudia Black, author of *It Will Never Happen To Me*

Mike Lew offers hope, encouragement, and practical strategies to promote healing. Professionals may wish to have several copies of this work available—one for the office and several to loan.   •   —*Virginia Child Protection Newsletter*

Supportive and practical . . . Intended as a "survivor's manual," it offers insights that counselors, clinicians, and therapists will appreciate.
—*Readings;* American Orthopsychiatric Association

Mike Lew has made an important attempt to address the effects of sexual molestation of males, and provides hope and direction for their recovery.

—*Guidepost*, American Association for Counseling and Development

An important book, and an outstanding guide to recovery.   —*Gay Community News*

What Readers are Saying . . .

What I've gotten from *Victims No Longer* is so wonderful and affirming! Out of all my gut/heart wrenching pain is *hope*.   —a male survivor from Michigan

I am so relieved to know that as long as I continue to work on this I might live a productive, healthy life. It's the nicest Christmas present I've received in years.

—a male survivor from South Dakota

I am overwhelmed by *Victims No Longer*. It applies as much to me as a survivor as to any man. Thank you for putting it all into words . . . It is devastating and soothing at the same time.   —a female survivor from Massachusetts who is the mother of a male survivor

Your book has given me new understanding and insight into my current relationship with a man who is an incest survivor. Your chapter for "pro-survivors" was most welcome.   —the male partner of a male survivor from New York

Victims No Longer helped me to know I was not alone with my feelings, and offered an objective viewpoint which has hopefully given my husband direction for recovery which I could never give him. Thank you.   —the wife of a male survivor in Massachusetts

Thank you, thank you, thank you for your book *Victims No Longer!*

—a male survivor from Oregon who is a priest

Victims No Longer

MEN RECOVERING FROM INCEST and
OTHER SEXUAL CHILD ABUSE

by MIKE LEW

Foreword by ELLEN BASS

HarperCollins*Publishers*

Grateful acknowledgment is made for permission to reprint:

Selected excerpts from *The Prince of Tides* by Pat Conroy. Copyright © 1986 by Pat Conroy. Reprinted by permission of Houghton Mifflin Company.

Selection from *The Survivor's Suite* by Keith Jarrett. Copyright © 1977 by Keith Jarrett. Reprinted by permission of ECM Records.

This book was previously published in hardcover in 1988 by Nevraumont Publishing Co. It is here reprinted by arrangement with Nevraumont Publishing Co.

First PERENNIAL LIBRARY edition published 1990.

Designer: Barbara DuPree Knowles

LIBRARY OF CONGRESS CATALOGING-IN-PUBLICATION DATA

Lew, Mike.
   Victims no longer: men recovering from incest and other sexual child abuse/by Mike Lew; foreword by Ellen Bass.—1st Perennial Library ed.
    p. cm.
   Reprint. Originally published: New York, NY: Nevraumont Pub. Co., 1988.
   ISBN 0-06-097300-5
   1. Adult child sexual abuse victims—United States—Psychology. 2. Incest victims—United States—Psychology. 3. Boys—United States—Abuse of—Psychological aspects. 4. Men—United States—Psychology. I. Title.
HQ72.U53L48 1990
362.7′6—dc20   89-45839

   01 02 DT/RRD 30 29 28 27 26 25 24 23

To my colleagues who care,
To the memory of abuse victims who were overcome by the struggle,
And to all incest survivors as they recover and flourish,
I dedicate this book with respect and admiration.

Contents

PART FOUR
ABOUT RECOVERY

Acknowledgments

It is impossible to give adequate thanks to the many people who provided me with information, help, advice, encouragement, solace and understanding during the writing of *Victims No Longer*. The book would not exist without them, and I am grateful for the part that each has played in my life.

I have been especially fortunate in having had more than my share of outstanding teachers, mentors and friends. The late Professor Carol Fisher of Syracuse University showed me that it is possible to push students to the limits of their intellectual and critical capacities without any loss of kindness, humanity or humor. Professor H. Daniel Smith, of the same institution, shared unstintingly of his love of learning and his openness to the great traditions of Eastern and Western cultures. The late Dr. Margaret Mead continually challenged, frustrated, confused, frightened, bullied, teased and encouraged me to be more than I thought I was—and kept on demonstrating that popularizing a subject leads to wider availability of information. Dr. Colin M. Turnbull expressed his deep love of humankind in all its diversity—in the beauty of his writing and the generosity with which he encouraged a young graduate student. Professor Joan Phillips Gordon took a chance on me, and kept on taking chances on "nontraditional" students and teachers. And my friend and colleague Professor Shalom Endleman, for more years than seems possible, has steadfastly helped me navigate academic and professional shoals. I shall always be grateful to all of them.

For sharing so generously of their expertise and insight, for specific information and suggestions, and for their unflagging support of this project, I owe special thanks to my professional colleagues: Mercedes Cabral, Betsy Moore, Jim Fereira, Andrea Soler, Carol DiGianni, Bob Poole, Tree Borden, Janet Yassen, Judith Herman, Dan Sexton, Linda Blick, Joel Becker, Laura Davis, Peter Dimock, Joe Doherty, Lee Ellenberg, Hank Estrada, Abe Feingold, Marshall Forstein, Mark

Gianino, Bernie Gray, Holly Hendricks, Michael Keane, Fay Honey Knopp, Sherry Leib, Hank Lerner, Susan Mayman, Luisa Medrano, Patrick Meyer, Roberta Pasternack, and Jean Chapin Smith.

Particular thanks to Zoya Slive, Steve Klarer, Leslie Fenn, and Thom Harrigan for the many hours they devoted to reading the manuscript in its roughest form and providing me with careful, thoughtful comments—liberally interspersed with hugs. Thanks to my original copy editor, Betty Anne Crawford, for her painstaking efforts to make this work correct and readable, and to Steve Hudson and Willy Welch for their extra effort in setting the type for the original edition of this book. And special thanks to my office manager, Mary Susan Convery, for her competence, intelligence, patience, and sunshine.

My literary agent, Charlotte Raymond, has been steadfast in her enthusiasm for this project. Rochelle Lefkowitz, of Pro-Media, is living proof that a publicist can be caring, insightful and fun as well as competent. I thank both of them.

I am also indebted to my friends and family for putting up with my moods, confusion, and periods of absence and for being rock-solid supporters throughout. Thanks Amy, Frank, May, Gers, Aimee, Peggy, Brenda, Larry, Cindy, Rebecca, Joanne, Tim, Alan, Martin, Hank, Barbara, Deb, Jack, Steven, Thom, Ron, Lenore, Jane, Craig, David, Lisa, and Eric.

I thank Ellen Bass for the poetry and generosity of her words and Alan Jon Carroll for the beauty and sensitivity of his artistic talent. Thanks to both of them for being models of loving and caring friends.

Thanks is given to Peter Nevraumont for suggesting the writing of this book and to my original publishers, Peter Nevraumont and Ann Perrini, for their gentleness and patience in guiding a fledgling writer in the right direction—and for their optimism when I was most discouraged. And I thank my paperback publisher, Harper & Row, especially Peternelle van Arsdale, who saw to the many details involved in organizing the paperback edition without ever losing her cheerfulness, and my editor Janet Goldstein for her intelligence, abundant energy, and ability to solve problems with creativity and undertanding.

T.W.—in hard times and good times—all my thanks and all my love.

Finally, my thanks to my clients, who must remain anonymous, but who continue to teach me about life, love, and recovery.

Preface to the Paperback Edition

It is difficult to believe that it's been exactly nine months since the original hardcover publication of this book. In that brief time, my life has changed radically. The response to *Victims No Longer* has been overwhelming, deeply gratifying, and profoundly moving. Since November 1988, I have worked harder, learned more, communicated with more people, been more exhausted and more exhilarated, and felt more deeply than I ever dreamed would happen. The book and readers' response to it have provided opportunities and experiences that are unusual for therapists. I have traveled to many parts of this country, doing workshops for male survivors, their partners and friends, and training programs for professionals in mental health, medicine, nursing, human services, law enforcement, teaching, and the clergy. I've been to large urban centers, and smaller cities and towns. In the course of these travels I've had the opportunity to meet with extraordinary men and women and have heard their stories—stories of strength, courage, and creativity in the face of childhoods which were filled with cruelty, confusion, chaos, and pain. I have met therapists and other helping professionals who have endured lonely struggles to focus attention on the issue of incest when almost everyone else was denying that a problem existed. I am still being swamped with letters and phone calls from survivors and their allies, telling of their pain, asking questions, telling me their stories, and generously sharing their insights and resources. Among the people I have met, heard from and spoken with are:

—a member of a motorcycle club in California who came to one of my workshops wearing his colors—"The Survivors MC"

—a seventy-year-old man in Tennessee who called in to a radio show, saying that he had been a good husband and father, citizen and church member, but that this was the first time he had told anyone he had been a victim of incest—and wanted to know whether it was too late to begin his recovery. After regaining my voice, I assured him that he had already begun—he had broken the silence.

—the mother of a thirty-year-old male survivor in Texas who, when she tried to get help and treatment for her son, was told that she is a codependent, and who went on trying until she found the resources she was looking for to support her son in his—and her—recovery

—a fourteen-year-old boy who was severely tortured by religious fanatics, who escaped into multiple personalities, and who continued to struggle against the abuse, insisting on finding himself the help he needed—finding it in California, New York, Florida, and Massachusetts.

We released the original edition of *Victims No Longer* at the First National Conference on Male Sexual Abuse in Minneapolis. At the time of this writing preparations are under way in Atlanta for the Second National Conference—this one focusing solely on male *survivor* issues.

I have watched organizations of survivors (even some specifically for male survivors) form, grow, and prosper. And I have seen heightening public recognition of the magnitude of the problem, along with considerably increased, although still inadequate, development of resources for support and treatment of recovering survivors. I've seen the beginnings of understanding that incest doesn't only affect the survivor—acknowledgment of the need for services and support for partners, friends and family of survivors. I've seen the dawning recognition of the problems affecting the enormous numbers of "wounded healers" (helping professionals—therapists, teachers, clergy, medical personnel—who are themselves survivors of childhood sexual abuse) and the particular stresses that these individuals face. And I see a few individuals who are beginning to talk about other incest-related issues that haven't yet been addressed in any systematic fashion:

Some courageous members of religious communities are starting to deal with the issues of abuse by members of the clergy and also are beginning to address the needs of clergy who are themselves survivors.

And the legal system is progressing slowly. Some judges and juries are starting to recognize the ongoing effects of sexual child abuse.

Sadly, we are going to have to pay increased attention to the issue of incest-generated AIDS. Not all children who are HIV-positive were infected before birth. We still have many difficult issues to face.

I've been treated as an expert at times when I knew that the person looking to me for answers was the real expert. If I have a special ability, it is that I can listen to those experts and communicate what they are saying so that others can benefit. To be able to do so is also my personal joy.

I've been through periods of being discouraged, overwhelmed, and confused. I've had people try to cast me in the role of guru or treat me as some kind of superhuman being. I am neither. I have fears, doubts, and weaknesses and I make mistakes. I am human. (And I urge everyone to resist being portrayed as superhuman because of the danger of abuse of power that such a position poses.)

However, not everyone has received the information in *Victims No Longer* and the growing survivor movement with equal enthusiasm. Wherever people are trying to overcome the hurts of the past, face up to problems, and improve the human condition, they will meet with opposition and hostility. There already is a strong and often vicious backlash to the survivor movement. Dr. Jon Conte, past president of the American Professional Society on the Abuse of Children (APSAC), in his final message before he left this position, warned of the virulence and sophistication of this backlash, and urged all helping professionals to stand up to those who would deny the existence of the problem or resist the creation of services for victims and survivors ("On the Backlash," *The Advisor*, APSAC, Chicago, April 1989). In past years, and especially since the publication of *Victims No Longer*, I've encountered this backlash from:

—those who deny the existence or the frequency of sexual exploitation of children

—those who view incest recovery as "this year's fad" and assume that "all the fuss" will die down

—those who think that men are always perpetrators and never victims

—those who do not understand that women as well as men sexually abuse children

—the apologists for sexual child abuse and intergenerational sex

—people who romanticize or minimize the harmful effects of child sexual abuse

—people who profit from the sexual exploitation of children and who have created a multimillion dollar pornography and child sex industry and a powerful "pro–incest lobby"

It has become increasingly apparent that it is essential that we stand up together, as survivors, pro–survivors, and helping professionals, and speak the truth about sexual child abuse. In that sense, your decision to recover, your insistence on arriving at the truth and being heard, is also a political statement. It is a statement against the most basic form of oppression, the oppression of children.

I want to address briefly some issues that have led to difficulty or misunderstanding in *Victims No Longer* and some points that need further discussion:

1 / Please *do not* attempt to read this book in one sitting. There is too much powerful emotional content here. Take your time, read it slowly, bit by bit, so that you do not get overwhelmed. You may find it better not to read the book at night or when you are alone. It helps to have someone (therapist, friend, another survivor) to talk with about it.

2 / I have been criticized for not including information for survivors who are also abusers. The fact that I have written this book for non–offending male survivors is a reflection of my area of experience. I have not worked extensively with perpetrators, and leave the topic of offender-survivors to the experts. This does not mean that I don't believe that these individuals need and deserve treatment. (Just as the fact that I don't work with children doesn't mean children don't merit help—simply that I don't have much professional experience with them.) My personal belief is that extreme care must be exercised when mixing offenders and nonoffending survivors in therapy, groups, and workshops. Many survivors are so starved for resources that they will attend anything that might offer some hope, even to the extent of putting themselves into situations that feel abusive and overwhelming. It is important that we offer nonoffending survivors a range of clear choices—without coercion or manipulation—always including the option of working in an environment that does not include offenders. I am appreciative of the letters that I have received from survivors who are also perpetrators, including several who have found *Victims No Longer* personally helpful. I wish them all success in their recovery from abusing and from having been abused. But I continue to believe that no one can recover from abuse while continuing to abuse another person.

3 / In the first edition of *Victims No Longer* I invited readers to write and call me with their reactions, and I replied to all letters and returned all phone messages. But I underestimated the volume of response to the book and overestimated my ability to handle it. I still invite your letters, and I will read all of them—and continue to learn from them. But I am not able to provide a personal reply to each. I will continue to be available to come to your local area for survivor workshops, professional trainings, and public lectures whenever people have the interest, energy, and resources to organize them. To make arrangements, contact The Next Step Counseling and Training, 10 Langley Road, Suite 200, Newton Centre, MA 02159, (617) 332-6601. If you do require a written response, please include a stamped, self-addressed envelope, and then please try to be patient.

4 / Since I wrote the section on recovery groups for male survivors, I have had the opportunity to offer groups and workshops that were not separated by sexual orientation. I am now convinced that the advantages of heterosexual and gay men working together far outweigh any difficulties. Male survivors have demonstrated again and again that we are dealing with issues of sexual child abuse, not sexual orientation. I continue to be moved by the solidarity with which group members come to that understanding and support one another in their diversity—and their recovery.

5 / We are learning that the extent of abuse by female perpetrators is far greater than anyone ever suspected. We must work toward understanding the particular issues facing survivors of sexual abuse by women.

6 / I also want to let my readers know that as of this writing all the male survivors who shared their stories in this book are still living, still growing, and still impressive. I wish I could have asked them all to update their stories for you.

People often ask me, "How can you do this kind of work? Isn't it difficult and depressing? Don't you burn out?" I usually reply, Yes, it is certainly difficult, and sometimes I cry about the sadness, pain, and cruelty that children endure—and I find that I have less and less tolerance for "slice-of-life" films and novels—I find myself putting off reading professional literature that deals with sexual abuse, and "forgetting" to tape TV programs on the subject—I increasingly look for complete escape and relaxation when I'm not working. But, overall, I love what I do, I find it inspiring and encouraging to work with survivors, their allies, and my professional colleagues in the sexual abuse recovery field—I can't think of anything else I'd rather be doing or any people I'd sooner be doing it with.

Most of the questions that I am asked by survivors—and by helping professionals—boil down to one question: Is recovery possible? Nothing I have experienced in the past months has changed my mind about the answer. Is recovery possible? Absolutely. How do I know? Because I have seen the evidence. Every day I encounter men and women who are actively engaged in the process of recovery from the effects of incest and other sexual child abuse. They are from all over the world and all backgrounds, ages and stations of life. Yes, recovery is *real* and *it matters*. *You matter*. It is still a long, difficult, and often painful process, but it is possible and it is worth the struggle. The pain diminishes and the survivor moves from surviving into thriving.

Another question that I am asked frequently is, "What do you mean by recovery?" It's taken me a while to answer this one. I have been depending on other people's definitions of recovery until I developed one that worked for me (just as you must develop one that makes sense for you). Mine is simple. For me, it is about freedom. *Recovery is the freedom to make choices in your life that aren't determined by the abuse.* The specific choices will be different for each of you; the freedom to choose is your birthright.

Once again, I thank you all for confirming my basic optimism about the nature of human beings. We must keep on reaching for one another's humanity—and for our own.

Mike Lew, M.Ed.

The Next Step Counseling
P.O. Box 1146
Jamaica Plain, MA 02130

Boston, MA
September 1989

Foreword
by Ellen Bass

I began working on the anthology *I Never Told Anyone: Writings by Women Survivors of Child Sexual Abuse,* when my daughter, Sara, was a few months old. Now, nine years later, I am writing this introduction to *Victims No Longer.* My seven-month-old son, Max, is practicing crawling in the living room. He gets up on his hands and knees and rocks back and forth. He pushes his legs straight, bends them again, rocks, briefly lifts his hands and feet, swimming in the air, and then settles back to all fours. Doggedly he continues, progressing slowly but steadily backward until he has scooted under the coffee table and backed up against the couch.

He wails and I scoop him up. His head is fuzzy and warm like the belly of a bird. His feet are fat and perfectly smooth, the pads of toes lined up like round peas in a pod. I pretend to eat them and he giggles, a delicious hiccoughing squeal. I want him safe in the world with the same fierce and tender love I first knew when my daughter was born.

I know there are other ways to learn about love but, for me, nothing startled my heart into caring like the birth of these children. We use lots of big words when we talk about sexual abuse. We speak about the vulnerability of children, the responsibility of adults, betrayal, humiliation, abandonment, powerlessness, violation. Multisyllabic words, but none of them convey how soft children are, how much they need our care. And innocence doesn't even begin to get at it.

My daughter was toting Max around one day when we were shopping. Although she usually likes to carry him, she didn't really want to this day. My arms were full of heavy bags, so she slung him over her shoulder and bounded along the sidewalk singing a cheerful, nasty little song, "Max, you're a pest. I don't like you best." Max's expression was one of utter contentment. Bounced and serenaded, he was oblivious to the fact that his carrier was annoyed, or that he was slipping down her side precariously. "Dropped" was not in his experience. Neither was fear.

We all came into the world this way—perfectly trusting. If "right" has any meaning at all, it must be that it is right that no one should harm children, that the young should be protected.

Yet people prey on their own young. You were a child once—crawling backward, learning how to ride a bike, taking the bus by yourself for the first time. You were this innocent, this trusting. And someone violated that trust.

You have lived with the wounds of that violation for a long time. You have suffered and you have struggled and, one way or another, you have survived. Now you have an opportunity to heal.

Until recently, there was little support for survivors of sexual child abuse and little information or understanding was offered. Finally, the problems began to be brought out into the open. Women began to talk about their abuse, books were written, and we began to learn how to heal. But even then men's needs were rarely addressed. When men called me there were no support groups I could direct them to, no books I could suggest.

The phenomenon of survivors of child sexual abuse working together to heal began as a woman-led and -oriented movement. It was—and still is—essential for women to have the understanding of other women and the safety of woman-only space in which to share their experiences and feelings. But now, as men are beginning to talk about their abuse and reach out for help, there is a parallel wave of men's healing that's been set in motion. For the first time in history men are coming together to share the pain of their childhood abuse; to be heard, comforted, and to help each other heal.

Victims No Longer is a significant contribution to this healing. Mike Lew talks to survivors with compassion, intelligence, and respect. I was particularly interested in reading *Victims No Longer* because I had just finished writing a book for women survivors, *The Courage to Heal*. Much of what I say to women is the same as what Mike Lew says to men, confirming again and again how similar the healing process is. There are, of course, some specific differences stemming from the different ways men and women have been treated in our culture but, on the whole, recovery is strikingly similar, providing a rich opportunity for men and women to be allies in their healing.

Victims No Longer speaks directly to men who were abused as children; addressing their pain, their needs, their fears and hopes. It contradicts the myth that all men who were abused grow up to be abusers. Although many abusers were abused themselves, it is not true that most abused boys grow up to be perpetrators. Rather, they grow up to be men who hurt, who need help, support, understanding, and information. *Victims No Longer* provides that support; offering clear, reassuring guidance, hope, and encouragement.

By reading this book, talking with other survivors, working together toward overcoming the effects of your abuse, you are joining a courageous community of men. Courage is a word that has been applied to men since recorded history—and its meaning has usually had something to do with risking one's life, health, or well-being to kill or save others. This standard has left men feeling compelled to sacrifice themselves (and sometimes destroy others) in order to be worthy. And this kind of sacrifice is incompatible with recovery from child sexual abuse.

There's another kind of courage, though. The courage to be vulnerable, to feel your feelings, to give and receive help.

Before my children were born, I was proud. I guarded my time like a precious jewel. I didn't want to accept favors, didn't want to get too close, because people might want something back. When my daughter was born, I was immediately humbled. I needed help. And I needed it so badly, I couldn't pretend I didn't. I had to ask. I had to learn to receive—and eventually to give. I could no longer stand aloof. I joined the human race.

For many men, the need to heal from child sexual abuse has a similar impact. The ways you've coped, the strategies for keeping your human need in check have been exhausted. You need help, you need connection, and you are willing to reach out for it.

This is courage. This is a special kind of bravery of the heart. It's a kind of bravery we as a society have not applauded—or even accepted—in men, but is crucial for healing. And crucial for our society.

Just by reading this book you are participating in a revolutionary act. You are part of changing the stereotypes of the tough guy and the wimp—and creating instead a vision of man as an active, responsive, feeling person. The implications of this are vast—and wildly hopeful.

The norm in our society has been for men to be strong, fearless, aggressive. As a man you know these expectations from the inside, while I see their results from the outside. Men are supposed to be powerful and in control. But "power" has often meant "power over." And "in control" has meant "controlling others."

In the process of healing from child sexual abuse, you are led to reconsider these concepts. As you allow yourself to get in touch with your feelings, you feel the hurt that you went through as a child. You feel the betrayal, the abandonment. You grieve. You learn that it wasn't your fault, that you aren't to blame. You feel angry—angry at those who abused you, who didn't protect you. You feel compassion for yourself—for the child you once were and the adult man now, still carrying the effects of the abuse.

Slowly, as you move through the healing process, you gain the skills to make changes in your life. You gain a sense of your own personal power and control over yourself—your body, your feelings, your ideas. You learn what's important to you, what your authentic needs are, how to meet them. You develop the capacity to form relationships that are intimate without being consuming. You become whole.

When I first began working with survivors, I received a call the night before a workshop from a survivor who had just recovered memories of abuse and was reeling from the pain. To make things worse, her lover had panicked and left. Then she'd lost her job. The group was already full and I felt terrible telling her there wasn't room. Finally, desperate, she said, "Then please, could you just answer one question?"

"I'd be glad to." I was relieved there was something I could offer.

"I just need to know," she asked, "is it possible to heal from this?"

Is it possible to heal? This is the question I am asked again and again. And the answer is, Yes. It is possible. It's a lot of work. It's hard. It's long. It's painful. But it's possible. And it's worth it.

Healing means reclaiming your life. It means living the rest of your life feeling like a whole person. Not just coping, not just getting by, not trying to pass for okay; but feeling, deep down, that you are okay, feeling comfortable with yourself and your life.

One of the things I've seen is that when survivors heal from child sexual abuse, they do more than "get over" the effects of the abuse. They become people who have thoroughly explored themselves; their strengths and their weaknesses, their hopes and their fears, their values, their commitments. Although they carry scars, many are healthier than people who never were abused, who never had reason to explore themselves so intimately and know themselves so well.

In the process of healing, all of our beliefs are brought out into the open for questioning. Abused children are given a lot of false information about themselves and the world. In the process of separating the lies from the truth, it is necessary to question much that our society takes for granted.

Survivors question the meaning of power: How can we empower

ourselves without dominating others? They question traditional roles of victim and victimizer, determined to find other ways to relate with mutual respect. They question what a man is supposed to be and what a woman is supposed to be.

This is an encouraging and fortunate process. And one of the more hopeful signs for the future. I want my son to grow up with the freedom to be himself, all the parts of himself—the tender parts, the feisty parts, the determined and the yielding. I want him to be able to cry, to work for what he believes in, to be able to admit fear—and not let the fear stop him. In short, to be a rich and varied human being.

We need to create a world that accepts and encourages men to be fully feeling human beings. When a child is sexually abused, he has feelings that are too painful and too overwhelming to acknowledge. In order to make the intolerable tolerable, children either repress the experience altogether or they remember the facts, but numb the feelings. Either way, we have a lot of people walking around who aren't in touch with their feelings. This is a dangerous situation. It's dangerous for each survivor and it's dangerous for the world.

Our world is in critical condition. We have always had war, greed, cruelty, rape and child sexual abuse, but as our technological capacities have increased, we now have the ability not only to devastate the lives of those close to us, but also to devastate life in its entirety.

I live in Santa Cruz, California. The air smells wet and fishy when the wind's blowing in from the Pacific—my favorite smell. I rarely notice it without wondering how long, even in this little bit of paradise, the air will be clear. And the water. These elements, precious, essential, the basis of life.

From where I look, it's all about the same thing. Children. The ocean. Fish. The earth. We either care about them or we don't.

As a society, it's clear we don't. And this is one of the reasons why I think it's important that people heal from child sexual abuse. How can you care about life, if you don't care about yourself? How can you feel you can do something to make a difference, if you don't feel you can do anything? How can you join with others, working to make a better world—or even just to preserve this one—if you can't trust anyone? How can you fight actively for what you believe in, if you think being active and assertive means being an aggressor, an abuser? How can you listen and learn, if you think being receptive is being passive, a victim? In short, how can we heal the world unless we heal ourselves?

My motives for doing this work are selfish. I want a better world.

I want there to be a world. For me. For my children. And their children. And for you. I am not willing to acquiesce in the slow death of this planet. I love the physicality of life—earth and leaves, bark, fur, wind, rain, eggplant, cornsilk, turtles, snake skin, flannel sheets, ginger tea, kisses, sunbaked sand. I want all of us to care enough to make choices which will keep this rich home of ours teeming with life.

In the past decade I've written a lot about women joining together. Women have enormous power, just barely tapped. We have enormous compassion and zest for life. I want us to work together to create a vision of a healthier world and bring that vision into reality.

But this cannot stop with women. Women alone can't heal this earth. Close to half our population is male. Men are an integral part of the fabric of society. They are making significant decisions not only about their own lives, but also about the lives of women, children, and all life. Too many of these decisions have been destructive.

I do not believe that healthy men could make such unhealthy decisions. And I do not believe that healthy men could allow others to make those decisions. No man who feels how tender and vulnerable he was as a child could miss seeing how tender and in need of protection other children are. When you start to own your feelings, you become aware that you care. You become aware of how precious life is *to you* and what a sacred responsibility we are entrusted with.

Child sexual abuse, injustice, and the devastation of the earth all are a part of the same desecration. And the healing of each comes from the same source. It comes from feeling. It comes from caring. Caring about ourselves and each other.

We all need healing. And healing is possible. As we heal ourselves, we have the energy, the vision, the power to join together to heal the earth. Healing moves out in a circle. And it begins with ourselves.

E.B.

Santa Cruz, CA

Victims No Longer

Introduction

It seemed to be a chance combination of circumstances that led me to start my first male incest survivors' recovery group. Some time ago I realized that a significant number of my clients, both female and male, were bringing up memories of childhood sexual abuse in their therapy sessions. Many of those memories concerned incestuous abuse. I began to realize that if a large number of the people I was seeing had been abused (and I wasn't at that time presenting myself as an incest specialist), then it was likely that most therapists, whether they knew it or not, were also working with survivors of incest.

When I tried to find clinical information about male incest victims, there was very little in print. What did exist wasn't very useful. The popular press seemed to accept the idea that most sexual abuse was committed by some weird stranger lurking around the schoolyard. That wasn't what I was hearing from my clients. They were reporting abuse by people who were well-known to them—people who had easy access. From reading books about and by female survivors of incest (particularly *Father-Daughter Incest* by Judith Herman, M.D., and *I Never Told Anyone: Writings By Women Survivors of Child Sexual Abuse* edited by Ellen Bass and Louise Thornton), I learned that most female survivors of incestuous abuse experience a range of effects similar to those reported by my male clients. I also found that group therapy is the treatment of choice for incest survivors. In consultation with Judith Herman (who, it turned out, practices in the Boston area) and other female therapists working in this field, I began to learn about models of group treatment for incest recovery.

In the process of looking for a survivors' recovery group for one of my female clients, I discovered that the Boston area boasts a wonderful network of women leading groups and providing other services for female survivors. Then I tried to locate a group for male survivors. There was nothing. I looked in Boston, and then I spread my search, first to eastern Massachusetts and then to eastern New England. I found nothing. I asked other clinicians, and they knew of nothing. Some were surprised that I even asked; they felt that there was no need for such services since "everyone knows" that little boys are rarely abused—most incest victims are female. Among those who recognized the problem, I found people who had attempted, without success, to start male survivors' groups. They had met with denial, resistance, hostility and ridicule. I found people who had organized peer support groups in the past but, despite the energy and skill of these organizers, the groups were no longer in existence. A number of factors, including leader burn-out and a sense of isolation, had led to their demise. The message was startlingly clear. There were no services geared to the needs of adult male incest survivors. This was outrageous!

I spent several months complaining about the lack of services for men, and my female colleagues listened patiently to my complaints. Finally, the light dawned. I realized that none of my outrage was going to do any good unless I translated it into action. I couldn't wait until someone who knew all the answers came along and started a male survivors' group. If I did that I'd be waiting forever. I had led other types of groups; I had experience in working with survivors; I probably knew as much about the topic as anyone else around. So, after trying to back out on the grounds that I wasn't ready to start a group (does this sound familiar?) and that I was terrified (several female colleagues "reassured" me that terror was a perfectly appropriate emotion), I began to put out the word that as soon as I had enough people, I was starting a recovery group for male incest survivors.

I was told to expect that, because of the fear surrounding the subject, it would take me ten times longer to get an incest survivors' group started than any other kind. In fact, men would probably not even show up for an interview, let alone actually join a group. I was told, "It's great that you're doing this, but men aren't ready to admit to being victims." I was prepared to have this take a very long time. I was wrong. I was unprepared for the overwhelming response to the small ad I placed in a local paper and the flyer I sent out to some of my colleagues. The time was right and in short order I had begun two male survivors' recovery groups and had waiting lists for each of them.

The news got around that I worked with male survivors, and I soon found myself being regarded as an expert in the field. I didn't feel much like an expert, but my only option was to learn as much as I could as quickly as possible. Since there was little written information available, most of my learning came from talking with my colleagues and listening to my clients. I attended every professional workshop I could find that related to sexual abuse. There weren't many. I joined with other therapists in putting together a group that meets monthly to discuss incest recovery issues.

I began to talk publicly about male survivors. I appeared on radio and television talk shows. I did newspaper interviews. I spoke to community groups and conducted workshops at professional conferences. I did staff trainings at mental health agencies, hospitals and prisons. And everwhere I went men told me their sexual abuse histories. For many of them it was the first time they had told anyone. It was becoming increasingly clear that the problem of incestuous child abuse (of both girls and boys) is of far greater magnitude than anyone had realized.

Returning home after an appearance on a nationally televised talk show, I found a message from a Peter Nevraumont, calling from New York City. When I returned his call, he told me that as an editor and publisher he had been wanting to do a book about incest recovery. He had seen the show and decided that I would be a good person to write such a book. Flattered but intimidated, I told him I was a therapist, not an author. He said he thought it was important, that I could do it, and why didn't I come down to New York to talk about it? This was the beginning of the end of my leisure time for a considerable period. The book is now complete. I hope the results justify Peter's faith in me.

What I Hoped to Accomplish

I wrote *Victims No Longer* as a handbook of recovery for men who experienced childhood incest and other sexual abuse—and for the people who care about them. My goals were to:

- Provide as much information as possible to as many people as possible about a subject that seems to be ignored as often as possible
- Present a framework within which male incest survivors can explore and share their experiences
- Reassure my readers that they can recover from the effects of incestuous child abuse
- Open discussion and investigation of the nature of incest recovery
- Share experiences (mine and others') of what has been helpful to men in their recovery
- Provide specific resources to male survivors, the professionals who work with them and the people who love them
- Invite the reader to join with other men in a shared odyssey of recovery

The first time I used the term *odyssey* to describe the recovery process, my publisher Peter Nevraumont responded, "I think this word is a key one . . . the word has many pertinent, positive connotations. Odyssey meaning voyage of discovery of a problem that has been hidden and discovery by the victims that they are not alone. Odyssey meaning heroic journey *in* (to the psyche) requires as much if not more bravery than a journey *out* (to the external unknown). Odyssey meaning journey of considerable length; the odyssey you envision is not like a trip to the corner for a quart of milk. The odyssey you are proposing requires strength of character, curiosity, a sense of adventure, and a willingness to stick with it. Odyssey is an accurate metaphor for what you have set out to accomplish in your book."

When I first read Peter's words of encouragement (or maybe warning) I had no idea of how accurate and prophetic they would be. Now, many months later, it is clear that he was talking about two journeys—that of the incest survivor in his recovery, and my own voyage of discovery. Writing *Victims No Longer* became an odyssey that paralleled the recovery process in significant ways. Beginning with a general idea of what I wanted to accomplish—and not the faintest clue as to how to go about it—the project began to take on momentum. It grew until there were times when I felt as though I had no life apart from this book. When I wasn't writing about incest recovery, I was thinking about it, talking about it, listening to other people's experiences, and working with incest survivors. Everything I heard, read and did became raw material. Every conversation seemed to turn to the topic of sexual abuse.

There were times of confusion and times when I felt totally overwhelmed. I would sit staring at a blank computer screen wondering how I had ever thought I could tackle a subject like this. I found myself agonizing over every sentence, concerned about being misunderstood and knowing how important it was to "get it right." But at other times, it felt as though the book was writing itself. The information kept coming. Every time I listened to a survivor or a colleague, with each group meeting, phone call, lecture, and article I learned more. I would touch the keyboard and the words seemed to flow automatically through me onto the display screen. There were periods of dejection and hopelessness. And there were occasions of great elation when I knew that the book was actually taking shape.

In the course of this voyage of discovery—as in a classical odyssey—I traversed a varied landscape, encountering "monsters" and "heroes." I heard stories of startling power: histories of physical violence, neglect, emotional and sexual abuse that at times left me crying, shaking—or numb. And I was equally moved by the courage, intelligence, and creativity with which incest survivors negotiate their lives. The children who were forced to create their own explanations of their irrational, abusive situations—who figured out how to survive in the absence of accurate information, support, encouragement, and love. And the adult survivors—often feeling as though they were clinging to the cliff edge by their fingernails—hanging on to their intuitive understanding that healthy humans treat each other with respect, thoughtfulness and cooperation—hanging on to the hope of someday experiencing that kind of relationship. I was (and continue to be) impressed by the gains that survivors have made in pulling together the pieces of their lives. The more I heard their stories, the greater my respect for them grew. And the more I felt the need to make this book a statement of that admiration.

This book isn't for everyone. I have aimed to write a book *for* male incest survivors and the people involved with them. It is not a work of scholarly research. It quotes few statistics and contains no footnotes. I leave it to others to write the definitive academic treatise on incest. (For those readers who are interested in technical, academic or statistically oriented material, I refer you to the resource section at the back of the book.) I have tried to present the information in "plain English" so it would be accessible to the widest possible audience. Because of the vastness of the subject matter, I had to be selective about what was included. I reluctantly realized that if I waited until I knew everything that can be known about incest recovery, this book never would be written. And it will continue to be written and rewritten by many individuals with many different perspectives— survivors and allies, professionals and nonprofessionals—as our understanding continues to grow.

The following pages contain what I have found to be true about sexual child abuse and incest recovery. It contains a great deal of information and a great many suggestions. I hope the information is helpful and the suggestions are practical, but you must make that determination yourself. What is contained in this book is neither law nor gospel. Please select what is useful to you and ignore the rest. It is clear to me that different pieces of information speak to people at different points in their recovery. There is a range of information in this book, coming from a wide variety of sources. It provides a rich banquet. I encourage you to consume it slowly, not moving on to another course before you are ready.

As a therapist, my primary interest is recovery. For this reason, I don't spend time arguing about (or trying to prove) the existence of the incestuous abuse of boys. It happens. This book addresses the effects of that abuse and ways to recover from them. In every chapter, you will find words of encouragement and suggestions for recovery.

You will find that some themes receive special emphasis. Among them are issues relating to *trust*, *isolation*, *shame*, and *intimacy*. They are given special attention because they are central issues for all incest survivors.

While I have tried to be as accurate as possible, *Victims No Longer* necessarily reflects my personal philosophies and biases. It is not a neutral book; I hope it is not dispassionate. I am passionately committed to the prevention of, and recovery from, child abuse. I have no patience with child abusers or apologists for child abuse. I believe there is a great deal wrong with a society that allows individuals to profit at the expense of children. I believe we have a long way to go in creating a world where child abuse is unknown and unthinkable— and I believe that we can do it.

There are other ways that this book isn't for everyone. There are some people who are still in deep denial about the existence of incestuous abuse. They will interpret this book as fiction or exaggeration. It is neither. There are individuals and groups who will resist what this book has to say because acceptance would mean change—and loss of their power and privilege. And there are other ways that abusive childhoods isolate their victims. Some survivors never learned to read; some cannot sustain a long-enough attention span. Others are so mired in hopelessness that they can't believe that anything will do any good, or have been so badly hurt by their childhood experiences that they need treatment far beyond the scope of a "self-help" book. And there are some people for whom the information is still too immediate or painful to look at.

But you have picked up this book. You're looking for something, and part of you—however small—knows that things aren't completely hopeless. In reading about the experiences and feelings that are commonly shared by incest survivors, you may recognize your own situation. You will find yourself in good company on the road to recovery.

The following chapters present information in several different ways. When I am writing about theory or general matters, I often use the somewhat neutral third person. However, when I am talking about personal experience or the specifics of recovery, I attempt to speak directly to "you," the reader. I will sometimes repeat or re-phrase material that I feel is particularly important, or when it fits into several contexts. Denial and fear connected to these issues are so

Focus

VICTIMS NO LONGER: ON THE USE OF
THE TERMS *VICTIM* AND *SURVIVOR*

There are difficulties involved in the use of either of these words when talking about adults recovering from incest.

The dictionary definition of *victim* ("one who suffers through no fault of his own; one who is made to suffer by persons or forces beyond his control") is an accurate description of the reality of childhood sexual abuse. But the word also suggests the emotional image of hopelessness and helplessness.

While this may have been true at the time of the original abuse, it is by no means reflective of your present situation. Regardless of how you feel about yourself, or how severely the abuse has wounded you, you are a strong, creative individual. You had the ability to survive to this point, and now you have the ability and the resources to recover. That doesn't sound like a victim to me. For that reason, in this book I shall try to use "victim" only when referring to the condition of the child during the time of the actual abuse.

There are similar limitations with the term *survivor*, which evokes pictures of people clinging to flotsam while their ship sinks, or hanging by their fingernails from a cliff edge. While this might be an accurate description of the feelings of the person who was incestuously abused, it neglects the reality that *survival isn't enough*.

Survival means enduring until something better comes along. The recovery process is one of learning to live a satisfying life—to *thrive* instead of merely survive. But, for now, "survivor" is the best word we have, and I use it until something better comes along. (Some people have suggested Adults Molested As Children (AMAC), but that feels even more passive to me than "survivor.") In this book, *survivor* refers to an adult who was incestuously abused as a child. But we must always be aware that survival is a *temporary* state, one that will be replaced by something better.

powerful that some information may need to be repeated many times before it is heard.

I also have tried to use pronouns in a conscious way throughout the book. Because this book is about male survivors, I tend to employ the masculine pronouns when referring to survivors. To avoid both sexist assumptions and an unwieldly dependence on phrases like "he or she" or "him/herself" I have alternated masculine and feminine pronouns when referring to therapists, family members, friends—

and perpetrators. Beyond these intentional idiosyncrasies (and despite the expert help of friends, colleagues and editors) stylistic difficulties reflect the limitations of the author.

Interspersed *within* chapters are special sections that I have called "Focuses." A Focus is set off from the main text because the information deserves special emphasis, bears repeating, or speaks to a specific experience or group. Each Focus is between a paragraph and about a page in length and its content will relate to the chapter in which it is found.

Interspersed *between* chapters are personal accounts, or "Statements," by adult male incest survivors reflecting their own experiences. I provided only the most general of guidelines to the men who wrote these Statements. I suggested that they include some combination of: (a) something about themselves; (b) something about what happened to them; (c) something about the effects; (d) something about what they have found useful in recovery; (e) anything they would like to say to other male survivors, who might not know anyone with whom they can talk. These Statements are anonymous, credited only by the approximate age of the author. Where names are given, they have been changed to protect the individual's privacy. Editing has been kept to a minimum.

As you will see, these Statements vary in scope and presentation, ranging from coolly detached to highly emotional, from a few paragraphs to several pages in length. Some time ago I saw a television interview with a Hollywood film maker (whose name I have unfortunately forgotten, as I'd like to give him credit). He was asked the difference between a "story" and a "plot." He replied that an example of a plot would be, "A man died and his wife died." An example of a story is, "A man died and then his wife died of a broken heart." The Statements provide the stories that give life and intimacy to this book. I am extremely grateful to the men who shared their experiences, ideas and feelings so powerfully.

Writing this book has meant a lot to me. It has challenged me, taught me, and changed me profoundly. I hope that you will find it a worthwhile companion on your own odyssey of recovery.

M.L.

Boston, MA
June 13, 1988

PART ONE

About Abuse

1

Incest: Myths and Realities

And those that create out of the holocaust of their own inheritance anything more than a convenient self-made tomb shall be known as "Survivors."
—KEITH JARRETT, *The Survivor's Suite*

Child abuse. The term has entered our vocabulary with an eerie everyday familiarity. It is an enemy that we can all rally against. Good people everywhere unite in their condemnation of the few evil, sick individuals who abuse children. We talk confidently about the need to protect our children from these weird, trench-coated strangers who lurk about schoolyards with molestation on their minds. We create programs that teach kids not to accept rides or candy from strangers. We assume that we know what child abuse is.

At the same time we create an image of the perfect family. Television shows and movies portray wise, caring fathers and loving, nurturing mothers imparting decent values to their children in an atmosphere of trust and openness. When problems arise, Dad has a fatherly talk with Sonny and gently guides him to the path of reason. Mom sits on the edge of Sis's bed and talks about her own childhood, dispensing motherly wisdom liberally laced with hugs. Or the family sits down together at the dining room table to solve the little problems of childhood through easy communication and folksy stories. We create a fantasy of family life and then we believe our own creation. We assume that we know what family life is.

If you have decided to read this book, it is likely that your own experience was dramatically different from the ideal. If you were abused as a child, your memories of family life present another picture. Dad's "fatherly talk" with Sonny was anything but reasonable, and his guidance far from gentle. Mom's own childhood memories may have been of violence and sexual abuse. And mealtimes were

What Is Abuse?

occasions to be endured or avoided. You may remember absent, un-available or nonprotective parents—unable to help you because they couldn't help themselves—as abused children or adult victims. A family evening at home might have included screaming fights, bouts of drunkenness, episodes of physical violence, cowering children hiding in fear, nightmares, tears, confusion, stony silences, unreasonable blame, ridicule, repeated beatings, missed meals, helplessness, attempts to protect a parent or sibling . . . or sexual abuse. Your memories may include not being believed and having no source of protection. You may have little or no detailed memory of your childhood, positive or negative, and wonder why you can't recall those happy times—those "golden childhood years." Some of you pretended that it was otherwise, imagining that your family was happy, wise, healthy, and harmonious. In this way you attempted to protect yourself from the abuse, holding on to the fantasies as long and as tightly as you could manage until reality forced its way into the picture. You may still find yourself tempted to rewrite your family history to bring it more in line with the way you wish it had been.

As a society and as individuals, the images of family life that we've created are pleasant and comforting. It is no wonder that we cling to them so fiercely—that we defend them against the intrusion of a harsher reality. Even when we are in the midst of an abusive situation, it is often easier to pretend that it is otherwise. In fact, your fantasy of an ideal family may have been the only refuge available to you as a child. Realizing this makes it easier to understand a child's insistence—in the face of blatant evidence of abuse—that nothing is wrong. In my clinical practice I have heard many people tell heart-rending stories of brutality and violence, only to have them react with surprise when I referred to their childhood as abusive. This begins to make sense only when we combine misinformation about the nature of child abuse with the mythology about perfect family life.

"The Family" is a sacred concept of American culture. Politicians are elected on the basis of their commitment to Family Values. Educators and clergy decry the "erosion of Family Life." No one is willing to risk violating the sanctity of The Family. Along with the value placed on the family, Americans cherish the concepts of Privacy and Independence.

"A man's home is his castle." Within this castle, the King and Queen can rule absolutely. Few people are willing to make suggestions as to how children should be raised, let alone interfere in their treatment. It is seen as solely the parents' responsibility. This combination of cultural values leaves parents (who may themselves be products of abusive childhoods) isolated in dealing with the stresses of family life. It produces an environment wherein children (and often wives as well) are seen as property. "Ownership" of a child confers license to treat him/her as one wishes.

Our respect for independence and diversity provides leeway for a wide range of parental behavior. The importance that we ascribe to individual and family privacy allows some harmful and shocking forms of behavior to go unnoticed (and extremes of abuse to go unreported). It is only very recently that the need to protect children from abusive parents has begun to be recognized. But change is slow and tentative. Interference with the family by child protective agencies is viewed with suspicion. Experts debate the boundaries between education, discipline and abuse.

The reality is that abuse exists. It is real and it is common. It takes many forms, some blatant and others more subtle. The spectrum of child abuse ranges from neglect to physical violence. It includes torture, beatings, verbal and psychological maltreatment, child pornography, and sexual abuse (ranging from seductive behavior to rape). The abuse of children is seldom limited to one of these manifestations. Abuse appears in varying combinations, durations, and intensities. What all forms have in common is their devastating, long-term effects on the child.

In the face of absolute parental authority, a child loses all "adult" rights—to privacy, independence, and even control over his or her body. We continue to maintain the fiction that abusive behavior by those closest to the child is less severe than that which is perpetrated by strangers. Without a doubt, the reverse is true.

Kids are remarkably resilient. With proper support, consistent love and encouragement, they recover from even the most severe hurts of childhood. When, however, the injuries are committed by the very individuals who should be crucial to the healing process, where can the child turn? The safety of the world is destroyed and the child is isolated in the abuse. When the perpetrator is a family member, the entire family—even those members who are unaware of the abuse—is affected. The relationships between the abused child, the perpetrator and the other family members become sources of anxiety and confusion.

I have not attempted to provide an exact description of "the abusive family" for two reasons. First, because there is no precise profile of the environment where incest and other forms of child abuse are to be found. While we can discuss cultural values and social climates that might provide a fertile environment for abuse, we can't describe the abusive family with the same precision that we present the fictional ideal "perfect family."

A second reason for not attempting to spell out the profile of the abusive family is the tendency of survivors to self-eliminate. It is natural to want precise answers and an exact framework within which to work. You may be saying to yourself, "If he only would give me a description of the incestuous family, then I can decide whether my situation fits the picture." What a relief to be able to say for certain that it wasn't really incest—or that your situation wasn't *too* bad because you didn't experience number seven on a list of characteristics of the incestuous family—but such self-exclusion wouldn't be helpful.

If you are a survivor of sexual child abuse, you've spent more than enough time feeling different, excluded, and isolated. Let us include you as we explore a range of possibilities. Let's assume that you are welcome here, that whether you have clear and exact memories of years of child sexual abuse or only picked up the book because "something told me it might be interesting"—whether your family was chaotic or "seemed so normal"—this book is for you. You have a right to read it, to have feelings about it, and to use it in any way that helps you to take charge of your life.

FOCUS
CURRENT EFFECTS

The following list was put together by the men who participated in a weekend recovery workshop for male and female incest survivors. The items on the list are in response to the question, "In what ways does the childhood sexual abuse continue to affect your adult life?" Not all of these responses apply to every survivor. I have presented them all, without editing, as they were listed by the participants.

- Nightmares (intense; violent)
- Fear that everyone is a potential attacker
- Shame
- Anger
- Guilt

- Fear of expressing anger/difficulties in starting to get angry
- Need to be in control
- Need to pretend that I am not in control (Helplessness)
- Fear of being seen/fear of exposure/agoraphobia
- Running from people
- Fear of intimacy/running away from intimacy
- "Avoidism"
- Pain and memories of physical pain
- Flashbacks
- Not being able to "think straight"
- Difficulties in communicating
- Intruding thoughts
- Compulsive eating/not eating/dieting/bingeing/purging/etc.
- Self-abuse
- Wanting to die
- Sexual acting out
- Feeling asexual
- Sexual dysfunction

The equation doesn't have to be exact. I invite you to use this book as a context or guide for exploring the experiences of your own childhood. As we look at many aspects of abuse, survival, and recovery, take what is helpful to you and leave the rest. As we talk of incestuous (abusive/dysfunctional/chaotic) families, recognize that the differences are variations, not reasons for discounting your own experience. You have had hurtful childhood experiences within your family or at the hands of other adults who should have protected you. This book is offered as a resource that you can use in your healing of those injuries.

How can we justify permitting family members to engage in hurtful behavior that would never be tolerated from strangers? Again, only by isolating parents in the name of independence, and maintaining a view of the child as property—devoid of feelings and without the right to physical or emotional autonomy. Seeing children as property is where the problem starts and is crucial to the whole question of abuse.

There are many theoretical perspectives brought to the question of what constitutes abusive behavior. Personally, I'm not terribly inter-

- Feelings of unreality/detachment
- Image of myself as a failure
- Need to be completely competent at all times
- Feeling that "It's my fault."
- Self-doubt/Feeling that I'm not good enough
- Jealousy
- Envy
- Feeling inadequate
- Wishing I were someone else
- Inability to receive comfort/nurturing
- Feeling ashamed when I'm complimented
- Low self-esteem
- Keeping unnecessary secrets
- Being "walled in"
- Finding it hard to connect with other people
- Isolation
- Difficulty in expressing vulnerability, being heard and cared about
- Feeling that "If they know me, they'll reject me."
- Escaping into addictions
- Frozen emotions
- Fear of other people's ulterior motives
- Fear that people will use me
- Inability to say "No."
- Lack of ability to recognize the truth
- Confusion about roles/identity/sexuality
- Ambivalence about wanting to be taken care of
- Fear of authority
- Fear of rules
- Fear of women
- Fear of men
- Fear of speaking out
- Inability to relax
- Disconnection from feelings
- Feeling stuck
- Linking abuse with love
- Forgetting/amnesia about parts of childhood
- Depression
- "Out of body" experiences
- Poor choices of partners

ested in arriving at an exact definition of abuse. I'm more concerned with recovery. As a clinical psychotherapist, I determine abuse by its effects. In the course of working with many incest survivors, I have come to recognize frequent adult manifestations of sexual child abuse. If you come to me with memories, feelings, and/or problems that may have resulted from incest, my responsibility is to help you to explore and understand how that childhood abuse hurt you and how it continues to affect your adult life. But understanding alone is not enough. The wounds of incest must be healed so that you can move on to enjoyment of a full and satisfying adult life. And I know that recovery is possible. I have seen it happen to survivor after survivor. It isn't quick and it isn't easy, but it is real.

As with my therapy and workshops, the purpose of this book is not to analyze or to come up with the definitive theory of abuse, but to talk about the effects of incestuous child abuse and how to recover from it. As for the question of what constitutes abusive behavior toward children, I can sum up my feelings briefly. I believe that children have a right to care and protection. This right is absolute. When anyone who is in a position of greater power—strength, authority, or experience—violates that right in any way, that behavior is abusive. There is no valid justification for the abuse of children. Abuse is *never* deserved, nor is the child *ever* responsible. It is only when we recognize as a living reality that children require protection from all forms of abuse—when we incorporate this recognition into the depths of our beings and reflect it throughout our social institutions—that we will become a truly healthy society.

Defining Incest   Incest is a particular manifestation of sexual child abuse. The traditional definition of incest is sexual activity between blood relatives. The degree of closeness that is necessary to constitute an incestuous union has been variously defined by different societies. In all cultures that I am aware of, sexual activity between parent and child and between siblings is viewed as incestuous and is prohibited.

The definition of incest that I use in my clinical practice (and in this book) is more inclusive. It is a definition shared in large measure by therapists who work with issues of sexual abuse and by support organizations of incest survivors. Incest is a violation of a position of trust, power, and protection. Sex between blood relatives is one part of this larger, more inclusive view of incest.

Incest differs from other forms of sexual abuse in that the perpetrator is assumed to stand in a protective (parental) role to the victim. The very person that the child should be able to turn to for care, comfort, and understanding violates that trust by sexualizing the relationship. For this to be a traumatic experience, it is not necessary that the "parenting" figure be a family member. Children naturally trust those adults who are closest to them—until there is reason not to. Sexual exploitation by any older caretaker is by my definition incestuous because it destroys that natural trust. This is true whether the perpetrator is a relative by blood or marriage, parent, stepparent, older sibling, neighbor, family friend, teacher, member of the clergy, therapist, physician, baby-sitter, camp counselor, or any other caretaker. In all instances the results are similar. The child's world becomes unsafe—confusing and frightening. In order to survive, the child must make sense of his/her situation.

By focusing on incest, I have no desire to minimize the results of other types of sexual abuse. No matter who the abuser is, relative or stranger, the effects of sexual abuse on a child are always serious. One of the aims of this book, however, is to look at some of the specific consequences when the perpetrator is someone close to the child—and why the scars left by incest are especially deep and difficult to heal.

The difference between sexual attack by a stranger and sexual attack by a family member (or other adult known by and close to the child) must be seen in context. We are taught from earliest childhood that family and friends are to be trusted. We are warned about the danger of trusting strangers. Home is equated with safety. The message is clear and widely reinforced. Recently, I watched a program of animated cartoons made in the 1940s and 1950s. The themes of these cartoons were surprisingly similar. A youngster (human or animal) strayed from the protection of home and family. In the course of his explorations, he found himself in danger (from the forces of nature or evildoers) only to be rescued at the last minute. The rescuer was usually the youngster's mother, although sometimes the father, both parents, another relative, or family pet played a part. The information conveyed to the child viewing the film was strong and unequivocal: Safety is with the family. Obey the rules. Do what your parents tell you. Stay with what is familiar. Similarly, in the classic children's film *The Wizard of Oz*, Dorothy returns to the safety of her parental figures, Auntie Em and Uncle Henry, by repeating the phrase, "There's no place like home." The enchantments and delights of the outside world have proven to be fraught with danger. The only protection is found in the familiar.

Sexual attack by a stranger therefore carries a different weight than attack by someone known to the child. We are somewhat more prepared for external dangers. Except in a very general way, the child victim never trusted the stranger in the first place. It is logical for a child who has been attacked by a stranger to turn to family for support, understanding, and nurture—and to begin the healing process in safety. If it is necessary to retreat from the world into the protection of loved ones, he can do so. The family can comfort, encourage, protect, and eventually guide the child back into the larger world. It can teach him how to better protect himself and how to determine a reasonable level of trust.

But what if Mommy or Daddy (or Uncle Henry or Auntie Em) are the attackers? Then who does the child trust? Where does he turn for understanding and protection? The closer the relationship of the victim to the perpetrator, the more certain is the loss of trust. This statement refers not simply to the biological relationship, but also to the *emotional* connection between the two. The more closely the child victim is tied to the abuser, the more the issue of trust comes into play. The victim of incestuous abuse has to deal not only with the results of a physical act, but also with the devastation of his ability to trust. If he cannot trust those closest to him, how can it be safe to trust anyone? The destruction—and rebuilding—of the *ability to trust* is a key issue for incest survivors. As such, it is a central theme of this book.

Incest in Context

"What sort of monster would sexually abuse a little child?"

"Isn't it awful that depraved incestuous families still exist!"

"How widespread is it really?"

"I can't imagine anyone we know doing such a thing."

"That sort of thing only happens among ———*."*   (Fill in your favorite stereotype)

"What do you actually mean by sexual abuse?"

"But they seemed like such nice people."

"How could I not have known?"

All of these quotes represent the type of questions that I am frequently asked about incest. They reflect a general assumption about the nature of sexual child abuse, stemming from widespread ignorance and the difficulty of looking directly at an upsetting subject. Rather than accept a painful and overwhelming reality, people tend to view incestuous abuse as though it were either some extremely rare manifestation of individual pathology, or another of the "distasteful heathen customs of exotic savages." In their desire to avoid unpleasant realities, human beings resort to doubting, denying, or distancing themselves from ugly truths.

We prefer to believe that "It can't happen here," maintaining our denial at a great cost—the repeated isolation and damage inflicted on millions of young people—yes, *millions*. Even if we take the more commonly accepted figures about sexual child abuse (that about one in three girls and one in ten boys are victims of sexual abuse) and assume that they have been inflated tenfold, we are still talking about millions of children. And it isn't likely that these figures are exaggerated. In fact, current evidence points to a strong possibility that they represent significant underestimations. We are talking about millions of victims, and millions of perpetrators. Who are they? Where are they found? It doesn't take much calculation to realize that we aren't just looking at a few "savages" and "lunatics." The savage and lunatic populations aren't that large, and would be exhausted long before we had accounted for those millions of victims and abusers. And we are clearly not looking at an isolated phenomenon peculiar to a particular ethnic group, part of the country, or time in history.

Anthropologists and historians have discovered that the prohibition against incest has existed in all known societies and at all times of history. These restrictions against sexual activity with someone defined as family must have been established for a reason. Psychiatrists, psychologists, cultural anthropologists and others have propounded many theories to account for the universality of the incest taboo. Some of these arguments are biological. (Incest had to be prohibited in order to prevent genetic defects resulting from inbreeding.) Others are economic (stressing the need to encourage breeding outside the family in order to broaden the base of power and wealth); sociological (solidifying a society through the widest possible network of connections, interactions and relationships); or psychological. (In *Totem and Taboo*, Sigmund Freud used cross-cultural data in his attempt to explain the prehistoric origins of this phenomenon.)

All these theories have their adherents and their detractors. They all have plausible aspects and flaws. There is no generally agreed-upon definitive explanation of the origin of the incest taboo. Volumes have been written on the subject, and the scholars still disagree. It isn't the purpose of this book to examine the various theories of the origin of incest and the development of its prohibition. If readers wish to pursue those topics, they will find ample resources for their research. This book seeks to explore more immediate issues—the nature of incestuous abuse, the ways that it affects the people who have been victimized, and methods of recovery from these effects. For our purposes, it is sufficient to acknowledge the universality of the incest taboo and the logical conclusions to be drawn from this acknowledgment. *There is no need to prohibit something that doesn't exist.* In short, there are incest taboos everywhere because every culture recognizes the need to protect children from incestuous abuse. The universal taboo against incest reflects the universality of the *act* of incest. That the incest taboo (at least in our culture) has been massively ineffective in protecting children from sexual abuse is evidence that we must take stronger measures. It shows that we have severe social problems that need to be identified, explored, and rectified. It is also a reason for my writing this book.

In addition to being found everywhere in the world and throughout history, incestuous child abuse is not limited to one particular segment of society. Despite our tendency to want to distance ourselves from unpleasant realities, incest is not something that is done by "them." It exists in "the nicest of families," among the wealthy, the poor, and the middle class. It happens in two-parent, single-parent, step, foster, and extended families. It occurs in religious and nonreligious, white- and blue-collar, northern and southern, farm and apartment-dwelling families. In fact, incest appears to cut across all racial, religious, ethnic, age, class, geographical, and rural/urban/suburban lines. It happens to people just like you. And for many reading this book, it happened *to* you.

If you are a male survivor, the essential thing to know is that there are many other men who were victimized. The exact numbers don't matter. Whatever they are, they are vast. And even knowing of the existence of just one other survivor helps you to break through the isolation. There are factors that are infinitely more important to the understanding of abuse and recovery than numbers and categories.

Patterns of Abusive Behavior

All behavior, including sexual child abuse, exists within a social and cultural context. We must examine this framework in order to further our understanding of the most fertile environment for the establishment and development of abusive patterns. We must also look at family attitudes, patterns of behavior, and other dysfunctional aspects of intrafamily interaction that allow for (and encourage) the sexual abuse of children. Finally, we must try to determine whether there are certain types of abusive experience that prove to be more hurtful than others.

Many researchers and clinicians believe that the relative severity of the effects of sexual child abuse is directly related to the age of the victim, severity of any physical violence involved, chronic nature of the abuse, closeness of the relationship between perpetrator and victim, sex of the child, whether the perpetrator was the same sex as the victim, and/or the way it was explained to (and perceived by) the child. I have no doubt that further research on these and other factors will guide us in our understanding of the nature of abuse and recovery. My hope is that we will continue to explore these factors without losing sight of the fact that *all* abuse of children is harmful, severe, and wrong. Our goal in examining different manifestations of incest should be to increase our understanding of prevention of all sexual abuse and recovery for *all* survivors.

I am reluctant to attempt to place much emphasis on exploring differences between the effects of various kinds of incestuous abuse. I have three reasons for my hesitancy:

First is the lack of hard evidence. While extensive research is being done on sexual child abuse, our knowledge of this topic is still limited. This book touches on some of the reasons why we know so little about incestuous abuse. In the case of male children, we have only the sketchiest data on the frequency of sexual abuse. While we can hazard some educated guesses, we still have much to learn about differences between a single (acute), isolated abusive incident and prolonged (chronic) patterns of sexual exploitation. We don't yet have a large enough population of male survivors able to talk about what it was like to have been subjected to one abuser or more than one; to seduction or violent attack; and to penetration, fondling, or sexual innuendo. We are limited in our understanding of the differences among men abused in infancy, early, middle, or late childhood, or adolescence. We don't know whether there are significant differences when the members of the abusive families are also alcoholic, violent, drug-addicted, or severely mentally ill. We have much to learn about what, if any, unique problems arise when there are several victims of sexual abuse in a family rather than only one. As you can see, we have a long way to go. These and other questions will occupy the research efforts of behavioral scientists for some time. Preliminary findings have already begun to provide us with information that sheds light on the nature of incest and the recovery process. No doubt their efforts will continue to increase our understanding of how to heal the wounds.

The second reason for my hesitancy to place much emphasis on differences is that I think it can interfere with the recovery process. The experience of incestuous abuse is an isolating one. The perpetrator must isolate his/her victim from possible sources of protection within the family. The perpetrator may also be successful in keeping the incestuous family unit separated from nonfamily members. The first step of recovery depends on breaking down the isolation in any way possible. Continued recovery requires sustained effort to overcome the effects of the years of isolation. The first time that an incest survivor hears someone else say, "That happened to me, too" or "I've always felt like that," his life changes. Listening to someone else tell of experiences and feelings that mirror his own contradicts a lifetime of being certain that no one will ever be able to understand. It appears to be far more important to recognize similarities than differences. I'm convinced that many of the distinctions that we cling to as important are, in reality, arbitrary and trifling. It is through the recognition of commonalities that connections are born, and the progress of recovery continues.

My third reason for hesitating to focus on differences is that the basic effect of sexual child abuse is damage to the ability to trust. This loss of trust is common to survivors of incestuous abuse, regardless of the specific forms that the abuse took.

Having expressed my reasons for believing that we shouldn't dwell too long on the differences, I'll briefly mention a few dysfunctional patterns that are frequently found in incestuous families—and offer some speculation about severity of effects. (**Remember:** If your experience doesn't exactly fit these patterns, it does *not* mean that you weren't abused or that your abuse was less serious than someone else's. We aren't attempting to set up a hierarchy of sexual abuse victims. You deserve full attention, consideration and support in dealing with what happened to you, regardless of the details of anyone else's experience.)

Many, but by no means all, incest survivors come from families where there were multiple patterns of abuse or dysfunction. I have had individual clients and group members whose parents (and/or other family members) were alcoholics, drug addicts, compulsive overeaters, child-beaters, wife-batterers, suicidal, severely depressed, paranoiac, manic-depressive, criminals, and/or were themselves survivors of incest. These other dysfunctions may even serve to help keep the incest from being discovered. If anyone perceives that the victimized child is troubled, it can be explained as the result of having a drunken father (or a crazy mother, etc.).

But incest is certainly not limited to multiple abusive environments. I have spoken with many survivors whose families would seem to the outside observer to be models of respectability: stable, financially secure, sober, clean, and reverent. Since, for abuse to be possible, secrecy must be maintained, what better camouflage than a model family? (And what better means of keeping the victim confused?) It is massively harmful for a child to be the keeper of the one painful secret in a "wholesome" family. And he will often keep the secret in an attempt to protect the stability of the family.

As with female survivors, many men report family situations where one or both parents were absent or otherwise unavailable for significant periods of time. Whether these absences were caused by chronic physical illness, mental hospitalization, job requirements, imprisonment, death, or other factors, the child may have spent significant periods of time in foster care, with other relatives or family friends, in institutions, or in the care of an abusive parent, sibling, stepparent, or other parent surrogate. This situation left the child vulnerable for victimization by the other parent or another adult.

In fact, the very unavailability of the absent parent to fulfill her (sometimes his) "conjugal duties" has been used as an excuse for the sexual exploitation of children. In these instances, the victimized child is forced into the role of replacing the absent parent and taking responsibility for assuming the "duties" of a spouse: companionship, housekeeping, child-rearing—and sex. And the absence is not necessarily physical. The sexual and emotional disinterest of a mate has caused both male and female children to be served up as substitutes. A patriarchal society fosters the idea—sometimes reinforced by law—that a husband has a "right" to receive sexual satisfaction. Many male perpetrators have attempted to use their wife's unavailability to rationalize and justify abusive behavior. Once again, we are looking at frequent, but not inevitable, patterns of incestuous families.

Sexual child abuse also occurs in families where the parents report that they sustain an active (sometimes mutually satisfactory) sex life. This may seem contradictory unless we remember that we are not talking about normal adult consensual sexual activity, but about *abuse* of children that takes a sexual form. A society that treats any class of its citizens as property—whether they are black, poor, disabled, women, or children—creates a social framework that is geared to perpetuating patterns of violence and sexual abuse. It is a cultural context that breeds incestuous families. It is only by changing our attitudes toward the rights of all individuals that we can eliminate incestuous abuse. This must be a long-range goal of all caring people. In the meantime, we must seek to protect all children from further abuse and to support all adult incest survivors in their recovery. You have been isolated by the abuse for too long; now is the time to overturn the effects of isolation. The path of recovery may be long, but it doesn't have to be lonely. You are not alone.

Speaking with hundreds of therapists and thousands of incest survivors has led me to one inescapable conclusion: The most striking feature about incest is the *similarity* of its effects on adult survivors. True, there are differences of specific situations and of how individuals are affected by abuse. There might be other factors that we haven't yet recognized. We will probably have the answers some day. For now, these matters are speculative. What we do know is that the effects of sexual child abuse result from the violation of what should be a loving, protective relationship. When this happens to a child, the hurts are profound. When they begin to share their stories, talk about and express their feelings, incest survivors—whether male or female, heterosexual or gay—recognize each other as brothers and sisters.

The commonalities provide a basis for understanding, sharing and connecting. They are a foundation for figuring out how to approach recovery. In light of these tremendous similarities, the differences no longer seem to be terribly significant. Themes that appear in later chapters will probably strike some uncomfortably familiar chords for the very reason that they reflect experiences that are shared by many survivors. They include:

- Issues of masculinity, gender, and sexuality in the context of abuse
- Feelings: how we learn to hide and deny them, and how to regain our ability to feel and express emotions in a healthy way
- Themes of loss of childhood and other losses
- Coping strategies that have helped survivors get through their abusive childhoods, and how to change these childhood strategies when they turn into adult problems
- Aspects of recovery—overcoming the fears and mistrust and moving on with the specifics of healing your life

The next four chapters of this book focus on what it means to be a man in the context of incestuous abuse. Their purpose is not to create divisions between men and women, and certainly not to imply that the abuse of boys is more or less serious than that of girls. In order to rid society of incestuous abuse, we must understand all its aspects. We must explore our attitudes toward men as victims, seeing how they differ from the way we view women. And we must examine how we view sexuality and feelings. Doing so creates a context for understanding the effects of incest and provides us with clues for recovery.

KEITH'S STATEMENT

Speaking directly to his fellow survivors—his
"brothers in suffering and courage"—Keith, a thirty-seven-year-old
survivor, writes of struggle and hope.

I would be dead today if there were not people who thought that incest, sexual abuse, and violence against children was a crime. I promised myself that whatever else I wrote for this book, that statement would be the first thing I wrote. I write today to you, my brothers in suffering and in courage, so that you can know that another feels as you do. I want to give you courage to feel what you know to be true—that a crime of violence was committed against you, an innocent. And I write for myself, too, because for hope to be real, it must be felt like a friend who touches us with a kind and gentle hand. If my words give you hope, they give you courage. The courage of knowing that not every human being is a beast who will hurt you, or a coward who will betray you. The courage of knowing that there are other human beings who understand just how much courage it takes for you to hold on to your dreams of love and being understood and accepted. And, yes, the courage in your dreams of wanting to love, understand and accept those who truly love you. Perhaps finally, the courage to act against your suffering—to win for all of us another life filled with innocence, gentleness, and courage. That is, a human life.

Incest is the story of silence. The silence of the innocent, of the vulnerable, of the trusting, of the sensitive, of the sweet, of the human. That silence alone thunders condemnation of the weak, sick, pathetic, cruel, and vicious individuals who destroy the expression of innocence, vulnerability, trust, sensitivity, sweetness, and humanity in another human being. This remains true even if our abusers were not the totally depraved individuals that some of our number suffered under. Even if there was some love in the hearts of our abusers, insofar as they abused us, they were not expressing love, but the disintegration and degradation of their humanity.

There is a violence in every betrayal of trust. That violence is at the core of the incest experience. Incest is not only a reprehensible crime of violence against the person of a child, but also a crime against the future of that child. There are three crimes in incest. The actual torture and/or using and/or neglect of the child is one. Denying that child an environment in which to express his childish love is the second. The last is denying that child a future based on the good things in life and the highest level of human achievement founded on the secure development of a human being. I was that child.

Like many survivors of abuse who have protected themselves by consciously forgetting, I struggle daily to turn my images of extreme sexual and physical violence directed against me—as well as my overpowering feelings of having been seductively overwhelmed—into memories. I have very clear images that are disassociated from the emotions I felt at the time they were happening, as well as very strong physical sensations that are disassociated from the events that engendered them.

I utterly reject the actions of those who forced me to drink at the trough of human experience, wanting humiliation to mark me forever so that they would never have to answer for or explain their actions. Instead, they saw in my suffering and confusion an easy way out of their guilt, or even a justification of their violence and cowardice.

Today I am not silent. Today I write with rage that speaks in a human voice about all the things that were forced on me and all the things that were denied me. To my question, who gave my abusers the right to make me suffer the way I did, I answer back that human beings have only the right to love each other and to care for each other.

I was abused by my mother. It is still frightening to me to say that, but today I can say it. Tomorrow, within the context of loving men and women who share my struggle against the violence of our childhood, I will be able to feel it.

Why is it that the community of survivors is so important? If we had lived lives of joy in childhood (which is our birthright), we would not even think of asking. We would know that the ultimate joy in human life is to share the love and the experience of life with other humans.

What we longed for—to be touched, loved, nurtured,

supported, understood, accepted, noticed, and appreciated, an innate human longing that speaks before words, is felt before feelings and is known before knowledge—was used against us, or given as reason for our punishment by those who could not live with the reality of their own humanity and sought to purge themselves of their feelings of guilt, or shame, or horror, or fear, or cruelty by blaming us for their feelings or desires. They acted cruelly and blamed us for their actions. To cover up their crimes, they made us participate in them. To make themselves seem less frightened and more powerful, they made us call it love. Is it any wonder, with these humans as teachers, we have all looked for a way to be human all alone?

We have all gone as far as we could, for as long as we could and as deeply as we dared, alone. If you have picked up this book, you know that you can never run far enough to make you happy. You have run—always with one eye toward the love of others—wishing to stop, to rest, to finally and deeply and simply and completely trust another, and so win back your trust in yourself. For who understands a call that is not echoed back? The joy in life is in fitting our song in the chorus of life.

It is only our abusers who value our silence and isolation. "If you are silent, you are not real," they say. "And if you talk I/ we will make sure no one recognizes your words as human, because you are crazy, ugly, stupid, dirty, stubborn, bad, selfish, weak, lying, unlovable, and unbelievable."

But we survivors—part of the chorus of humanity—answer back, "We believe *you*, not them. We believe you before you feel the outrage of what was done to you, before you know for certain and forever that *what* was/is a crime, before we have met, because you are ourselves and your story is our story."

And so it begins. I speak to your hands that hold this book, to your eyes that read these words, and to your heart that jumps—ever so slightly, cautiously—or perhaps even leaps at the sound of my love, which is a call to battle. And your hands respond, feeling that this book feels good in your hands. Your eyes respond, going back to that one sentence in this piece that didn't filter through your brain, but leapt directly to your heart. And your heart responds; your tired, weary heart, sick of all the violations, silences, denials, betrayal, and cowardice. Your heart has loved life so much you have never completely given up your hope that there might be human beings who would love you for the whole truth of who you are, and where you have been, and not hurt you or deny you because of it. Your heart has stood ready to forgive humanity as a whole despite what some among its number have done to you, if only someone would step forward and tell the truth.

On this day, at this moment, on this page, in this book, I am that person. And I say to you: You *are* innocent. If you are holding this book in your hands; if you have allowed your heart to express the boundless courage that beats within it and the hopes you have refused to let die, then you already have within you all that is required to carry this struggle through to the end.

Ours is not an easy struggle, taking place as it does at the most fundamental levels of human character. But remember this: If you have been abused, you are already engaged in the struggle.

The core of our being was not destroyed by our abuse, but the lengths we had to go to survive left us very vulnerable to life. To act in the world takes an innocence based on trust. The more completely we avoid fighting the battle to find the human beings we can trust and so begin to learn to trust our own judgments, feelings, and thoughts to make sense of the world, the more completely our abusers will have robbed us of our innocence and the more guilty we will feel and act in a world that seems confusing, impenetrable, and frightening.

What you lack is help, and help is something you can get. If we do not reach, however, the kind of help that allows us to connect our experience to that of humanity as a whole and not just the particular perversion of it expressed in the actions of our abusers, we suffer tremendous losses in the real attempts we make to connect with the good things in life. We have no way of using the best we humans have come up with to dispel our ignorance, calm our fears, soften our pain.

Life does not remain static. Some losses and some mistakes cannot be undone and the continued defeat of our hopes over time takes a toll that for some of us leads to death. There are those among our number who did not get the help that would have allowed them the support and understanding to act in such a way as to get the love they needed and so to experience hope in the only way it can be experienced: to have something real—really ours—now, here, right now, today and tomorrow.

I know what I'm talking about because I was almost one of

those human beings. My denial of the effects of incest/sexual/ physical violence in my life cost me the love of a woman I really loved, a family (her daughter), and a move into what was going to be a deeper level of adulthood. I could not protect the gains I had managed to make in life despite my incest history. I could not make the move I wanted to make to win for myself a deeper level of satisfaction in life, without looking incest squarely in the face. I bargained with time to face that fear and lost a deeply crucial and inexpressibly dear set of relationships and hopes, as my lover and friend lost her faith in me (in combination with whatever pulls there were in her own history and the development of her own life in relation to mine).

One year ago, in the immediate aftermath of the breakup, I did make a move to Boston to join a group I had heard about for male survivors of incest. It was do that or die by ending my life. I hope this book helps you to decide to get the help you need to really go after incest and get it out of your life completely. There is no compromise with an enemy who has no pity. Take your time; find the ways to proceed with kindness and safety for yourself, but do it. It is an illusion to think that once we begin there will be no turning back, because there was no turning back from the day our abuse began. Our only choice is to live in fear or to live with courage.

We were not the lucky ones, but because of our experiences and our integrity in the face of them—which is the deepest form of self-knowledge—we bring a special tenderness, a special gentleness, a special courage, and a special joy to the realm of human experience. If we take up this battle with courage and truth and follow it to the end, we bring that joy not only to others but also to ourselves. We have something true to say about human love. No human could ask for more.

I used to dream of the day when I would not feel shame in my heart at the fact that I existed. I used to dream of the day when my shame at being a human with human needs that seemed so "awful" would be dispelled by the love of others and my love for the life that flowed through me. I have always lived and died with my heart. I have always longed to be a man who would live and die with the truth of that heart. Today, I am becoming that man. Tomorrow, I hope to join you on the other side of our current struggle, where your voice and tender story of love and hope sound like the sweet protecting embrace and call to action that I hope my voice sounds to you.

I also promised myself that the last sentence I wrote would read: "And this goes for all the women, too."

PART TWO

About Men

Messages
About Masculinity

The tone I use on my son will be the tone he uses on himself.
                                    —A MALE SURVIVOR

No experience exists in isolation. The way we respond to the sexual abuse of children is the direct result of how we define sexual abuse and what we think about children. By the same token, our society's response to the sexual abuse of boys and the aftermath of that abuse reflects how we define maleness. Not only does our perception of men (and of victimization) set a context for abuse, it provides a backdrop for our perception of the male survivor. To understand the context in which abuse, survival, healing, and recovery take place, we must examine a number of our cultural beliefs. We need to look at the nature of our ideas about abuse, victims and perpetrators, children, and women. And we must be aware of what we think being a man is all about. Examining the messages we receive about being male lets us see how gender stereotypes affect the recovery process.

Seeing Through Stereotypes

Some years ago, when I taught a college course called "Sex Roles and Sexuality," one of the assignments I gave my students was to choose a mass-circulation magazine or to watch three hours of television. They were to ignore the content of the articles or programs, focusing their attention instead on the commercial advertisements. What they were to look for was what the media were telling them about how to be a man or a woman. With very few exceptions, the messages showed little variation, regardless of the nature of the publication or the time slot and type of program. That the media were presenting us with consistent messages about masculinity and femininity came as no revelation to the students. Neither were they surprised at the themes, which offered traditional stereotypes of male and female temperaments, interests, and roles.

What came as a shock were the frequency and persistence of the communication. Many of the students realized that they had no idea of the extent to which they were subjected to this information. Students who chose to expand their investigation further found the same messages in other advertising media: billboards, radio, newspapers, direct mail, etc. But these messages are not limited to the advertising industry. They abound in the content of films, literature, textbooks, theater, song lyrics, music videos, fashion, and children's toys, games, and stories. Everywhere we turn we are learning about what we "should" do to be acceptably male or female.

The training begins at birth, often supplied unconsciously by parents and other adults who were themselves raised according to similar standards. Studies have shown that male and female babies tend to be held differently, treated differently, and given differing degrees of attention. The words of appreciation and admiration for infants of different sexes are as different as blue and pink baby blankets. Even parents who strive diligently to purge their children's environment of gender-stereotype limitations cannot keep them insulated from the outside world. Other adults and peers will offer rewards for "gender-appropriate" behavior and punishments for the reverse. All but the most unusual of schools further reinforce these ideals. Children will learn what is expected of them in order to gain acceptance and approval. They are quick to figure out how they can fit in, and equally astute in their understanding of the ways that they can't "measure up." Continual frustration of a child's striving for belonging can lead to resentment, hopelessness, or even revengeful behavior. The child who feels "different" most often feels inferior and isolated as well. And no matter how persistently parents strive to rid themselves of these conventions, they rarely have complete success.

If our ideas of appropriate maleness (and femaleness) are ever questioned, it is only in the most superficial manner, since we are seldom aware of how deeply we have internalized these cultural stereotypes. (Just as a fish, having known nothing else, can have no perspective on water, it is the rare individual who is able to step outside his/her cultural conditioning.) Since these cultural ideals are reinforced everywhere we turn, we are most likely to accept them as "natural" and universal, rather than see them as what they are—one expression of human possibilities. Instead of opening ourselves to the virtually unlimited potential and flexibility of which human beings are capable, we concentrate our energies on trying to live up to an ideal. The fact that ideals are absolutes (and therefore never completely attainable) leaves us open to feelings of frustration and inadequacy. Nonetheless, we continue in the hope that if we only could get ourselves to look, act, or feel differently (better), we would be OK (perfect). These negative self-judgments are reinforced every time we look outside ourselves for confirmation of our self-worth. Once we accept that we fail to meet the standard of masculinity (or femininity), we carry a sense of inferiority into most areas of life. Men have spent their lives trying to "prove" their masculinity, or have succumbed to the feeling that because they aren't "all man," they aren't men at all.

If you have any doubts about what I'm referring to, try the experiment yourself. Pretend you are a Martian trying to learn about Americans. Pick up a copy of the first magazine you come across at a newsstand, supermarket checkout line, or waiting room. Watch an hour of prime-time television, another of daytime shows ("women's programming"), and a third of sports offerings ("men's programs"). If you're ready for a real shock, check out some Saturday morning cartoons ("children's programs"). Listen for the words that are used to describe men and those that refer to women. (The differences are equally apparent for boys and girls.) Look at posture and body positioning. Who appears to be dominant more often? Who is portrayed as being "in control"? What possessions do men (or women) appear to have? What careers? And in what frequency? Even the background music in commercials may be different if the advertisers are trying to sell a "male-oriented" product. It won't be long before you have a pretty good idea of "what it means to be a man." Multiply these messages by literally thousands of times a day, every day, in a multitude of forms, and you can appreciate their power—and the difficulty involved in recognizing, understanding and contradicting them.

Another experiment can be done alone or with friends. Come up with a list of adjectives such as strong, pretty, silly, competent, mechanical, passive, dizzy, dominant, seductive, athletic, nurturing. Ask people to list their first response to each word as masculine or feminine. Even individuals who know that none of these adjectives is limited to either gender will have a hard time denying that they have internalized some feelings about them. The most "ardent feminist" or most "liberated male" was also raised in a sexist society that unquestioningly accepted stereotypic views of masculinity and femininity.

In order to free ourselves from the limitations of these definitions, we have to be aware of their existence and recognize their negative effects. This calls for work and attention. Automatic judgments about masculinity and femininity are everywhere. Even our supposedly neutral, judgment-free reference books display our cultural biases. A look at a major thesaurus reveals the following synonyms for the word *feminine:* delicate, tender, docile, submissive, effete, sissyish, and faggy. For *womanly*, listings include: mature, soft, ladylike, refined, sympathetic, tender, and motherly. Turning to synonyms for *masculine*, we come across macho, robust, muscular, athletic, strong, vigorous, lusty, energetic, powerful, potent, brave, fearless, unafraid, hairy, and butch. The entry for *manly* yields two-fisted, he-mannish, hairy-chested, mighty, broad-shouldered, red-blooded, rugged, intrepid, audacious, daring, tough, unflinching, ready for anything, honorable, decent, and ballsy. The message is clear. What is expected of one sex is denied to the other. A woman cannot be "masculine"; no true man displays "womanly" attributes. To be a woman one must be passive, soft, nurturing . . . and weak. Men, in turn, must not evidence these "softer emotions." They must be strong, devoid of fear, unflinching, and capable ("ready for anything"). Any lapse into doubt, confusion, tenderness or emotionalism is perceived as weakness—a female characteristic.

Reference works don't create cultural attitudes; they *reflect* them. Perhaps there really is a "rule book" for being a man—it just isn't called that. And it isn't written down in one place; these "rules" are found everywhere. You only need to listen to our speech patterns to understand the restrictions that these distinctions place on us.

In the process of becoming men, little boys watch, listen, and learn. They mimic the postures, gestures, speech, and behavior of adult males. They are exposed to the values, ideals, and norms of their culture, neighborhood and family. They are punished for behavior that is considered unacceptable and reinforced for desirable responses. Some cultures are more flexible about the range of permissible behavior and less punitive when the rules are broken. But every society has ideas about what constitutes masculinity and femininity. To keep their cultural viewpoints intact, each group places limitations on individual expression of diversity. The traditional American (northern and western European) view of men as physically strong, powerful, dominant, controlled, independent, self-reliant, and successful may be fine for those who legitimately fit that picture—although this stereotypical male role model certainly has some serious limitations.

Restricting the range of permissible behavior and emotions compromises a man's creativity and his ability to respond flexibly to life situations. (How this creates problems for abuse survivors will be addressed later.) Moreover, for the man (or boy) whose temperament is incompatible with that image, life can be hell. He may be teased, ridiculed, shunned, or even brutalized. It may be difficult for him to achieve credibility in social, educational, and professional environments. He may be rejected by his family as a source of embarrassment. Faced with this type of pressure to conform, he may continually strive to meet society's expectations of a man, exhausting his energies and denying his essential nature in order to gain acceptance. Failing to develop into the male ideal, some men pretend to be what they are not, turning themselves into a parody of traditional machismo. Others give up the attempt, rejecting themselves because of their perceived failure as men.

The specifics don't much matter. However it manifests itself, the traditional view of the "ideal" man leaves every man isolated. Forced to depend only on himself (for fear of seeming less than a man) cooperation becomes a virtual impossibility. Vulnerability, seen as weakness, is equally impossible. What we have left are isolation and pretense. The difficulty of a restricted view of what it means to be male (or female) is that we are confined to limited resources. Women are kept from realization of the stronger, lustier, more reckless, and "tougher" aspects of their natures. Men, in turn, do not have access to their tender, emotional, nurturing, and sympathetic qualities. And everyone loses—in deference to a competition that sets men against men, women against women, and the sexes against each another.

We have to stop being concerned with determining the "right" way to be a man. There is ample room for diversity of interests, personalities, temperaments, and capabilities for women and men. What disturbs me is the inevitable result of an attitude that *limits* human diversity. We have accepted a collective mind-set that limits our range of choice. To curtail freedom of expression of our variety weakens us as a people. It creates a climate that enables us to accept and justify the victimization of anyone who is different. It isn't wrong for you to be a certain way. Freedom means the right to be who you *are*, whether or not you are compatible with an acceptable image. You must have the absolute right to fulfill any stereotypes, reject them completely, or select only the parts that fit—without fear of ridicule or rejection.

Rigid adherence to a particular view of masculinity not only increases the incidence of victimization, but severely inhibits prospects for recovery. It does so by equating "different" with "wrong." If we view diversity as bad, it is only a small step to sanctioning the punishment, rejection, or abuse of those who look or act "unacceptably." We stand a far better chance of becoming healthy (individually and collectively) when we come to appreciate who we are and applaud our human diversity.

Intolerance inhibits the full expression of our humanness. Allowing others their differences (and celebrating their uniqueness) opens the

FOCUS

OUR DEBT TO THE WOMEN'S MOVEMENT

It is important to say a few words about feminism and the "women's movement." Feminists have received a great deal of criticism based on misunderstanding of their aims and ideas.

I believe that men recovering from incest have no greater ally than the feminist movement. In exploding the traditional view of what it means to be a woman (or a man), feminists have opened greater possibilities of realizing our full potential as human beings than ever existed before. They have challenged the inevitability of a patriarchal system that accepts the exploitation of smaller and physically weaker individuals. They have explored ways of interrelating through cooperation and mutual respect, rather than seeing violence and competition as the only means of resolving differences. They have attempted to change our attitudes and behavior toward children. And, to an amazing extent, they have succeeded.

Change is slow and difficult. Power and privilege don't yield easily. But, more and more, our laws, social behavior, institutions, and ways of interacting reflect a new awareness of possibilities. There is no doubt that the active work of the feminist movement has forced our society to recognize the existence of incest. Feminists have continued to resist and contradict the forces that would seek to deny the realities of abuse, sweep them under the rug, or minimize their effects.

door to self-acceptance and self-appreciation. As will be seen later in this book, self-appreciation is a cornerstone of recovery.

Men As Victims   In looking at what happens to a man when he is victimized, we have to be careful to set up no artificial distinctions between abuse of boys and girls. The effects of abuse are equally profound whether the victim is male or female; they are also generally similar. It is likely that a greater number of variations can be attributed to individual personality characteristics than to differences between the nature of men and women. There are, however, differences in the ways that we raise male and female children, based on how our culture views the sexes. It is reasonable to assume that since we have different ideas about the nature, temperament, and capabilities of men and women—our different expectations of boys and girls are reflected in

People are skilled at ignoring what they don't want to deal with. In order to effect a change of attitude and behavior, a climate must be created that recognizes the need for change and encourages correction of problems. Change has to occur in context.

Judith Herman, M.D. (author of the book *Father-Daughter Incest*), has referred to the need for "a movement" to insure that information about trauma doesn't need to be "rediscovered" every hundred years. Without a movement to remind and reinforce, the best research data are ignored. Society at large (including mental health professionals) finds it less stressful to look the other way.

Proponents of feminist theory and action haven't permitted this ostrichlike denial. They continue to insist that we deal with the realities of many important life issues, including incest. They have forced recognition of these issues in the face of resistance and misunderstanding. It is no accident that only now has the sexual abuse of boys and girls become a topic of widespread public discussion. Years of struggle by feminists have set the stage.

Adult male incest survivors are among the beneficiaries of the work of the feminist movement. We must ignore the stereotypes we have heard about "women's libbers"; these stereotypes arise out of fear—and the fear comes from ignorance of the facts. The fact is that feminists have improved life for all of us. By helping us to realize our potential as humans, they have touched every woman, man, and child.

When we can really look at what these changes mean to us, we will be well on our way to creating a world where abusive behavior is unthinkable. That will be the ideal climate for recovery from past hurts, and the safe nurturing of all children. We are still a long way from realizing these goals, but we would be a lot farther from them if it weren't for the work of the feminists. Indeed, it is no exaggeration to say that the women's movement is enabling us to become "real men."

how we raise them—we will also have somewhat different ideas about male and female victims of sexual abuse.

Male survivors are not immune from viewing themselves through the lens of culturally determined male stereotypes. You are likely to have some different perceptions and expectations of yourself than if you were a female survivor in similar circumstances. Recognizing that these generalizations do not apply to all men or all women, this chapter looks at particular emphases and perspectives regarding men as victims.

Human babies, male and female, are born with equal capacity for feeling and expressing the full range of human emotion. Shortly after birth, however, adults begin the process of teaching children the ways of their culture. Much of this training is unconscious, the adults not even realizing that they are teaching the child (by their words and behavior) what is considered appropriate to their group. Part of this training (anthropologists call it *enculturation*) includes learning the different ways that men and women are supposed to behave. All societies differentiate between behaviors and roles they consider "male" and those they consider "female." The specific definitions of masculine and feminine, however, vary tremendously from culture to culture. Behavior and personality traits considered masculine in one society would be thought of as feminine in another and as gender-neutral in yet another.

The culture and personality school of anthropology investigates ways in which being raised in a particular cultural tradition influences a person's adult personality structure. The work of these psychological anthropologists provides us with ample evidence that human beings are infinitely adaptable—capable of a great range of behavior, personality characteristics, and emotional styles. Each society develops its beliefs and behavior from a vast spectrum of possibilities. However, the members of a particular society are usually unaware that their ideas about masculinity/femininity are choices. We assume that the system by which we view the world is the only logical and normal way (and, by extension, any other way is strange and illogical). This limited vision (anthropologists call it *ethnocentrism*) fails to recognize that our ideas about ourselves are not "natural," but are *learned*. We must, therefore, look at what our own culture teaches us about gender.

In no area of life is the difference between our expectations of men and women more obvious than in sexuality. The male is expected to be the confident, knowledgeable, experienced, aggressive, dominant sexual partner. Women, in turn, are supposed to remain passive, "virginal," tentative, and submissive. Men are to be the seducers, arousers, and controllers, whole women are passively swept away by passion. In sex (as in ballroom dancing) men have been expected to lead and women to follow. A woman who freely enjoys sex is viewed with some suspicion, particularly when she initiates it. The traditional ideal is that women remain virgins until marriage, whereas men should have prior experience. Young men "sow their wild oats," while young women are said to "go wrong."

The fact that these ideas are the result of self-deluded male fantasies, with little basis in fact, hasn't prevented them from showing a remarkable persistence in male-female relationships. (Even the "female" fantasies found in romance novels and "love comics" serve to reinforce the idea that men are the romantic seducers, and women are initiated into sex by the more powerful, controlling males.) On the surface it would appear that this is a system where men benefit and women are oppressed; however, the reality is that no one benefits from a sexist structure. When a society limits individual diversity, everyone loses. Setting up arbitrary distinctions between the sexes inhibits the development and expression of individual talents. None of us can freely explore our potential. This is true for both sexes; men as well as women fall victim to the rigidities of sexism.

In one rather odd way, these distinctions between what we expect of men and women have added to the difficulties of male survivors. Since women are expected to be passive, weaker, powerless beings, there is room for sympathy when they are victimized. Again, this does not mean that female victims have an easier time of it. (On the contrary, the very acceptance of victimization of women perpetuates abuse and inhibits their recovery.) But there is a particular focus of the problem that is faced only by men. It arises from the fact that our culture provides no room for a man as victim. Men are simply not supposed to be victimized. A "real man" is expected to be able to protect himself in any situation. He is also supposed to be able to solve any problem and recover from any setback. When he experiences victimization, our culture expects him to be able to "deal with it like a man." Unfortunately, "dealing with it like a man" usually translates as avenging the hurt (preferably violently) and then forgetting about it—moving on. When he cannot—or is unwilling to—resort to this mode of problem-solving, he is called a coward and scorned as unmanly. As much as we are aware of the lack of logic in this sort of macho thinking, it is the rare individual who hasn't unconsciously internalized these attitudes to some degree. A male survivor may know that violent revenge would be a dangerous response to his situation, but still feel like a weakling for not resorting to it. Men are also supposed to be in control of their feelings at all times. The survivor's ongoing feelings of confusion, frustration, anger, and fear can become further evidence of his failings as a man.

Since men "are not supposed to be victims," abuse (and particularly sexual abuse) becomes a process of demasculinization (or emasculation). If men aren't to be victims (the equation reads), then victims aren't men. The victimized male wonders and worries about what the abuse has turned him into. Believing that he is no longer an adequate man, he may see himself as a child, a woman, gay, or less than human—an irreparably damaged freak.

Some survivors resort to broad parodies of "acceptably masculine" behavior in order to counteract this self-perception. Men in my recovery groups have talked of the lengths to which they have gone in order to prove their masculinity, including daredevil activities, sexual promiscuity, violent behavior, law breaking, military exploits, and the like. Others report having "given up," accepting repeated victimization as inevitable. Frequently, a male survivor will feel that he must conceal the fact that he was abused, for fear that he will be rejected, disdained, or exposed to ridicule. Having internalized the view of victims as being less than men, he is certain that others would view him in the same way. The lack of available information about sexual abuse of male children leads him to imagine that he must face his difficulties alone and that few if any other men share his situation. (Some men who have attempted to receive help have in fact had their problems discounted, ignored, or treated insensitively. This treatment serves as confirmation to them that they should not be considered worthy of respect as men.)

Seeing himself as less than a man, the incest survivor may view such "male" attributes and accomplishments as strength, power, and success as beyond his reach. Success seems like an impossible dream; the most that he thinks he can hope for is survival by conscientiously (and exhaustingly) keeping up appearances. His only success, he believes, lies in keeping other people from discovering the true extent of his shortcomings. As long as his act isn't exposed, he can get by. He lives in continual anxiety, feeling certain that his exposure is only a matter of time. He discounts any success that he does achieve as temporary at best—since it is based on deception. Similarly, he devalues his strength and power because he alone knows how weak and defenseless he feels. Whether his strengths, power and successes are physical, financial, professional, romantic, sexual, emotional, athletic, academic, intellectual, or social, he finds cause to write them off. No picture of reality is able to penetrate his wall of self-negation.

Alternatively, the male survivor might exert himself beyond all reason to prove himself a man. Feeling that he must conceal his shortcomings through worldly success, he strives for (and often achieves) wealth, recognition, and power. But even massively impressive attainments leave him feeling uncertain. There is always the possibility of discovery and humiliation. He fears that if anyone truly found out who he is (a fraud) and what he is (a victim of abuse), all of his accomplishments would mean nothing. The no-win situation appears again. If he achieves success through traditional education and hard work, he feels that the system has worked despite his personal inadequacies. If he forges his own path to success, he views it as a fluke, and feels that he never could have made it the way most (normal) people do. Whichever path he takes, the male survivor is certain that his knowledge, skill, strength, courage, personality, and aptitude are different from (and inferior to) other people's.

The male survivor didn't receive the same information as other children. Not having been issued the "rule book" about how to survive and prosper, he may spend his life figuring out how to achieve success, power and strength. Obsessed with hiding his faults and pretending to be normal, he is not apt to appreciate (or even notice) his *actual* successes and strengths. If he does recognize that he has made it, he still can't let down his guard. He must strenuously protect what he has built. Taking time for rest and enjoyment would cause him to be overtaken, displaced, and revealed as a failure. However the world views him, he knows the "truth." He is a victim; his only hope is in striving to keep that information hidden for as long as he can. It is exhausting to maintain his image and keep people from seeing his "true" self. If anyone gets intimate with him, there is the danger that they will see through the act. The survivor feels he must either sustain an illusion with anybody who gets close to him, or keep everyone at a distance so they won't see that he is a fraud.

The price of his "deception" is exhaustion and isolation. He never stops to consider another possibility—that his accomplishments and attributes are genuine. He is so busy worrying about being "found out" that it never occurs to him that other people might admire him *despite* his act, rather than because of it. He is so certain that he is unacceptable that the idea of someone liking him for himself is alien beyond consideration. People who like him are either fools or are being fooled. A major challenge of recovery for most incest survivors is rebuilding their self-esteem to the point where they begin to see in themselves what others see in them and recognize that those percep-tions are *accurate*. As they accomplish this, they move toward liking themselves as much as others like them.

Another difficulty faced by the male incest survivor arises from the confusion between power and abuse. The progression of this confu-sion is as follows: As a child, he had the experience of powerful adults abusing that power. In fact, the perpetrator may have also been his primary role model. Because of this, he is likely to draw the conclu-sion that to be a man he must be abusive. It isn't necessary for *all* powerful adults to behave abusively—one such experience can easily be generalized. The old saying "Once bitten; twice shy" operates most powerfully when the child was "bitten" by someone who meant so much to him. This logical misconception that confuses masculinity with abusiveness can play itself out in various ways. The survivor may set himself up as:

1 / A perpetrator. He feels that he must achieve power so as to avoid further victimization. In a world divided into victims and per-petrators, abuse can be interpreted as power. The only way of mas-culinizing (empowering) himself seems to be by turning someone else into a victim. As terrible as it feels to be an abuser, it feels like his only possibility of leaving the role of the victim. And he never wants to play the victim again. I have no doubt that this is much of the reason why so many child abusers are found to have been abused themselves.

2 / A victim. Once again, the survivor feels that the only options open to men are the roles of victim or perpetrator. Knowing how he felt as a victim, he is determined that he will never victimize another human being. So he resigns himself to remaining a victim. Since power is abusive, he reasons, the way to avoid being an abuser is to remain powerless. The role of victim has become familiar to him, and he carries it into all his adult interactions, expecting to be (and often being) taken advantage of. He finds confirmation of the inevitability of his position in each revictimization.

3 / A protector. Feeling that children are in constant danger from adults, many male survivors deal with their fear of being abused by taking on the role of protector. On a very basic level they may be attempting to give others the protection they needed as children (or still want for themselves). They may see their role of protector as the only way to achieve nonabusive closeness to other people. Our culture assigns the role of nurturer and caretaker to women. Men, too, have a need to be nurturing. They can sometimes meet this need by taking on the role of protector in human service professions, or by following "nontraditional" male pursuits, such as nursing or day-care work. My first incest recovery group consisted of six adult male survivors. Five of them were human service professionals; all of them dealt professionally with people in emotional crisis. I believe that it is no accident that there are great numbers of incest survivors (male as well as female) in the helping professions. Some incest survivors remain victims, others become perpetrators, and many become protectors.

I have called the belief that men have to be abusive a "logical misconception." What I mean by that phrase is that abused children have a limited perspective on the world, based on having received incorrect and incomplete information. I often refer to sexual abuse of children as *lying* to them. The lies that are taught through incest include misinformation about the nature of power, control, intimacy, sex, love—and what it means to be a man or a woman. If you are an incest survivor, then you have been lied to. These untruths were instilled forcefully over a long period of time.

As an incest survivor you will find that a significant aspect of your

FOCUS

WHY DID I WAIT THIS LONG?

Try not to punish yourself for not having dealt with the incest sooner. There can be many excellent reasons why you didn't do it until now:

1 / *The abuse was still too fresh.* You needed time and distance to regain your equilibrium and gain enough perspective to begin your recovery work.

2 / *You hadn't defined it as abuse.* It takes time and correct information to undo lies. What might be obvious to an outsider is not necessarily apparent to someone in the midst of a situation.

3 / *You were still caught by the ways that the perpetrator got you to keep silent.* It is difficult to question what we learned as children.

4 / *You were afraid.* Although the abusive situation is over, it can still feel dangerous. Even a dead perpetrator's presence can be felt strongly.

5 / *The time and place weren't right.* Not everyone is ready to hear about incest. You were right to wait until you found a safe and supportive environment for recovery.

6 / *You didn't know that you had options.* Women have only recently begun to work on incest recovery. This is a brand new area for men.

7 / *You were feeling too weak, battered and hopeless to take action for yourself.* Or you felt like such a terrible person that you didn't feel deserving of anything better.

8 / *There was too much else going on.* When you are dealing with daily crises and a basic struggle for survival, there are few resources and little energy left over for anything else. You had to get your life under better control in the present before tackling the past.

This list could go on, but I hope you get the point. Forget about self-blame. The reality is that *you couldn't have done what you are doing one minute sooner.* The time wasn't right, and for whatever reasons, you weren't ready. Punishing yourself about it isn't realistic. Neither will it decrease your recovery time. If anything, it will get in the way of your progress. There are solid reasons why most survivors don't begin to deal with these issues until they are in their thirties, forties, or fifties. Men in their teens and twenties usually are still too locked in denial and confusion to take much action on their recovery. If you started this work in your teens, you're off to a good start. But don't worry if you didn't. People start their recovery in different ways and at different points in their lives. We have no choice but to work in the present. The future is promising. *You are exactly where you "should" be in your recovery process.*

recovery consists of learning to identify the ways that you have been lied to. You must come to recognize what you were taught about masculinity, power, and abuse—and what was wrong with that information. You must deal with your feelings about having been lied to, and all the time that you lost because you believed the lies. You must grieve lost opportunities and failed relationships. You must express hopelessness about ever achieving a balanced life, confusion about whether you will be able to pick up the pieces, and fear about trying alternatives. And you will probably need to express further outrage at the lies and anger at the liars.

All of these endeavors will help you (as they have helped other survivors) understand what happened to you, clear your thinking, and allow you to begin to explore some different perspectives on human nature. Having had your trust so severely shattered, it isn't easy for you to accept new possibilities. You must move slowly, testing every person and every new idea.

In order to effect recovery, adult survivors must come to believe that recovery is possible *for them*. No one can accomplish this feat on faith alone. As an adult survivor, you have to know that what you are doing makes sense. You must test your perceptions against your own experiences and those of other people, including other survivors. All of this constitutes the process of recovery. It is a means of building a solid foundation of understanding, good judgment, experience, and some trust. With this as a base, adult survivors set out to build self-esteem, positive relationships, and a satisfying life.

Recovery is difficult, but exciting. You are not alone in what you are doing. As you proceed with your own recovery, you will be able to make use of the support, experience, knowledge, and understanding of many allies: male and female, incest survivors and pro-survivors, professionals and friends. Yes, recovery involves hard work and pain, but there is lots more. You will also experience wonder, renewed energy, and the delight of discovery. Every time the dark curtains part—even for an instant—to reveal the reality that awaits you on the other side of the struggle, you will know why you are doing this work. You will have had a vision of recovery. The world can never be again quite as bleak. You will come to know safety, belonging, and welcome. Recovery also involves lightness and joy. There is hard work, but there are pleasures along the way.

Men and Feelings

If fire could be contained in ice, that's how I get angry.
—DAVID, A MALE SURVIVOR OF ABUSE

We have all felt the effects of stereotypes about men and emotions. When we have feelings that are "inappropriate" to our gender, we are apt to worry about whether we are masculine/feminine enough. We may pretend to feelings that we don't actually have, dramatizing the "correct" emotional expression (or lack of expression) in a parody of how we think we should act. These limitations serve to make us suspicious of our own feelings, seeing them as having to be kept under rigid control, so that we aren't seen as weak, cowardly or "overemotional." We are turned into emotional "one-note songs" (angry men whose reaction to any difficulty is to rage, bluster and bully; women who burst into tears at any frustration) or, worse, adults who are incapable of recognizing that they have feelings, let alone expressing them.

"Real men don't cry." When you think about this statement, it is as silly as saying, "Real women don't laugh," or "Real dogs don't bark." Yet this line has been repeated so often that many of us accept it unquestioningly—much to our detriment. We have heard this kind of mistaken notion so many times that both men and women have been fooled into believing that:

- Men *can't* cry.
- Men shouldn't feel any emotion.
- There are "male feelings" and "female feelings."
- Feelings are weak or unhealthy.
- Expressing emotions is juvenile.
- Adults outgrow their need to cry.
- Women have free access to their feelings and men do not.
- Logic is masculine and feelings are feminine.
- Feelings get in the way of thinking.
- Expressing your feelings means you are out of control.

Most of the male incest survivors I have spoken to have spent a great deal of frustrating time trying to *think* their way out of their feelings. It is an exercise in frustration because the trauma of incest doesn't yield to reason or logic alone. The trauma of child abuse isn't just a "mistake" brought about by "illogical thinking." Perpetrators of sexual child abuse aren't simply behaving illogically; they are harming children deeply. It is not illogical to hurt a child: it is wrong. And harming a child in this way wounds him emotionally. These injuries are caused by people who themselves have emotional problems. You can't "reason" with abusive behavior and you can't "think" the hurts away. Incest is a highly emotionally charged situation. To understand it and heal its scars requires the "logic of emotions." Until you understand and work through your history of incest on an emotional as well as a logical level, it will continue to interfere with your enjoyment of life. This chapter looks at the myths and realities of our attitudes toward our feelings. It explains why we must change our ideas about emotions in order to successfully recover from sexual abuse.

Buying into erroneous ideas about emotions without examining where they are incorrect places you at a tremendous disadvantage in your recovery from abuse. Looking at the reality of emotions enables you to reject misinformation and get on with the business of healing.

As I noted earlier, each society teaches its children (consciously and unconsciously) the traits and behaviors that it considers appropriate to males or females. The expression of emotions is subjected to the same determinants as any other aspect of behavior. Therefore, we must look at what our own culture teaches us about gender and feelings in order to understand the relation of men to their emotions.

It would be easy to conclude that, in our culture, women are allowed to feel and men aren't. But that would be an oversimplification. Both men and women are limited in their expression of emotions, but in different ways. It is considered inappropriate for either men or women to freely express their full range of feelings. Women are given permission to experience those feelings that we tend to label as feminine (grief, fear, embarrassment). They are therefore allowed more freedom to express these emotions by crying, trembling, blushing, and giggling—activities generally considered to be a display of weakness in a man. Since it is considered less seemly for women to feel the more masculine ("stronger") emotions (anger, hearty excitement, powerful joy), they consequently receive less encouragement in expressing rage or full-throated laughter.

The learning of what constitutes acceptable male and female emotions begins early. Adults are quicker to shame young boys for being "crybabies." In fact, the form that the shaming takes often likens them to girls—the ultimate insult. Boys learn to repress certain emotions in order to avoid the stigma of appearing weak and feminine. Little girls are not unaware that they are considered inferior. Yet members of "the weaker sex" are punished more frequently when they assert their anger. A little girl who is strong and self-confident is criticized as being a "tom*boy*." The message is clear. There are ways that male and female children are supposed to behave—there are appropriate and inappropriate emotions for each sex—and woe unto the child who expresses the wrong kind of behavior or feelings.

The sanctions continue even more strongly into adolescence and adulthood, reinforced by pressure from peers. Social institutions and role models evolve to reinforce our image of the stoic, strong, sometimes angry, logical, and insensitive (sensitivity being suspect as a feminine virtue) male and the emotional (sometimes hysterical), illogical, weaker female. Our movie heroes and heroines, commercial advertising, children's (and adult) literature, family, schools, and the work world all abound with examples that support these views of the sexes. Although some of these ideas are changing, changes come slowly.

For the individual who was raised in an incestuous family, especially one that is also violent (or otherwise dysfunctional), the problem of feelings is further complicated. In such a family, emotional expression tends to be associated with abuse. Feelings often will build until they burst out in a torrent of anger, leading to further verbal, physical, and/or sexual abuse. To respond emotionally to these assaults only makes matters worse. Crying, trembling, or even laughter is likely to provoke renewed attacks. One client reported to me that he had been severely beaten as a child because his mother had overheard him laughing from the next room. She assumed that he was laughing at her, and he didn't have time to tell her that he had been reading a comic book. His voice was flat when he told me, "It probably wouldn't have mattered anyway. I was always getting it for something."

A boy's crying or trembling is even more likely to provoke a violent response. The behavior is considered weak and unmasculine, and becomes a justification for the adult's brutality. Many of my clients have talked about learning to control their tears and fears to avoid triggering renewed physical or sexual attacks. One said, "My father told me, 'Stand up straight and stop that cringing. You look like a whipped dog.' Then he whipped me." The phrase, "Stop crying or I'll give you something to cry about," is familiar to most children, although few children cry without reason. Once again, the abused boy is receiving a clear message. Keep your feelings in check and try to prevent other people from expressing theirs. Feelings can only hurt you. The boy is learning to hide, deny, and control his emotions and to help others to do the same. By the time he reaches adulthood, the technique has been mastered. Learning to thaw this emotional ice jam is a difficult process, but one that is essential to recovery.

An abused child will often pick up an additional message about feelings. His perception of the world is that there are only two kinds of people, abusers and victims. It is clear to him where the power lies; only the abuser is permitted to express anger. The child is not allowed to express his angry feelings. Any angry response by the child will more than likely provoke further abuse. Anger is an emotion that is reserved for those in power. This leads the abused child to equate anger with power. (He has also witnessed that crying and trembling are perceived as weaknesses and lead to victimization.) He draws the logical conclusion that to be powerful, he must be angry. If only the powerful are allowed to be angry, he reasons, then only the angry can be powerful. Since anger is allowed only to men, the prohibition against his own angry feelings serves to further diminish his sense of his own masculinity. In an attempt to counteract his feelings of vulnerability and impaired masculinity, the adult male survivor can end up feeling that his only protection lies in intimidating the world with a theatrical display of anger. This works, with varying degrees of success, in keeping potential abusers at bay. Unfortunately, it also keeps everyone else away, leaving the survivor angry . . . and isolated. This dramatization of anger seldom represents a pure emotion. It is more likely to be a protective mask, hiding what lies behind it (usually fear or sorrow).

"True" anger is a powerful and "juicy" emotion. It takes the form of righteous indignation in the face of abuse and other injustices. I have not seen it expressed nearly as often as the other, "theatrical" variety. It only seems to present itself after a great deal of other recovery work has been done. But, when it is present, it is impressive, and everyone who sees it recognizes it as genuine. When a survivor reaches a point of feeling and expressing this form of anger, he feels alive and powerful, perhaps for the first time in his life. There are many emotional steps to be taken to reach that point. First, there will be tears, trembling, and even laughter. It may also be necessary for the survivor to engage in the other, more theatrical display of anger—especially if he has never before had permission to do so. This will be helpful as a path to the underlying fear and sorrow.

When I refer to the dramatization of anger, I don't mean to imply that it is a consciously contrived act. The survivor may or may not know that his anger is a show of bravado. He simply feels that he has no choice. It is too dangerous to risk letting go of his "protective" display of anger.

Feelings are a source of great confusion to the male incest survivor. He is afraid to have them (because they would lead to loss of control or reveal his weaknesses) and he is afraid of not having them (because that would be evidence that he is a numb, barren, incomplete person). No wonder it is a difficult and frightening topic. Chapter 8 concerns the ways that survivors find to numb their feelings. For now, it is important just to say that recovery of feelings is a major part of the healing process.

It is difficult to unlearn misinformation we were taught as children. The adult male survivor must explore what feelings are really about. He must slowly come to accept that he is capable of emotions (yes, the entire range of human feelings), that it is alright to feel and even to express his feelings. He must understand the difference between appropriate and inappropriate expression of emotions, and how feelings can be sources of healing rather than adjuncts to abuse.

It is a tremendous breakthrough when the male survivor can begin *to talk* about his feelings more and more openly. Initially, this may happen in therapy or in a group. Although the ultimate goal is to be able to do it with family and/or friends, this may be too much to expect in the early stage of recovery. The safety isn't there; neither, perhaps, are the friends.

Laura Davis, coauthor of *The Courage to Heal*, tells about how, in the early stages of her recovery, she was completely obsessed with the process—and that only another survivor could have had the interest to listen as much as she needed to talk about it. The survivor may need to talk about feelings in individual therapy or in a recovery group in order to bring himself to the point of making friends that he can talk with. As important as this talking is, it is even more exciting (though terrifying) when the survivor also discovers the safety to actually *acknowledge*, *feel*, and *share* his feelings. No one ever died of feelings, but a life devoid of emotions is a form of living death.

How is recovery of the ability and permission to feel accomplished? My best answer is, "Slowly and patiently." It took a long time to teach you to deny your emotions; it will take a while to recover them. The process is a natural one. You haven't lost your ability to feel—that is an innate part of being human. It has just been hidden away. It needs to be found, dusted off, and brought into the open. You don't even have to search. It happens of its own accord as you establish sufficient safety. When you are encouraged and offered aware, nonjudgmental caring, the feelings will present themselves.

At first, as you begin to shed a few tears, shake a little, let yourself laugh out loud, or even permit yourself to get a little angry, you are likely to be frightened. It will feel as though you are completely out of control, and it will feel dangerous. But the reality is quite the opposite. You will cry until you no longer need to, having worked through a piece of your grief; shake until the fear is gone; laugh and tremble your way through the embarrassment and shame; rage through your anger; and yawn away the physical tensions and body memories of abuse. (**Note**: Survivors are often amazed that they find themselves experiencing wave after wave of yawning—one yawn following the last uncontrollably. They wonder whether they are being rude or if they are tired or bored. Feeling impolite, they will apologize for yawning, or try to hide or stifle their yawns. But yawning is to be encouraged. There is evidence that this type of yawning is a way that the body releases muscular tension and works its way through the *physical* aspect of abuse. Since part of the hurt of incest was installed physically, healing must also have a physical component. Yawning is one aspect of that physical part of emotional recovery. Humans are the only animals that try to stifle yawning. I suggest that you do not attempt to control your yawns. Let them roll and experience how much better you feel afterwards.)

In the right environment, all of these expressions of emotions are therapeutic. The problem is that we confuse the *healing* of our hurts with the injuries themselves. Crying is not grief; it is a way of *getting over* your grief. Trembling isn't the same as fear. Rather, it is part of letting go of fear. In the same manner, embarrassed laughter, yawning, raging, and even rapid, excited talking are parts of the healing process that get mistaken for symptoms of the problem.

While not every setting is appropriate to the expression of feelings (it may not be a great idea to yawn a lot when talking to your boss, to shake your way through a job interview, or to burst into tears at a dinner party), it is important to find settings that are safe enough to let you relearn how to feel, and—through your feelings—how to heal. This is why much of the early part of your healing may need to be done in the company of other survivors. Later, you will focus part of your energy on how to integrate your gains into the everyday world.

Don't worry that it is hard at first. Your ability to feel and express emotions will improve with experience. The first tear running down your cheek can feel as powerful as Niagara Falls. And don't worry about duration and intensity. There will be times of intense feeling and expression of emotions—and other periods of calm. You won't cry, shake, laugh, yawn, or rage forever. You won't even need to talk about it forever. But it *will* take some time. Janet Yassen, a Boston-area social worker who leads groups for female incest survivors, talks of the necessity of at least "1500 hours of crying" to get over the hurts of incest. Now, you don't have to set your watch for the countdown. This is not a precise measure. Rather, it is a statement of recognition that: (a) It's OK to cry. (b) Crying is a valuable and necessary aspect of recovery. (c) Recovery is an ongoing process that takes a long time. Don't allow other people to pressure you to "get over it" or to stop crying and "making such a fuss." They don't understand; their impatience is *their* problem. And don't pressure yourself, either. Cry as long as you need. Everyone has a different timetable; your recovery will take as long as it takes.

Finally, try not to berate yourself for not having done this sooner, or to feel that the task is hopeless. You couldn't have done this a minute earlier. You simply weren't ready. You now have the determination, the hope, and the resources. As you come to accept the reality of a safe, welcoming environment for your healing, the emotions will begin to appear. Each time someone listens to you with awareness and interest, the walls will come down a little more. It will feel sudden and magical, but you've actually been working toward it for a long time. Everything else that you did in your life has led you to this moment. Now is the time that you have. Can you let yourself feel the excitement?

4

Sexuality, Homophobia, and Shame

I feel like an alien.   —SURVIVORS EVERYWHERE

Male survivors of incest often deal with confusion about their sexuality. Since the abuse was committed sexually, it is often mistakenly seen as an act of sexual passion instead of what it really is—an aggressive, destructive violation of another human being. Survivors who were sexually abused by other men question what this experience means about their sexuality. (**Note:** Since the great majority of reported cases of incestuous abuse—of both boys and girls—involve male perpetrators, most of the attention of this chapter will be on men who were incestuously abused by other men. This is not meant to deny the reality or minimize the severity of the many cases of boys being abused by female perpetrators. See the Focus later in this chapter for a discussion of issues specific to male survivors of abuse by women.)

Questions about their sexuality are faced by male survivors regardless of their sexual orientation. Although the specific form of these questions varies slightly, the upshot of them is the same whether the survivor is heterosexual, gay, bisexual, "asexual," undecided, or confused. Many survivors, in fact, have moved among these categories in search of answers. The essential question is, "What did the abuse do to my sexuality?" Heterosexual survivors wonder whether a "victim" can ever function successfully as a sexual partner to a woman—"Am I Man enough?" This concern can lead to sexual "performance anxiety" or promiscuous behavior in an attempt to "prove his Manhood." The anxiety may be acted out in fear and avoidance of gays (lest the survivor himself be identified as gay) or by more active, sometimes violent, forms of homophobia. For most of the men, the question also involves whether being sexually victimized by a man *causes* homosexuality. The tone of the question for heterosexual men is, "Does this *mean* I'm gay?" For gay men, it more often takes the form, "Is this *why* I'm gay?" or "Did this happen to be *because* I'm gay?" (struggling with reinforcement of the stereotype of gays as victims). These are difficult questions, and it would be wrong to attempt to solve them with easy answers.

A great deal of research and theorizing have been done about the "causes" of homosexuality. Some investigators begin with a bias for or against homosexuality. Others look for origins in the attempt to find a "cure." It is not within the scope of this book to propound a theory of the genesis of sexual orientation, gay or heterosexual. There is an extensive psychological, biochemical, sociological, anthropological, philosophical, medical, and religious literature on the subject— all of it inconclusive. We don't know what "causes" homosexuality. What we do know is that apparently, throughout history and in all cultures, approximately 10 percent of the population was (and is) sexually oriented toward their own gender. This figure appears to be consistent whether or not the individuals were sexually abused as children. We don't have adequate figures about adult male incest survivors. There are too many difficulties that stand in the way of obtaining them:

- Sexual abuse of male children is only beginning to be accepted as a reality.
- Many men will not accept or disclose their sexuality.
- Many men will not disclose or recognize their history of abuse.
- There is no universal agreement as to what constitutes a particular sexual orientation—there are many possibilities and shades of gray.
- There is disagreement as to what constitutes sexual abuse.
- There is no way of determining a direct correlation between abuse and the establishment of sexual orientation.

What we do know is that both heterosexual and gay men are survivors of incest. My general sense is that abuse is probably not the *cause* of sexual orientation, but it almost always leads the survivor to have *confused feelings* about his sexuality. Survivors tend to worry about sexual feelings of any sort, so that any feeling of attraction toward someone of the same sex can cause great anxiety. It feels like a set-up for further abuse. Since all feelings of intimacy are likely to be sexualized, just to *like* another man can feel like a sexual act. Virtually all the gay men in my incest recovery groups report that they have tried to trace their homosexuality to the abuse. Most have (sometimes reluctantly) concluded that they experienced attraction to other males prior to having been abused.

Another question asked was, "Did this happen to me *because* I'm gay?" The assumption that homosexuals will be victimized and that such victimization is permissible leads us to deal with a much deeper issue, that of *homophobia*. Homophobia is variously defined as:

- Hatred of gays
- Fear of gays
- Fear of contagion (fear of becoming gay)
- Fear that people will think you are gay
- Dislike and denial of your own homosexuality (known as "internalized homophobia")

Whatever its definition, it is abundantly clear that adult gay men and lesbians face rejection, discrimination, ridicule, stereotyping, and even violence because of their sexual orientation. A homophobic culture does not limit its fear and hatred to adults; the oppressive behavior is extended to children. Adults, gay or straight, speak of the tortures that they were subjected to as effeminate "sissy boys" or tough little "tomboys." It is only reasonable to assume that the sickness of homophobia hasn't been confined to ridicule and beatings of children who don't conform to acceptable behavioral norms. It is likely that weak, effeminate, and gay children (yes, researchers believe that sexual orientation is established well before puberty) have suffered sexual abuse simply because of who they are. It is also possible that an incident of sexual abuse could activate awareness of a sexual orientation that might otherwise have manifested itself later on in a less traumatic fashion.

Still other male survivors feel completely unable to define themselves as sexual beings. Any sexuality has become so associated with abuse that to be sexual means to define oneself as abuser or victim. Male survivors may attempt to present themselves as asexual or simply confused about their sexuality. Whether or not they see themselves as sexual beings, it is unlikely that they will feel sexually desirable. Their low self-esteem (coupled with the fear of further abuse) doesn't allow them to feel attractive. When the issues of self-esteem and sexuality come up in recovery groups, male survivors are amazed to discover the understanding and support that are available to them.

Another issue that causes major difficulties for male survivors is the fear of becoming an abuser. There is a popular mythology that men who have been sexually abused inevitably become abusers them-selves. This belief springs from the studies that have shown that most child abusers were themselves abused as children. While this is so, the reverse does not follow. In fact, many men who were abused as children dedicate their lives to protecting others from abuse. Again, it is no accident that so many incest survivors enter careers in human services. They provide what they needed to receive as children. Some individuals, of course, become both protector and abuser, as is evi-denced by stories of sexual abuse in the day-care, teaching, scoutmas-ter, clergy, and therapy professions. But it is not inevitable. And many men join recovery groups because they have (or are about to) become fathers and are determined to end the cycle of abuse—so their children will not have to go through what they have experi-enced. Feeling like potential abusers, male survivors often fear and avoid any affectionate contact with their own or other children. This is a loss to everyone. A recovery group provides a forum for distin-guishing between fears, feelings, and behavior. Group members sup-port each other in sorting out myth from reality, and in figuring out how to allow themselves to be loving, caring, nonabusive men.

It is impossible to understand the effects of incest without con-sidering shame. Adult survivors of sexual abuse live their lives in the face of massive shame. As was previously stated, "men are not sup-posed to be victims" in our culture. If they have been victimized (even if it happened to them as infants), they conclude that they are failures as men. Survivors face shame that they "allowed themselves" to be demeaned, demasculinized, and weakened. If they enjoyed any part of the abuse (see the Focus: What If I Enjoyed It? on page 132), they see it as further confirmation of their shortcomings—they have failed as human beings and as men.

Since our culture has institutionalized sexism as well as homopho-bia, to be less than a man is seen as feminization. The heterosexual survivor, clearly not a woman, worries about whether he is that even more shameful being—a feminized man, a homosexual. Gay men as well internalize our culture's homophobia. Raised in a society that teaches them that it is shameful to be gay, they must work extremely hard to overcome negative messages and build self-esteem. This task is made considerably more difficult when a person carries the shame-ful feelings arising from sexual victimization. At its worst, internal-ized homophobia can cause gay men to wrongly blame themselves (or their gayness) for their having been abused. This ultimate form of blaming the victim (the victim blaming himself) says that just by being who he is—gay, weak, needy, or otherwise flawed—he brought the abuse on himself. It is important for such individuals to

FOCUS

IF THE ABUSER IS A WOMAN

A boy faces a particular form of confusion and isolation when he is sexually abused by a woman. Sexual activity between older women and young boys is rarely treated as abusive. It may be ignored, discounted, or disbelieved. Men (even boys) are supposed to be the sexual aggressors, strong enough to protect themselves against unwanted attention from members of the "weaker sex." What is ignored in these cases is that there is more involved than physical strength, and sexual abuse is not limited to sexual intercourse.

The boy is probably aware of cultural attitudes toward sex between women and boys. In many instances it is romanticized, being seen as "scoring" or initiation into manhood. (The French are particularly fond of romanticizing this type of intergenerational sex in their literature and films.) A boy who talks about his having been sexually abused by a woman is often greeted by disbelief, denial, trivializing, and romanticizing of his story by police, doctors, therapists, media, and the general public. Faced with a society that seems to be celebrating his pain, the incest victim is unlikely to risk talking about it. He may try to redefine the experience to fit in with other people's perceptions, even to the point of bragging or joking about it. He knows that no one will understand what he is feeling, so he might as well just try to fit in.

Society's blindness to this aspect of abuse places him in a powerful double bind. If he enjoyed the experience, then it wasn't abusive. If he didn't, he must be a homosexual. Once again we see the result of confusing sex with sexual abuse. It is shameful for a man to admit to not having enjoyed any form of sex with a woman. The victim is faced with the expectation that he should enjoy his victimization. (This has parallels with romanticizing the rape of women.)

Not knowing how to cope with his confusion, he may push it into the recesses of

learn about homophobia and rebuild their damaged self-esteem so that responsibility for incestuous abuse can be laid where it belongs.

Sexual abuse of children forges a connection between sex and shame. For an incest survivor, heterosexual or gay, any sexual activity with a man or a woman (or even a sexual reference) can restimulate shameful feelings. Sex has been so strongly associated with victimization (and therefore with shame) that it takes great effort to break the connection. Homophobia adds another link to the chain and makes the task of regaining self-esteem even more complicated. Separating sexuality from shame is a major goal of recovery.

his mind, losing all conscious memory of the event until years later. It is my impression that male survivors are more likely to repress memories of abuse by women than by men. It is not uncommon that previously forgotten or partially occluded incest memories are recovered in the safety of an incest recovery group. Memories of female perpetrators seem to be more resistant to recovery; when they do come up, they appear to be more devastating and emotionally draining.

Men have entered with clear memories of male perpetrators and, during the course of the group, have recovered additional memories of having been abused by a woman. One male survivor, who had gone to his father's bed to escape his mother's, had never consciously thought of the sexual activity with his mother as abusive. One man, during a group meeting, blurted out, "Oh, my God, my mother, too!" His anguish and dismay were apparent to everyone in the room. This type of discovery is not all that unusual once sufficient safety has been provided.

I can't speak to whether the situation is greatly different for women survivors, but I believe it is likely that the effects and implications of abuse by a woman take on a particular emphasis for men. Being victimized by a woman appears to bring up an added level of shame; men are more likely to blame themselves or discount it as not really being abuse.

This is especially true when the perpetrator is the survivor's mother. This may be due to a cultural stereotype that says that mothers are to be trusted more than fathers. Mothers occupy a special, almost sacred place in any culture. For many people, it is unthinkable that a mother would not be a nurturing, protective, loving figure. Even children who have experienced extreme forms of physical, emotional and sexual abuse at the hands of their mothers may find themselves protecting their tormentors through pretense and self blame.

Outsiders commonly dismiss a child's report of abuse at the hands of his mother as fantasy or exaggeration. If we are to effectively deal with incest, we must create a climate that recognizes all sexual abuse for what it is. Incestuous abuse is harmful regardless of the gender of the perpetrator or of the victim.

A frequent result of the sexuality–shame connection is sexual dysfunction, a problem that is found among both male and female survivors. Some type of sexual dysfunction is so common among male survivors that if a client enters treatment for sexual dysfunction of any sort, I ask about childhood sexual abuse and keep alert for signs of abuse in his history. The survivor's problem may take any number of specific forms (e.g., inability to achieve or maintain an erection, premature ejaculation, inability to ejaculate, fear of specific sexual acts, sexual obsessions and fetishes, compulsive masturbation, inability to separate sex from humiliation, shame, pain, or physical injury).

However, whatever form it takes, I am convinced that the source of the problem lies in sexual child abuse.

It is the devastation of trust that occurred when he was abused as a child that turns adult sexual activity into an encounter fraught with anxiety for the male survivor.

The problem of sexual dysfunction is one that generates feelings of depression and hopelessness for many male survivors. They despair of ever being able to "get over this problem" and lead a "normal" sex life. But the situation is far from hopeless. If you get at the root of a problem, the symptoms tend to lessen and eventually disappear. I have seen survivor after survivor overcome their sexual dysfunction as part of the natural course of recovery. It doesn't happen magically or overnight, but as they move through their shame, as they continue to rebuild trust and self-esteem, and as they forge healthy friendships and intimacies, their sexual problems begin to diminish. (Yes, even yours! You are not a unique, hopeless case.) Much to their amazement and delight (usually tinged with a little nervousness and mistrust) they find themselves moving into a healthy sexuality.

The only reasonable way to begin to release yourself from the shame that results from connecting abuse and sexuality is to recognize that we are not dealing with an issue of sexual attraction or sexual orientation. *The issue is abuse!* Repeat it to yourself as often as you can. Write it on your bathroom mirror. Post it on your bulletin board. Have friends remind you. Be clear about it. The issue is not sexuality, it is abuse. It always was. It doesn't matter whether you are gay, straight, bisexual, all of the above, or none of the above. You were sexually abused. You didn't bring it on yourself, no matter what kind of child you were or what you did. It only got confused with sexuality because the abuse wasn't limited to physical violence or emotional exploitation. It also had a sexual component. But the real issue for the male survivor (as for the female) isn't sexual orientation. What we are really looking at is trust, intimacy, and self-esteem. As these elements are explored, understood, and strengthened in healthy, encouraging, nonabusive relationships, the issues of sexuality will become clearer and more comfortable. You will be happier with who you are, and you will develop a new perspective on your sexuality. Sexuality is one aspect of a total (and worthwhile) person. Your shame will increasingly yield to self-acceptance and self-appreciation.

Since this is a book for and about incest survivors, and because I don't work with abusers, I have been reluctant to devote much time and attention to writing about perpetrators. But it is relevant to this chapter to say a few words about sexual abusers in the context of sexuality. When a boy is sexually abused by a man, it is often incorrectly seen as a homosexual act. Once again, this is a mistake. We are not talking about sex, but about *sexual child abuse*. (As I once heard someone say, "If you hit someone over the head with a frying pan, you wouldn't call it cooking.") An adult male who abuses a little girl is not engaging in heterosexual behavior; he is sexually abusing a little girl. The same is true when the victim is a little boy. The issues of anger, hostility, and power are the same; the effects are equally harmful. The question, then, is not one of homosexuality or heterosexuality, but of sexual child abuse and its results.

Just as a young male victim of sexual abuse is not—nor will he inevitably become—gay, the male perpetrator is not necessarily homosexual. In fact, all available statistics indicate that the reverse is true. The vast majority of perpetrators of sexual abuse of boys (as well as of girls) are heterosexual men. Most of them would be shocked and surprised that they might even be considered homosexual. Pedophilia (sexual attraction to children) can focus on the same sex or the opposite sex, or be indiscriminate. The attraction is to children, not to males or females. Same-sex child abuse is only seen as a homosexual act when we deny the reality that sexual child abuse is not about sex, but about abuse and power. (We have begun to accept that adult rape is about violence and power rather than about sex. We must make the same distinction regarding sexual abuse of children.)

The perpetrator, *whether male or female*, is a sexual abuser of children. It doesn't matter whether the children he (or she) abuses are male or female. It doesn't matter whether or not the abuser relates sexually to other adults as a heterosexual or a homosexual. Worrying about sexuality only confuses the issue and misses the point; we're dealing with adults harming children. Only when we are ready to accept this reality—and stop treating incest as anything other than sexual child abuse—will we be able to begin to create a society where children are afforded the protection and nurturing they deserve.

ROBERT'S STATEMENT

Robert, a twenty-eight-year-old survivor,
tells of the echoes of incest in his adult relationships—and the
challenge of learning to love himself.

I am a survivor of an incestuous family. It hurts to say that
because I still want to believe, at twenty-eight years old, that
my parents' myth of their perfect family is true. It is not true.
It has never been true. My family was far from perfect. I
hesitate to even call it good. It has been very difficult to realize
the pain that I carry within myself. I have not wanted to look
at how much I hurt and how much that pain has influenced
my whole life.

I started writing this with a question, "Where do I begin?"
It is very difficult to know where to begin to explain the depth
of the fear and the pain that I still carry when it is so all-
encompassing in my life. It is hard for people who are not
incest survivors to realize and to understand just how much it
forms the core of my whole way of looking at life. Each and
every minute of my life is full of fear and mistrust. I am
always afraid that someone is going to abuse me.

My mother was my emotional and sexual abuser. My father
abused me with physical beatings and emotional absence. They
played me off of one another. My mother literally took my
food away from me to give it to my father. She also sent me
to him for "disciplining" when I behaved poorly (which meant,
from her perspective, that I refused to take care of her). My
father could not deal with my mother's emotional instability
and her great needs. She often talked of committing suicide.
He couldn't deal with her. Early on he recognized that
somehow I "got along with and understood" my mother.

He periodically sent me into the bathroom where she would
be screaming and wailing and expected me to calm her down
and "take care of her." It got to the point where she so much
counted on me to assuage her painful feelings that she began to
have her outbursts in my bedroom. She would then get into

my bed and wait for me to come into my room to make her feel better. I still remember the smell and the feel of her in my bed, and it repulses me. My father seemed to appreciate the whole arrangement. He escaped dealing with her anger and anguish and great depression by making me do it. She more and more appreciated my attention to the point that she wanted all of it. She didn't want me to date. She told me to watch out for girls because they only had sex on their minds.

My girlfriend/romance relationships have been difficult from the beginning. The moment I first start feeling attraction or excitement over a female companion I start getting nauseous. I have vomited my way through every relationship I have ever had that was at all interesting to me. I have finally realized some of the cause of that intensity. My whole system has been rebelling against the intrusion of another relationship on my own well-being. My relationships with my parents have made the impression on me that being in a relationship means being dangerously close to death. Because of the beatings from my father, I have been afraid of men, thinking that they are all violent. Because of the sexual and emotional abuse from my mother, I have been constantly afraid of women, thinking that they all want to use and abuse me. This has left me feeling that all relationships result in me being hurt. I have tended all my life to have few friends and to spend a lot of time alone and avoiding people.

I am working hard this time at taking care of myself. It is a difficult process to learn. I always wanted someone to take care of me, but since no one ever would, I felt as though I must not be worth taking care of. I am now struggling to learn that I am valuable. This includes doing therapy in group and in individual forms, feeding myself good meals regularly, and trying to recognize how *I* feel about people and situations and then acting according to my feelings rather than the feelings of others.

I am trying to learn to love myself. It is really hard to love myself when the things I have been shown about loving are so abusive. Even now, when I am more than 2000 miles away from my family, I can feel their abuse of me. Even when I don't talk with them, or see them, or hear from them, my sense of self is so low that I carry on my own abuse. It is hard not to be self-abusive when abuse is most of what I have ever known. I need to learn not to be so hard on myself before I will ever be comfortable with the intimacy of being in a relationship with someone else. I desire to be close to someone, to trust someone, and really to love someone so much. I want to show someone the love that I have, that it is a pleasure—not an obligation; that it is beautiful and free—not oppressive and demanding. I am working on feeling positive about myself in ways that feel good to me. I need to feel good about myself before I can really feel good about someone else. Hopefully the day will not be too long in coming when I will feel strong and healthy about myself rather than unhealthy and abused. I have to believe in that hope.

PART THREE

About
Survival and
Aftereffects

Loss of Childhood

I grew up hating his guts because I was always afraid in his house and because it's difficult to forgive anyone who has robbed you of your childhood.
—PAT CONROY, *Prince of Tides*

"Loss" feels to me like a very imprecise word to use when we are talking about the childhood of an incest survivor. How can you lose something that you never had to begin with? Can a childhood be lost if it was never allowed to exist?

We have created a mythology about childhood. "The best years of your life" are supposed to be carefree and happy, protected from the harsh realities of adult life. These fantasies are reinforced by movies, literature, and television shows that idealize family life and the childhood years. Any departure from that image is treated as an aberration, the exception that tests the rule. The trials of childhood are minimized and seen as temporary. They are tempests that will subside with the advent of adulthood. (No one seems to see any contradiction between viewing childhood as a carefree time and expecting that adulthood will solve all of its problems.)

The reality of the situation is quite different. Even the best childhood is no picnic. There is a whole universe to be made sense of. Children are continually exposed to confusing and conflicting messages. They are faced with information that is beyond their level of understanding—not the least of which is the incomprehensible behavior of those most peculiar alien beings: grownups. The world is not tailored to their size or level of ability. They must endure rules that make no sense to them, often imposed without any attempt at explanation or clarification. Every adult appears to have the right to criticize or discipline them "for their own good." Any attempt to resist, disagree, or even understand may be punished as "backtalk," insolence, or rudeness. They are unlikely to be consulted in any meaningful way about even those decisions that affect them personally; their problems are often ignored, trivialized, or discounted. Children may be seen as cute, amusing, or entertaining, but are seldom taken seriously. They may be loved and cared for, but it is unusual for them to be respected by adults.

It is small wonder that children aren't impressed by grownups who rhapsodize about the joys of youth. They have evidence to the contrary. They chalk it up as one more unfathomable grownup behavior. No, it's not all it's cracked up to be—and I'm talking about a "good" childhood. I'm talking about a relatively stable family, where the children are afforded love, caring, and protection. Even a child raised in this benign an environment is faced with difficulties that test his or her strength and resilience. As we think about these issues it becomes clear that even the luckiest of children have a hard time.

But, as we have seen, few if any families begin to approximate the ideal. The happy, loving, financially secure, nuclear family—the traditional image (of hardworking, sober, strict-but-fair father; mother as nurturing, attentive, wise, pretty homemaker; two healthy children; dog and cat; neat, clean home with protected yard)—may not be a complete myth, but it is certainly not the norm. Only a tiny minority of American families fulfill that picture. Increasingly, pressures are added to family life by economic, social, and political realities. In more and more families both parents must work to provide an adequate living standard—or choose to work in order to realize their potential as human beings.

A huge number of single parents don't have the luxury of choosing not to be working parents. While their families may be quite happy and well-adjusted, the children as well as the adults are faced with added pressures. Children in poor or single-parent families may be forced to take on adult responsibilities earlier than in the "traditional" family. They may become more serious and self-sufficient at an earlier age. Although not necessarily a bad thing, it departs from our popular image of the carefree child.

Many other children are born into less fortunate circumstances. Not all children are wanted; not all adults are willing or able to care for them. People have children by accident, in response to family pressure, and for a variety of other questionable reasons. Indeed, having a baby may be easier than preventing the birth of an unwanted child. There are fewer requirements for parenthood than for driving a car or catching a fish. Children are born into alcoholic, drug-addicted, violent, and otherwise dysfunctional families. Babies are born to addicts, to psychotics, to children, and to people who hate them—and children are exposed to adults who sexually abuse them.

If a "normal" family presents difficulties, it is far more difficult to survive an incestuous childhood. You may, in fact, still be experiencing some of the reactions of the abused child. The fact that you are now an adult—and that the original abuse is far behind you—does not mean that you *feel* safe, secure, or adult. The hurts of your abusive childhood have ripples; you will feel the loss of childhood long after childhood's end. Adult incest survivors report feelings and behaviors that are the direct result of their childhood losses.

What pieces of childhood does the sexually abused child actually lose out on? And how are these losses manifested in the survivor's adult life? Unfortunately, the list is extensive:

1 / Loss of memory of childhood. Sexual child abuse is extremely difficult to endure. One way of dealing with the pain is to put what is happening out of mind. If a child has to deny or forget what is happening to him in order to survive an abusive situation, he may find, as an adult, that he has literally lost his childhood. A great many incest survivors have little or no memory of their childhood. In fact, this method of dealing with childhood trauma is so common that when clients tell me they have no recollection of whole pieces of their childhood, I assume the likelihood of some sort of abuse. When childhood memories begin to be recovered, it is usually clear why they were forgotten. People tend to remember the good things. We have a tendency to glorify the past. One of my clients cried when he recalled that the only positive memory he had of his childhood was when he was alone. These were the only times he could be sure that no one would be hurting him. Protection, then, was only to be found in isolation.

2 / Loss of healthy social contact. When a little child feels that his only safety is in isolation, it seriously impairs his ability to respond to others. Protecting himself from abusers by keeping to himself, he also misses out on the possibility of positive, healthy social interaction—with peers or with adults. This isolation is often reinforced by the perpetrator. As a way of keeping the abuse secret the abuser may, usually successfully, attempt to isolate the child from other people. The child may play an active role in maintaining this isolation, feeling the need to protect the family secret. As an adult he may continue to feel isolated, no matter how many people care about him. He feels that he must maintain protective barriers and put on an act for other people. Only when he is alone can he let down his guard and allow himself to feel. And the way he feels at those times is not good or safe; it is lonely, different, and sad.

3 / Loss of opportunity to play. If you were to ask people what children do with their time, the most frequent answer would probably be "Play." This is not true for many abused children. True play is interactive; it requires playmates. This can be extremely difficult for the abused child. He cannot relax or trust others enough to enjoy playing. Easy, active, spontaneous playfulness feels too much like loss of control. And loss of control, in his experience, only leads to abuse. He is reluctant to move too close, and he knows that life (survival) is serious business. His seriousness and reticence interfere with his ability to make friends. And there is another reason why participation in relaxed playfulness can be so hard; it puts the reality of his own situation into sharp contrast. It may be easier to endure an abusive childhood if you can believe that it is normal. Experiencing the contrast between playfulness and abusiveness can be too painful. The loss of opportunity to play leads to difficulties in adulthood. The adult survivor may experience stiffness and tension when he is in a playful situation. Many incest survivors tell me they "don't know how to relax." Vacations, weekends, and social situations become occasions of discomfort and anxiety. They see themselves (and may be seen by others) as stiff and somber.

4 / Loss of opportunity to learn. Childhood play is more than frivolous enjoyment. In every society children learn through play. Childhood games incorporate cultural values. In the course of their games, children learn to understand and take charge of their environments. They learn communication, cooperation, competition, problem solving, coordination, motor skills, creativity, and age-appropriate and gender-appropriate behavior, and they share information. "Child's play" is a major part of learning. Through their games children help one another to figure out what the world is all about. By playing at being adults, children lern to become adults. The abused child, however, must make sense of the world by himself. He has learned that people lie, and that it is dangerous to trust anything but his own direct experience. And his own experience has been isolation and pain. He has lost the opportunity to learn in the company of his peers, and this also causes problems for the adult survivor. Filtered through the lens of abuse, the survivor's picture of the world is clouded. Having been robbed of the opportunity to learn as other children do, the adult survivor feels naive, stupid, and socially inept. He feels that he must always play catch-up with people who have learned how to successfully negotiate the world.

5 / Loss of control over one's body. Childhood is a time when individuals learn to differentiate between what is theirs and what belongs to others. The most intimate aspect of oneself is one's body. Sexual abuse violates a child's sense of himself in the most basic way. Someone else takes control of his body against his will. He feels that he has neither the right to his body nor the ability to protect himself from attack. The childhood loss of control over his body that robbed him of other protective abilities also has its adult aftermath. He may go through life being revictimized—being taken advantage of in any number of ways. Not expecting anything but abuse, he goes through life looking for—and finding—confirmation that the world is an unsafe place. Despite his adult strength, size, and agility, the survivor feels small, weak, and helpless. When he looks in the mirror, he sees a puny (or fat), cringing, ugly, weak child. Despite all evidence to the contrary, he has bought the lies that abuse teaches. It is important to remember that all abuse involves lies. Children are being lied to about themselves, about love, and about the nature of human caring. They are being taught that there is no safety in the world, and that they have no right to control over their own bodies. Loss of control over their bodies leads to control being a major issue of their adult life. They can become inflexible, controlling, and suspicious—or helpless and indecisive. How can they be expected to be trusting as adults when their natural desire to trust was so badly taken advantage of?

6 / Loss of normal, loving nurturing. I've said it before, but it can't be repeated enough. Every child deserves to be loved. Every child needs to be cherished and nurtured. Childhood should be a time when every child learns that he is good, that she is lovable, that he is wanted, that she is welcome, and that information, understanding, and protection are available from loving adults. Child abuse prevents all of this. Whatever genuine loving and nurturing that may be available to the child is diminished, belied and negated by the abuse. Perhaps the greatest loss of an abusive childhood is this loss of safety in the world. It leads the survivor to have tremendous difficulty in developing healthy adult intimacy, a feeling of belonging, and a strong sense of his own value. Not having been valued as a child makes it extremely hard to create positive adult self-esteem.

7 / Other losses. Clearly, this list could go on and on, recounting how the loss of many aspects of a normal childhood—the loss of family, loss of identity, loss of certainty and so on—causes the adult survivor to face further losses. He deals with loss of control, safety, playfulness, trust, calm, self-confidence, self-esteem, sexual maturity, intimacy, comfort, and security. No doubt you can add to this list from the losses that you have experienced. It may be difficult for you to imagine that life can be any other way. But we will explore roads out of the abuse. The way is difficult, but far from im-possible—and the rewards are worth the struggle.

Previously in this chapter, I spoke of child abuse as *lying* to a child about the nature of love, safety, and caring. When these lies are so powerfully instilled and reinforced, it is extremely difficult to unlearn them and begin to make room for the truth. So, perhaps I was impre-cise in talking of "the loss of childhood." What victimized children experience is the *perversion of childhood*. What they lost was *every child's right to a normal childhood*—loving, protective, and nurturing. The abusive childhood hasn't been lost at all. It remains with the survivor every minute of his adult life.

The effects of the loss of childhood play themselves out in many different ways. Although the scenarios differ in their specifics, what they have in common is that they all represent responses to loss—to the perversion of a normal childhood that is caused by incest. In order to understand how childhood losses affect the adult survivor, we must look at what actually happens to a child when he is faced with sexual abuse. The fact that he cannot trust his environment to be safe and protective doesn't allow him to feel comfortable or secure in any situation. The need to take care of himself and to be ever-vigilant turns him into a serious, watchful person, unable to display the play-fulness of other children. He may seem to be suspicious and remote, having few friends. This is a direct consequence of the confusion and isolation that results from the abuse. He has reason to be distrustful; his innate trusting nature has been taken advantage of. Indeed, he may reject overtures of friendship by other children and adults, fear-ful of what could lurk behind the friendly gestures and kind words.

Experiencing violence and abuse, he may learn only this mode of relating to others. Rejected by other children for his aggressive behav-ior, the abused child will often act out in order to get attention. Alternatively, he may retreat further into his isolation and with-drawal.

A child may also latch on to a friend's family. In doing so, he is attempting to compensate for his loss of childhood and family by finding a substitute. This creative attempt to change his situation can be a lifeline for the abused child. Unfortunately, it is usually only partially successful. Unable to tell them why he is reluctant to go home, he will remain within this protective family until he has over-stayed his welcome and is forced to return to his abusive home. The contrast between the two families can be painful and confusing.

At worst, he may feel that the only person he can get close to is the one who is abusing him—and that the only possible intimacy is sexual. Faced with the apparent choice between isolation and abuse, he may allow himself to be revictimized in order to be close to someone. He may refuse to acknowledge the reality of the abuse, because the perpetrator is the only person he has been able to (or been allowed to) get close to. One of my clients, who was sexually molested by a camp counselor when he was a child, vigorously defends the counselor and the experience. This client came from a home that was physically violent, verbally and emotionally abusive. The fact that the counselor "only had sex with" him, and didn't beat, berate, or scream at him, made the molestation feel like a caring, tender act. To relinquish this image of "tenderness" would leave my client bereft of any positive childhood memories. He discounts the coercive and seductive nature of the abuse by saying that afterward he looked for a repeat of the contact. He has yet to understand that children will seek tenderness and closeness, and will put up with a great deal in order to obtain it. His low self-esteem does not yet permit him to recognize that all children, including himself, deserve caring and protection that is non-sexual and nonabusive. The counselor took advantage of this child's needs, and another child bought into a lie about sexual child abuse.

The abused child has no opportunity to learn to establish reasonable protective boundaries. Not having experienced safety, he cannot distinguish dangerous people and situations. He may throw himself into wildly perilous circumstances or, at the other extreme, refrain from daring any level of risk.

He may learn the trick of seeming to disappear without leaving the room: The good, quiet child may be trying to escape notice for fear of attracting abusive attention. Alternatively, an abused child may go to tremendous lengths to obtain approval, notice, and recognition. He is attempting to "learn the rules" so that he can survive and be accepted. Bright, clever, and funny, no one would ever suspect the tremendous secret burden that he carries every waking moment.

When I spoke of this secret burden to one male survivor, he wrote the following to me:

"Secret burden": Isn't the main thing that is lost . . . the freedom (innocence) not to have to concern himself with sexuality in its adult mode. He loses the opportunity to emerge into a full sexual being at a "normal" pace. The victim of sexual abuse is unceremoniously snatched out of childhood innocence into the world of adult sexuality—which the victim is not ready or prepared for—and worse yet, into the world of thoughtless & dysfunctional adult sexuality. This creates a "schizophrenic" situation for the young boy. In one part of his life he is brutally thrust into the world of adult sexuality at its worst. On the other hand he continues in his regular life relating to his peers and their collective coming into sexual awareness and function. These two worlds are set apart from one another. His relationship with the adult is secret and the adult does not want to hear about the boy's sexual life with others the child's age. In fact the adult doesn't want to relate to the child except as an object of sexual gratification. The boy, of course, finds it impossible to carry the abusive situation back into his childhood life—it is not something he can share—he has been frightened into secrecy by the abuser. Even if the boy is aware of another child being abused by the perpetrator, there is very little sharing of information between the two children. Shame and a lack of real understanding of what is happening prevent communication. And with friends who are not being abused (as far as he knows) there is no forum for sharing this secret imposed on him by the adult world. "The Secret Burden."

The abused child may become a superior student, star athlete, class clown, or popular comrade in his attempt to deal with his hurt. But the sense of shame and failure never really goes away. Loss of childhood? It certainly is. But, contrary to popular wisdom, the losses don't disappear with the end of childhood. The effects are felt well into the adult years.

When you first become aware of what you have lost through having been subjected to an abusive childhood, you may react with a sense of hopelessness. You feel that you have been cheated, robbed of any hope of attaining a satisfying life. Because of the abuse, you feel you have lost your chance at happiness. Take heart. While it is true that you have been cheated, your recognition of this fact puts you on the road to recovery. What has been lost can be found, but first you have to know what you are looking for. You can't create a happy childhood for yourself; to pretend that you had an idyllic childhood would be denial of what really happened. And denial doesn't allow you to let go of the pain. Neither can you find as an adult the love you needed as a child. However immature you may feel, you are no longer a child.

It will be important to seek the caring that you need *as an adult*. It isn't fair that you didn't get the love you needed and deserved as a child, but it would be far less fair to allow that fact to keep you from *ever* getting your adult needs met. You may need to express feelings of sadness and anger at what has been lost (or, perhaps more accurately, *stolen* from you). But this anger and sadness are a recognition that you deserved better treatment. It is a sign of self-esteem—a hopeful sign. After all, if you felt completely hopeless about your chance for recovery, you wouldn't be reading this book. Childhood,

Focus

FREQUENT ISSUES AND PROBLEMS
FACED BY INCEST SURVIVORS

Not every incest survivor experiences all of these. And this list is not exhaustive, but includes many of the problems most commonly reported by male survivors:

- *Anxiety* and/or confusion; panic attacks; fears and phobias
- *Depression*—often including suicidal thoughts or attempts
- *Low self-esteem*—a feeling of being flawed or bad
- *Shame and guilt*—over acts of commission and/or omission
- *Inability to trust* themselves or others
- *Fear of feelings*—a need to control feelings and behavior (their own and others'); compulsive caretaking
- *Nightmares* and *flashbacks*—intensely arousing recollections
- *Insomnia*—and other sleep disorders
- *Amnesia*—memory loss, forgetting pieces of childhood
- *Violence*—or fear of violence
- *Discomfort with being touched*
- *Compulsive sexual activity*
- *Sexual dysfunction*
- *Hypervigilance*—extreme startle response
- *Social alienation*—feeling isolated and alone
- *Inability to sustain intimacy* in relationships and/or entering abusive relationships in which they are revictimized
- *Overachievement* and/or *underachievement/ underemployment*—feeling like an imposter professionally
- As adults, becoming *abusers* and/or *protectors*
- As adults, becoming *victims* of other abuse
- Having *split* or *multiple personalities*—or feeling as though they do
- *Substance abuse*—drugs, alcohol, and so on
- *Eating disorders*
- Unrealistic and *negative body image*—feeling distant from their own bodies
- Feeling like a *frightened child*
- Hyperconsciousness of *body and appearance*

once lost, cannot be recovered. As hard as it may be to accept that fact, it is the truth. As one survivor put it, "There is no way to go back and have a 'Leave It to Beaver' childhood. That was ruined by a thoughtless, selfish adult." But even though what was lost cannot be recovered, *there is recovery from the effects of the loss.*

As part of your recovery, it will be important to return to your childhood—not to make it right, but to understand what really happened and what your actual role was in it. You will, in essence, be getting to know and befriend a little boy—yourself as a child. You've been carrying him inside you for your entire adult life. And you haven't ever really understood him. Self-understanding is one of the parts of your childhood that you lost. It was stolen from you by the person who abused you. He lied to you when he told you that you were bad. He perverted your need for human love and physical nurture. He confused you about who you were. And you lost perspective on the child within you. You owe that child a lot, you know. If it wasn't for his courage and survival skills, you wouldn't be here. What he deserves from you is reassurance.

As you come to understand this little boy, you will be redefining him in the light of the truth. You will understand completely and explain to him that *he was always good*. What *happened* to him was bad. He was always doing the best he could, trying to figure out what was going on. But he was faced with situations that no kid should have to handle. As an adult, you can see the lie for what it is, and expose it. In doing so, you won't recapture what you lost as a child, but you will be able to put the losses into perspective—and stop beating yourself up about your childhood. You can actually talk to that little child within you, and reassure him that there is a world beyond the abuse, and that he is going to live to partake of it. After all, who knows that better than you? You are living proof of his survival.

In the process of getting to know a pretty special little kid—while learning about his courage, intelligence, insight, and goodness—you may begin to rediscover those qualities in yourself. You are, of course, related to him. As you build your self-esteem in this way, you will also start to recover your ability to relax and even to play. A return to your childhood is not just a journey into pain. At best, it can be an assertion of power and pride.

The changes are not accomplished without struggle. Returning your attention to the abuses of your childhood may evoke a sense of hopelessness. (And while you remain in a state of hopelessness, there is little chance that you will be anything but *helpless* to effect positive change in your life.) But the hopelessness is temporary. As you continue to work on your recovery, you will begin to move out of the despair. At that point a welter of feelings will arise, including sadness, fear, and anger. Don't be discouraged; you are not going to stay stuck in these emotions, either. Uncomfortable as they may be, having these feelings is another hopeful sign. Recognizing the losses and acknowledging them are the first steps in emerging from hopelessness. That process is always accompanied by strong feelings.

As you acknowledge your losses, you can begin to mourn them. Through the grief process, you will begin to recognize the ways that you were lied to and ripped off. This recognition that you were completely the victim and never the perpetrator will bring up your outrage—the righteous indignation at what happened to you. Directing your anger toward the perpetrator, rather than toward yourself, leads to determination. You become determined to recover, determined that the abuse will no longer run your life, that you will stand up to the abuse by taking charge of your life in a satisfying way. Instead of sitting in the pain, you have begun to bring it up and experience it in order to move through it. You are recovering from incestuous abuse, and your recovery is the ultimate overturning of the lie.

Recovery doesn't involve regaining the specifics of what you have lost, but the essence. Recovery means taking charge of your life in a satisfying, adult way. It means feeling positive about yourself and creating mutually satisfying relationships with others. It means feeling your strength, intelligence, and creativity. And it means helping the world regain something we have all lost—an unwavering commitment on the part of all human beings to provide children with a healthy childhood. Recovery means understanding the past and using your awareness to create a brighter future. All of these are well within your power, and you are already on your way.

PHILIP'S STATEMENT

This story is eloquent testimony to the power of the
human spirit. Although his statement is wrenchingly difficult to read
it commands respect and admiration. Philip is forty-four years old.

Hello.

Although I'm a proper Bostonian and of the strata of Cabots
who spoke only to Lowells and the Lowells who spoke only to
God, my family spoke to everyone, yet rarely said anything at
all.

My name is Philip. It's not the one I'm using now. I
actually have several choices (Edward, George, Bruce),
indicative, I suppose, of the initial marital unrest and inability
to agree on the part of my parents. In my forty-fifth year, I
am a war baby who has only recently begun to fight. But,
perhaps I'm getting ahead of myself. I offer this brief
autobiographical sketch. I'll consider it a success if it has
engendered an empathetic response, caused utter disbelief, or
pointed out the perversity, perseverance and humor of the
human spirit. Please feel free to hiss, boo, and applaud. I've
always played to the balcony (anything closer and they'd see it
was all sham).

Curtain:

Born to a twenty-five-year-old woman and a sixteen-year-old
man, I was an unwelcome "circumstance" of a romance on the
rebound and the yearnings of a neo-Don Juan. An unlikelier
pair would have been hard to come by: my mother from
genteel—if recently tarnished—Brahmin stock; and my father,
at best, considered a "bead-rattling" French Canadian.

I was three when I met my father for the first time. He had
returned home from the war. He was a member of the
Merchant Marine (the U.S. Navy felt he was too unstable for
their ranks). At the time, we were living in my grandparents'
town house on the Hill (it being the end of war and an acute
housing shortage). My initial and ongoing recollections of that
time are of a liberal, intellectual, and libertine philosophy

78

coupled with a need to put a good face on everything, no matter what the cost. It wasn't until years later that I realized that the "cost" was often myself.

Mother had to get married. Although I had surmised this by the page of thirteen, she did not confirm it until two months before her death. From the beginning I was *something* special to her, something she had sacrificed for and something for which she had great expectations . . . regretfully not just in the area of accomplishment, but also in an intense intimacy and ongoing symbiotic relationship which survived until her death. From the time my father arrived home from the war it was understood that she and I suffered his presence, tolerated his rudeness and paid the price of "legitimacy" by giving lip service to the myth of good marriage and solid family.

For the first three years I was spoiled rotten. The household consisted of doting maternal grandparents, a great-aunt, a second cousin (who for some unspoken reason could not return home), my mother, a housekeeper/cook, a butler, a series of maids fired weekly by my grandfather as "incompetents," and myself. Initially, I shared my mother's room. From age two until my father returned, I shared her bed. Upon his return I was given a cot in the same room until a room on another floor could be found.

My parents hardly knew one another. Tension was quite high and often accompanied by violent arguments and equally violent lovemaking. I became "psychogenically" deaf from age three to four-and-a-half. Coincidental with the return of my hearing was the relocation of my bedroom.

My father never really fit in. He was uneducated, performed menial labor, spoke broken English and was a total illiterate (remains so to this day, only recently having been diagnosed as dyslexic). He was the product of a broken home, a fair amount of early deprivation and a disastrous adolescence. It seems he had few choices. Forced to participate in the Civil Conservation Corps or go to jail for assault and battery and later charged with involuntary manslaughter, he joined the Merchant Marine rather than serve a two-year jail sentence. At age sixteen he married my mother under the threat of rape charges.

Mother was hardly a saint herself. She was grossly obese, a rebel, and a social misfit throughout her childhood and adolescence. She was the fifth child born to a mother who was forty-three years old and a father who was fifty-seven. Needless to say she was a mistake; her next oldest sibling was fifteen years her senior. Early on, she learned the facile skills of jolliness and denial. Her diaries lead me to believe she was the recipient of unwanted affection and anger from her father, who was frustrated by his wife's youth and vitality as he approached old age. Mother attended but never graduated from high school, finishing school, and college. She finally got a doctorate in clinical psychology in 1968. Although a brilliant woman with a host of close friends, she suffered from chronic low self-esteem and depression.

My brother was born when I was five. We shared a room until I was eight, when I finally inherited my second cousin's now-deserted bedroom. Throughout this period my father had many jobs from which he was either fired or which he left. He had an explosive and violent temper which, coupled with a good measure of paranoia, made him nearly unemployable. I am sure that remaining dependent upon my grandparents must have been terribly stressful. There was absolutely no way he could ever hope to duplicate the lifestyle of my mother's family.

I was six years old when I received my first real beating from my father. Every Sunday morning he would read the funny papers to my brother and me. Being illiterate, he made up the stories according to the pictures. I had just started to learn to read. I corrected him. It cost me a split lip, three stitches, and four years of remedial reading classes. I was sent to a child psychiatrist who, in all his wisdom, decided that it was "tense" at home and recommended that we all share a glass of wine together before dinner.

My mother and father had been bitterly fighting and in marriage counseling for over a year by the time I was nine. In April of that year my mother confronted my father with various marital infidelities (grandfather had hired a private detective in order to gain some control over my father after having received a bill from the family physician for treatment of my father's V.D.). His "wings were clipped," she would no longer make love to him, and his comings and goings were closely watched. Given that my father was already paranoid, this new turn of events made life nearly untenable. The tension was extremely high.

It was the habit of the house that when my father came home from work my mother would retire for a nap and my brother and I would play with my father from five until half-past six, at which time my mother would sit with us while my brother and I ate supper. My father bathed and changed for dinner with the adults at seven. During the play periods we would often roughhouse. Once my father's wings had been clipped, this time took on a whole new aspect. My father became increasingly more attentive to me. Within less than a month (my brother was away overnight at a friend's), my father, while roughhousing, pulled my sweatshirt back over my head pinning my arms behind me, pulled down my jeans, forced me on my stomach, put some "3 In One" oil on his penis and (I still don't know what word to use here) Fucked me, Raped me, Screwed me, Buggered me, Made Love to me. It hurt awfully bad. As I began to scream he threatened to kill me. When I could no longer control whether I screamed or not, he forced my head to the side and bit down hard on my lower lip, breaking the skin. When he was finished, he insisted I fellate him to clean him up. At supper my mother put a bandaid on the lower lip. (I'd like to think it was a slip, referring to parts of my body as if they weren't mine; it's not, I've been doing it for years.) She reprimanded my father and me for playing too hard. The routine was quickly established. Within a week I had (what do you call it when it's repeated?) been with him twice more.

I ended up in the hospital with a high fever. Initially, the doctors thought it might be polio (it was during the period of the epidemic). After careful examination, however, they repaired a tear in my large intestine and, with antibiotics, the peritonitis cleared. No one ever asked me what had happened, or how. Just recently, I requested copies of the records. All that is listed is high fever and anal repair.

Upon my return home, he resumed his assaults as before. I grew to anticipate how and when they would come. If he could not get to me, he would become verbally and physically abusive to my mother and brother, eventually escalating the level of violence until he was throwing things and slapping us around. I became quite accomplished at getting my mother out of the way quickly, of convincing my brother that he and I should play with dad separately, and always me first. If lucky, I could get away with fellating him; if unlucky, I submitted to anal intercourse. It's funny how quickly I learned "not to be there," to numb out. I could, within three or four minutes, shut off my mind and go on "automatic." It wasn't till much later in my life that I lost control of this ability and became increasingly "not there." I would come around, usually in a great panic, trying to piece together what I had missed. For a time, however, it served me well, thank God.

By the time I was eleven, my father was becoming quite disturbed and had been psychiatrically hospitalized twice for paranoia. It was not uncommon when accompanying him in the car to the local store for him to become quite paranoid, be convinced someone was following him, and end up in New York City as an avoidance technique. It was on one of these trips that my father and I ended up in New York late on a Friday. He had calmed down enough to realize that he was no longer in danger and decided we should eat in the Village. It was here I first acted as a decoy for my father. I was told to ask a young man standing on the street to come join my younger brother and me in the car. He did and ended up fellating father. Between the age of eleven and thirteen, this happened six additional times.

At age thirteen, I came home from school one day and found mother packing our bags. She said she'd had enough. Mother had discovered that father was having an affair with the marriage counselor. He had taped an individual session during which he and the counselor had made love. He played this the night before at the dinner table for all of us to hear. Dad had demanded his marital prerogative, asked her to perform an "unnatural act," and she had refused. He'd threatened to kill her and that was the final straw. For the first time in my life, I realized that, maybe, I wasn't crazy. I was inwardly thrilled to be leaving. (It is only recently, as I look back, that I have become bitter when realizing that only when it came to her welfare did my mother take action.) She had known of my father's assaults on me. When I was in the hospital, they had come to visit. She had gone out for ice cream and, upon her return, had interrupted my father in the process of forcing me to fellate him. I could never get her to talk about any aspect of this incident. Well, we did leave and moved into the summer house. I soon became my mother's keeper.

The town we moved to was a small, exclusive seaside community of the overprivileged, old-monied, politically conservative. It was promiscuous and two-faced in all other respects. Children went to boarding schools. There were ski trips and island trips and the New York Yacht Club cruise.

Mother was ill-prepared to be the breadwinner. Having committed the unpardonable sin of divorcing her husband, she was promptly cut off from all financial and emotional support.

We were quickly flat broke, literally dependent upon "the kindness of strangers." Mother drank heavily for the next two years, often coming home either loaded or with a perfect stranger (perhaps I should say a not-so-perfect stranger). This was one of the most difficult and desperate times for me. I thought I had finally escaped and instead I found I had inherited an entirely new and complex set of problems.

I was a quick study. I'd already learned to give whatever it took to get by. Mother increasingly turned to me as confidant, seeking approval and emotional support. Her new friends included me as her chaperone/escort. At age fifteen I was driving the car without a license, drinking at parties, restaurants, and bars. The illegality of it was never an issue. To this day I am amazed at how easily I made the transition from son to gigolo and how easily my role was accepted. I was treated as an equal by her friends and my mother alike. People often assumed we were brother and sister or that mother had again taken a young lover (I wish this were an exaggeration, but it is not!). For the first time my grades at school suffered, and I began to have marked fluctuations in weight (gaining and losing fifty pounds regularly; dieting, bingeing and purging episodically).

I took complete charge of running the household: shopping, cooking, cleaning, and when not acting as a chaperone, babysitting. I quickly learned how to put off bill collectors, juggle three checkbooks, forge signatures, and write excuses for school with authority and bravado. The only function I did not perform was that of lover. I believe mother was keenly aware of the danger that would have been for me (and I do remain thankful for that small favor). The manner in which she avoided it, however, was nearly as devastating. She had a series of indiscreet love affairs, at times insisting that I witness various forms of her lovemaking as I drove her and her beau home. Thankfully this stopped at fellatio. I only dared complain once and was told I was too conservative, a stick-in-the-mud. To prove the point she promptly tried to seduce the delivery man in my presence. I never challenged her again. In retaliation, I slept with my mother's best friend and lost my heterosexual virginity at age fifteen.

I grew to cherish the turmoil, the difference between my peers and myself. I had entrée into an adult world that was far beyond anything they could even anticipate. I had only one friend during this entire time. He was also gay and living a similar lifestyle, being brought up by his grandparents. We often shared stories and (I like to believe) provided a safety valve for one another. I learned early on to keep my mouth shut. My mother and her friends would say I was the essence of discretion (at times, however, I felt like the invisible man). Included in this lesson was the discovery of the force of my will power, that I could accomplish nearly anything. All I really had to do was figure out what someone wanted (and, if possible, why) and then play to it. I successfully maintained (I still do) two, if not three or four, separate lifestyles. I was at that time (still am) inwardly quite confused because all realities became viable. At any given moment I had to remember and maintain several facades. I think this was near the acme of my ability to totally divorce myself from feelings. (To this day I'm often not sure what I'm feeling, whether or not I've manufactured a called-for response.)

In late adolescence I went to three different prep schools (only two were boarding schools; mother wanted me home nights and weekends to attend to household and chaperone duties). Changing schools so regularly allowed me to be whoever I wanted without fear of someone knowing my past. I discovered amphetamine for weight control and quickly found it helped support an increasingly diverse/disparate lifestyle. My first real stint away from home was freshman year in college. I chose (over objections of all aunts and uncles) to attend an extremely liberal, small college in upstate Vermont. Drugs, dope, sex, and academic freedom. Sophomore year I began the round of Ivy League colleges. My uncles, in combination with my ability to gain scholarships, convinced me to transfer. I did so yearly for the next three years. I always maintained a 4.0 average and was given full credit from school to school. As I've said, I was a quick study. When brains didn't work, influence and my persuasion did. I decided I wanted to become a social worker and chose a graduate school in the Midwest (miles from the safe and sane northeast) in a large urban city. I wanted to work with disadvantaged youth, but was instead placed in the Welfare Department at the time of the steel strikes and massive layoffs at the automotive plants. Needless to say it was nearly disaster. For the first time in my life I barely scraped by (barely living up to my academic record of achievement and totally unable to adjust). I bowed to family pressure and the recollection of being broke as a teenager and applied and was accepted to medical school, graduating in 1968 with one residency in surgery and another in psychiatry. I couldn't stand the arrogance of the surgeon, and I was increasingly seeking answers to what had gone wrong with my life. I was chronically depressed, sexually promiscuous, pan-sexually so, drug abusive, and in general a great success. Rewards were no longer keeping up with gains. I, however, was still convinced that if I could just get it right, everything would be okay.

I married the year I graduated from medical school. I was absolutely terrified that if I didn't do it soon, I'd be lost. Someone would surely find out about me: my gayness, my fakery, my vulnerabilities. My mother graduated the same year with a doctorate in psychology and was entertaining fantasies about forming a joint practice with me. I needed to put as much distance between us as possible. I married a woman who had done volunteer work with my mother, was introduced to me by my mother, and was the first woman I dated of whom my mother approved. Julia was a fine midwestern (read unsophisticated/naive) young woman from a Waspy family. A child of the sixties, Julia had made one small "sad" mistake by getting herself pregnant out of wedlock and had borne a child. (Ignore the echoes of my mother's marriage—I was too scared to care.) The father of the child was a man with whom I had slept and continued to sleep until my marriage to Julia.

All was not gloom. Although I was a gay man, afraid of my own shadow, I was also a graduate of medical school and an adoptive father to a beautiful red-headed little girl named Susan. It didn't dawn on me that I was also father to a dependent wife who was just as scared as I was—she eventually became a little sister to me. Susan, however, was something I did right. Perhaps in my entire life, she was the only person I loved without guilt and trusted absolutely and wholeheartedly. For me she was a child of choice, without blame on my part. I do not want to overly romanticize this period. I was just starting out and Julia was going full time to pharmaceutical school. I assumed total responsibility for running the household as well as making a living. I often felt like I was living a rerun of my late teens.

Susan inherited the best of both worlds: her mother's solid midwestern honesty and openness, coupled with a good dose of New England sophistication/cynicism and an appreciation for the finer and absurd things of life. High points were sitting at breakfast on Sunday on Newbury Street watching the parade and acting wicked as we rated all who passed by. Susan and I spoke the language of Best Friend/Uncle and Daughter. (Susan had always known her real father.) She made me so very proud, providing me with a touchstone that often deflated my balloon and laughing with me as the air ran out and I began to wrinkle with age. Once Susan was in college, Julia and I parted good and committed friends (not without rancor, but certainly without a bang). After all, we had always pretended to be mature adults; we were too proud to be otherwise at divorce.

Susan died in the summer of 1982 in an automobile accident in France. Julia had joined her there at the end of the summer, intending to spend August with her. I had recently switched jobs and could not get the time to join them. They had squabbled and Julia returned early. I located Julia and, between the two of us, we literally forced her onto an already fully booked plane bound for France. It was the only time in my entire relationship to Julia that she was single-minded and assertive. A day later, seventy-eight hours after the accident, I received a call at work from Julia. (Julia and I had always agreed that extraordinary means were not to be used to prolong life when life was no longer viable.) She and the doctor were in Susan's room. While I sat at my desk at work, with the help of the nurse, Julia put the receiver to Susan's ear and the three of us sang her a lullaby as the doctor shut down the life-support system.

In the mid-seventies I took a male lover for the first time. He was a nice formerly married man with two school-aged children. For me this was my first monogamous relationship and my first gay one of any significance. Bob was Italian— volatile, warm, outrageous, and confrontative. He was also promiscuous and a true tramp. I wonder if I didn't go from being figuratively married to my mother to being married to my father. I cherished the turmoil. Bob was one of the first gay men to be diagnosed with AIDS in the Greater Boston area. My medical training had given me enough warning to steer clear of sexual liaison with Bob once it became clear that multiple sexual partners might be a cause of the (then new) disease. (To date I remain seronegative.) Bob became increasingly ill and despondent until one god-awful Monday morning in April. While we were speeding to Boston for chemotherapy, he, in great despair, turned the car into a granite wall at about eighty-five miles per hour. I was thrown clear, he died.

My next three years were spent in plastic surgery and physical therapy. I got to choose a totally new look. Such a mixed blessing. I suppose if I had known who I was, it would have been an easier adjustment. I was depressed and, in a real sense, at times totally unable to care for myself emotionally and physically. My mother came to the "rescue," moving in with me and going about the motions of caring. Now in her sixties, she had lived life, if not in the fast lane (she used to say her soul was in the clouds, but her mind was in the gutter), at least recklessly. It has been costly physically. She was quite obese, smoked four packs of cigarettes a day, had numerous dependent friends and patients. Her emphysema required daily suctioning, nearly constant oxygen, and often functional immobility. She moved a cot into my room so that I could monitor her breathing. (After forty years I was again sharing a room with my mother.) Within six months I was feeling well enough to want some privacy. I rented her an apartment and sent her traveling at my expense for several months (not an inexpensive proposition when medical supplies must be arranged everywhere she went). She returned to my house on Labor Day, informing one and all of her wonderful time, poured herself a Manhattan and went to bed. She died early the next morning dashing to the toilet.

During the spring prior to Mother's death, encouraged by her admission of my illegitimacy, I endeavored to confront her about Father's abuse (one final time) in order to gain some insight into why it wasn't stopped and why it had gone on so long before we left. Her response was woefully inadequate (or perhaps I was seeking the impossible) and yet terribly accurate. With emotional resignation in her voice and tears in her eyes, she said, "Ya had to be there to appreciate just how bad it was."

"But! Ma! I was there! I do know."

She replied, "I thought you did, I know you did. We shared that didn't we? I have often felt I made a mess of things, ya know. Oh my goodness, perhaps you should now talk with your father."

Fairly soon after mother died, I wrote to my father, requesting a meeting and outlining a protocol for the meeting. I left it that I would be calling him in two weeks, once he had had a chance to think it over. Within twenty-four hours of his receiving the letter, I got a phone call from him saying he was on the Cape. I agreed to meet at a local restaurant within the hour. Already I had given in and broken the outlined protocol I had hoped to follow.

When I arrived at the restaurant, there was no sign of him or his car. I tried to cool my heels leaning on the hood of my VW Beetle. I was "not too scared," just absolutely terrified. I was becoming keyed up and, in a real sense, beginning to "numb out." After about half an hour he pulled up. I was not prepared for the man who stepped out of the new Caddy Seville wearing a red sportscoat, gray flannel slacks, gray silk shirt, and an ascot and leading two golden cocker spaniels on a tangled leash. (I was to find out later that he had named them Nanette and Louisa after his present wife and my mother.) He walked directly in front of me without recognizing me (I'd had so much plastic surgery, he didn't know me right off). When I realized what had happened, I called out to him and was immediately launched into a frenzy of broken French/English and tears. He rushed to his car to get his camera and insisted that a passerby take a picture of us together. He was laughing, crying, and quite out of control. I became outwardly more and more reserved, while inwardly overwhelmed and frightened.

I had hoped to find a table in the back of the restaurant, but had to scratch the idea as a busload of tourists headed in for breakfast, increasing the likelihood that his emotionality would draw attention to us. I thought the two of us might sit in my car, however, I'm 6'2" and my father is 6'4", so I agreed to sit with him in his car. I had again broken my own protocol about being alone with him.

Once in the car, he said he understood that I might have questions. He offered that he had questioned his paternity from the very beginning. Without being able to get a word in edgewise, I sat there trying to re-form my questions. Suddenly he automatically locked the doors of the car, raised the armrest dividing our seat, and while starting to fondle my leg, unzipped his fly. Grabbing the back of my neck and twisting it sharply downward toward him, he said he thought I called because I wanted to get together again to do it. While yelling, "No, not on your fucking life," I struggled to sit up, only to have the side of my head banged solidly against the steering wheel. As I yelled, he forced my open mouth down on the steering wheel, burying its rim so far back in my mouth my lower and upper back teeth on both sides were smashed. I pushed my way out of the car, swallowing blood. I ran for my car, locked myself in, and drove home. I tried to pull myself together and found myself slipping in and out of "being there." I reached my psychiatrist and set up an appointment that morning. By the time I arrived I was quite suicidal, damning myself for my poor judgment, convinced that somehow I had led my father on and caused it all to happen again like when I was nine. My psychiatrist was reassuring. He assured me that, at age thirty-nine, I had survived far worse and he was sure I would go on. He could only give me fifteen minutes. At the dental service, they removed several pieces and made an appointment for me the next day. I never went back to that psychiatrist and have yet to have the broken stubs in the back of my mouth repaired. One year later I had my neck rebuilt for the second time in my life. I can now "look straight ahead," barely able to turn to the right or left. I have a partial hearing loss in my right ear. I've switched jobs four times since, finally removing myself from clinical practice, taking the time (who's kidding who?), needing the time to finally address the question of *ME*.

I entered therapy for the eighth time. Having had one somewhat successful attempt at coming to grips with aspects of my problem, I decided to address some of the incest issues. Approximately a year before, I had met a young therapist associated with the AIDS Action Committee for which I was also a volunteer. We had had one nasty run-in, and he had successfully stood up to my rather arrogant and off-handed manner of dismissing him. I was impressed. Within a year, he was running two advertisements in the local gay newspaper. One group was for gay men in their forties, who wished to explore issues of middle age and relationships. The other group was for survivors of incest. Of course, I was interested in the group dealing with incest and not the least bit interested in the middle-aged men's group. I therefore interviewed him and questioned him and watched him closely for an additional six months, then approached him about the middle-aged men's group. At that point, I decided to be honest and talk about the incest issues. I was struck by his lack of preconceived notions, or at least the care taken not to put them forth, thus freeing me from having to pander to them and accommodate them. My second major concern was the fact that I was an M.D. and he was a master's-level clinician. The concern was twofold: would he be threatened by me and could he be trusted with the issues of confidentiality? Of course, ultimately therapy involved relationships, transference, countertransference, all the therapeutic garbage that came with the two of us being clinicians—wildly clouded by the incest issue of trust.

Two years later, I've taken a lover (also an abused male and child of alcoholic parents). It isn't the least bit easy for either of us. Trust is hard to come by, intimacy something as alien as living on the sun, and sex something to hope for as my lover is seropositive. My ex-wife is again pregnant and I've been diagnosed with Hodgkins Disease.

I ask myself, are there echoes? Thankfully, yes, and depending upon my mood I cherish them and call them memories and file them under wisdom; or alternately run agitatedly from ghosts, too scared to say "help," feeling too unworthy to trust responses.

I used to think, "live a day at a time." Progress means now planning two weeks ahead, with fantasies for the future. I still suffer from TUD (The Unknown Dread)—but then, who doesn't?

Survival Strategies: A New Perspective

We do not see the world as it is, we see the world as we are.   —THE TALMUD

"Do you know what I mean?" This would appear to be a matter-of-fact, straightforward question. In the course of everyday conversation, people check to make certain that they are being understood by their listeners. For many, this line becomes a figure of speech, a mannerism of their conversation, in a class with "Y'know," or "See?" It is a simple way of affirming the connection between speaker and listener, and may mean no more than "Are you still listening?" The speaker is probably unaware that he or she is using the phrase.

As I worked with survivors of abuse, I found myself increasingly conscious of this question and others like it. I was hearing it more frequently and with a greater intensity. It seemed to carry with it a sense of urgency. The question took several forms: "Do you understand what I'm saying?" "Does this make sense?" "Is that nuts?" I began to listen for the questions and to wonder about them. What was really being asked? What was behind the force of the questions?

It soon became apparent that what I was hearing was no mere figure of speech. I was becoming aware of the appearance in adulthood of a child's need to make sense of the world. I was once again discovering the extent to which the abused child needs to compensate for the loss of a healthy childhood. I was witnessing the outgrowth of a strategy for dealing with having grown up in an environment that lacked sane guideposts. (**Note:** Your own family experiences are bound to be somewhat different from the examples I present. They are representative of the many ways children figure out explanations of abuse and survive abusive situations—and how these survival techniques show up later in life.) No, this was anything but a figure of speech, I was being enlisted in the survivor's attempt to comprehend a complex situation. I was being asked a vital question, "'Will you help me to understand?" I was being told that the world of the incest survivor is a confusing one. He feels as though everyone else was issued a "rule book for living" and that he never got one. Other people appear to be confident in their opinions and perceptions. They seem to move powerfully in the world, secure in word and action. It feels to the survivor that he will never be as confident about *anything* as others appear to be about *everything*.

When the incest survivor asks me, "Do you know what I mean?" I take the question seriously. He is sharing with me his confusion and feeling of isolation from others. He is inviting me to help him to make sense out of the world. By asking me, "Is this crazy?" or "Am I crazy?" he is telling me that he goes through his life *feeling crazy*. Never confident that his perceptions are accurate, never sure that other people perceive things as he does, he continually questions his normalcy and sanity. Yes, I take these questions quite seriously. When what is being presented makes sense to me, I tell him that it does and why it does. When it doesn't, we discuss the parts of it that are unclear to me and attempt to resolve the confusion into clarity.

FOCUS
MASKS AND IMAGES

Masks have many functions. You can hide behind them, disguise or decorate yourself with them, and use them to achieve a desired effect. Many incest survivors, disliking what they perceive to be their "real" selves, will carefully cultivate another image—one that they feel is more acceptable, attractive, or self-protective.

The purpose of these assumed identities is to hide what the survivor thinks are his character flaws, and to "fool" other people into liking him. The problem with masks is that they conceal the positive as well as the negative. Masks are rigid and unchanging. They always look the same, and the wearer appears to have the same response to all situations.

A mask can also offer clues as to what lies behind it. For those who are willing to look carefully, masks can reveal as well as conceal. Your choice of a persona tells a great deal about your self-image and the way you perceive the world.

Male survivors have brought a variety of images into the incest recovery groups. (One group member even suggested the *actual* wearing of masks during the group. It would be interesting to see what the choices would be.) Some of the more familiar masks include:

- *Blustering:* Filling the room with words, "ragtime" speech that leaves no room for anyone to pierce his fragile defenses
- *Ominous:* Silent and glowering, presenting a dark image of barely repressed violence and great physical strength
- *Invisible:* So silent and self-effacing that he seems to disappear before your eyes
- *Intimidating:* Intelligent, glib, sharp-witted and so psychologically savvy that no one dares challenge his verbal barrages
- *Angry:* Radiating rage, criticism, and

This may involve examining the content of what is being discussed or the style of presentation. Often as not, what is being talked about is perfectly clear, and all that is needed is acknowledgment that it is.

Another aspect of the insecurity felt by incest survivors is expressed in their precision of speech. Feeling confused and inarticulate, the survivor assumes that is the way he is presenting himself. To compensate for this perceived lack of clarity, he may speak with a slow, measured tone and grammatical precision that robs his message of spontaneity and feeling. Conversation then takes on an academic tone, which serves the double function of overexplaining and ridding the words of the frightening reality of emotion. The secondary effect of this type of delivery is that it distances the listener from the speaker. The information is conveyed as material in a lecture rather than what it is—the profound and vital expression of the reality of a human life.

Another example of a childhood survival technique that has mani-

---

intolerance—attacking to keep from being attacked
- *Outrageous:* Shocking in word, appearance, or behavior—using the bizarre to create protective barriers
- *Placating/Pleasing:* Being so nice, caring and helpful that all the attention is directed toward others
- *Comedy:* Relying on superficiality, banter, and irrelevancies to distract attention from his underlying pain
- *Tragedy:* The Lost Cause. Presenting an image of such severe disability that no one is likely to attempt such a Herculean task as trying to help him
- *Polyanna:* The rosy pretense that everything is just fine—a mask usually constructed of the most insubstantial material
- *Teddy Bear:* The warm, comforting, nonthreatening, amorphous (and usually asexual) creature that is the opposite of Ominous
- *Academic:* Retreating into his head to keep from riskier contact with the emotions— often taking the form of writer, lecturer, or analyst. Tries to be observer, explainer, or cotherapist in the recovery group.

All of these masks are probably familiar to you. You may be wearing one of them right now.

What they (and many other images) have in common is that they get in the way of face-to-face connections. They keep us from getting to know our natural allies. But fortunately they tend to be insubstantial.

Built of flimsy materials, our disguises dissolve when exposed to powerful concentrations of caring and encouragement. As we spend more time with them, they become increasingly transparent, until not even the wearer can fool himself into believing that they still work.

We present our masks to the world hoping they will be pierced. There is tremendous relief in letting them down and revealing the true beauty behind them.

fested itself in adult life is the "throwaway" style of delivery. In order to keep his own feelings under control, the survivor may talk about his experiences as though they were of no consequence. The most disturbing stories of brutality and neglect are told with what amounts to a verbal shrug of the shoulders. Again, the reasons are understandable. The survivor may be convinced that the listener would be frightened off by his whole story with the feelings attached. He has been trying his best to keep the feelings at bay for so long that it has become second nature. And there is the fear that, once opened, the floodgates of emotion will be uncontrollable, washing away both speaker and listener. Now that he has found someone to listen, the possibility of frightening him or her away is too great a risk.

The effect on the listener can be confusing or chilling. It is strange to hear stories of human suffering told as though they had no more significance than a laundry list. But it is necessary to understand how important it is to be heard, even in a limited fashion. With patience and understanding on the part of the listener, the feelings begin to reappear and the recitation of a plot outline becomes transformed into the story of the genuine experiences of a real person. (**Note:** Although seemingly opposite to the previous example of precise speech, this throwaway style is identical in source. Equally common and equally disconcerting, the two may even be found together—exactitude of speech delivered with a sort of "verbal shrug.")

Why would an intelligent, articulate person appear so insecure about his ability to communicate? Why would he fear that his perfectly reasonable perceptions and conclusions are the ravings of a lunatic? What has so destroyed his confidence? How is his fear of being (or going) crazy another legacy of the abuse? And how do these adult examples represent holdovers of childhood survival strategies?

Every child must make sense of his/her environment. Children do this by watching and listening to what is going on around them. They try to understand the world by playing out what they see and hear. In a stable, healthy situation, the child has opportunities to deal with confusion. The adults in his environment behave in a reasonably consistent fashion. Inconsistencies can be resolved by asking questions. There is a sense that the world is safe and can be understood. The abused child must attempt to function in an irrational environment. Rather than explaining and reassuring, the adults in his life become sources of confusion. Adult behavior is, at best, inconsistent; at worse, it is brutal and terrifying. The words of explanation and reassurance which come from the grownups are at odds with the child's experience. He knows "something crazy is going on!" but he doesn't have a context for figuring it out.

FOCUS

EXAMINING YOUR SURVIVAL STRATEGIES

Coping methods can be healthy and positive or injurious and addictive. Any repeated behavior bears some examination. Here are four questions you can ask yourself to help determine whether what you are doing is what you want to be doing:

1 / How did I feel afterward?

2 / Has it helped make my life more satisfying?

3 / What have I seen other people do in similar situations?

4 / What are some other options that I might try?

Trying new strategies doesn't commit you to the changes. You can always go back to doing things the old way. But the more you explore options, the more you free yourself to take charge of your life.

The abused child has to develop explanations for what has happened (and what is happening) to him. And what has happened to him is crazy. (**Note:** I am consciously using the word "crazy" in place of more clinical terminology in order to present it as perceived by the child.) Since he has been isolated by the abuser, he has little or no recourse to normal sources of information. He can only depend on his own resources. (Jealously, perpetrators frequently will isolate their victims from other social interaction in an attempt to keep the abuse secret, or for reasons of domination and control.) In light of the limited and twisted reality available to him—full of contradictory messages—it is easy to see why the child feels crazy. If he behaves on the basis of what he knows to be true, his behavior will be at odds with that of other children. Once again, his perception of himself as different from other kids will be reinforced (and he is forced back into isolation or further abuse). Adults who are unaware of the abuse will see him as a strange and disturbed child—and he will internalize their reactions.

The abused child has no opportunity to attain perspective on his situation. Where can he learn that he is not crazy, but his situation is? There is no one to tell him: IT IS CRAZY TO SEXUALLY ABUSE A CHILD. The child may not even know that he is being abused. He may not know that anyone lives any other way. He does know that something is wrong. Since the world is so confusing, why not believe that there is something wrong with him? Able to depend only on his own resources, convinced that these resources are severely flawed, the child works to develop explanations for what has happened to him and skills for daily survival.

Extreme situations call for extreme measures. In light of the need to make sense of a crazy situation, behavior that may appear dysfunctional can be understood as an effective survival strategy. I am in continual admiration of the creativity with which children figure out ways to survive an abusive childhood. Working against powerful odds, with limited resources and incorrect information, that they survive at all is amazing. (And, of course, many do not.) No matter that some of the adaptations are bizarre, they are functional. They permit physical survival. The child deserves absolute respect for having figured out a way to get through his childhood. It is only later, in adulthood, when there is distance from the abuse, that the individual can contemplate change. The actual abuse is no longer taking place, he is removed from it in time and distance, and the very strategies that enabled him to survive have become barriers to a satisfying life. Strategies have turned into problems, and the survivor will most likely blame himself for creating the problems by seeing them as further evidence of his deficiencies.

But the survivor deserves neither criticism nor blame. That bravely struggling child managed to figure out a way to make it through, and for that he is eminently deserving of complete admiration. He negotiated a sea of insanity despite a lack of adequate training—and with a broken compass. His limited strategies moved him through his abusive childhood to a point where, as an adult survivor, he can begin, however fearfully and timidly, to entertain the possibility of change. This is the beginning of his process of recovery. The child as survivor must be celebrated by the adult he has become. Like that child, you are more than an incest survivor. You are fully human, with all the attributes, imperfections and complexities that go along with that definition. You possess intelligence, creativity, humor, and ability. Proceeding with your recovery will enable you to accept your full and rich humanity.

Chapters 7–11 examine in greater detail some specific childhood survival strategies and their cost to the survivors' adult functioning. The chapters discuss how and why these strategies were developed, what functions they served, and how, when they are no longer needed to insure survival, they become impediments to achieving a satisfying adult life. I hope that, in the course of reading these chapters, you will see these strategies for what they are—creative solutions discovered by intelligent young human beings caught in terrible, senseless situations. And I trust that, through this understanding, you will (as I have) come to respect the creativity and innate goodness of all survivors—including yourself.

GERALD'S STATEMENT

Sometimes a seemingly simple insight sets off skyrockets,
as in this statement from a forty-four-year-old survivor.
Gerald's work of computer art (the original is in many colors)
expresses the joy of dawning awareness.

7

Forgetting, Denying, Distancing, and Pretending

The memories first appeared when I was on my honeymoon. I had a new family and I didn't have to pretend that nothing happened.　　—A MALE SURVIVOR

It's easier to think of myself as a liar than to admit that these things really happened to me.　　—A MALE SURVIVOR

"Wouldn't I remember it if I had been sexually abused as a child?" It is reasonable to assume that something as frightening as incest would be indelibly engraved in a person's memory. But this is frequently not the case. In reaction to the trauma of childhood sexual abuse, people often forget the entire event and anything related to it. This repression can even extend to events which occurred over a period of years. (See the discussion on page 69, "Loss of Memory of Childhood.") When memories aren't accessible, the individual feels as though he is working in a vacuum. He feels that something is wrong, doesn't know exactly what it is, and will very likely assume that *he* is the problem. He will ask questions like: "Am I just looking for an excuse for my failures?" "Am I just a terrible person and trying to blame it on someone else?" "Is there something wrong with me that I can't remember my childhood?"

Recovery of "lost" memories is one of the most common reasons for entering treatment. The client feels that *knowing what happened* would take care of all the confusion and bewilderment. "If only I knew for certain—then I could deal with it. It's the uncertainty that's so hard." The survivor enters a search for the key that will provide access to the memories. He may work with hypnosis, psychodrama, guided imagery, psychoanalysis, meditation, massage, or any other combination of mind and body work in order to attain the ultimate prize—remembering.

There are some problems associated with setting remembering as the all-important goal. It creates a mind-set that believes that recovery of the memories is a prerequisite to any other recovery. "I can't go on with my life until I know *exactly* what happened." Maintaining this belief serves to distract the individual from the task at hand—healing the hurts of childhood. He becomes obsessed with remembering. Success or failure, health or pathology, normality or abnormality—all are judged by the degree to which the abuse can be recalled.

You are understandably curious; it is human nature for you to want to remember your own life. But turning into a memory sleuth is more likely to be frustrating than helpful. While I understand how hard it is to live with the uncertainty of not knowing, I urge my clients to try not to focus on regaining the memories. I have seen many people do profound and important recovery work despite uncertainty that anything happened to them. Continue with your recovery program. A great many survivors recall memories spontaneously while engaged in other aspects of the healing process.

To understand how memories can be recovered, it is necessary to look at some reasons why they are hidden. As I have discussed in Chapter 6, survival is the first order of business for the abused child. Possessing limited resources and faced with ongoing assaults on his physical and emotional well-being, he has neither time nor ability to weigh options. He just has to make it through. When the world is overwhelming, when the pain is too intense to endure, all that may be possible is to distance himself from the situation.

This is one reason why so many of the runaways—the "street kids" of our cities—turn out to be escapees, physically distancing themselves from abusive homes. They adapt to the abuses of the streets—drugs, prostitution, violence, brutality—because they are no strangers to abusive situations. In fact, they know little else. And, as hard as life on the streets is, there is some illusion of control over their situation. They are among others who understand their feelings. They no longer have to pretend that everything is fine. They don't need to put up a facade of normality. They aren't faced with the contrast between the apparently happy, normal families of their schoolmates and their own situation. They have finally been able to make some sense of their situation. That the price of understanding and acceptance may be further abuse, addiction, disease, and death is simply another factor to be accepted. Return to the abusive family isn't an option. If nothing else makes you understand the magnitude of the trauma of childhood incest, this should. There *are* "fates worse than death." For many young people, death holds less fear than the family from which they ran.

For many other children, running away from the abuse isn't an option. They may be too young, too scared, physically incapable, or otherwise unable to leave home. These children figure out creative ways to *distance* themselves from the abuse while it is occurring and after it has ended. Physically unable to get away from the abuse, they remove themselves psychologically. The child may retreat to a trance state or a fantasy world. Some of the "dreamy" or "spaced-out" kids we encounter are dealing with far more than an "overactive imagination." Men in my incest survivor groups talk of ways that they removed themselves from the abuse while it was happening.

> *"I was always having out-of-body experiences. I could float up to the ceiling and look down on my father and me."*
>
> *"I imagined that it was happening to someone else."*
>
> *"I just tried to think of other things until it was over."*
>
> *"I gave myself another name and another personality."*
>
> *"I knew that they weren't really my parents. Someday my real mother and father would come and take me away with them. She would be kind and beautiful. He would be tall and strong and would lift me onto his shoulders and we would live happily ever after."* (This last was said with an embarrassed smile. It seemed as though the speaker felt that, although I might find this childhood fantasy silly, it was important that I hear it—and that I know what it meant to him.)
>
> *"I just focused on how much I hated him. If I could do that, I didn't have to think about what was happening."*
>
> *"I pretended that my friend Joey's parents were my real family. I spent as much time as I could over at Joey's. They were always nice to each other and laughed a lot. I tried to get them to invite me to dinner with them a lot and I always wanted to stay over. My mother didn't want me to spend so much time there. I think she was hurt that I was happier there than at home."*

Further along the continuum of ways of dealing with pain is blocking it completely. In the case of emotional trauma, this can be accomplished by *forgetting*. If I don't remember my abusive childhood, then it never happened. If it never happened, then I don't have to deal with it. Not remembering the parts of his life that are too confusing, painful, and overwhelming enables the abused child to deal with as much as he can. It is logical to solve huge problems by breaking them down into manageable bits. When the abuse is especially severe or ongoing, enormous pieces of childhood may be pushed into hiding. (I am no longer surprised when clients tell me that they remember little or nothing of childhood.)

When an adult client tells me that he can't remember whole chunks of his childhood, I assume the likelihood of some sort of abuse. Memories are blocked for a reason. That reason is usually protective. Removing that protection must be done carefully and patiently, in an environment of safety and caring. It is unreasonable to think that getting the memories back will take care of everything. Just as we wouldn't think of opening up a physical wound and then leaving it to become reinfected, we must know that we have a new strategy ready to replace the forgetting. It is important to point out that the amnesia *has worked*. It has enabled the child to get through the abuse, and to physically survive to adulthood. The dressing on the wound was a temporary one. But it sufficed until something more permanent could be found. So, once again, we can appreciate the creativity of the child in figuring out a way to "play for time." He has survived until recovery became possible.

The adult survivor carries the legacy of these strategies. He discovers many other ways of protecting himself from painful memories. In addition to forgetting portions of his childhood, he may rewrite history, a strategy that contains elements of both *denying* and *pretending*. The adult survivor may remember his childhood as having been perfect. He may paint over the grim details with softer colors. When a client presents "too perfect" a picture of childhood, I find that it is usually a good idea to look further. When something appears too good to be true, it often is. This doesn't mean that he is lying. He chose a view of the world that he could deal with; he came up with a version of reality that allowed him to function in the face of abuse. He is only now starting to be ready to let go of his picture of a perfect childhood and look at what really happened.

Related to the strategies of forgetting and rewriting history are rationalizing and minimizing. Like rewriting history, these techniques contain aspects of denial and pretense. The survivor may excuse the perpetrator, explaining why he couldn't help it—she was driven to it, he didn't know what he was doing, and that she "really loved me." Justifications incude alcohol, drugs, mental illness, a bad marriage, and so forth. In fact, all the rationalizations given by perpetrators to justify their abuse may also be employed by the victims to excuse it. This, too, must be recognized as a way of breaking down the enormity of abuse so that it can be handled. As such, it must be respected as a survival strategy, but not accepted as reality.

The survivor may reduce the feelings of overload by denying the seriousness of the abuse (minimizing). "It really wasn't so bad." The most extreme stories of sexual, physical, and psychological abuse have been presented by their survivors in a casual, matter-of-fact, almost throwaway tone. I'm always surprised to hear people assume that survivors dramatize their histories. (I've even heard survivors themselves worry that they're being overly dramatic—making too much of it.) It has been my experience that survivors tend, if anything, to minimize what happened to them and need slow and careful encouragement before they accept that their childhood was truly painful.

One of my clients, a man whose father would burn him with cigarettes, was startled when I referred to the behavior as abusive. He had never thought of it that way. To him, it was just something that Daddy did. It was only when I asked how he would react if I told him that a child he knew was being burned that he was able to recognize that, indeed, he had been abused.

Abused children have to endure grim realities. That they survive at all is testimony to their strength and creativity. Having had to cope with more than most children, they may take their coping abilities for granted. And, when the old strategies prove insufficient to the current situation, they feel as though they are incapable of "normal" problem solving.

As much as a survivor may want to remember the details of his childhood (every bit as much as others may wish to *forget* theirs), his mind continues to protect him from the painful memories. I believe that the only reasonable approach to recovering occluded memories is to respect the reasons why they are unavailable. Memories can best be recalled when certain conditions are met. These include:

1 / Time and distance from the abuse. This is why it is more common for people to be dealing with the effects of incest when they have reached their thirties, forties, and fifties. By then enough time has passed to recognize that they are no longer in danger of being further abused *as children*. It is unusual for men in their teens and twenties to feel that same safety. The abuse is still too recent. The danger still feels present. Physical distance may be necessary as well in creating the right environment for recovery. Several of my clients came to Boston from other parts of the country because they felt that they couldn't work on their incest histories at home. Only by getting away from the perpetrators (or the environment in which the abuse took place) were they able to let down their guard enough to do the work they needed to do.

2 / Creation of a safe environment. Safety can have many meanings. A feeling of comfort is often mistaken for safety. The recovery work undertaken by survivors of incest is seldom comfortable. Any environment is likely to feel scary, especially one where painful emotions are brought up. When I refer to a "safe environment," I mean an atmosphere that is nonabusive, nonjudgmental, accepting of the individual and his story, and open to the expression of a full range of feelings. Despite a diversity of backgrounds, education, ethnicity, wealth, occupation, age, and life experience, the men in my incest recovery groups struggle to create a safe atmosphere to work on healing. (See Chapter 17 on "The Group.") This is no easy task, involving as it does a need to trust virtual strangers. That these strangers are also men can make it even more difficult (a) for survivors who were abused by men and (b) for those who have adopted a negative view of their own maleness. The struggle to overcome fear and suspicion and to push through years of emotional isolation is intensely painful. The success with which survivors have managed to create powerful, meaningful support systems in the face of these obstacles speaks to their courage as well as the strength of their desire to recover.

3 / Sufficient emotional discharge. The importance of the availability of feelings and their expression is addressed at length elsewhere in this book. It is important, however, to mention it in the context of recalling blocked memories. Part of the recovery process involves the need to express feelings. The survivor may need to cry, rage, shake, and even laugh or yawn as part of this process. His need and right to do these things must be unquestioned. In fact, it is often necessary to reassure him repeatedly that it's OK. He will be feeling fear, embarrassment, confusion, anger, resentment, and physical tension during this process. He must be encouraged to do so. There is no timetable for getting at (or through) these feelings. It can't be accomplished in isolation; patience and encouragement from others are vital to the process.

4 / A catalytic situation or event. Although not always necessary, many survivors point to a specific event which triggered their awareness of the need to do something about their situation. This can occur whether or not the survivor has conscious memory of the abuse. The catalyst may seem mundane and trivial (such as a television commercial that evokes a childhood memory or seeing a child in a playground), or it can be a major life event (the birth of a child or the death of a family member). I have heard men say:

"When I became a father I was overwhelmed with sadness. I knew that I had to protect my child from something terrible."

"When I saw you on that television show I couldn't stop crying. I knew that something terrible had happened to me, too."

"I was having a massage and when he had me turn over onto my stomach I began to shake uncontrollably."

These catalysts may evoke full-blown memories or simply the feeling that something happened. For many it is the first clue that they were abused.

Memories are released and recovered when the individual is ready for them. When the conditions are met, it is unnecessary to pursue specific means of recall. Memories will reappear, sometimes as vague images and at other times with a blinding clarity and breadth of detail. They may return all at once or in a slow, piecemeal fashion. Just as when a piece of information is "on the tip of your tongue," going after it directly seems to make it move farther away from awareness, while putting your attention on something else allows it to return. The best way for the incest survivor to recall forgotten events is to concentrate on his program of recovery.

It is important to remember that forgetting, denying, distancing, and pretending have been valuable survival tools. The process of recovery involves finding tools that fit the job at hand. These old tools, having served their purposes, can be put away with care and respect.

JOHN'S STATEMENT

The abuse almost killed John, a forty-eight-year-old
survivor. His determination enabled him to survive.

I cannot remember, but I have been told that when I was four
years old I drank ammonia. I know now that was my first
attempt at suicide.

I do not remember much about my childhood except that I
was mostly unhappy. I was overweight and very feminine. I
can remember my grandmother asking me how I could eat ice
cream knowing it would make me even fatter, and no one
would love me if I got any fatter.

When I was in high school I was sent to a psychiatrist
because I was suicidal.

I wanted to go to college, but felt too insecure even to apply
for admission. Instead I went to trade school to learn baking.
(Also, it didn't cost anything, even though my parents could
have afforded to send me to college.)

I was acting out sexually, being promiscuous with older men
from the time I was in junior high school. I wanted a lover,
but was too needy and sexually wild. Then, at age twenty-five,
I met the perfect mate.

He was a very successful older man who was in complete
control at all times. He was also always angry and homophobic
and he didn't give me credit for knowing enough to come in
out of the rain.

This ideal relationship—I felt like dirt and he treated me like
dirt—lasted twenty-one unhappy years.

I worked very hard. I had a nine-to-five job, bought and
sold antiques, and in my spare time renovated houses. We had
a ten-room town house and a ten-room eighteenth-century
vacation house. That way we could work evenings, weekends,
holidays, and vacations. Both houses were totally restored by
us.

I was becoming more and more unhappy. My life was not
worth living. I could think of nothing that would ever make

me happy. It was getting worse and worse and the only out that I could see was suicide. I was drinking more and more and using pot, but even that wasn't working. The only thing drugs and alcohol were doing was giving me the escape of blackouts. I had days that I functioned OK, but I don't remember being there.

Then on Nantucket in May 19—, I could see no hope. I decided this was it: no more fooling around, *just end it*.

But somehow God had other ideas. I got so drunk that the police picked me up and put me in protective custody. I don't remember any of it. The next morning they didn't just let me out—they put the local psychotherapist in with me.

He suggested I go to Alcoholics Anonymous. I told him he did not understand and that the only way I stayed alive at all was through the use of alcohol and pot. He finally convinced me to go to an AA meeting. Somehow, at the first meeting I was given hope that AA could make life worth living.

Two years sober and happier than I had ever been before I still felt emotionally shut down, so I started treatment with a psychotherapist. I was also going to Adult Children of Alcoholics (ACOA) meetings on a weekly schedule.

Four months after I started psychotherapy, I was at an ACOA meeting where a man spoke of being sexually molested by his father when he was two years old. I thought it was very sad and I started to cry. I could not stop crying.

My therapist went to lunch at twelve noon, and the next day (still crying) without an appointment, I was outside his door. When he came out to go to lunch, I told him I had to see him . . . *now*.

I explained that I was still crying over the story I had heard the night before. He said that was good. It meant I must be ready to face my own past incest.

I still don't remember, but I know it happened and I know what happened. It was with my father when I was three years old.

It is now three years ago that I first became aware incest was what was in the way of my living a happy life. I have now gotten past the most difficult part. I have felt the rage and the fear. I am not finished with it, but now I know it doesn't have the power to ruin my life.

I feel I am available for love and all the good things life should be full of. I have good close friends and my life is worth living.

8

Numbing

I never smiled until I was twenty-three years old.

—CARL, A MALE INCEST SURVIVOR

When the strategies of forgetting, denying, distancing, and pretending work, they allow the child to survive his abusive situation by putting it out of his conscious awareness. But what does a person do when he remembers the abuse and the memories bring nothing but pain?

Part of being fully human is to be open to the range of life's experiences and emotions. To a child who hasn't been severely hurt, the world is an exciting place, full of new and wonderful things to do, see, explore, and *feel*. The unhurt child approaches new situations with zestful curiosity, eager to see what life has in store, confident of his ability to master his environment. He knows that the adults in his life are benevolent and ready to help him overcome the frustrations and injuries that are a part of childhood. If he is aware that there are dangers in the world—that people may be irrational and hurtful—he is secure that the grownups who are closest to him will protect him from the worst of these dangers. He is free to feel excitement, joy, fear, anger, grief, or confusion, because he knows that they are all temporary conditions and that family, neighbors, teachers, and older friends will be there to provide guidance and comfort.

Loving parents do their best to protect their children from extreme danger, while permitting them to take some risks. Risk-taking lets the child learn valuable lessons: that many problems can be solved and that some can't; that one's actions have consequences; that adults can't fix everything; and that all endings aren't happy. A child who is not permitted to take risks may feel invulnerable (and perhaps put himself in mortal danger), or may fear any risk-taking (and end up leading a stifled, constricted existence). Parents must push through their own natural fears for the safety and well-being of their children. Fearing the worst and knowing that even their very best efforts and continual vigilance cannot insure the safety of their children, they provide what guidance they can as their beloved children begin to move out into an imperfect world.

The process of growing up involves an interplay between being nurtured and becoming independent. The healthy child moves back and forth between dependency and independence. The healthy parent provides a safe base from which the chid can depart, explore, return to process his experience—and then depart on another journey of exploration. When, in the course of his explorations, the child encounters pain, he learns that the adults in his life are there to help him understand and deal with the hurt. The child grows to adulthood with a sense of security. Confident in his ability to function in a fundamentally benign world, he meets other people as potential allies and friends. His basic self-confidence is sufficient to carry him through difficult times and to allow him to enjoy the good times.

The situation is quite different for the abused child. Finding himself in a confusing and painful situation, he has no one to whom he can turn for help, understanding, and comfort. The very people who would normally provide protection are often the cause of the pain. If they are not the perpetrators themselves, they may be aware of the abuse (consciously or unconsciously) and allow it to continue. Or the perpetrator may have effectively isolated the child from any adult who might provide protection from the abuse.

There are any number of ways that this isolation is established and reinforced. The perpetrator may have forbidden the child to have contact with nonfamily members and thoroughly intimidated those within the family, preventing them from supporting one another. He may insure the child's silence by means of coercion, threats, or actual physical violence. She may frighten the child with images of what will happen to him (disapproval, punishment, imprisonment, removal from the family, or even death) if "her part" in the abuse is discovered. He may likewise promise injury to himself or another figure who is important to the child if the abuse becomes public knowledge. (Remember that it is not safe to assume that the child does not love the perpetrator.) She may enlist the child in a pact, promise, or conspiracy of silence. Or he may bribe his victim into compliance. There are many ways to keep a child quiet. But whatever means is used to maintain the secrecy, silence serves to isolate the child from potential allies. He sees no way out of this situation, and his isolation can last well into adulthood. Faced with the prospect of a life of chronic pain, confusion, and isolation, and (for whatever reason) unable to forget what is happening to him, the child may attempt to reduce the pain by numbing.

This is how the numbing process operates. When abuse is present, a child can become suspicious of any feeling. Emotion is so often connected with pain that, in order to avoid any painful emotions, he may attempt to deaden *all* his feelings. When the feelings mean pain, then the absence of feelings becomes a working definition of *pleasure*. Based on the misinformation that all emotion must be painful emotion, the abused child sets himself the task of ridding himself of all feelings by diminishing them, destroying them, or distracting himself from them.

We have all seen numerous examples of well-meaning adults who attempt to numb (usually seen as "soothing") a child's feelings with ice cream and cookies or to distract them with toys, comforting sounds, or entertaining activities. Many of these adults have also bought the idea that feelings are to be avoided at all cost. By these means the child receives further evidence that the proper response to a feeling is to kill it. He finds an activity, object, or substance that lulls him, distracts him, and diminishes the pain, and he employs it as long as it achieves the desired effect. If the specific strategy ceases to be effective in numbing the pain, he may increase the duration of the activity, the quantity of the comforting substance, the intensity of the behavior, or turn to another form of numbing—one designed to be stronger or longer-lasting. If this looks like a description of addiction, *it is*. The child is setting an addictive pattern that will very likely follow him into adulthood. Unless recognized and interrupted it will persist throughout his life.

It is unusual to encounter a survivor of abuse who isn't addictively or compulsively engaged in some form of numbing behavior. Although everyone, at times, has a need to numb—to escape the pressures of life by diminishing the intensity of their feelings—the addict feels that ordinary life is so painful that, in order to survive, he must diminish or redirect *all* intense emotions. I am not simply referring to chemical addictions here (although a high percentage of drug addicts and alcoholics were abused as children, often by addicted or alcoholic adults). I am talking about any consistent, ongoing, intensive pattern of behavior designed to numb feelings.

Clearly, some numbing activities are more socially acceptable than others. Some, in fact, may even be valued by society. Rather than being interrupted, socially acceptable addictions and compulsions may be rewarded and reinforced. These numbing behaviors are not recognized as such, much less seen as addictions. The man who directs all of his energy into his career may jokingly refer to himself as a *workaholic*, but he seldom is conscious of the import of that definition. And, of course, as his career and income increase—as others recognize and reward him as a "pillar of society, wonderful provider, and wealthy, sober, upstanding citizen"—there is no awareness of the pain underlying the drive to work. The workaholic's pattern is doubly reinforced: (a) the time spent at his work occupies his energy and distracts him from the need to deal with painful emotions; and (b) appreciation by others makes him feel as though he is a more worthwhile (less damaged) person. Of course, that very appreciation has an addictive quality, spurring him on to greater achievement in his work life so that he can appear even greater in the eyes of others. The workaholic becomes trapped by the very strategy he devised to escape from feeling bad about himself. He now feels he can never slacken his drive to the top for fear of the loss of acceptance and admiration of others, as well as the reemergence of the painful feelings. Even when the workaholic achieves the pinnacle of success in his field he cannot rest, both for fear of losing what he has achieved and because the awful feelings and memories are still waiting to entrap him.

This is not to say that a person shouldn't put energy into his career. It is important to derive satisfaction from our work—it is one of the cornerstones of life. But when a person completely derives his identity and worth as a human being from his work, he has erected a very fragile structure. We have all seen the results of such an orientation: the executive who retires and loses all will to live, or the person who "takes a drink" after being fired. One drink doesn't make one an alcoholic, nor does being excited about and invested in one's career turn one into a workaholic. We are talking about the degree and quality of the behavior. Whenever one aspect of a person's life becomes the overwhelming focus of attention, it is a good idea to take a look at it. Most addictive behaviors taken in moderation are either acceptable to society or attract little attention. However, it is the nature of addiction that it rarely remains at a moderate level. The solution (strategy of numbing) intensifies until it becomes a problem. This is why numbing is only a temporary solution to the problems of the survivor, ultimately creating additional problems. Addictions and compulsions are the extreme extensions of any numbing behavior. If the alcoholic and drug addict faces health problems, loss of family and friends and psychological difficulties, so does the man who is addicted to his career.

There are many other examples of numbing patterns, carrying varying degrees of social acceptability. In my groups for male incest survivors, I have had recovering alcoholics and drug addicts. I have seen compulsive overeaters, gamblers, shoppers, spenders and workers. There are men who are "addicted" to sex, masturbation, credit card use, television, danger, sleep, body building, and marathon running. There are fanatic collectors of art, automobiles, clothing, money, academic degrees, and friends. There are people who are driven to take care of others and there are religious fanatics of every philosophical stripe, both Eastern and Western.

Few of these activities or interests would arouse anyone's concern if kept in perspective and indulged in moderation. It is the quality of the behavior and the underlying reasons for it that are troublesome. When a pattern of numbing of feelings is undertaken by a survivor as a strategy for surviving abuse, he may feel better for a while. Ultimately, the behavior gets out of control and causes more pain than it alleviates. At that point, the survivor must add one more difficult part to his program—overcoming addiction. He must learn to live without numbing and experience the range of feelings necessary to recovery and to a healthy life. The way out of the pain is *through* it. Ultimately, pain can no more be numbed than it can be avoided. Instead, the survivor must find a safe and encouraging environment in which to feel his emotions, including the painful ones. In this setting he can gradually begin to let go of his numbing techniques and experience the reality of feelings—they are rich and wonderful and nobody ever died from having them.

9

Compartments

Everyone gets a piece of me, but no one has all of me.   —PHILIP, A MALE SURVIVOR

For most of human history daily life existed as an integrated whole. Even where there was a culturally established division of labor (men hunting and women gathering food) the divisions were known by and visible to all members of society. Life wasn't divided into work vs. play, religious vs. secular, or career vs. family. Everyone knew who they were and where each person fit into the fabric of social life. Celebrations and special events formed a part of the rhythm of life. There was security to be found in the belief that life in the present was an extension of what went before, and would continue into the future in much the same manner. When we became an agrarian peasant society, this integration continued. The family unit was the unit of work. Extended families worked the farm, ate, played, and worshiped together. Although the seasons changed, the rhythms of life remained constant. And neighbors lived in ways that were pretty similar. You not only knew who you were, you knew who everyone else was.

As we became an increasingly technology-based civilization, the natural integration of daily life began to break down. Work became more specialized, so that we no longer knew what everyone else was doing. And work began to take people out of the home, so that even family members were leading very separate lives and moving among different people. Children were educated outside the home and encountered schoolmates and teachers with dissimilar ideas, values and experiences. For men, this transition was especially isolating. Men were the first group to work away from home. This was in sharp distinction to the traditional role of the man as the head of a family-based work force, which was also the basic social, religious, educational, leisure and celebratory unit. In modern society the schools educate, the clergy prays, and the man most frequently spends the bulk of his time at work, removed from family, neighbors, and friends. He is encouraged to keep career, family, friendships, and leisure activities separate from one another. Since everyone he knows is living the same way, it seems natural to do so. The modern man can find himself feeling isolated from those closest to him without realizing why.

When someone feels strong and healthy he strives for an integrated life. He sees himself as a whole person who brings together diverse aspects of personality, training and experience. Although his responses to different people and situations may vary, the face he presents to the world is fairly constant, whether he is currently occupying the role of worker, friend, neighbor, or family member. Of course, he will not treat an employee in the same manner as he does his child. He will certainly not interact with his child in the same way as he would a lover. But, whatever the interaction, the same basic person is in evidence. This being so, he is able to deal with those times when the various parts of his life intersect (such as having the boss over for dinner or running into a coworker at a party). Part of becoming an adult involves learning how to adapt to the requirements of a range of social situations *while remaining true to one's essential personality*. It has been said that "the advantage of telling the truth is that you don't have to remember what you said." The secure individual has accepted himself enough to act on the assumption that he doesn't have to change *who he is* in order to interact with different people. It is enough to be sensitive to the needs of the situation—and to be himself.

Most incest survivors find it very difficult to integrate their lives in this manner. For one thing, they lack a visible model of integration. The adults who abused them showed them faces that were very different from those they presented to the rest of the world. Abused children are told to pretend that nothing is amiss, and they learn how to keep secrets very well. The abused child realizes early on that, to survive, he must become a master of pretense. It makes little difference when he receives conflicting information. If one experience contradicts another, he can simply keep them separate—each in its own little compartment—so that they don't interfere with one another. The child, then, has learned to accept an infinite number of coexisting realities. It is small wonder that he feels grounded in none of them, or that reality is seen as fluid and insubstantial.

Sexual abuse leaves a victimized child with a fragmented life. He has had to learn ways of keeping the parts of his life separate from one another. The sexual abuse must be kept secret, locked in a compartment that cannot be shown to peers, teachers, or even other family members. If he needs to escape temporarily from the pain of the abuse, he moves into another compartment. When an event occurs that doesn't fit into any of the existing categories, he simply creates a new compartment to account for it. This need to compartmentalize his life gets carried into adulthood, the survivor ending up with an adult life of fragments that he is unable to integrate.

Even if he is devoid of memories and numbed of feelings, the survivor of abuse lives in an isolated world (as discussed in Chapters 7 and 8). He feels that no one can understand him. Since he doesn't know whether he can trust his own memories and perceptions, he's not sure that he can even understand *himself*. Carrying the self-perception that he is hopelessly flawed as a person, an integrated life seems beyond reach. Each social interaction, every new situation, feels *completely* different, and he feels frighteningly unequipped to cope with the new demands. It doesn't feel like a matter of adapting one's experience and intelligence to somewhat different requirements. Instead, the survivor fears each new situation because it has to be learned afresh, from step one—and he doesn't know whether he is up to the challenge. Fearing new people and new situations, the survivor may find himself increasingly isolated, dealing only with the familiar, afraid to risk—and reinforcing his sense of unworthiness and unacceptability.

Increasingly, even within the life that is familiar to him, the survivor may separate one part from another. Keeping all the parts of his life in tight little compartments, isolated from one another, feels both easier and safer. It is easier to act a role if you are sure of the play that you're in. If you only have to interact with one person at a time, you only have to *be* one person at a time. No matter that the relationship becomes static and dull; it is safer that way. There are fewer surprises; surprises are not always pleasant. And the more compartmentalized your life is, the less information needs to be shared with any single individual. Conversely, the more information that gets out, the less control you have over how that information is used . . . or abused. And, most important, if the abuse can be kept in a compartment it is less likely to spill over into all parts of your life. It can be kept under control. It's much easier when you know where the abuse is to be found, instead of never being sure of when and where it might pop up.

One of my clients, who is academically, professionally and socially adept, said to me, "Everyone gets a piece of me, but no one has all of me." He felt that he had to maintain rigid control over who saw what, and that it was necessary to present inaccurate, intentionally distorted, and radically different faces to others in order to protect himself. It is significant that when he referred to others in his life he said,

"No one *has* all of me," rather than "No one *sees* it all." It reflects the assumption that knowledge is power, and that power will always be used to hurt. If someone knows who I am (he reasoned) then they will have more control over me and I can't risk that. I know what happens when someone gets too close.

For this individual the course of his recovery necessitated gradually sharing more of himself, both in group and individual therapy. As he did so, always terrified, always certain that the openness would lead to further abuse, he began to explore the possibility of leading a healthier, more integrated life. Along with the terror came the feeling that when he had revealed enough of himself to me or to the other group members, he would certainly be rejected. We would then see how imperfect, stupid, evil, and ugly (all *his* words) he really is. We would be angry with him for having fooled us, and would be repulsed by him. The reality was, and continues to be, quite the opposite. Freed of the need to maintain rigid control, no longer having to expend vast amounts of energy on keeping people apart and remembering who knows what about him, he could begin to relax. As he did so he became more, rather than less, attractive. Showing some vulnerability made him real and accessible. He found himself beginning to feel welcome for the very first time. It is important to state that these changes did not happen quickly or easily. Each step in the process involved his moving through terror and doubt. There were times when the fear became too overwhelming and he slid back to the safety of one of the old compartments—but the compartment no longer fit and was certainly far less comfortable than it had been. So the retreats lasted for shorter and shorter periods. And, although the recovery process is not over, he is now very clearly working to integrate the diverse aspects of his life.

The day he told me, "You have more of the pieces than anyone else," I knew that I had been given an important and valuable gift. The trust he had placed in me was (and always will be) something to be cherished and nurtured. As this process continues to progress, his face and body relax more and more. He looks younger and less strained. He no longer needs to cringe or strike intimidating poses. His voice has become softer and he shows emotions more easily. And most important, as he allows people to get to know him, he is no longer able to accept the misinformation that has helped to keep the isolation in place.

As long as he kept himself hidden from others, he was able to discount any expression of caring on the grounds that, whatever the other person was seeing, it certainly wasn't *him*. But whatever the reason, it wasn't real. He had fooled yet another individual into liking him. And if he could fool him—if this other person couldn't see through the act—then he surely couldn't be smart enough to be of any real help. So he was faced with an apparent double-bind. He felt that if he wanted people to stick around, then he couldn't be real. He had to pretend, caretake, or buy their friendship. If he couldn't be real with someone, why have him around? Social contact brought up the feeling that the situation was hopeless. Now, as he increasingly lets go of the controlling behavior, the masks, and the compartments, he is finding that people were attracted to him *despite* these things rather than because of them. People like him because he is truly a good, smart, kind, and interesting person. They like him because he is likable. They are attracted to him because he is attractive. And *that* is reality. What a challenge to trust that this might be so! What fear in testing that belief! What a relief to begin to let down the defenses and controls! And what a triumph to begin to turn around life-long rigidities!

These changes are available to you. As you proceed with your recovery, you will encounter similar challenges, fears, relief and triumph. You will experience the same doubt and mistrust, and you will sometimes find yourself slipping back into old compartments. But these slips are temporary. Increasingly, you will find the compartments breaking down, being replaced by something that is far more satisfying and far more real—an integrated life.

10

Self-Image, Self-Esteem, and Perfectionism

I have two teams that I take everywhere with me: the FBI to check everything out and a film crew to record and make sure I did everything right. And they are both me.
                                                              —A MALE SURVIVOR

An incestuous childhood shatters the survivor's self-esteem and causes him to be left with an unrealistic picture of himself. Regardless of how he is perceived by others, he has a negative self-image. He feels ugly and unlovable. Since these feelings don't reflect any kind of objective reality, they aren't subject to change through rational argument. Despite all evidence to the contrary, the survivor "knows" that he is ugly, stupid, incompetent, uncreative, weak, sick, and/or evil. If people perceive him in any other way, he takes it as evidence that he has fooled them. This means that he can discount them because they are so easily taken in by what is, to him, an obvious deception. If they do see the ugly "reality" and don't seem to be bothered by it, then several explanations are possible—none of them positive. They are laughing at him behind his back. They are treating him kindly because they feel sorry for him. They are "losers" themselves and thus not worth his time. They are enduring his presence because they want something from him. Or they haven't perceived the full scope of his unacceptability. Any explanation that occurs to him confirms his lack of worth. That a normally perceptive and intelligent person would find him likable or desirable (in any way that isn't harmful) is inconceivable to him. He never entertains the possibility that others may be correct in their perceptions of him, that they like him and want him around because he is an interesting person. He has had to rely so completely on his own view of reality that the possibility of accepting any other reeks of danger. After all, look what happened when he was subjected to the perpetrator's definition of reality.

As a child, the incest survivor realized that he had little or no control over whether or not the abuse would take place. Smaller, weaker, and less experienced than the adult perpetrator, he was forced to submit to his or her greater power. At best he learned to manipulate the situation to shorten the duration or lessen the intensity of the abuse. One survivor reported the following:

"I knew whether he was going to want sex as soon as he walked in the door. I learned how to get my mother out of the room so that we could get it over with as quickly as possible. If I did it fast enough, then he might not beat us up. I was angry with her when she didn't leave right away. It meant that he was going to hurt me more."

This man learned at an early age that his power to control his life was severely limited—and that because of his inferior position, his best chance at self-protection was to limit the scope of abuse through manipulation. Not having the ability to protect himself or to significantly alter his situation led to a general feeling of inferiority and powerlessness. "If I were only smarter, stronger, quicker or nicer [the child feels], this wouldn't be happening to me." It is clear to him that, because he cannot adequately protect himself, he is inferior, and no one can preserve positive self-esteem while feeling powerless and inferior. As the incest survivor carries this sense of inferiority into adulthood, it manifests itself in a variety of forms.

He may completely accept his own lack of positive attributes, seeing himself as hopelessly flawed. Given this perspective, it seems foolish to even try to take charge of his life. Career, relationships, academic achievement, athletic prowess, and enjoyment of life all are perceived as unattainable. So why bother to even try? People will respond to him as a failure because that is how he presents himself. Any success he achieves can be written off as accidental, or discounted as incomplete—not good enough. And what difference would small successes make, anyway? Only perfection will provide protection. He is safe only if he is the smartest, strongest, quickest, *and* best looking. This is impossible to achieve, so why bother trying? Nothing less will do. Nothing less will protect him. Nothing less than absolute perfection will satisfy him. And, since no one can be perfect, his need to be so will surely destroy what is left of his self-esteem.

In these ways, feeling flawed and incomplete, believing that his only protection lies in complete power, strength, intelligence, and competence, the incest survivor has become a perfectionist. The world has become one of extremes. Relationships as well as achievements are idealized. People must be perfect or they are worthless.

Since it is clear to the survivor that he is massively imperfect, he knows that it is just a matter of time before other people recognize his worthlessness. Faced with division of the world into "perfect" and "worthless," the survivor finds himself in another no-win situation. The perfectionism presents itself in this form: "In order to be OK, I must be perfect and do *everything* right." Anything short of perfection is interpreted as further evidence that, "I can't do *anything* right." Since partial success is seen as no success at all (and humans are, after all, imperfect beings), there is no way to overcome his shortcomings.

There are four specific ways that perfectionism plays itself out in the lives of adult survivors:

First, having become a perfectionist while perceiving himself as "damaged goods" leaves the survivor feeling even more hopeless. He may respond by giving up entirely. Convinced that he has no chance

FOCUS

ALL-OR-NOTHING THINKING

To "see both sides" of a problem is the surest way to prevent its complete solution. Because there are always more than two sides. —IDRIES SHAH, from his *Reflections*

Incestuous abuse narrows a child's perception of the world. Having come to see people as either perpetrators or victims (Chapter 2), he tends to grow into adulthood with a similarly constricted view of life. The world is divided into black or white, all or nothing, life or death dualities. There is no room for flexibility or nuances in his rigid world view—the stakes are too high. There are examples of the extremes to which the all-or-nothing thinking can be carried throughout this chapter.

Recovery for the incest survivor involves a piece of electrical work. He must remove the on-off switch that limits the way he responds to the world, and install a dimmer. Most people are neither heroes nor villains; most events fall somewhere between triumph and tragedy. When we only allow two options for any situation, two solutions for any problem (the right way and the wrong way), we are cutting ourselves off from most of life's richness.

I once commented to an incest survivor client that there is a vast territory between black and white. He replied, "Oh, you mean shades of gray." "Yes," I agreed, "but also red, blue, green, orange, and magenta . . ." Expanding the possibilities that we allow ourselves opens us up to the rich and colorful spectrum of human experience. It lends variety to an otherwise drab palette. As survivors move through the hurts of incest, they discover that new and exciting options have opened for them. Recovery is a matter of expanding horizons.

for success, he may not even try to achieve in school. Since he believes that a successful career is completely beyond his grasp, he settles for just getting by, taking any job that comes along. And, of course, nobody would want such a "failure" as a friend, lover, or husband—so it would be foolish to even bother. Thus the prophecy fulfills itself. He becomes the failure that he always knew he was.

A second scenario for the perfectionist survivor is to settle for an average level of achievement while putting himself down for his mediocrity. He is able thereby to live a perfectly acceptable life while maintaining an overwhelming sense of being a failure. His need for perfection doesn't allow him to take pleasure in "modest" accomplishments; they only serve to further lower his self-esteem. In this form of perfectionism, we can see most clearly the difference between the image that the survivor presents to the world (external) and his (internal) self-image. Outwardly, he is leading a comfortable, responsible, and reasonably well-integrated life. Who would suspect that he views these very things as evidence of his failure? He knows that he has settled for second best.

A third manifestation of perfectionism is overachievement. Many adult incest survivors are tremendously talented and accomplished. They have achieved enormously successful careers, amassed sizable fortunes, become well-respected members of their communities, formed deep and long-lasting friendships and relationships, been caring family members, and done great good for humanity. They are, in the eyes of society, successful. But their success brings no solace. If they are not at the absolute top of their professions, it is not enough. No level of income is enough to allow them to relax.

One of my clients, a single man with no dependents, said, "If I don't make over one hundred thousand dollars a year, I might as well commit suicide." He meant it. Anything less was evidence of failure. However, the fact that he earned far more than that was not seen as evidence of success. Again, a no-win situation.

Another client, a multimillionaire with a loving family and a winning personality, found himself conspicuously amassing possessions so that "people will think I'm rich."

Even if he reaches the absolute peak of his profession, the perfectionist incest survivor remains driven, lest he lose what he has attained and thereby reveal his "true nature" to the world—a failure.

Even if he has achieved a perfect career, family, friendship or honor, the perfectionist is able to discount it all by selective comparison. "I may be rich, but I'm not handsome." He compares himself to others in ways designed to find him wanting. He compares his intelligence to Einstein's while measuring his biceps against Schwarzenegger's. He would never dream of doing the reverse, comparing himself to a whole person, or even not judging or comparing himself at all. He has judged himself inferior and continues to find evidence to justify that judgment.

Fourth, other male survivors become chronic "underachievers," finding themselves in menial, ill-paid positions for which they are tremendously overqualified. I have seen male survivors who have several advanced degrees working in clerical or manual jobs *because they felt inferior* to people with far weaker abilities and qualifications. I'm not judging the relative merits of different careers. If an occupation is freely chosen, it can provide satisfaction. But if an individual feels stuck in a job that provides nothing but frustration and confirmation of his failings, the situation needs to be reexamined.

Whether the adult survivor is a medical doctor who "feels like a fraud," a multimillionaire who worries about feeding his family, a talented musician who helps others achieve success while he remains in the background, or a skilled and insightful psychologist who moves from one menial temporary job to another, the underlying issue is *self-esteem.* Although female incest survivors also struggle with career and success issues, there is a cultural bias that says that men are supposed to be aggressive and fearless in pursuit of professional success. Feeling passive and fearful, the male survivor is able to sabotage or discount any career achievement. An important aspect of recovery is the development of a more positive self-image. This is most effectively accomplished through building trust in others. In therapy, in recovery groups, and with friends, the survivor gradually begins to accept a more accurate view of what is a reasonable and clear picture of himself. This, in turn, opens the possibility of enjoying career success as part of a satisfying, well-integrated life.

Until such time as the survivor is ready to begin to let go of perfectionism and start to accept a more reasonable self-image, his life is one of anxiety, tension, and the torture of self-doubt. The effects can be enormously unhealthy. Since only perfection will do, the perfectionist hates himself for his perceived shortcomings. Having set himself impossible standards, he sees how he doesn't measure up to them. His unrealistic standards can lead to dangerous behavior. Feeling, for example, that his body is ugly and unattractive, he may resort to self-destructive eating habits (including rigid dieting, anorexia, or bulimia). He may attempt to perfect his physique through compulsive body building coupled with the use of steroids. If he was once overweight, he is ever-vigilant in his war against calories. No evidence of mirror, height-weight charts, or the reactions of others will convince him that he is not grossly obese or in imminent danger of becoming so. A client of mine, who would be described by almost anyone as tall and elegantly slim (perhaps verging on gaunt), showed me photographs of himself taken many years ago as evidence of how fat he *is!* He feels that he must continually purge himself of food (a condition known as bulimia) so that he doesn't show the world his true nature.

The "Catch-22" of this situation is that it also feels dangerous to appear too attractive. If other people find the incest survivor attractive, he believes, they will abuse him. The compulsive overeater may feel his obesity is a buffer, providing insulation from a dangerous world. Food, for the overeater, serves many purposes. It provides nourishment and dependable comfort. It numbs negative feelings. The resultant obesity keeps people from taking a sexual interest in him, at the same time that it provides visible evidence to confirm his negative image of his inner self. He feels that he is (always was and always will be) ugly. He uses this evidence as another stick with which to beat himself. When he attempts to bring his weight under control, it brings up massive terror. That the only way he can still the fear is with food destroys any hope of success. This, once again, confirms his sense of failure. It is important to remember that the survivor feels a need to project an image that is at odds with his self-image. He is faced with two conflicting pressures: (a) a need to be (and appear) perfect, in order to conceal his perceived flaws (imperfections) from the world; and (b) the need to conceal anything that would make him attractive, so that he will not invite abuse.

If the survivor is to be attractive in any way, he must find something to protect him from the resultant threat of abuse. Thus, the body builder may attempt to protect himself by presenting a powerful and intimidating image to the world. The martial arts expert tries to be the very best so that no one can overpower him. Perfectionist survivors are likely to be obsessive and extreme in their athletic pursuits. Runners may be drawn to ultramarathons or triathalons. The underlying, often unconscious, goal may be safety; it may be acceptability. Neither feels attainable. And it isn't attainable, because (to the perfectionist) safety means *total security* and acceptability means *complete and absolute acceptance.* These do not exist in the world, but the pefectionist either continues to struggle, gives up completely, or berates himself for his mediocrity. His insistence on absolutes prevents him from achieving a reasonable, healthy level of self-esteem. A healthy self-image and a satisfying life are attainable, but not without giving up unrealistic standards of perfection.

Living at the extreme of shame and hopelessness, the survivor can see no way to overcome his monumental deficiencies. Ultimately, if the level of his self-esteem falls low enough, he may be led to contem-

FOCUS

SUICIDAL FEELINGS

If you have ever felt this way, then you know that it is almost impossible to move out of the suicidal feelings by yourself. You need perspective on the painful emotions. That perspective can only come from outside yourself. Survivors need to be able to express the hopelessness that leads them to consider doing away with themselves. They need to share mistaken notions like: "Everyone would be better off if I were dead." "It would be the ultimate solution, I wouldn't feel the pain anymore." "I could finally relax and just stop struggling." This is another reason why contact with other survivors, therapy, and participation in recovery groups and workshops are so important. Sharing the struggle with other survivors provides a safety valve for suicidal thoughts. It shows you that you are cared about—that whether you live or die makes a difference. Incest survivors need to talk about their hopeless times, and what they have found useful in moving out of despair. They may create their own "suicide hotlines," making themselves available to receive phone calls or visits from one another when things get too overwhelming.

If you feel like killing yourself, call someone—a friend, a neighbor, a counselor, a crisis hotline and move yourself away from your suicidal isolation. Make a contract with your therapist (or a friend) that you will not act on suicidal feelings until you have spoken face-to-face. Give yourself a chance to turn your life around. Your feelings of low self-worth are the outgrowth of the way you were abused. *If you kill yourself, then you are letting the abuse win!* Don't allow that to happen. No matter how bad you feel about yourself, you are worth more than the abuse! The painful emotion and the low self-esteem can be overcome. Recovery is real. You can heal. And the results are worth the effort.

plate or attempt suicide. At this point of despair, killing himself seems to him to be a reasonable option. He feels that he could give up trying, let go of the pain, and the world would no longer have to put up with him. He could put an end to the striving, the frustration, the failures, and the self-hatred. And, he feels, no one would really care anyway. People could go on about their lives and stop wasting their time on the likes of him. Thus, the logical extension of this unrealistic perfectionism is, "If I can't be perfect, then why should I *be* at all?" Incest survivors frequently report feeling like killing themselves. Many have attempted suicide; some have succeeded.

Your process of recovery will involve the gradual breaking down of misguided perfectionism. It will entail learning to distinguish reasonable goals and expectations from unreasonable ones. All people must come to recognize that to be human is to have human flaws—and this is as true for you as for everyone else. In the course of your healing you will begin to discover that people *do* like you, not because of the perfect face that you have struggled to present to the world, but often *despite* that facade. By testing your perceptions against those of others—in individual and group therapy, with friends and allies—you will find out who you really are. You will understand how your childhood experiences led you to accept misinformation as the truth. You will be better able to spot the negative, self-defeating thoughts as soon as they appear, and to learn how to contradict them. The face that stares back at you from the mirror will come to look less like a hideous monster and more like an ordinary person, with a range of interesting strengths, weaknesses, talents and problems. You will begin to explore the rich and varied landscape that lies between worthlessness and perfection.

STEVE'S STATEMENT

Pushing through his fears of not being good enough and his desire to minimize, deny, and numb, Steve, a thirty-eight-year-old survivor, shares the importance of his feelings.

My name is Steve, and I almost did not write this. Not that I could not; as you can see, I can write. Nor that I should not; my experience of being sexually abused by my father for well nigh ten years, followed by my road to recovery, the insights gained as a result of those experiences, as well as extensive research on the subject, make me well qualified. No, it simply boiled down to the fact that I know, deep down, I cannot write it well enough to say what needs to be said, to reach those who need to be reached. It simply had to be perfect, and I know I am further from being perfect than any man.

That demand for perfection in myself, while forgiving any and all frailties and foibles in those around me, is just one of the character defects I know I must have. Low, nay, a lack of self-esteem, self-worth, and self-confidence, as well as inabilities to trust, to form intimate relationships, to engage in sexuality, or even admit to my sexuality, are all common residues of my incest trauma that I share with many others.

Also, like many others who have experienced incest, I have adapted so well to these deficiencies they often go unnoticed. It is only when I am in a group of other survivors that, seeing the ravages of incest in their lives, I can clearly see it in my own. To see a need to control in others, and then to find it such a pervasive trait in myself is truly eye-opening.

None of this should be so alarming to survivors or those who wish to help them as to prevent them from beginning or continuing down the road of recovery. Usually the trauma is so extensive that all areas of the person's life are in some way affected. This need not rule out recovery; rather it underscores the difficulties and obstacles along the way. To hope never to feel the pain and anger and sadness is not a realizable goal of recovery. Not to have the sadness, anger, and pain prevent one from truly being happy, loving, and caring is.

Sex, Trust, and Caring

When Reason knows the heart and soul are troubled
   But thinks that happiness would look better
And Reason makes the body react accordingly, then
     Reason is unreasonable.
          —A MALE SURVIVOR, from his poem "Something Old, Nothing New"

It has been widely noted that rape is a crime of violence, not a sexual crime. However, since the anger, hatred, fear, and violence are acted out sexually, many people continue to view rape as an act of sexual passion. I raise the subject in order to emphasize how easily a connection can be made between two different phenomena when they occur in close proximity or when they have common aspects. Some time ago I was watching a television comedy special during which Carol Burnett asked Robin Williams, "Are you laughing at me?" He replied, "No, I'm laughing *near* you."

The distinction between laughter and ridicule is not readily apparent to someone who has experienced the embarrassment of being laughed at or teased. To someone who has been attacked by a dog, *all* dogs, no matter how cute and friendly, may be objects of terror. If a child was subjected to beatings for talking during mealtimes, he may as an adult become a morose, uncommunicative dinner companion. He may not realize why dinner table conversation makes him uncomfortable, but it does. The connections were childish connections, perfectly logical in the context of his limited experience, carried unconsciously into adult life. Similarly, incestuous child abuse delivers a message to the child that equates caring with sex. A trusted adult violates a position of responsibility by sexually victimizing the child. An adult who is supposed to care about the child becomes his attacker. The child learns to mistrust any caring overtures, fearful that they will lead to further sexual victimization.

These associations aren't necessarily being made consciously—we aren't always aware of the lessons we are learning—but the connections are being made. Our childhood perceptions, whether accurate or incorrect, are incorporated into the ways we view and respond to the world.

Any form of incestuous child abuse generates confusion, which profoundly influences adult relationships. We have spoken of how children make logical assumptions based upon what they are told and what they experience. People in the world of computers are familiar with the phrase "Garbage in, garbage out." When the child receives correct information, he is able to draw conclusions which are also correct. If, however, he receives misinformation, he will develop a world view which—although consistent—is based on inaccuracies and distortions.

The incestuously abused child comes to make many connections based on the abuse. When a protective, caring relationship becomes sexualized the child can come to the conclusion that any expression of caring will lead to sex. The converse is that he feels that, in order to be cared for, he must be willing to submit to sex. All touching (or a particular type of touch—gentle or violent—depending upon the child's particular situation) may be interpreted as sexual. If there was physical violence attached to the incest, then touch, caring, and/or sex may feel like a violent act. If touch means sex, and sex means abuse, the child may feel as though he is being abused whenever anyone touches him. Having incorporated this misinformation into his understanding of life, the child may go out into the world fearing and avoiding any expressions of caring. When treated affectionately, he reacts with mistrust, becoming withdrawn, suspicious, or antagonistic. Having learned to connect caring with sex, he might attempt to sexualize the interaction—and become confused when his behavior is regarded as inappropriate. After all, that is what was being demanded in the past.

Acting on internally logical conclusions based on childhood sexual abuse, the child (and later, the adult he becomes) receives confusing messages from the world—and, in return, behaves in ways that are strange and confusing to people who were not victims of incest. If he manages to learn appropriate behavior and isn't seen as a misfit, he may still be confused. He goes through the motions without really knowing why his behavior is appropriate. He has learned to give people what they want without questioning their desires too closely.

In her workshops, Claudia Black refers to how children raised in alcoholic families develop the ability to shift their reality at a moment's notice. The survivor of incest, often from an alcoholic family himself, must also develop this skill. He has learned this skill in order to survive. He becomes very adept at figuring out what people want

so that he can supply it. If the other person doesn't want anything—
or doesn't want anything *sexual* from him—he is intensely confused.
Convinced that all displays of caring and affection must become sexual, the individual who doesn't want to be sexual is viewed with
distrust. "He/she must want *something* from me. If it's not sex, then
what is it? If it is sex, then why pretend it isn't?"

On the other hand, the absence of a sexual response may be seen
as rejection. When a person sees his only value as that of a sexual
object, and his partner isn't interested in sex, then he feels that he has
no value at all. As much as he may not want to have sex, the incest
survivor may redouble his efforts to sexualize social interaction. He
has learned "what people really want." If the other person yields to
the pressure, the survivor is confirmed in his belief that, after all, all
closeness is sexual. Resistance to sexual overtures is interpreted as
abnormality, denial, or rejection. When someone chooses not to sexualize an interaction, the survivor will very likely interpret that as
recognition of his undesirability. "Of course she/he doesn't want to
have sex with me. Who in their right mind would be attracted to
someone as messed up as I am?" Once again he is faced with a no-win
situation.

Sex is seen as inevitable, whether desired or not. But whether or
not sex is involved, the survivor writes himself off as undesirable. He
is *only* a sexual object, attempting to prove his worth and desirability
through repeated sexual encounters which are neither satisfying nor
uplifting. Or, if he doesn't engage in sex, he sees himself as worthless,
unattractive, and undesirable—once again confirming a negative self-
image.

If the negative and erroneous messages about caring, affection, and
sex are not powerfully contradicted, the incestuously abused child
carries them into adolescence and adulthood. Studies of sexually promiscuous teenagers, prostitutes (male and female, teenage and adult),
and sexually compulsive adults have turned up large numbers of individuals who report childhood incest. Many survivors describe
themselves as not liking to be touched while, at the same time, engaging in compulsive sexual activity. This appears contradictory only to
someone who is unaware of the way that sexual abuse leads to the
sexualization of any expression of caring. It isn't contradictory because it represents genuine needs—the need to be cared for and the
need to be close. Compulsive sexual activity depersonalizes sex, and
makes it possible to engage in physical closeness—and even the appearance of caring—without requiring the survivor to be intimate.
Intimacy involves trust, and that is too threatening for the survivor to
risk.

Trust is the paramount issue for incest survivors. Since the information he receives from external sources so strongly contrasts with his own experience, trust is a stranger to him. Why, indeed, should he trust? Who could he trust? It feels as though all that trusting ever got him was abuse. Having learned to depend on his own resources in order to survive, he sees nothing but danger in trusting others. This lack of trust and dependence on misinformation about caring are carried into all adult relationships. I say "misinformation" about caring because he hasn't experienced true caring. Genuine caring is respectful of an individual's needs and boundaries. Abusers put their own desires ahead of the well-being of their victims. No matter what the justification or how gentle the behavior, it is still harmful.

It will take the survivor a great deal of time and effort to learn that people *do* care. It takes even longer to accurately distinguish true caring from the perversion of caring that he learned from the perpetrator, and to trust that his perceptions are accurate. This involves slow building of trust, and learning how to form intimate (not necessarily sexual) relationships with caring people who will be able to respect the intimacy and not violate the trust. Building trust and establishing intimacy are extremely difficult tasks, but they must be done. If they aren't, the survivor will continue to live out patterns of unsuccessful relationships generated by his abusive childhood experience.

In my work with incest survivors I have encountered five common patterns:

1 / Isolation. Fearing and distrusting intimacy, the incest survivor may distance himself from *any* relationships, living a lonely and isolated life. He may not know why he is unable to connect with people, seeing it as further evidence of his own unworthiness. Other people are seen as happier, smarter, and better adjusted. Relationships may be perceived as ideal states, perfect and perfectly inaccessible to someone like himself. He sees his inability to "figure out" how to sustain relationships as further evidence of his stupidity.

2 / Short-lived and volatile relationships. Some incest survivors push through their isolation and enter into a series of short-lived and highly volatile relationships. Suspicious and afraid, they wait for their partners to abuse them. Some will goad their partners beyond endurance, never realizing that they are behaving provocatively. Expressions of caring are rejected, as trust is necessary in order to let caring in. Since they have learned to mistrust words, open communication is impossible. Partners who attempt to discuss problems in the relationship are met with silence, hostility, or withdrawal. Finally, the survivor finds sufficient justification to leave the relationship, often abruptly and without explanation. He feels hurt and misunderstood, but quickly moves on to another relationship which follows a virtually identical pattern to the one he just ended. If he remains in the relationship, the incest survivor may unconsciously push his partner away. Through silence, criticism, unreasonable demands, emotional outbursts, promiscuity, or other means, he may wear down his partner's ability to keep trying. Since there is very little open communication, these issues aren't worked on. When the partner, hurt and confused, leaves the relationship, the incest survivor feels—once again—abandoned. He has received further evidence that nobody cares; that people can't be trusted; that he is unable to find someone who will really love him; that all women/men are undependable; that all anyone wants from him is sex; that relationships are impossible; and/or that he is totally unlovable. No insight or understanding comes from the breakup because there was neither trust nor communication involved.

3 / **Abusive relationships.** In other cases the incest survivor enters into abusive relationships. Whether he is the victim or the abuser in these relationships, they tend to follow a pattern that closely resembles the original abuse. His chosen partner may resemble the perpetrator physically or in some aspects of behavior, mannerism, occupation, age, voice, or personality. Or he might find someone who resembles himself as a child and proceed to treat her/him as he was treated by his perpetrator. This type of relationship may continue for some time if the chosen partner was hurt in ways which lend themselves to acting out her/his chosen role. This creates a neat fit, with the partners in agreement as to how each of them should act. Or the partner may rebel against the victim (or perpetrator) role, demand a change, or end the relationship. Whether this type of relationship is ended by the survivor or his partner—or if it continues for a considerable duration—it provides confirmation of the survivor's belief that relationships must be abusive. Once again, little understanding can result from an interaction that doesn't allow for open discussion between individuals who trust one another's basic caring and good intentions.

4 / **"Settling for crumbs."** Another type of relationship involves settling for very little. Not trusting that anything better is possible, feeling useless and inadequate, believing that he is lucky to have any relationship at all, the incest survivor may find a partner in a life that is tedious, unsatisfying, unchallenging, and humdrum. The incest survivor interprets this type of existence in a variety of ways. He may

see it as all that he can hope for, since he is himself such a boring person. He might even find a humdrum life infinitely preferable to one of violence and abuse. He may feel that this represents normalcy. Or he might see his life for what it is, but feel inadequate and powerless to change it. If his partner feels similarly, the relationship may continue in its grinding dullness for a considerable length of time. He may hate his life but feel bound to his partner, their children, or his ideal of commitment. If one or both partners are dissatisfied with the arrangement, it is still necessary to communicate the dissatisfaction in order to effect change. This is no easy task, as this type of arrangement is seldom based on open discussion. If the survivor leaves the

FOCUS

WHAT IF I ENJOYED IT?

It is not unusual for sexually abusive experiences to arouse some degree of pleasure in the victim. For many survivors, these pleasurable sensations are more upsetting than painful ones. This response to an otherwise negative experience confuses the meaning of enjoyment and the understanding of pleasure. It is likely to set off a chain of emotional reactions that lead to mistaken conclusions about the nature of abuse. If you have been confused about pleasure or arousal during incestuous abuse, you may have gone down one of the following paths of reasoning.

One faulty path arrives at the belief that if any part of it was pleasurable, it wasn't really abuse. That you can even consider this possibility is evidence of how incestuous abuse warps reality. It allows perpetrators to confuse their victims into thinking that their participation in the abuse was of their own volition.

Reality is quite different. There is no such thing as a "willing victim"—to be a

victim is to have your will destroyed. The act of victimization damages the human spirit. An element of physical pleasure does not diminish the destructive nature of sexual child abuse.

"You enjoyed it" is a self-seeking statement by the perpetrator that attempts to mask the nature of abuse and enlist the victim as an accomplice. What you enjoyed was a physical sensation that represented the kind of closeness that you needed—not the abusive act itself.

Human beings deserve to be offered pleasurable experiences that do not rob them of their autonomy and self-respect. It's how you should have been treated and it's a legitimate goal of your recovery.

A second mistaken connection leads you to the belief that pleasure can only be found in abusive situations. Having experienced some enjoyment from the original abuse, you may have allowed the abuse to continue (and even sought out further abusive encounters in order to reexperience some de-

relationship, it is often with feelings of guilt and inadequacy about his ability to sustain a nonabusive relationship. If his partner leaves, he is confirmed in his isolation and the feeling that, to endure, relationships must be abusive. He is left without even the meager partnership that he had.

5 / Two-survivor relationships. There are many situations where both partners in a relationship have experienced childhood sexual abuse. Just as significant numbers of adult children of alcoholics end up together, it is not uncommon for incest survivors to enter into relationships with other survivors. Although there is very little infor-

gree of physical pleasure, however small). Thus, the perpetrator has not only inflicted abuse directly, she or he has set up a pattern of victimization that can continue into adulthood.

Where this pattern exists, recovery requires breaking the connection between abuse and enjoyment. As you explore nonabusive means of experiencing physical pleasure, you begin to open the possibility of leaving your victimization behind.

A third conclusion arises from confusion about what it means to be an abuser. It leads to a logical but *false* progression of thinking about your role in the abuse. The progression moves this way:

1 / If I enjoyed it at all, then:
(a) I'm a perpetrator; (b) I'm a bad person; (c) It's all my fault. This leads to:
2 / If I get any pleasure from sex of any kind, then I'm bad. Sexual pleasure has been connected to abusive behavior. The ultimate extension of this derailed train of thinking is:
3 / If I derive any enjoyment out of life, there's something wrong with me. Any positive experience becomes a source of suspicion, self-doubt, mistrust, shame, or fear—because it opens the possibility of abuse.

A child who has been given love and protection feels secure in his enjoyment of life. The boundaries and distinctions between caring and hurtful behavior are clear. And even an abused child has a fundamental understanding that things should be otherwise. An adult incest survivor said to me, "Do you know when I got up the courage to tell my mother about the abuse? It was the first time that I started to enjoy it."

It is vitally important that, as an adult recovering from incest, you do not punish yourself for whatever pleasure you were able to derive in the midst of the abusive experiences of childhood.

You did nothing wrong. You deserved better treatment. What was wrong was that you were subjected to a damaging environment that blurred the distinction between loving and child abuse. Some perspective on the abuse can be gained by thinking back to your childhood and asking yourself:

• What was I really needing?
• What was I really enjoying?
• What was I settling for?
• What do children deserve from adults?

Understanding these distinctions will help you to move toward acceptance of the healthy pleasures that life offers.

mation available about two-survivor relationships, it is likely that they face challenges and strains similar to those of adult children of alcoholics. (And there are a number of excellent books on that subject.) If your relationships have tended to follow the other patterns I have described, you may be hooking up with other survivors. For these two-survivor relationships to be successful, it will be necessary for both partners to work on their own healing. It is not enough for one of you to recover. You can't do the work for your partner, and you certainly can't expect your partner to do your healing for you. But you can use one another as resources, supporting each other in a program of mutual growth and healing. Each of you is likely to understand what the other is experiencing, having had similar experiences yourself. Again, this won't be easy, but it will be rewarding—and you won't have to do it in isolation.

The hopeless picture presented by some of the preceding paragraphs reflects the feelings of many adult survivors. Contemplating "normal" sexual relationships, friendships, intimacy, and trust only underscores their difference from the rest of humanity. They either fail to recognize gestures of caring, or can't trust that they are genuine. Sex feels like too confusing a topic on its own, without the frightening additions of caring and trust. Their options feel extremely limited—to remain in isolation, to accept abuse as a given in relationships, or to go through the motions of what they perceive as "normal" sexual relationships without ever feeling the caring, understanding the communication, or trusting what is going on.

I don't want to leave this chapter without providing some balance to the tone of hopelessness. Healthy relationships are difficult for anyone to achieve. They involve continual dedication and hard work. Even though this is particularly true for people who were abused, many adult survivors have learned how to maintain healthy, satisfying relationships. You can do the same. This achievement requires time, patience, and understanding of the issues by both partners. It cannot be done in isolation. After all, it was isolation that first set you up for misinformation and hurt. You must be able to test your thoughts, ideas, feelings, and reactions in a safe, welcoming, nonjudgmental environment. You need people to listen as you work through your confusion and fear. (Information for people who are in relationships with survivors is provided in Chapter 21.)

You are starting to perceive your positive qualities, figuring out the world on the basis of new information and learning that this information can be trusted. You will start talking to people who will believe you, instead of treating your memories as though they are sexual fantasies. You will need to test, sounding out your perceptions in an understanding arena, asking question after question. You will doubt that friends have the patience and interest to listen to all that you have to say, and to respond to all you need to ask. In fact, some will not, but others will be steadfast in their caring. The opening of trust will usually be slow and tentative, and at times you will retreat into old patterns—especially when you feel that you have gone too far or that someone has gotten too close. When old feelings take over, you may want to pull back or lash out. This can occur just when things seem to be going well. Forgive yourself when this happens. Understand that it is those developing feelings of trust and caring, which are so unfamiliar and threatening, that trigger the reaction. You are learning how to build healthy, trusting, caring relationships.

It is vital that the pace and intensity of your trust-building be completely in your hands. You are in charge of your recovery. Too much change at too fast a pace is overwhelming and will inevitably lead you to shut down and retreat. It has been my experience that incest survivors tend to have an excellent sense of how much is too much, and when they need to speed up, slow down or take a rest. Trust your own sense of timing. Allow your friends to facilitate your recovery by listening to you, providing nonjudgmental feedback and respecting your physical boundaries. It's OK for friends to make some mistakes and have some conflicts. What is a friendship without them? Remember that mistakes aren't usually disastrous and disagreement is a normal part of a relationship. It may be necessary to reassure yourself that difficulties can lead to understanding and strength.

Building trust in relationships will take other forms. Just as you must regulate the pace and intensity of sharing your ideas, perceptions, and feelings, you will need to be in charge of your physical world. Since the nature of the incestuous abuse involved loss of control over your own body, you must be completely in charge of when, how, and by whom you are touched. Remembering that, in the past, touch was inappropriately sexualized, it is easy to see how even casual touching can feel threatening. Having the freedom to decide whether or not to engage even in such "innocent" interactions as a handshake or an arm around the shoulder helps to provide you with an atmosphere of safety. Under no circumstances should a friend engage in physical exchanges that rob you of control over your body (such as tickling, bear hugs, pinning you down, or hugging you from behind). State your needs clearly, assuming that a friend will want to be as helpful as possible. Let him or her know that, no matter how playful the motivation or how innocent the intent, these behaviors can be a source of intense restimulation of negative memories. The rule of thumb is not "no touching," it is, rather, "no touching *without permission*." Any touch should be by *mutual consent*, with either person having the complete right to terminate it at any time. If feelings are brought up by the touching—or the limitations on touch—it is very helpful to take the time to feel them and talk about them *without negative self-criticism*. The greater the degree of communication involved in the interaction, the more helpful and loving it is. Learning how to communicate in relationships contradicts the isolation and leads to insight and understanding.

When the relationship is one that has a sexual component, it is even more important to think clearly and communicate openly about what feels (and what is) abusive. It is essential that each partner determine absolutely what is acceptable to him (or her). When there is any doubt it is always appropriate to err on the side of caution. If you are not comfortable with something your partner wants, it is best to refrain from doing it. If it feels abusive to you or your partner, talk about it. It is neither loving nor sophisticated to pretend to feelings you don't have. Abuse is never a loving act. You can always do more in the future, but behavior can't be undone. A loving partner will communicate how he or she feels and encourage the other person to do the same. Questions like "May I touch you this way?" "How does this feel?" "How do you like to be touched?" are always appropriate and greatly aid in communicating caring and showing consideration for the needs of one's partner. Letting your partner know what you enjoy and what you find unpleasant allows him/her to be a more sensitive lover. Thus, opening communication enhances the sexual experience as it increases the safety and trust level of the relationship.

It is far from easy to overcome fear and reach out to other human beings. It takes time to unlearn years of misinformation and isolation. There are inevitably slow periods, mistakes, and setbacks. But it doesn't have to be figured out all at once. And it doesn't need to be done alone; there is lots of help available. It is worth all the effort to learn that people can express feeling in ways that don't hurt others. The struggle to separate the mistaken connection between affection and abuse leads toward the creation of healthy, affectionate interactions. Learning to establish and maintain satisfying relationships is a primary goal of recovery.

Ellen Bass and Laura Davis, authors of *The Courage to Heal*, talk about needing to open wounds in order to clean them out and heal them. This cannot be done with the old tools. New tools are required—tools that are suited to the task of healing. Some of these tools for recovery, and their uses, are discussed in the chapters that follow.

PART FOUR

About Recovery

Is Recovery
Possible?

My eyes are open, but I want to blink.
—A MALE SURVIVOR at a recovery workshop

I'm not going to keep you waiting for an answer to the question posed in the title of this chapter. This isn't a mystery novel, and the question is too important to play games with. My response to that question is a resounding yes! Absolutely. Unequivocally. Without a doubt. Recovery is possible. And not only is it theoretically possible, it is possible for *you*.

In earlier chapters, when I wrote about the nature of sexual child abuse and its effects, I wasn't attempting to prove the existence of incest. That children are incestuously abused is a given; it happens all the time. My purpose in describing sexual child abuse and its aftermath was to give you a basis for understanding your experience and to offer a framework for your healing. Similarly, I do not doubt the reality of recovery. That, too, is a given.

This book is meant to provide you with tools, resources and encouragement in your recovery process. When Ellen Bass and Laura Davis called their book *The Courage to Heal,* (emphasis mine) they presented their confidence in the availability of healing. In the same way, this book, *Victims No Longer: Men Recovering from Incest* (emphasis mine) assumes the reality of recovery.

How can we be so certain that healing and recovery are possible? From our own experiences of working with hundreds of incest survivors and talking with scores of counselors and therapists who work with survivors, we have seen the reality of recovery. We have seen many survivors grow and change—creating better, healthier, more satisfying lives. I speak confidently about healing because I've witnessed it. I know that it is true. And that growth and change are available to you. It isn't quick or easy, but it is real. The remaining chapters of this book do not attempt to prove the existence of recovery; instead, they offer you specific guidelines to assist in your recovery process.

Many people consult me professionally because they know that I work with adults (particularly men) who were victims of childhood incest. They have heard about me through various sources: referrals from professional colleagues, television and radio appearances, workshops, newspaper interviews, and word of mouth. Whatever the source of the contact, when men come to see me for incest-related issues, they often display a certain kind of urgency. It isn't difficult to understand why they feel this way.

Incest survivors have lived with pain and confusion since childhood. Most have tried many different ways of getting past the experience. They may have numbed themselves (see Chapter 8) with alcohol, drugs, sex, food, or any number of other addictions and compulsions. They may have tried to change their view of life through religion, various psychotherapies, meditation, mysticism and philosophies (both Eastern and Western), workshops, retreats and personal growth practices. Many have thrown themselves into work or play with an intensity that is incomprehensible to anyone except another survivor (see Chapter 10.) They have attempted diets of deprivation and of overindulgence. They have sought serenity through yoga, release through marathon running, and protection through martial arts. They have attempted to escape geographically, some moving several times a year or whenever the feelings began to get too overwhelming. Some have changed their appearances, jobs, friends and lifestyles. Many have pursued academic degree after degree (often in psychology or other human services) in order to gain understanding of their situation. They have avoided (or pursued) men, women, children, authority figures, older people, friends, and lovers. Some of these practices have proved very helpful and a source of significant relief, learning, and comfort, but there always seemed to be something missing. And through it all they have tried and tried to *think* their way out of the feelings that they have never been able to shake off completely.

No doubt some of this list is familiar to you. Whatever strategies you have undertaken to help you endure, survive, identify, fit in, or feel better, they (and you) are deserving of complete admiration and respect. The fact that they are no longer what you need doesn't negate one simple fact—they helped you to survive to this point. Appreciate yourself for having figured out a way of getting yourself here—ready to dare to take the next step in your recovery.

When you undertake the process of recovery, it must be a conscious decision that has been arrived at through a great deal of soul-searching. Having attempted every imaginable way of working around, over, and under the feelings, you have reluctantly come to the conclusion that the only way out of the pain is straight ahead . . . through it. The abuse and the pain created by the abuse need to be confronted directly. Those awful feelings must be felt. This is no easy matter. Even though it is unlikely that anyone has ever died of feelings, it can *feel* like dying. (And there are those who have chosen death rather than face what they perceive to be a lifetime of painful emotion.) It takes tremendous courage and determination to undertake this confrontation, especially when you feel there are no guarantees that its outcome will be any more successful than all the other things you have tried. Beginning a recovery program may not lessen the pain immediately. In fact, it often feels worse before it gets (and feels) better. But it *does* get better. And it continues to improve as you move from surviving to *living* and *thriving*.

An alcoholic, in order to recover, must first admit to being powerless over the disease of alcoholism. He must let go of the illusion of control in order to take genuine charge of his program of healing. Control is an equally central issue for the incest survivor. Similar to the recovering alcoholic, the recovering survivor begins to relinquish the rigid controls over his feelings—and the familiar avenues of escape—that have felt like his only protection against being overwhelmed by terror, rage, or grief. He must risk depending on other people's experience, judgment, . . . and caring. He may be asked to think, react, and behave in ways that feel impossibly dangerous. When an incest survivor first comes into my office, his level of anxiety, tension, and fear is often so high that it feels like a physical force in the room. He has overcome the impulse to cancel the appointment or to just not show up, and is probably struggling against an urge to bolt out the door. My usual first question, "How do you feel being here?" may come as a relief or as confirmation of his worst fears, "He is going to force me to *feel*." I listen very carefully to his answer, and I believe it. It usually gives me some gauge of his anxiety level.

In the face of his fear and distrust, the incest survivor has decided to move forward. Indeed, he may feel that having tried everything else, this is his last resort. He doesn't *want* to be there; he feels that he *needs* to. And since he has to be there, and knows that it's going to be a terribly difficult experience, he wants to get it over with as quickly as possible—preferably yesterday. While understandable, this desire to speed through recovery is unrealistic. Recovery from incest is a long-term, ongoing process. It takes time. I wish it were otherwise, but I know of no other way. (I keep several "magic" wands in my office, and offer to try waving them in hope of an instant solution. But the wands seem to be defective and only succeed in eliciting an occasional smile. Maybe that's enough to make them worth waving.) Although I understand my clients' feelings of urgency, I try not to buy into them. I try to help the survivor arrive at a realistic picture of what he can expect of his recovery process. Having realistic expectations makes the prospect more bearable. It allows for some structure, order, and reassurance. It takes recovery out of the realm of the imagination and puts some of the worst fears to rest. ("Other people have been through this. There *are* things that have worked for them. Maybe . . .") Having this reality base also allows for the setting of specific, realistic goals—something that hasn't felt possible before.

In addition to impatience, many survivors undertake the recovery process with feelings of anger and resentment. ("It just isn't fair that I should have to go through more pain. After all, I was the victim. The perpetrator doesn't have to pay money, spend time and feel pain in order to get over this. And it was her/his fault!") Once again, these feelings reflect unfortunate fact. If the survivor waited for the perpetrator to apologize, repent and make amends, he would very likely be waiting forever. Although it truly isn't *fair*, it is *necessary* that his recovery be his alone. (This does not mean that he must go through the process in isolation; it only means that his recovery cannot depend on anyone else's actions or inaction.) I wish it could be otherwise— that there were some way that I could reach in and pull out the pain. If there were, I would do it without hesitation. But that is beyond the scope of a therapist. I (and others who care about survivors) can only provide my best thinking, experience, . . . and caring. I can reassure my client that, although he does have to go through this experience, he has allies in the struggle. He doesn't have to experience it again the way he did as a child. He now has protection. His resources are real and powerful. There are paths through the woods. When he returns to look at the hurts of childhood, he can do it as an adult man, able to reassure a frightened child that he will survive. He is, of course, living proof of that survival.

The most important reassurance that I can offer the courageous individual who embarks on an odyssey of recovery is that, although there is pain, it is not unceasing. There are also times of rest, relief, and even joy. Recovery can be undertaken with humor and humanity. There is time to forge ahead and time to stop, look back, and gain perspective on your progress. When the process feels too overwhelming, or the progress too unimportant to matter, it may be time for a rest or a celebration. After all, a major part of recovery is learning how to be kind to yourself. As you begin to accept the fact that it is alright to feel good, enjoyment of life ceases to be some far-off goal— to be realized only after "completion" of the recovery process. In small steps you continue to unlearn all-or-nothing thinking. Enjoyment of life no longer represents time taken away from your recovery. On the contrary, taking pleasure means *participating* in life. It is evidence that the recovery process is working.

Once the recovery process has begun and as you begin to accept its reality, you will start to trust that change is possible. Even tentative acceptance of the possibility of change ("Well, I'm not sure I believe you, but you haven't lied to me yet") represents a major step toward taking charge of your life. This is not the old rigid need for absolute control. Rather, it is recognition that human beings have the ability to make decisions that affect their lives . . . and the power to put these decisions into action. This is a tremendously important insight. Power to change your life had seemed inaccessible—something that was only available to other, healthier beings. Although you may not *feel* it completely, you are now ready to move out of your isolation and make decisions about how you will live your life.

Having accepted that change is possible, it is difficult to control the desire to change everything at once. Although you may be making changes at breakneck speed, you will probably feel that things aren't moving nearly fast enough. How can you be comfortable with "small" changes when you want "everything" in your life to be different? You are tempted to consume change with the fervor of a starving man coming upon a banquet. If this enthusiasm gets out of hand, it can lead to disappointment. Once again, it is necessary not to fall prey to all-or-nothing thinking. Unrealistic expectations will set you up for failure. To achieve a healthy life you must learn to determine which goals are realistic. It is important to turn to other people for help in goal-setting and checking of your progress. Doing this helps you cut through the feelings of isolation while providing perspective on what is reasonable. Setting goals that are reasonable makes them possible to achieve. Thus, success builds upon success, and each successfully attained goal becomes further evidence of the reality of recovery. It keeps the process from becoming overwhelming.

The combination of taking charge of your life in specific ways and breaking through isolation to reach out for support represents powerful and profound growth. It makes a host of other changes possible. Perhaps for the first time, you will be able to achieve a perspective on how some of your coping methods have served to keep you stuck. You can then look at how to replace these with healthier, more satis-

FOCUS

FOUR MYTHS THAT INTERFERE WITH RECOVERY

One of the most intelligent, self-aware, and insightful men I know frequently describes himself as "stupid" because he can't think his way through his incest history.

Men are taught that logic and rational thought will solve any problem. This is a persistent and frustrating piece of misinformation that impedes incest recovery for men.

If sexual child abuse yielded to clear thinking alone, most male survivors would have gotten over their experiences long ago. The reason why it doesn't work is not a matter of intelligence, it is that *more* than logic is required. Other pieces need to be added to the logic.

All too often men attempt to reason their way into denial and minimization of the abuse. They "think" that it really wasn't so bad, or that the pain they are feeling isn't so terrible. They are hesitant to take the next "logical" step toward understanding their situation for fear of what it might stir up. A vitally important step for many male incest survivors is to let go of the following myths:

MYTH 1. Vulnerability = Weakness

MYTH 2. Rigidity = Strength

MYTH 3. Comfort = Safety

MYTH 4. Under Control = In Charge

Many men talk about being "afraid to be vulnerable," as though vulnerability were some hideous flaw. Fearing what might occur if he were to allow himself to be vulnerable—what uncontrollable destructiveness would be unleashed, what dire aspect of his character could be revealed, what fur-

fying behaviors. As your outlook on your life shifts, you become ready to question some other premises. Having accepted that the world is not a totally dangerous place, you can explore, with other people, ways to distinguish genuine dangers from irrational fears. You can talk about safe boundaries—how to set and maintain them. And you learn to "check out" your feelings. Instead of "mind reading" (assuming that you know what other people *must* be thinking and never finding out if your assumption is correct), or "separating" (believing that you must be the only one in the world who has these feelings and perceptions), you find that you can talk about what is going on in your mind. You become less and less surprised to discover that others share your thoughts, values, and perspectives. Once

ther abuse he would be opening himself to —the male survivor seeks to maintain tight control over his emotions and behavior.

He may attempt to adopt the image of the rigid, unfeeling, taciturn, self-sufficient, macho male that our culture so frequently mistakes for strength. But this posturing is not true strength, and deep in his heart, the survivor knows it. If he is really that strong, why does he feel like a scared little kid?

True strength lies in his risking vulnerability—for vulnerability is not weakness, it is *openness*. To be vulnerable is to open yourself to feeling pain and to looking at uncomfortable, unpleasant realities. It is letting go of the need to control all situations. It means showing yourself to other people and inviting their responses. It is allowing your feelings to be felt—finding the safety to experience the uncomfortable emotions—sadness, fear, anger, shame, embarrassment—and even joy.

Feelings are not the enemy, they are important healing resources. Allowing yourself to be vulnerable won't happen instantly. It took a while to shut your feelings down, and you've been holding a rigid pose for a long time. It takes time and courage to open yourself in this way, but it is the path of recovery. Undoing the myths and stepping out of your emotional isolation will provide you with genuine information to "think through."

When all the misinformation has been contradicted, you will see rigidity for what it is—a feeble attempt to portray strength that you don't feel you possess. You will be able to risk vulnerability, realizing that it represents genuine strength. Comfort and safety will take on their correct meanings—so that you will find real safety instead of settling for comfortable illusions. And having learned that being "in charge" means responding flexibly to the demands of a given situation, you will cease to substitute the rigid control that you mistakenly thought provided strength and safety. In short, you will have achieved genuine strength and safety; you will truly have taken charge of your life.

again, the recovery process becomes one of increased inclusion and participation. In gradual, sometimes small steps, you are able to achieve tremendous growth and change. Although not always dramatic, the recovery process is real and impressive.

PAUL'S STATEMENT

At sixty-two years old, Paul is living evidence
that recovery is *real* and that it's never too late.
His statement describes the feelings that followed
a major step in his recovery.

It is the day after a workshop for male survivors in Santa
Cruz, and I want to write this while the reactions and feelings
are still fresh—if I wait too long, I am afraid they will fade
away, so here goes.

As I write this, I am sitting in my garden—a beautiful and
peaceful environment of flowers, oak trees and surrounded by
tall Monterey pine trees. I am listening to Beethoven and
enjoying the company of two neighborhood cats who have come
to visit. I am at peace for the moment. Not so this morning as
the weeping which started on the drive back continued.
Actually, the tears began to flow during the workshop—I
remember the shame over my "lack of control"(!), but my
attitude toward those tears is changing. They are *my* tears,
which are the expression of *my* sadness, and I am trying to be
grateful for being able to weep for and *with* my child within. I
cried uncontrollably for a long time in the car and then,
miraculously, began to scream and rage at the people who
"took care of me" when I was an infant and a child. I say
"miraculously," as I have been unable to express my anger and
rage—I've had no difficulty with expressing pain, fear, and
sadness, but have been terrified of my own and others' anger.
After I had exhausted myself with the yelling and raging in the
car, I had a short period of relief—a feeling of having
empowered myself! However, the tears resumed until I got
home to the peace and serenity of my little house in the pines.
And then a long phone call with a woman survivor friend here,
who patiently allowed me all my tears and feelings that the
workshop had released in me—she didn't try to "fix" me—just
listened and shared some of the similar experiences from her
own history. The workshop *was* a gift—to hear the pain,
sadness, joy, and hope of the other men touched my heart—for
a short time I got out of my "intellectualism" and grandiosity

and opened my heart (the tears are starting again). Also the sight of that many men, *straight* and gay, being patient, open, and cooperative with each other, really moved me. To share with all these other gentle, wounded and, I think, brokenhearted men, certainly contributed to my healing—not to mention the warm and supportive way in which the leaders conducted the workshop. Enormous feelings of love were surfacing for me during the course of the workshop—feelings that I have kept buried and hidden for many, many years. I had almost given up ever feeling or expressing love—I had no concept of what that word meant—after all the years of receiving(?) their "love."

I couldn't understand why I wasn't experiencing euphoria at the close of the workshop. I don't know where I got the idea I was *supposed* to feel euphoria! I was simply in touch with *my feelings*, and I am getting closer to being able to let go and just *feel* without censuring or blocking. So for now my hope and faith are invested in that process. I pray that I have the courage to survive the days (and nights) which may be painful or uncomfortable due to surfacing feelings—the workshop leader did warn us of the temptation to resume our addictions (mine being alcohol, pornography, and sex), and I remember shaking my head to indicate to you that it could not happen to me (more grandiosity). I have changed my mind after experiencing the emotional roller coaster of the past three days (the day before the workshop, the workshop, and the day after, today). I am going to pray for the courage to go through the healing process and to find the appropriate people and resources, as I know I cannot do it alone. I certainly *want* to do it alone, as I have survived alone most of my life—but the isolation has become too uncomfortable to endure.

I know it's not "too late" to recover, and now I have feelings of hope. My goal is to love and cherish "little Paul" in order to allow the loving, caring, and creative adult Paul to emerge—released, finally, from all those shame-based "caretakers" of the past. I want to return all of the shame to *them*—they are entitled to it—it was never *mine*.

I certainly hope these are not just words on paper—I pray that I mean them, and can maintain my resolve to persevere in the healing process. P.S. The touching image of the grown men cuddling teddy bears is still with me.

A loving survivor,
Paul

13

Breaking Secrecy

There are no secrets in families, only denial.

—TERRY KELLOGG

Secrecy is the cement that holds incest firmly in place. It allows sexual abuse of children to continue despite the presence of concerned family, friends, and neighbors and despite the existence of child protective legislation. It is certain that the extremely high incidence of child sexual abuse could be greatly reduced by bringing the topic fully into open discussion. As long as the subject remains hidden—a source of shame and embarrassment—children will continue to be victimized in great numbers. Like mushrooms, incest grows and spreads when kept in the dark. We know that this is true, yet not nearly enough has been done to bring the subject out into broad daylight.

Before writing this book, I asked several people to read my outline and offer comments. On the topic of secrecy, one incest survivor wrote: "What is it that makes this subject so difficult to talk about—not only within the family in which the abuse took place, but with friends made and kept in adulthood? For the victim, having been abused is like having cancer—something he doesn't want to admit; and for others, something they don't want to acknowledge—for fear of 'catching' it? I suppose the answer is obvious, but it wouldn't hurt to spell it out in some detail." I'm not sure I agree that the answer is obvious, but I know that there is a great deal to be gained by discussing it . . . out loud, often, and "in some detail."

In order to create an environment where he or she can abuse a child without getting caught, the perpetrator must make sure that no one who might interfere with the abuse knows about it. The logical first step is making certain that the child won't tell anyone. There are any number of ways that silence is installed and maintained. The perpetrator may make direct threats to the child, promising dire consequences if he should tell anyone. These may take the form of threatening to kill or hurt the child himself or his loved ones. There may even be the promise that harm (imprisonment, violence, or death) would befall the perpetrator if the incest were discovered. At first glance this would appear to be reason for the child to speak up. But it must be remembered that the perpetrator is often someone who is very important to the child, and the fear of losing him/her is enough to insure silence. At times, the threat of harm may be reinforced with actual violence expressed toward the child or other family members. Many children bravely endure abuse in order to protect siblings or other loved ones from harm. In this situation the child soon learns to suffer in silence rather than to risk the threatened consequence of seeking help.

If it is in their power to do so, perpetrators may insure secrecy by physically isolating their victims. Children have been jealously protected from contact with playmates and, later, not allowed to date or participate in social activities. In extreme cases, children have literally been held prisoner by abusive adults. If this treatment is explained to the child at all, it is usually presented as punishment for his wrongdoing or evidence of his being a bad boy. As with physical violence, physical and emotional isolation add another harmful dimension to the sexual abuse of children.

The perpetrator may also tell the child that nobody would believe him—that he would be called a liar and punished if he told anyone. Unfortunately, this is often the truth. Adults are reluctant to believe that anyone they know would molest a child. Because of their own denial (or sometimes through bewilderment, helplessness, or fear), they refuse to believe that the story is anything more than the result of a child's lurid, overactive imagination. The child may even be chastised for making up "such an awful fib." This serves to confirm the child's view of himself as an evil person who needs to keep his "true nature" hidden. Even if the report is believed, the trusted adult may be too frightened, confused, or disinterested to take any appropriate action to protect the child. It doesn't take long for the child to get the message that there is nothing to do but accept the situation. He learns that it is easier to go along with the abuse than to make futile attempts to stop it. He learns that since there is no help to be had, his best hope is to behave in ways that will minimize the abuse—get it over with faster and with less violence. Ignoring or disbelieving a child's story serves to reinforce and perpetuate the abuse. It effectively isolates the child with the perpetrator. In so doing, it constitutes further child abuse. Whatever problems may result from giving credence to and investigating a child's report of abuse, they are insignificant when compared with the results of allowing abuse to continue. It takes tremendous courage for a child to disobey an adult's commands and risk the anger of a large, intimidating figure. If a child's pleas are ignored, it is not likely that he will take further risks.

Perpetrators do not always resort to threats and violence. Secrecy may be maintained through bribes, either actual or promised. The child who accepts such gifts or special treatment (bribes are not always material) in exchange for his silence about the abuse is virtually certain to grow up feeling like a co-conspirator or a prostitute. (This may even become a self-fulfilling prophecy. There are few prostitutes who do not report a history of sexual abuse.) And the gifts may not be interpreted as bribes. As one of my clients said, "When you've got nothing at all, anything feels like something."

Still another way to insure that the child will maintain secrecy is to misrepresent the nature of the incestuous relationship. Desperate for love and comfort, the child will accept an adult's words of assurance: "This is our special secret" or "This is how a father loves his son." By the time the child realizes that he has been lied to, he is often too ashamed, intimidated or hopeless to tell anyone. One of my clients, after years of working on his feelings of anger and loss, was finally able to let go of his attachment to the perpetrator when he discovered that he was not the only victim. A sense of betrayal overwhelmed him when he found out that there were other victims. "He always told me that I was special. Now I see that this was just another way I was lied to. He never cared about me. He only wanted his own pleasure." Coming to this realization allowed my client to give up his last illusions about the incest and move on with his life.

Mistaken notions of family loyalty (sometimes taught by the abuser) further serve to reinforce the silence. When abuse is shared by a family, it is often kept as a family secret. A facade of respectability can effectively mask the chaos within a family. "Everyone thought we were the perfect family. My father was a deacon of the church. He was a boy scout leader. We looked like *Father Knows Best*. Who would ever believe that Jim Anderson would be having sex with Bud?" Thus, consciously or not, the entire family cooperates in sacrificing one or more of its members to the abuse. Incest becomes truly a "family affair," affecting all family members. When the incestuous behavior is interrupted, family unity (which is based on accommodating to an abusive system) is destroyed.

For healing to take place within the family context, it is necessary for all family members to receive extensive help. This takes time, resources, and commitment. It is more common for the family to be torn apart, sometimes blaming the victim and forcing him out of the family. "Whistleblowers" are seldom rewarded in our society. The incestuous family that has settled for "comfortable" does not take easily or kindly to the family member who insists on embarking on the uncomfortable road to health. The more family members who ally themselves with each other and insist on putting an end to the pretense (no matter what the cost), the greater the chance that the family will recover intact. It is far more common, however, that the family members continue to accept the abuse until each is in a position to escape it alone. The abused child has learned to keep his own counsel. He may never have discussed the incest with anyone— even his own siblings who very likely were victimized themselves. The adult survivor who chooses to violate the family conspiracy of silence and pretense is likely to be defined as "the problem":

> *"You always were a difficult child. You were never happy. Nothing seemed to satisfy you."*
> *"You never knew when to keep your mouth shut."*
> *"Can't you ever leave well enough alone?"*
> *"Things were fine until you started in with this business."*

If this happens to you, don't be confused by these tactics. Things *haven't* been fine until now. The family hasn't been "well enough"; it's been sick. You know very well how to keep your mouth shut— you've been doing it for many years. Accusing you of having been a "difficult" child is unconscious recognition of the effect of the abuse. *You are not the problem.* The problem is incestuous child abuse and its effects. It must be acknowledged if it is to be dealt with. You are right to be breaking the secrecy. But it is difficult. What you are doing is contrary to all you have been taught.

The abused child grows into an adult who knows how to keep a secret. He plays his cards very close to the chest, and may feel uncomfortable about disclosing any information, no matter how harmless. How much more dangerous it feels to share his shameful secrets. The adult incest survivor has learned his lessons well. Convinced that he is a severely flawed person, he maintains secrecy to keep others from discovering just how bad he is. The pattern of protecting the perpetrator has been so deeply ingrained that it is likely to persist even after the perpetrator dies or otherwise is no longer a threat. And the survivor is certain that "normal" people would be unable to hear his story. They would find it too shocking, disgusting, or frightening. They would scorn him, reject him or, even worse, treat him with pity. At best, the survivor sees no good coming from telling his story.

Even when talking to a group of other incest survivors, he can find reasons to maintain his silence. These can range from "My story is less important than anyone else's so I'll keep quiet" to "My story is so much worse than anyone else's that I'd better not tell it." He may feel

FOCUS

FINDING YOUR VOICE

The taboo against talking about incest is stronger than the taboo against doing it.
—MARIA SAUZIER, M.D.

It is no accident that:

- The national support organization of incest survivors calls itself VOICES.
- Many survivors find loud sounds upsetting and loud-voiced people intimidating.
- Survivors often find it impossible to yell or shout.

Perpetrators of incestuous abuse must silence their victims in order to keep them powerless and allow the abusive behavior to continue. Many survivors carry memories of raised voices inaugurating a cycle that led to their being sexually exploited. In adulthood if they speak loudly, they feel as though they are being abusive. If someone else raises his or her voice, the situation feels dangerously out of control.

There is a phenomenon that is so common that I have become very aware of it when talking with a new client. Although I know of no research about its frequency, when I mention it to other people who work with incest-related issues, they recognize it instantly.

It is so familiar that I've named it. I call it "The Voice."

Incest survivors often speak in slow, measured, soothing, lulling tones. They have cultivated a soft and pleasant voice quality which, when combined with a precision of word usage (it is quite common for even uneducated incest survivors to select their words with correctness and precision), produces a calming, hypnotic effect.

When I find myself feeling as though I'm being soothed by a person who is talking to me, that I am receiving a "verbal massage," I assume that the speaker may have a history of abuse.

I am also aware that if I have to strain to catch the words, lean forward in my chair, or regularly ask the speaker to repeat himself, there is a good possibility that I am talking with a survivor. Any interaction where loudness and/or emotions are expressed can feel unsafe, and "The Voice" represents an attempt to calm a potentially volatile and dangerous situation. I think that "The Voice" is used to prevent anger from getting out of control.

Male survivors fear the consequences of unbridled anger—their own or someone else's. Being men, they fear that their anger, if released, will be a harmful, destructive force. "My anger is so strong that if I let it

that no one is really interested or that they would derive morbid pleasure from hearing details of the abuse. Finally, although all logic tells him that he is now physically safe from being abused, it just feels too frightening to risk. The initial breaking of secrecy may be the

out I'll kill somebody." Their fear is that any expression of anger, however small, will be so overwhelming that it never will be brought back under control.

When men in my incest recovery groups first begin to express anger—whether it is directed at the abuser, their families, the leader, or other group members—they are certain there will be dire consequences. Even a harsh word can feel like a devastating attack. It takes a long time to realize that strong words and a powerful (even angry) delivery are not necessarily abusive.

Since a person's voice reveals a great deal about him, it is no wonder that it plays a major role in the life of incest survivors. One man in my recovery group talked of feeling as if "everyone can hear the conversations that go on in my head. I feel like I'm talking all the time." (In fact, he seldom spoke in group, but watched and listened carefully to the other group members.) Another survivor reported that he loses his voice when he is frightened. Several group members said that they use their voices to "control" other people.

An important aspect of recovery is finding your true, full voice, both literally and symbolically. You may need to spend time regaining your ability to yell. (If the prospect of shouting terrifies you, then it is almost certainly called for.) You can start by speaking with your full voice when you are alone at home. You may try a shout or two in the shower.

Having practiced on your own, try it out

wherever you have a good opportunity. Ask a friend if you can practice yelling at him or her; try raising your voice in your individual therapy or your recovery group, and experience the feelings that it brings up. You can shout into a pillow or someone's shoulder to muffle the sound. (Some of my clients have suggested that it feels more comfortable to yell in their cars on the highway, or to have their shouts muffled by ocean surf or forest foliage.) You may begin with sounds, words, or phrases.

As you become more comfortable with your newly rediscovered voice, allow yourself to attach feelings to your speech. Don't be surprised if you find yourself crying, shaking, or laughing as you do it. Don't let the feelings stop you—keep on shouting, raging, crying, laughing—at full volume.

Once you learn to do this, you can experience the exhilaration of telling your story—out loud—with the full power of your voice. As you move on to loudly expressing your anger at the perpetrator, you will be amazed at how spirited you feel.

After growing more comfortable with expressing your voice, you will find that your everyday speech has become stronger and more confident. Finally, you will find a forum for your voice. It may be in helping others to recover their voices, or simply by making your voice heard more powerfully in every aspect of your life. However you choose to do it, I encourage and celebrate your moving on with your recovery—at full voice.

most terrifying—and the most important—step in recovery from the effects of incest.

When someone who is being (or has been) abused asks, "What should I do?" the best answer is "Tell somebody." Incest survivors as well as the therapists who work with them insist that this is the essential first step toward recovery: "Find somebody," "Tell your story," "Break the silence."

This may sound like simple, logical advice, but it is anything but easy to accomplish. In order to break the silence, you must stand up against years of training in isolation. You may have tried in the past and been disbelieved, rebuffed, or punished. This is not a course of action that you will enter lightly. What if you are still not believed? What if they think you are weird or sick? And what good would it do to talk about it now? Fighting against all the pulls to keep silent, you are still faced with the question of who to tell. Again, the simplest answer may not be as easy as it sounds. Not everyone is willing or able to listen to reports of incest. Some might respond in an unhelpful or even abusive manner. And even a person with the best of intentions may have neither the resources nor the ability to respond to the issue.

So who *do* you tell? Sometimes the answer provides itself. Someone raises the subject of abuse or identifies him or herself as an incest survivor—and the story comes pouring out. The subject of incest is increasingly addressed in books, articles, films, and television programs. Regardless of the quality of these programs, they help to provide an atmosphere where it is all right to discuss the topic. Your story has been waiting for years. Sometimes all that you need is a catalyst. And whoever is around becomes the first person to hear your story. It isn't unusual for the first person learning of the incest to be a total stranger. You may open up to the person sitting next to you on a bus or to the friend of a friend. "Something about the person" may make you feel safe, or the situation might just be right—who knows why? In fact, the very impersonality and anonymity of a passing acquaintance can create a safe enough setting for disclosure.

Who do you tell? The answer must be: "Somebody," "Whoever you can." What is most important in breaking the secrecy is not *who* is the first one to be told, but that you tell *someone*. The log jam of silence, fear, and intimidation must be broken. Where you start is less important than *that you start*. You don't have to wait for the perfect person or the best possible circumstances. Tell someone. If she or he is unable to listen, tell someone else. Get into the habit of disclosure. Share information all over the place. If the abuse is still happening, keep on talking about it until you find someone who can help. If the actual sexual abuse has ended, the effects remain. Talk about them. You will find someone who can listen. You'll probably be surprised at how much support there really is in the world.

Don't worry about getting the story right. All the details aren't necessary. You may not even know them yourself. What is important is starting the process, reaching out to someone. It is good enough to tell someone, "Something happened to me." If that is all you know for certain—or if that is all you're able to say—then it's enough for now. If you don't know that much, it is enough to say, "It feels like something could have happened to me." Just once. Once the first log or two starts to move, it is amazing how quickly the others follow until finally the jam has broken up completely and the logs flow easily.

Once the silence is broken—and you see that the world has not ended—it is important to maintain the momentum. Tell your story again and again. Repeating your story:

- Makes it more real to you
- Underscores the fact that it is important
- Allows for shifts of focus and access to new perspectives on your experience
- Allows a forum for more feelings to come up
- Provides a reality base that continually contradicts the lie that talking about the abuse will result in dire consequences

Don't assume that you have found the only person in the world capable of listening to you. Rather, begin with the assumption that you have a right to speak and that people are eager to hear you. If anybody is unable to listen, don't assume that *no one* wants to hear you. Look for someone else. The fact that not every conversation or social situation is appropriate for discussing incest doesn't mean that it is never OK to talk about it. If you keep talking, you will find a helpful support network. You will create the safety. Once the secrecy is broken, you never again need to return to the isolation.

Each time the story of abuse is told—whenever a survivor is listened to with caring and awareness—another piece of healing takes place. As the story is repeated, more details are recovered. Whole chunks of childhood which had been forgotten can be recovered. This is not always a pleasant experience, but it is immensely valuable. This is especially true as the story begins to be told with more and more of the *feelings* attached to it. When survivors first start to tell their stories, descriptions are often delivered in a flat, lifeless, or factual tone (as though the topic being lectured on was of purely academic interest, without any personal connection to the speaker). This reflects the degree of fear attached to talking about the incest. The survivor is so terrified of releasing powerful and painful emotions that he keeps his voice (and feelings) under rigid control. The detachment of his presentation is simply an attempt to create distance between the speaker and his emotions. The subject may even be presented in a light, offhanded, almost joking manner—as if it were no more important than the baseball scores. This delivery serves the double purpose of keeping feelings at bay while reassuring the listener that she or he doesn't have to worry about this story—or even take it too seriously. "Don't worry (the survivor seems to be saying), I won't lose control. It really wasn't that bad." The listener may be left more confused than reassured. The content of the story is shocking; the presentation is calm and lighthearted or devoid of feeling. Which is to be believed? But don't let concern over confusing your listener stop you; it doesn't really matter *how* the story comes out. Any confusion can be straightened out later. For now, it is important that your story be told to someone any way at all.

As you become more comfortable with talking about the abuse, you can begin to attach more feeling to your story. Beginning with a few tears, a nervous giggle, or a slight shudder, you gradually connect your emotions to what happened to you. This is a true exercise of trust. For some people it comes relatively quickly in the recovery process. For others, it takes years to create sufficient safety. Some men succeed in sobbing, shaking, or raging their way through their stories. For others, having a "funny feeling" when talking about incest represents a tremendous accomplishment after years of feeling nothing at all. Whatever emotions are accessible to you should be encouraged and celebrated. Feelings are the lubricant that allows recovery to move ahead. All incest survivors (including yourself) need to tell their stories over and over again—in as much detail as they can recall—with as many of the feelings attached as are accessible. It is no use pushing for the feelings. They will arise spontaneously when sufficient safety has been created.

When you first break silence about the incest, you will experience powerful and conflicting emotions. You may feel frightened that you (or someone you love) will be hurt. You are likely to think of yourself as having betrayed someone close to you. Disclosure can feel like weakness of character. You may feel as though you are falling apart or going crazy. You may have panic attacks or fall prey to periods of worrying. You may struggle with bouts of depression. Changing the pattern of secrecy that you have depended on for so long can leave you confused and disoriented. Disclosure is no picnic. But these effects are temporary. Gradually, as you tell more and more of your story, as more emotions become available, and as your isolation is replaced by healthy interaction, the healing process continues. You start to see that change is possible. As your self-esteem increases, you begin to accept the possibility of something that had only seemed available to others: Hope. The process is often slow and takes a long time; there are setbacks. But the overall growth is consistent and the rewards are real. It all begins with breaking the secrecy.

In summary, there are many reasons why it is important to break secrecy:

- If the abuse is still going on, talking about it will help to stop it. It can solidify a family and lead to healing.
- Talking cuts through isolation and creates support. By building support you learn that not all trust is abused. You learn to trust.
- Through breaking the silence you bring up feelings and, by doing so, help to heal your wounds.
- Telling your story is an important part of taking charge of your life. It leads to greater self-confidence—an important aspect of recovery.
- Talking about it leads to greater public awareness of incest and its effects. This creates an atmosphere that is more responsive to the needs of people in recovery.
- It helps others by paving the way for them to tell their stories— reassuring them that they are not alone.

Once your silence has ended, the recovery process has begun in earnest. The pattern of abuse has been broken. Nothing will ever be quite the same again.

ED'S STATEMENT

Ed's story is one of courage and perseverance
in the face of family denial, pretense, and resistance.
At twenty-three years of age, his determination and success
in standing up to abuse provide a model of healing.

I was molested by my oldest brother when I was nine and he
was fifteen. I can remember it like it was yesterday, because
my mother caught us the very first time it happened.

My brother had crawled into bed with me and started
fondling me. I didn't know what to do. I was scared and
excited at the same time. How many nine-year-olds know about
sex? I lay there and let him do it. As far as I was concerned,
he knew what he was doing and it couldn't be wrong. He was
my older brother. I trusted, respected, and loved him. I
couldn't believe he would do something to hurt me. Was I
wrong.

My mother came upstairs and caught him. She ordered him
out of bed and downstairs. She didn't say anything to me, but
the look in her eyes was enough to let me know that
something terribly wrong had happened.

Later on that day, she pulled me aside and told me if he
ever did anything like that again, I should tell her. I promised
her I would. I wish I had kept that promise. If I had, I
wouldn't be writing this. But he came back and I didn't say
anything.

When he did it again, I pushed him away and told him
what our mother said. He told me that it wasn't wrong, but
that I shouldn't tell her. It had to be our secret. I didn't know
what to do. Could my mother be wrong? My brother said she
was. I looked up to my brother, so I told him I wouldn't say
anything. I didn't want to hurt my mother. I knew I would, if
she found out. She would be mad at me. He told me that. I
believed him.

I learned about sex when I was nine years old. I was giving
blow jobs at ten. While other kids were out playing with guns,

I was learning how to "please" a man. I was taught how to be a "woman."

My brother liked to act out fantasies in which he was the "man" and I was the "woman." That was fine by me. When I acted out these fantasies, I was somebody else. It wasn't me taking the abuse. I wasn't feeling the pain. I built up a wall as high as possible. It protected me from the hurt. When that wall went up, I felt nothing. I still use it. When it goes up, nobody can get in.

Unfortunately, it didn't protect me as much as I wanted it to, because I soon started to have bad feelings. Guilt, shame, anger, hurt. I hated myself for what was happening. I started blaming myself for letting it happen. I hated myself for liking it. There were times when I actually enjoyed it. That usually lasted about five minutes.

But liking it made me hate myself even more. If I initiated it by going to him, I would cry after it was over. I told myself it would never happen again. But it did. I'd go on lying to myself every time.

One night he brought some friends over and proceeded to tell them that I gave great blow jobs. I had to go down on his friends. I was ten at the time. I also started having sex with some cousins, both male and female. Sometimes I would initiate it, sometimes they would. I had sexual fantasies about other members of my family. I thought that was how it was; I didn't know any differently. The only sex I knew was with family members.

My first thoughts of suicide occurred when I was twelve. I knew what was happening was wrong. The feelings inside were often too much for me. I wanted to die. I convinced myself that I would be better off dead. It would be easy, right? Wrong. I don't know if it was a survival instinct, but every time I wanted to kill myself I always chickened out. It wasn't until I was almost sixteen that I actually cut myself. Again, I got scared about dying and I stopped. Once I got into my car, locked all the doors, started the engine, and began to fall asleep. I was happy that it was going to be over. Fortunately, some friends found me and talked me out of it. But the thoughts about killing myself stayed with me for a long time. I was bound and determined to end it sooner or later.

I thought of ways to make myself unattractive, especially to my brother. I was always depressed, but that didn't stop him, so I turned to food. It "helped me" during my depression. Not only did it help to make me a *little* happier, it also helped me gain 120 pounds by the time I reached freshman year in high school.

The abuse had gone on nonstop during my twelve years of school. High school was the worst. I already felt like a different person. Nobody else was doing things with their brother. I was the only one this was happening to. Who would understand? I weighed close to 300 pounds in high school so, naturally, I was the brunt of a lot of cruel jokes.

Of course, I hated myself even more for this. A lot of times I would come home in tears, or close to it. Sometimes I would tell my mother what was happening and she would tell me to just ignore it. I don't think she ever fully understood how badly I was affected by the kids at school.

I started seeing a counselor at school. He was a nice guy but, because he was a man, I couldn't trust him. I was being hurt by a man so, to me, men couldn't be trusted. I never told him what was happening to me.

When I did turn to him and told him I wanted to die, he told my mother. When my mother asked me why, I couldn't tell her. I told her it was because of the kids at school. She told me to ignore it. Later, after she came from the shopping mall, she handed me a white stuffed baby seal and said, "You think you have problems, just think what this poor thing has to go through."

That was the end of it. But my thoughts of suicide didn't stop. The incest didn't, either. Through four years of high school I was being used by my brother. It would happen during the day or at night. It didn't matter if the rest of the family was home or not.

If it happened while my family was home, I would pray that we would be caught. Then it would finally end. But my brother knew what he was doing and made sure there was no chance we would be caught.

If no one was home, I knew it would happen. I sometimes wanted it to happen. There were times when I enjoyed it. "Enjoyed?" No, not really. As I got older, it was the only sex I knew and, as my own sexual desires surfaced, I turned to my brother. There really was no joy in it. I would go until I had an orgasm, then it would be over. Right after I had an orgasm, the feelings would all come up. Guilt was the major emotion. Even now, if I am having sex with a partner, my partner has to reach orgasm first or I just shut off.

It would start in different ways. If I was in bed, my brother would come in and start rubbing my leg, moving up my body until I woke up. The first time someone else did this to me while I was sleeping (this was after I had moved out), I must have jumped about twelve feet, screamed, and scared the hell out of the person who did it.

If I were awake when he came home, he would go into my room and lie on my bed, or I would go into my room and pretend to be looking for something. He would come up behind me, reach around, and start fondling me.

Other times he would knock on the wall separating our bedrooms. This was my signal to go into his bedroom. If I were taking a shower, he would come into the bathroom, tap on the shower curtain, tell me to get dried off and "get ready." To "get ready" meant to go to my bedroom, lie down naked and wait for him to come in.

If we went on a vacation, my brothers and I would share a room. I would end up in the same bed with my oldest brother. My second oldest brother would be in the next bed. At that time I didn't think he knew what was going on. Now I remember he did. It happened between us only once. He is a year older than me. We were in his bedroom and I gave him a blow job. I can't remember who initiated it, but it happened.

I wanted it to stop, but I felt powerless to stop it. A couple of times I told my oldest brother "no more," but it would start again. One time, when he was trying to have anal intercourse, I started crying. It was just too much. He asked me what was wrong. I couldn't believe he was asking me what was wrong. I told him we couldn't do this anymore. It was wrong; we were brothers. I pulled away from him. He looked at me and said, "We are not brothers. We are lovers."

That devastated me. He saw me as his lover. I said, "No way." I had to walk away or kill him. I was going to stop it. I had to. It was killing me emotionally. And I wanted to kill myself.

It stopped for about three months. Then he came into my bedroom one night and started again. I let him. I don't know why I couldn't stop it. Why couldn't I just tell him that he was the biggest asshole I'd ever met and walk away? Maybe I'll never know, but at that time I couldn't do anything.

When my brother informed the family he was getting married, it was the happiest day of my life. If he was getting married it meant he would be moving out. I didn't have to stay awake nights wondering if he was going to come into my bedroom, or finding someplace to go, or worrying about how I was going to fight him off if my parents went out. I could go on with a "normal" life.

The night of my brother's bachelor party we had sex. We had to drive someone home. I went for my mother. She didn't want my brother driving alone, since he had been drinking.

On the way back he pulled a rubber penis out from under the seat. I groaned in . . . pain, can only describe it. I didn't want to. I had enough. He put it up to my lips and told me to suck it. I didn't want to, but we were alone on a deserted street and I was afraid of what he might do if I refused. I was afraid of him. I did what he wanted me to. I sucked on that for awhile, then he told me to suck him.

When I went down on him, I wanted to bite it off. It sickened me to know that he was getting married in two days, yet still wanted me to satisfy him. I couldn't wait for him to get out of the house. I wanted to be left alone.

After he was married, I only visited a couple of times, always making sure my sister-in-law was there. Once I went over and she wasn't there. I started it; I wanted it. We had sex in his bed. After that time it never happened again during his marriage. A year after he was married, his wife left him and he moved back home.

I moved into the bedroom downstairs, and when I found out he was moving back, I freaked. My parents slept upstairs. When he came home, he could come right into my room. I wanted a lock on my door, but my mother refused. I couldn't explain why I wanted one. I was sure she wouldn't believe me and/or blame it on me. I was in my senior year of high school. I was seventeen years old. I didn't know what to do.

I wanted to move out, but I only had a part-time job and there was no way I could afford to get an apartment. What could I do to stop it? Kill him? I thought about it. But I didn't have the courage. I trained myself to stay awake until he came home and went up to his own bedroom. Sometimes he wouldn't come home until one or two in the morning. I would stay awake until I was sure he was asleep. When my alarm went off at quarter-to-seven, I would be exhausted.

My schoolwork wasn't that great and it got worse. My mother yelled and screamed at me to do better work. I was more worried about my brother than my schoolwork. A couple of times he came into my bedroom. I would tell him I wasn't feeling good, or I would let him do what he wanted, then tell him to leave.

Around the time I was seventeen I went through a major change. I did a lot of thinking about myself. I had a girlfriend for awhile, but it didn't work. Yes, I loved her very much, but I had mood swings. I wouldn't tell her anything for days, then I'd want to share everything with her. It got to the point where she couldn't take it anymore, and I don't blame her. I knew it would end, anyway. What sex we had, I always felt there was something missing. I thought it was either a phase I was going through or it was because of my brother. Maybe I just had to find the right girl? But I knew that wasn't it. I was different from other guys at school. I found men attractive. I wanted to sleep with them. I acted more like a girl than a guy. I knew I was gay. I also knew this was something else I couldn't tell my parents.

To my family homosexuality was a sick, abnormal disease. Gay people were jokes. I was trapped. I had no one to tell. I sank more deeply into myself. I couldn't stand looking at myself in a mirror. When I walked by a store window, I couldn't look at my reflection. I loathed my appearance. I hated myself and I was convinced everyone else hated me. I was a Failure.

It was at this lowest point in my life when something good happened. I was accepted to a women's college. Although it was small, it was a good school. The best part was that it had recently gone coed. I would be comfortable; I would "fit in," and I did.

Although it was occurring only once or twice a month, the incest, however, didn't stop. Despite this, college was great. I was in the human services field. I wanted to be able to help people. Even though I couldn't help myself, I wanted to be able to help others in some way.

During this time I met someone who would help me more than anyone. I met Mary through another friend. After we met the second time, we clicked. Although she was seventeen years older, I could talk to her. She listened and she cared. We were out together one night when she asked me to move in with her. I knew she was living with another woman, but that didn't seem to matter. She needed me just as much as I needed her. I, however, couldn't move out of my parents' house unless I could afford it. Mary told me I could move any time I was ready.

By the time I reached my second year of college, I had basically stopped the incest. If my brother came into my bedroom, I would tell him to get out. If he pleaded, I would refuse. Without my parents or anyone else knowing, I got a gun. I vowed that if he ever tried to force me, I would shoot him. If I were watching TV and he came home and started, I would walk out. Sometimes I would walk the streets for a couple of hours. Other times when he failed, he would go right to bed and I would go back and watch TV. As far as I was concerned, it would never happen again. If it did, one of us would die and I was through thinking it would be me.

It was also my second year of college that I met a really nice guy, someone who would change my life. I dated this guy for four months before we went to bed together. I put him through a lot with my moods, but he stuck by me. I finally agreed to sleep with him only because I was afraid of losing him. It was the night before Easter and we went to a motel.

The night was wonderful. I finally felt fulfilled. This was what I had been longing for. I finally had a real man. He was the exact opposite of my brother. Tall, slim, great personality, very handsome, and I loved him. All of this did not prepare me for the next day.

The next morning we said our goodbyes and agreed to meet that evening. I went home and called Mary. She asked me how everything went. I told her good, but I wasn't feeling good. Everything I had ever felt after my brother was done, I was feeling now. I felt so guilty about making love. I felt ashamed —like I had done something wrong to someone I loved. During the whole day I felt that way. I wanted to be alone. I went out for a drive. When I got back, I stayed in my room. I didn't want to see or talk to anyone.

I had promised to meet this person at the club we frequented. Mary and some other friends were meeting us there. I knew I had to go. All the hate I was feeling toward my brother, I was directing toward this guy. I knew it wasn't his fault, but I felt I couldn't see him. All day I went back and forth about going. I finally decided to go. Maybe seeing him would make me realize it wasn't him.

When I got to the club, he and my other friends were all at the downstairs bar. I went down, took one look at him, turned around, and went back upstairs. I couldn't face him. It was too much. I sat down at a table.

Mary and another friend of mine, Alice, came upstairs. They wanted to know what was wrong. "Nothing," I told them. It was obviously something. My "lover" was upset. He didn't know what he had done. He hadn't done anything. It was me.

I looked at the two of them. They were angry and concerned, but I didn't know what to say. Could I trust them? Would they believe me? Would they still love me? A million questions ran through my mind. I didn't know what to do. All I knew was that I couldn't go on like this anymore. I wanted to be able to have a normal relationship. If this happened every time I had sex with a man, I knew I had to get help. But who to trust?

I told Mary and Alice because they were women and because I couldn't take it anymore. I gathered any strength I had in me, took a deep breath, and told them.

"I was molested by my brother."

I cried, torrents. I cried like I had never cried before. Alice held me in her arms and let me cry. Mary said she was going to tell my "lover" that it wasn't his fault and that I just needed some time. It felt so good knowing they believed me and didn't hate me. Alice asked me if I wanted to get professional help. I said yes. I needed it. I knew the only way I was going to live a half-way normal life was if I got help. Alice said she knew a therapist who might be able to help me. I agreed to meet him.

I had to tell my mother. She had to know. But would she believe me? Just because my friends did, didn't mean she would. I would have to take my chances.

The following week was the worst. I couldn't concentrate on anything. My schoolwork suffered. I was only a couple of months from getting my Associate Degree, but my studies were going downhill. I cried constantly. When people asked what was wrong, I swore it was nothing. By the end of the week I couldn't stop crying. I couldn't stand it anymore. I had to tell my mother. I was scared, but I knew it had to be done. I decided to do it that night.

All the way home I changed my mind several times. I was afraid that my brother would be right and my own worst fears confirmed. I was, however, on the brink of a nervous breakdown and, no matter what the outcome, I had to tell my mother.

When I got home, I brought her into my room. As gently as possible, but without beating around the bush, I told her.

Through her tears, and my own, I explained how I was affected. I also told her that my brother may have been molested.

When I told her this, she said she knew who probably did it: her brother, my uncle. Ironically, this uncle was the first person I talked to about being gay. I also had gotten together with this uncle to discuss the molestation. Again I was hurt, betrayed, by a man I trusted. Never again would I let that happen. From then on, I decided, I wouldn't trust a man unless I knew him for a long while.

Anyway, my mother was hurt, naturally very upset, and mad at me. Not for telling her, or for letting it happen, but for not telling her in the first place.

"Why didn't you tell me sooner?" was the only question she asked. I explained why I couldn't. I had been convinced she would hate me and blame me. She took me in her arms and we held each other and cried. She told me that she loved me. I really needed to hear that from her. It was probably the best thing she could have said. I told her I was gay. I figured, why not? I might as well lay everything on the line. We discussed everything I had told her.

I moved out that night. I hated leaving her alone, but I couldn't stay there any longer. I drove over to Mary's and rang the doorbell. She opened the door and smiled, but immediately stopped smiling when she saw my face. She asked what was wrong and I said that I had told my mother about my brother. We talked about it for awhile, then she went to bed. It was about one a.m. and she had to work the next day. I lay down on the couch, but couldn't sleep. There were too many thoughts running through my mind. What would my dad do when he found out? Would he defend my brother? Would he turn against me when he found out I was gay? I didn't know. I was scared.

When my mother confronted my brother, he denied it. She wrote me a note saying that she had to believe me and she had to believe him. I was very angry at her. Didn't she know that he was going to deny it? She made me feel like he had been right when he told me that she wouldn't believe me. I was the one suffering and he was the one getting away with it. I couldn't speak to my mother. I had always considered her my friend. Now she, too, was betraying me. I never wanted to see or speak with her again.

While I was living with Mary, I started seeing a therapist. He was very gentle, very caring. The only problem was that he was a man. He promised me that he would in no way ever try to molest or hurt me. How could I believe him? I had been hurt, very badly, by two men I had trusted. I couldn't trust this therapist. Not unless he earned it.

I tested him. I would sit in his office for forty-five minutes without saying a word, staring out the window. I was convinced that sooner or later he would ask me to leave and not come back. I was trying to prove to myself that no man could be trusted and that I wasn't worth it to anyone. I'm glad I was wrong.

My therapist proved himself to me and as I got to know him, to trust him, to love him, I opened up more and more until forty-five minutes wasn't long enough. We worked together on some things. He made me work alone on others. I always knew he was there for support. He put up with a lot from me, and I kept thinking that one day he was going to turn around and say goodbye, but I knew deep down that wasn't true. I hope it's not anyway.

In the meantime, I had been living with Mary for nine months when some trouble started at the apartment building and we decided to move. At first we were going to try and find a place together, but I decided to save some money and try later. I didn't know what I was going to do. I couldn't move back home, not with my brother there. I asked my mother to phone an aunt to see if I could stay with her. My aunt said, "Okay."

My dad was a little upset because I wasn't moving back home. My mother made me promise I would never tell him about my brother because "it would kill him." My dad has a bad heart. Reluctantly, out of guilt, I promised. Previously, my dad accepted the fact I was gay with no problems, but now I had to "protect" my father. By doing so, I was protecting my brother.

I lived with my aunt for awhile, then moved in with a cousin. Unfortunately, I couldn't stay there very long and had to leave. The only place left was home. I asked my mother if I could move home. She said yes. I made some rules. I wanted a lock on my door. I wanted to be able to come and go as I pleased. I had been on my own for almost a year, and I had gotten used to doing things my way. I was twenty-one and felt

I should be able to run my own life. My mother still insisted my father not know about my brother. I still protected my brother by not telling my father.

I was home for a couple of months when I met a really nice guy. He was possibly someone I could trust. Before we started seeing each other, I explained about my brother and how I dealt with things. He promised me he would stick with me. I moved in with him. Things were rough at times, but we managed. He even came to therapy with me once to try and get a better understanding.

The only problem was that I still didn't trust people. I didn't trust him most of all. I couldn't; I was in love with him. One night he decided to go out alone. I had to work. I didn't want him to go. We got into an argument about it, and I told him I didn't trust him. No more was said that night.

For three days we didn't speak and I was falling apart. On the fourth night I had to work and he was going out. I got home early and tried to wait up for him, but fell asleep around midnight. When he came home the smell of liquor was so strong I felt sick.

The next day, I called him at work and asked if we could talk that night. He agreed. I asked if we were going to be okay. He said he didn't know, but that we could talk.

He picked me up after work. We drove to the dead-end street and he told me he wanted me to leave that night. I tried to make him change his mind, but I knew he was right. I called my mom again and cried, trying to explain what happened. She told me to come home.

I left his apartment that night. I walked part of the way home vowing never to trust anyone again. People who weren't my true friends could go jump in front of a speeding truck. Trusting people wasn't worth the pain. I called my mom again from a pay phone. She picked me up. I got home and fell asleep on the couch.

The next day, I was sitting on the picnic table when my dad drove up in his truck. He got out and said hello, and I said hello. He asked me if I was going to live at home again. I said yes. He said we needed to talk.

We went inside and my dad told my mother and I to sit down. At that moment my brother walked in and my dad told him to sit down. I knew right away what was going to happen: a confrontation.

I had already confronted my brother again with my mother

there. This time he admitted molesting me and also admitted having been molested by our uncle. He refused, however, to get help. Apparently he didn't have a problem. His beer, coke, and pot made him happy. But he had "no problem."

When we were all seated, my father asked me why I didn't speak to my brother. I have never started to shake so badly in all my life. I could barely hold my cigarette.

I looked at my mother, who looked at me as if to say, "Please don't tell him." I looked back at her thinking, "To hell with you. He has to know and I won't hide it anymore."

Surprisingly, my brother started it by telling my father it was something that happened a long time ago. With tears streaming down my face I explained what happened. Dad was dumbfounded. He was also very hurt. He didn't say anything for a while. Then he quietly asked me why I hadn't said anything before.

I had never felt close to my father, not only because he was a man (another one I didn't trust), but also because I never felt like he loved me. Maybe it was just me, but my father and I always fought. If I couldn't tell my mother, who I loved more than anyone, how could I tell him?

I explained to my father that when one of my cousins talked about being molested, she was thrown out of the family. My dad said the reason he didn't talk to my cousin was because of the way she treated her father. I couldn't believe he didn't know. I told him that she treated her father like that (not talking to him, not even caring if he were alive) because he molested her.

This surprised my dad. He really hadn't known. There was so much happening in our family, but none of the adults seemed to notice or, if they did, they ignored it. Keeping the "Family Secret" quiet is an old tradition in my family, one that's being broken down now as more and more of my cousins come out about who molested them.

I told my dad about our family and who had done what. I told him about the aunts and uncles who molested my cousins. I told him about the brothers who molested sisters or vice versa. I told him a lot. Not everything, but what I felt he could handle. I was becoming drained emotionally.

After I finished, he turned to my brother and told him to get some help. My brother insisted he didn't need help. I tried to tell my dad that a person can't be forced to get help; he has to want to get help. Unfortunately, my brother doesn't want help. He still insists he has no problem. I know he does, but I can't force him to get help, either. I've learned to worry and care about myself.

Every day is a fight to survive. In therapy, I was told that incest survivors view their lives as failures. Some are underachievers and some are overachievers. I am an underachiever. I don't do half of what I can. Things that I do, usually fail because of something I've done to screw them up.

I am trying to get my life together. I have a couple of cousins who I can talk to. One lives in California. She works with incest survivors. I hope to do the same some day. I call her for advice and/or support. My therapist is a great help still. I don't see him that often because of work. When I do see him, however, forty-five minutes is still not enough time.

I'm taking one day at a time. I feel I'm becoming stronger every day. I want to put what happened behind me. I'm so . . . gung-ho about incest and sexual molestation and getting it stopped, especially in my family, that I'm trying hard (sometimes too hard) to get people to talk about it. In this area I feel I'm overachieving. I want it stopped. It messed up my life and I want to stop it at my generation. Maybe someday my family will all get along and love each other. Maybe there won't be any denial in my family, someday.

My parents don't talk about it. I do feel that if and when I need support, my dad will be there for me. My mother is deep in denial. We were talking one day about the incest, and she admitted to being molested by an uncle of hers. I asked her why she never said anything. She said she couldn't. I believed her. When my mother was seven, incest and molestation were not talked about at all. If it had been talked about, it probably could have been stopped a long time ago.

My mother freaks out every time I mention it. If I say I'm going to talk to someone, she gets mad and asks why. She still feels it shouldn't be talked about. I don't think she'll ever understand that the only way to stop it is to talk about it. She's so afraid something will come out about the family secret that she doesn't want me to say anything. Her motto is forgive and forget. God will take care of it. I'm not going to wait until people die to say anything or to get the incest stopped. I want them alive so they can get help and maybe help others in their family. Helping is much better than hurting.

Relationships
and Social Support

Child abuse can exist in adult relationships.
—A THIRTY-THREE-YEAR-OLD MAN IN RECOVERY

Allies aren't a crime. —A MALE SURVIVOR

T he previous chapter discussed why it is necessary to break secrecy about the incest in order to begin the healing process. Since the abuses are committed in private and the child feels he has to maintain silence, he is effectively trapped by (and with) the perpetrator. The abuser may even convince the child that she or he (the perpetrator) is the only one who cares about him.

The abused child feels isolated in a world that he is helpless to change. Adults are either unaware of the abuse or unable (at times unwilling) to do anything to put an end to it. Someone who is isolated in this manner cannot learn to trust. Suspicious of others' motivations and doubtful that they could do anything even if they cared enough to try, he grows to be an adult who relies only on his own abilities and resources. Offers of help and support are viewed with suspicion. "What will they demand in return?" Friendships only go so far. If someone gets too close, the survivor will shut down emotionally, become cold and distant, or end the relationship. People will say things like, "You can only get so close to ———. I've been his friend for years and I don't feel as though I really know him."

In order to maintain the relationship, friends will respect the incest survivor's emotional boundaries, staying away from topics that make him feel uncomfortable. These limits on intimacy are not talked about; the survivor is probably unaware of their existence. But they work as effectively as a moat around a fortress. The survivor maintains absolute control over when and for how long the drawbridge is lowered. If there is any hint of danger, it is quickly raised again, leaving the friend standing bewildered on the outside. If the friend becomes worn out by having his/her attempts at intimacy rebuffed, the incest survivor interprets the diminished friendship as proof that people can't be depended on. Here, he thinks, is further evidence that caring about someone only leads to abandonment and pain. Not having a model of trusting, nonabusive relationships, he has no way of seeing how his behavior has contributed to the estrangement. "After all," he reasons, "my behavior was no different than before."

The survivor is left where he has always been—emotionally isolated, confused and fearful. He is once again dependent on his own resources; he views the world through a lens that has been clouded by his history of abuse. He always needed intimacy, but sexual child abuse prevented him from getting the nurturing he required. These unmet childhood needs cause problems in the survivor's adult relationships.

The requirements that are basic to human survival are the needs to love and to be loved. When a child's basic needs to be loved *and to be allowed to love* are stifled, they do not disappear. Whenever a parent doesn't love his or her child (or when that love is perverted into sexual abuse), the child continues to search for that love. He will seek a loving parent in all relationships. The need for parental love has become "frozen." A *frozen need* is any unmet childhood need that is carried into adulthood. It is incapable of being filled, no matter how hard the adult survivor (or his partner) may try. Hard as it is to accept, you can never get the love that you missed when you were three years old. No one will ever be able to parent you as a five-year-old, because you are no longer five. This does *not* mean that you cannot be loved, just that you can't be loved *as a child*. There is an important reason for letting go of the frozen childish need for parental love. Not only is this need impossible to fill, it interferes with something more important. As long as you insist that your partner becomes your loving parent, you prevent him or her from being able to offer you a genuine adult love. Even if she or he tries to meet those frozen needs, the effort is doomed to failure. Your partner isn't the one you needed love from when you were a child. It is only possible for her or him to love you *now*, as you are, in the present.

At the same time that he fears intimacy, the incest survivor yearns for close human contact. Humans are social beings. Although we occasionally crave solitude, to be *solitary* is to be something less than human. Children who are raised in isolation don't learn the social and emotional skills necessary to live healthy lives. The isolation of incest deprives the child of the normal experiences necessary to the establishment and maintenance of warm, caring, and mutually satisfying human contact. Although he has not developed the ability to form these relationships, he is aware of their existence. He sees other people who seem to enjoy normal friendships. He knows of relationships that appear to be satisfying. He reads and watches and listens, and wonders whether he will ever experience the closeness that he desires . . . and so fears.

Intimacy involves questions of trust. The conflict between wanting and fearing closeness is a central theme in the life of the adult survivor of incest. Since his most powerful interactions have been chaotic and abusive, he wonders if caring, nonabusive relationships aren't just a Hollywood myth. If he accepts that human intimacy is theoretically possible (or even actually attainable by others), he may assume that it is unavailable to him. Seeing other people who seem to be happy becomes further proof of how flawed and unattractive *he* is. That he cannot "figure out" how to form relationships confirms his feeling that he is stupid. If he decides that perhaps he should try to get close to someone, he doesn't know how to go about it. How could he? Where would he have developed the skills? If he begins to move close to somebody, the perfectionism takes over—at the first sign of a problem he is ready to give up. Any conflict can become proof of failure. Accustomed to idealizing friendships, he hasn't had the opportunity to learn that no relationship is perfect. They all require work and they all have problems. But his experience has been limited to abuse. He is an expert on the subject. And he will always be looking for signs that he should run and hide. He will feel a pull to protect himself in situations where he is in no danger. He will misread signals because, in the past, they always meant danger. Or he will unconsciously seek out abusive relationships because they are more familiar and less confusing to him.

Incest survivors have told me that they can never hope to sustain successful relationships because their needs are too great:

"When someone pays attention to me, I just want to hang on and never let go."

"I feel like I'd fall apart if he left."

"I wanted her with me every minute. I was jealous of her friends, I resented her job, and I wanted us to do everything together. When she wanted to be alone, I felt like she didn't love me and wanted to leave."

"I get so scared and I feel like a little kid. I just want to hold on tight."

This kind of intense, clinging neediness is easy to understand. The first expression of warmth and affection after a lifetime of deprivation feels precious and unique. It feels like your only chance at a happy life. The stakes are impossibly high. "If I blow this opportunity I'll never get another chance." Part of that perception is correct—human connections *are* precious. They should be treasured and nurtured so that they can flourish. And each relationship is also representative of what can happen when people connect with each other. What is learned from one can be applied to others, but no relationship has it all. A full life contains a rich variety of human interactions. No one person is capable of fulfilling your every need. That he or she is unwilling or unable to do so is not failure, nor is it evidence that the person doesn't love you enough. A profoundly loving partner may not be able to bake a cake or understand world politics. She or he may have no interest in folk music or be passionately involved in something that you find boring. This is not proof of incompatibility. Nor is it abandonment if your partner chooses to pursue some of his or her interests with other people. Relationships flourish in an atmosphere of encouragement. Each partner supports the other's interests without needing to take on every one. Time spent apart, alone or with other people, fosters diversity of experience. Rather than pulling the two apart, it can allow each to develop strengths that they can then utilize in helping the relationship to grow. Instead of being two frightened children, clinging to each other for comfort, they become strong, independent adults who have *chosen* to share parts of their lives with each other.

When someone clings to another person—when they are overcome with jealousy and feel frightened and needy—it usually has very little to do with present reality. Insisting that your lover be "the parent you never had" will only leave both of you feeling frustrated and unhappy. Caring between two adults, although it can never replace what was lost in childhood, is a wonderfully affirming experience. To achieve it, it is necessary to stop blaming your partner for not being what she or he can never be—and to begin to appreciate what *is* possible. It isn't fair that you were never loved the way you deserved to be. Nevertheless, you must let go of the insistence that somebody must love the little child that you feel yourself to be. Giving up this frozen need isn't easy to accomplish, but doing so opens the door to accepting support in ways that weren't possible before.

There is another aspect of blame that you have to let go. To move ahead with recovery, you need to stop blaming yourself for not having been a lovable child. Many incest survivors find that an important component of their recovery involves acceptance of themselves as children. *No child ever deserved to be abused!* Although you can accept this truth about other people, you probably have difficulty believing it about yourself. As you look back to your childhood, it is a fair bet that you don't like what you see. You may have accepted the lies that you were ugly, stupid, evil, unlovable, manipulative, seductive, or otherwise "deserving of the abuse." It isn't comfortable to remember a small, frightened, and confused little child. It is understandable that you would want to distance yourself from association with your abusive childhood—and the child who reminds you of it. But getting to know that child in a new way—befriending him—can prove to be a key part of creating a supportive environment for the adult you have become. Understanding that your "child within" always deserved to be loved moves you toward being able to accept yourself as a lovable adult, deserving and capable of achieving healthy adult relationships.

As an abused child you had no guarantee that your struggle to survive would be successful. You got through the abuse the best way you could, relying on your intelligence, creativity and courage. That you survived at all is an accomplishment deserving respect. That you became a functioning adult is testimony to the resiliency of the human spirit—reason for admiration and celebration. (I have discussed my admiration of the strength, courage, and creativity of incest survivors in Chapter 9, but I believe that it needs to be repeated again and again. Are you starting to be able to hear it?) It can be a powerful experience to go back to your childhood and befriend yourself as a child. You can reassure and appreciate the child within you. You can tell him that he is fine and brave and good. You can tell him that he is right to expect to be treated with respect and caring. You can tell him that it isn't fair that he is treated abusively. And you can let him know that he will survive his situation. After all, you are living proof of his survival. *You* can become the loving, nurturing adult that he (you) always needed. In short, you can break down his isolation and form a loving, respectful relationship with him. By cherishing yourself as a child, you become able to give up expecting others to do so. Relieved of the burden of parenting you, the energies of others are freed to provide you (and you become free to accept) the kind of support that adults can offer one another. In that way your adult isolation is broken down, opening the way to healthy adult relationships.

Having begun to take care of the needs of the past, it becomes possible to address present concerns. As you start to support yourself, you also can reach out for realistic support from others. You still may not be able to get support from your family. They may have remained abusive and chaotic. They may still be locked in denial and pretense. Or they may not be physically or emotionally accessible. Some incest survivors have made great progress in joining with their families in

FOCUS

FINDING THE CHILD WITHIN

One of my clients who is an incest survivor carries in his briefcase a framed photograph of himself that was taken when he was a child. He treats the picture with respect, keeping it wrapped in a soft cloth and handling it gently. Sometimes we look at the photograph together, while he tells me about himself as a boy.

Another client will sometimes prop up an early childhood photograph on the sofa during his session, as a reminder of a time before the abuse.

Thom Harrigan, a Boston social worker who works with incest survivors, asked each member of his men's recovery group to bring in a childhood picture. He reported to me that most group members showed up with several pictures of themselves and sometimes snapshots of their families. They all knew that it was important to them to make these connections.

It is clear that part of your incest recovery work needs to focus on your childhood. That is, after all, when the abuse took place. The boy that you were is an important source of information about the man you have become. You carry him with you in the form of memories, feelings, reactions, attitudes, personality, and physical characteristics. There are a number of reasons to get to know him.

At times you still feel like a scared, lonely, abused child. Part of your self-concept was frozen at the time that you were abused. Emotionally, you don't recognize that you have gotten through the ordeal. The world still feels like a risky place. When you are confronted with a difficult or frightening situation, try to ask yourself, "How old do I feel?" Chances are that you feel young, small, and weak. Returning your attention to childhood helps you to get a better picture of who you were—and who you are.

Initially, you may have some difficulty finding something positive to say about your younger self. Many survivors have carried their negative self-images from childhood. They blame themselves rather than the abuse for their unhappiness, shyness, fear, confusion, and isolation. Nothing could be farther from the truth.

The fact that you survived into adulthood is proof that, as a child, you were

sharing the difficult process of reconciliation and recovery. Others continue to battle to extract recognition and caring where none exists. They have taken on a thankless and hopeless task—one which leaves them stuck within their isolation. Still other survivors have decided that, since their biological families are incapable of providing the needed support, they will create their own "families." These support systems take many forms. They may consist of only those biological

resourceful, creative and strong. (Yes, I'm talking about you!) You owe a debt to that little boy. It is because of his courage and determination that you are moving on your recovery today. And it is a debt that you are able to pay. He deserves your respect and friendship. You are an adult he can count on absolutely. You are living evidence that he will make it through his difficult, lonely childhood. Recognize that he was working by himself with limited resources, and he overcame tremendous odds. What a terrific little guy! If he could do all of that without help and support, imagine what he could have accomplished with the right kind of care, love and encouragement. Getting in touch with the reality of yourself as a child will help you turn around your equally inaccurate picture of your adult self.

There are many ways to reconnect with the child within you. Here are some suggestions:

1 / *Make use of photographs.* If you can, take a look at pictures taken before you were abused as well as afterward. Notice how they are different.

2 / *Write a letter to yourself as a child.* Tell him how wonderful he is and that he never deserved to be hurt. Reassure him that he will survive, and that the abuse will not go on forever.

3 / *With the help of friends, or in a workshop or group, create a drama or fantasy about your childhood:*

- You can have someone else take the role of you as a child while you reassure him that he is fine and everything will be OK.
- You can play out returning to the scene of the abuse as your adult self, protecting the child by standing up to the perpetrator. Take along allies or reinforcements if you like, but be your own hero.
- You can set up a scene of yourself as a child the way it always should have been. Imagine a safe childhood, peopled with kind, loving, protective adults.

4 / *Learn new ways to play.* Don't worry about appearing foolish or feeling silly. That's what it's all about. There's nothing like playfulness to bring out the child within you.

I recently saw a button that said, "It's never too late to have a happy childhood." While you can't change the past, you can forge a new perspective on it that will allow you to have a happier adulthood. Befriending and reassuring the child within strongly reinforces adult recovery by creating new insight into past experiences.

relatives who are able to respond in an open, caring way. They may be the survivor's own spouse and children. Or the family may be formed of unrelated people who commit themselves to thinking and caring about one another. The new "families" may be made up of other incest survivors who have decided to learn how to support each other.

I'll describe one interesting (and unexpected) example of how this kind of support system can come into being. Some of my 12-week recovery groups for male survivors have spontaneously turned themselves into longer-term groups. At such times, all the group members have elected to continue for an additional cycle, allowing no room for adding new participants. What occurs in these continuing groups is extremely powerful, speaking to the advantages of ongoing work in an environment of established safety. These groups move from the retelling of their incest histories to raising specific life issues. Members bring more details of their current life struggles into the group and enlist group support in dealing with them. In this way, the continuing groups begin to resemble general issues groups—but with a very specific difference. For recovery group members, their safety is grounded in a level of trust that can only come from a shared traumatic experience. (This is similar to the intensity of support felt by groups of Vietnam combat veterans.) Although it is important that this trust eventually be extended to people outside the group, that issue can be dealt with at a later time—often with the active assistance of the other group members.

The members of these ongoing groups have made sense of their experiences and are using their insight to bring about real changes in their lives. These group members are more likely to go out for dinner or coffee together after the meetings. They invite one another to parties and meals at their homes. They send each other notes and make phone calls. Group members have provided active support during intimidating life situations; such as accompanying one another to medical and dental appointments, attending court appearances and funerals, helping in preparation for job interviews, attending family events—and confronting perpetrators. During the breaks between the end of one cycle and the beginning of the next, group members have met informally as an interim support group. In this process it is clear to me (and to them) that something very special is happening. These adult incest survivors are taking genuine charge of their recovery. They are accomplishing this feat by creating a healthy, functional *family*. This is the way family always should have been. On some level they've always known it, and now they are figuring out what to do about it. They are actively rejecting the experiences that told them that there is no closeness without abuse.

It is no exaggeration to say that, in accepting support from one another, they are rediscovering their capacity for love. And they are reaffirming what they originally knew—the possibility of nonsexual, nonabusive loving of other human beings. This is a profoundly thrilling discovery, opening infinite possibilities for male survivors. What has been done can be repeated. They are able to recognize that if trust and love are possible here—with this group of men—then it can be found elsewhere as well. Survivors, now starting to *thrive*, can (with the certainty of experience) say, "Change is possible, and I have the ability to turn my life around." The power of this transition from surviving to living—from hurt to health—deeply affects everyone who experiences it. I feel touched and privileged to be witness to what these men have accomplished. And this is only one (admittedly special) example of how survivors support each other by creating new families. There can be any number of foundations for these associations. They may be religious, neighborhood, school, or special interest groups. Most frequently, the new families are less rigidly defined, taking support from a range of safe, supportive friends, wherever they can be found. Creating a support network requires trust. Like trust, social support grows slowly, one interaction building upon the next as relationships are formed. This development of adult support systems is crucial to the recovery process. It means that you are no longer alone.

The route to recovery begins with putting an end to your isolation. And the only way out of isolation is, of course, the company of others. The logical question is, "How do I go about it?" You may feel as lost and unskilled as a child. Asking you to form intimate relationships seems as unrealistic as asking a baby to talk or a five-year-old to write a sonnet. This is not an idle comparison. To ask a child to behave as an adult is unrealistic in the extreme; to *require* that he do so is cruel. The basic information and social experiences—the building blocks of relationships—simply aren't in place. It is short-sighted to expect the incest survivor to know intuitively how to negotiate the confusing tangle of emotions, expectations and skills involved in maintaining an emotionally satisfying social life.

But the situation isn't hopeless. It is not stupidity or incompetence that keeps you isolated. You never had the opportunity to develop normal social skills. Social relationships are possible; skills can be learned. But it can't all be done at once. Moving toward other people must be done in gentle, logical steps. Whenever a new bit of progress is achieved it must be examined, felt, thought about and savored. The only way to tackle an overwhelming task is to break it down into manageable bits. When one step feels solid, it is possible to move on to the next. Now and then it makes sense to stop and look at what you have accomplished. If you only focus on what you still need to do, the task will always feel impossible. Looking back at where you were last year or three months ago allows you to see the progress you've made.

Building a relationship takes time and experience. Everyone makes mistakes, and very few mistakes are fatal. When people are willing to acknowledge that something went wrong—and don't waste a lot of time in blaming the other person *or themselves*—they can get on with the business at hand. That is the business of correcting mistakes, figuring out a better solution, and thereby forging a stronger relationship. Human interactions that have survived tests can be more solid for them. By meeting challenges together, people forge a history of successful communication, one that they can fall back on when things get rough.

HARRY'S STATEMENT

Harry, a forty-year-old survivor, tells of
removing himself from abusive situations through
out-of-body experiences and running away—and
how he stopped running to start healing.

I am five years old. My parents have just completed their
umpteenth screaming match. I've gotten used to it. I can fall
into a trance while they fight, a state bordering on sleeping and
waking.

A noise grows out of my own heartbeat. It squeaks and
thumps in regular rhythm, getting closer and closer. It's at the
window now.

I get out of bed and move toward the door. My terror
grows. If I can just reach Mom and Dad in time—I make it to
the hall and run. Run, Harry, run!

I can feel the floor begin to slip under my feet. A creature I
cannot see is getting closer. I can see the kitchen light and the
shape of my mother's head. My mouth forms a soundless
scream. There is no escape.

To this day, terror stuffs down the word "help" when I
need it. Sometimes my soul still spins into a half-dreaming,
half-waking state as my mind conjures up monster-movie
dreams.

I am a forty-year-old gay male, a musician by trade. The
forty-year-old part is not a pleasant prospect. I'm still running.

Looking back I can see a lot of reasons why my life has
gone the way it has. My father left when I was four. The
unspoken reason: marital separation.

I couldn't grasp any of the situation except the fact that he
was gone. I began my own brand of separation: mental
separation.

Dad is gone. I am lying in bed for a winter's nap. I gaze at
the sun filtering through the "webs" at the base of my fingers
and drift away. Soul leaves body.

My mother and I joined my father in Houston a year later. Together again! But drinking and fighting begin. Violence erupts into our outwardly "Ozzie and Harriet"-type family life.

Mother senses trouble the first time Dad drinks heavily. He picks at her with a cold sarcasm. The sounds begin to crescendo and Mom and I head for a motel to weather the storm.

A day later we return to an absolute shambles. Furniture is broken, musical instruments smashed, and clothes thrown about. In later instances we stay home and learn to take it.

I also learn that anger can destroy, and I reject it as a valid expression of emotion, become a true Southern gentleman. Little do I realize that the depression I adopt to survive can maim, cripple.

A similar process operates at school. I have a difficult time adjusting socially, and am labeled "underachiever" by teachers. My father circles grades under an "A" in red. On the other hand I am beaten up by other kids for being "bookish."

My mother has a long history of drinking. She began as a teenager when her stepfather made life miserable for her; perhaps she was a victim of abuse. She drinks day and night by my eleventh year. I return home from school to find a locked front door, the television blaring, and Mom passed out in front of it. I learn to leave my bedroom window undone so that I can get in. Basically the neighborhood streets and the field behind our house become home.

Earlier, I mentioned my separation technique. I perfect it so I can disappear at school, too. By my fourteenth year, my guidance counselor has me classified something like "out the window." She asks often if anything is wrong at home. I answer no. I have learned my lesson well.

In this same time period I return home one day to the usual scene. Mom is snoring away in front of the television and I feel a wave of rage. I don't need to think twice about what I am going to do. I grab a butcher knife out of the kitchen drawer, creep to the sofa, and raise the knife to her throat. I falter, redirect the knife to myself. Again I falter. The separation starts. I don't know how long I have been staring at the knife while soul left body.

I join Scouts at age eleven, hoping for some escape from home. I work hard to earn the money and rank to attend so I can attend my first summer camp. My reward: a scoutmaster, male hero-image, sexually molests me. The major part of the experience is in an outhouse and we are totally silent. I learn sex is a dirty, secret experience.

I feel guilty, afraid, responsible. I leave the troop and join another, attempting to escape my shame, but run headlong into a group of older boys who are drawn to me like radar. I can read their thoughts; new meat.

I am initiated into the troop the following summer by five members of this older group. My next-door neighbor is within earshot and I listen to his screams as he receives a "normal" initiation consisting of being blindfolded, rolled in mud, sprayed with shaving cream, and receiving a series of punches and whacks.

J———, who I am fellating while my neighbor screams, whispers, "Isn't this better than what's he's getting? Now relax, kid."

Relax.

N——— continues to scream. I relax as soul separates from body.

In high school there is not much to report. I try to reform myself in this new place, but I am too far gone. I live up to my underachiever status most of the time, except in music and drama.

In my late teens, however, I discover religion and become part of an Episcopal church that bears the earmarks of a cult. There is a system of extended families and I become a part of one in order to find safety for myself. My separation ability becomes spiritual experience, my ability to separate is sanctified. My inwardly directed anger and self-hatred are redefined as self-mortification and perfection.

It is possible that the separation experiences are willful attempts at psychotic split, the ultimate refuge of the tortured. However, the depression continues, deepens. Suicide looks pretty good as an alternative.

Finally at age thirty-three I leave community life, determined to discover what my long-repressed gayness is about. As far as I can tell from the behavior of those around me in the late seventies and early eighties, one is supposed to sleep around. I discover a certain prowess in that activity. My musical and acting abilities developed in music school and perfected in the church community serve me well as I now perform in bed, often to packed houses in gay baths, rest areas, parties, but always with strangers.

Every time someone gets too close, I move and/or change

jobs. I've had eight jobs in three countries during the last ten years, and have lived in forty-seven homes in my lifetime. Panic alternates with depression, despair with hopelessness. I am alone in crowds. But I keep running.

After watching a television show describing the long-term effects of child abuse on its victims, I talk to a counselor whose name is advertised in a local gay newspaper. We review my symptoms, compare them with those of adult incest survivors and I enter group and individual therapy. I begin to change certain unhealthy life circumstances.

It has taken me a long time to plug into the group and to trust even my therapist. But at last someone understands my horror story and does not minimize it, nor allow me to. I am slowly allowing a few people into my life in significant ways, sharing feelings while they happen. I'm working at committing myself to living in the Boston area and putting a stop to the running. I have a new job (church music!) where I feel professionally significant and socially accepted.

I am in the middle of establishing a monogamous, mutually life-giving relationship with another survivor. We know each other's assets and liabilities clearly, try to live openly and honestly. We blow the whistle on the tradeoff game each of us learned to play in order to survive.

I have recently taken the HIV test. The result: positive. But I feel pretty good physically and mentally.

I am determined to feel whatever is left of my life rather than separate and dream it away. I look for hope in tiny doses. Hang on, Harry, hang on.

Sexual Feelings

It's hard to be passionate when you're trying to maintain control.
—A MALE SURVIVOR

One of the most perplexing questions faced by an incest survivor is, "What should I do about sexual feelings?" In spite of all he has done to ignore, deny, control, redirect, hide, discount or explain away his sexual feelings, they have a way of appearing, unbidden, with alarming persistency. I have mentioned some of the elements of his consternation in earlier chapters:

1 / He has come to associate sex with abuse. When sexual feelings arise, he is apt to feel that he is about to be abused—or that, if he acts on the feelings, he will be abusing someone else.

2 / Since displays of affection have been inappropriately sexualized, any show of affection has the potential to be sexually charged. This can bring about avoidance of any kind of affectionate interaction, lest it lead to arousal and then to inappropriate behavior. Finding himself aroused in situations which have no obvious sexual component makes him feel like a pervert—sex-obsessed and out of control.

3 / The incest was committed by someone who was unwilling or unable to recognize and respect normal boundaries. The perpetrator, in meeting his or her own sexual desires, taught the child that people act on impulse, regardless of the pain that this action may inflict on others. The incest survivor has learned that any arousal will inevitably result in sexual activity. Never having had the power to keep the perpetrator from abusing him, the survivor feels powerless to prevent his feelings from leading him into sex—whether or not he wants them to.

4 / The idea that it is necessary to act on all impulses blurs the distinction between feelings and behavior. Thinking about murdering someone is not the same as committing the crime. Wanting to hit someone raises no welts. In the same sense, sexual fantasies are not the same as sexual acts. When he has not yet learned to make this distinction, an incest survivor punishes himself for crimes that he hasn't committed. He has "lusted in his heart" and feels like a rapist or sexual deviant. His sexual feelings have become, for him, further proof of his wickedness.

5 / Fear of his sexual feelings can lead the survivor to excessive preoccupation with sex and arousal. Having begun with a commendable wish to behave toward others in a nonabusive manner, he finds himself without adequate guidelines as to what constitutes abuse. He has been lied to in the past. And if he talks to people about it, what will they think of him? Will they suspect that he is having these feelings and expose him to ridicule and punishment? Thrown back on his own resources, the incest survivor becomes increasingly scrupulous about monitoring and controlling his feelings. Every impulse is scrutinized and judged. Each thought is examined for potential sexual content. The prophecy has fulfilled itself. In his attempt to avoid becoming a perpetrator, the incest survivor has become obsessed with sex. He can't seem to get his mind off the subject—a fact that he sees as further proof that he is flawed beyond recovery.

6 / The incest survivor may attempt to deaden all feelings in order to avoid sexual arousal. He may avoid situations that have the potential to be arousing. He may deny that he has sexual feelings or, when they do appear, label them as something else. In his distrust of sexuality, he may go to great lengths to protect himself and others from his sexual feelings.

Many survivors keep sex rigidly compartmentalized—separate from other areas of their lives. They may confine sex to solitary masturbation, thus protecting others from being sexually "victimized." Masturbation has the powerful secondary benefit of being completely under one's own control. Since the only other people involved are fantasy objects, they present no physical threat. Ironically, even this harmless form of sexual release can become overwhelming. As it turns into a patterned, compulsive activity, it becomes one more part of life that feels out of control. The masturbatory fantasies may replay aspects of the original abuse, reinforcing the feeling that sex—even when performed alone—is abusive. There is an ample body of pornography dedicated to fantasies of sexual and physical abuse. The term *self-abuse* becomes, in this case, a description not of the act, but of the feelings attached to it. It underscores loneliness and provides survivors with further proof that they are unacceptable human beings with no hope of normal relationships. (I do not mean to criticize masturbation, which is not necessarily an unhealthy activity. In fact, masturbation may be the only safe way that the survivor has been able to allow himself to enjoy sexual feelings. My concern is when the activity becomes a compulsion, serving to isolate the survivor and reinforce his negative self-image.)

Another form of compartmentalizing is to confine sexual activity to situations that are purely sexual in nature. These may range from frequenting prostitutes and massage parlors to anonymous—sometimes furtive—encounters in parks, public toilets, or highway rest areas. What these activities have in common is that they are divorced from any other area of the survivor's life. There is no need to develop a relationship. There is no requirement of tenderness, humanity, or self-revelation. It is a simple gratification of a sexual urge. Or is it? There would be no problem if it could be accepted as simply meeting a physical need. But there is more to it than that.

Compartmentalizing sex reflects the belief that it is wrong, dirty, evil, abusive. That is why it must be hidden. "Nice, normal" people must be protected from this activity. The old morality that states "good girls don't" carries the corollary that "bad girls *do*." The next logical step is easy to take. If only the dregs of humanity engage in this kind of sexual activity, and if the survivor's sex life is limited to it, then surely (he reasons) he is beneath contempt. (These beliefs may not be held consciously. The survivor may feel himself to be a completely liberated, liberal individual, and be unaware of how severely he is judging himself.)

Taking this belief system a bit further shows how seriously it can affect the survivor's life. Having defined himself as flawed or perverted, he may attempt to protect other, "better" people from contamination. Assuming that his sexual feelings are dangerous to himself and others, he backs away as soon as he begins to feel them. Any attempt to add a sexual component to a relationship is met with suspicion and fear. The illusion of control is threatened. Order must be established. This is accomplished by running away. The survivor finds a reason to end the relationship abruptly, leaving his partner bewildered—particularly if she or he doesn't share or understand his situation. If he does become sexual with his partner, he may negate all other aspects of the relationship, redefining it in keeping with his previous sexual experiences. His abuse history, then, has sabotaged a potentially satisfying relationship, relegating it to the level of a sexual encounter.

In order to lead a satisfying life you have to figure out what to do about your sexual feelings. You must break down the barriers that keep sexuality separate from the other parts of your life. This process is one of acceptance and integration. It is never easy, but there are ways of accomplishing it.

Just as with breaking the silence about abuse, you begin to deal with your sexual feelings by talking about them. As long as sexual feelings and activities remain hidden, they become shameful secrets. It will be hard to share them. It can feel like a horrible confession of your sins or an embarrassing revelation of weakness. It may be easiest to begin by sharing your feelings with a counselor or therapist. In this setting you are assured of confidentiality and (it is hoped) of not being judged. An experienced, sensitive counselor will provide safety and encouragement as you begin exploration of your sexual feelings. (Chapter 16 includes a discussion of how to find the right therapist for you.) As you begin to be more accepting of your own sexuality, you will begin to communicate thoughts and express feelings with others. In this process you will discover that they have concerns, fears and interests that are similar to yours. It is especially helpful to share your thoughts and feelings with other incest survivors. (Chapter 17 explains why interacting with other survivors is a powerful aspect of recovery.) As you become more comfortable with your sexual feelings, they won't need to be kept hidden. Neither will they be constant intrusions that prevent you from relaxing and enjoying life. It will become easier to accept them as another part of the richness of human experience. The acceptance of sexual thoughts and feelings paves the way toward integration of healthy sexuality into your life.

I don't mean to present this simplistically. It isn't simple. Sexuality is a highly charged topic for everyone. None of us is as "cool" about sex as we would like others to believe. Sex is still a topic fraught with embarrassment for many of us, and it is common to attempt to cover it up with pretense or jokes. It may take years before you are comfortable with your sexual feelings. But the benefits of taking the first steps are numerous. And you begin to reap these benefits long before the process is complete.

To talk about feelings is to acknowledge their existence. You may be asking yourself, "OK, now that I've acknowledged them, what do I *do* about my sexual feelings?" The answer, at first, appears to be painfully simple. When stated, however, it may seem to be the reverse—simply painful. The best thing to do about feelings, sexual or otherwise, is to *feel* them. This idea can seem threatening and feel frightening. As an incest survivor, you have experienced what happened when feelings weren't kept under rigid control. They always were acted on—and the actions were abusive. So you are rightly suspicious of any suggestion that you allow yourself to feel sexual. Wouldn't that make you an abuser, too? My answer is a resounding NO! You have been given misinformation. You have been lied to. Feelings are not the same as behavior. (And sex is not the same as abuse!) You are not at the mercy of your feelings. You don't have to act on them unless you choose to do so—*no matter how it feels*. Learning to acknowledge them, accept them, and *even enjoy them* allows you to stop being a victim of your own feelings. Again, feelings are to be felt. Nothing more. There is no harm in that. Neither are feelings alone the best basis for action. The most useful guide to behavior is your own best *thinking*, taking into account all available data, including (but not limited to) your feelings. When you accept that, you can cease to be afraid of your feelings. Only then does the unlikely concept of enjoying your sexual feelings make sense.

Start to talk about your feelings to someone who will listen (and share) without judgment or criticism. As you begin to allow yourself to have sexual feelings, to share them and even to celebrate them—as you accept that you have a choice as to which of your feelings you will put into action—you will begin to see how it is possible to be *a feeling, caring, and sexual person*. As the process continues, and you recognize that you have the choice not to act on all of your feelings, you can also accept that it is possible to act on *some* of them. You have charge of when you will be sexual and when you will not. Sexual feelings—even sexual arousal—do not have to lead to sexual activity *unless it makes sense for you and your partner*. This revelation is tremendously liberating. It enables you to explore all ranges of feelings and activities at your own pace and in your own way.

Having given up rigid control over your feelings and actions, you become free to really *take charge* of your life. You experience what it feels like to touch and be touched in ways that don't automatically lead to sex. You learn how a hug can be enjoyed as a warm expression of human caring. Instead of responding to every touch by tensing up or drawing away, you allow yourself to be held, to be caressed, to be reassured physically. You see how it is possible to express (and receive) affection on many levels. And you learn to make the distinction between abusive contact and caring touch. Most important, you become able to state clearly when (and how) you want to be touched, and when you don't. As you recognize that everyone has a right to absolute control over his or her body, you exercise that right without worrying about hurting someone's feelings. Having given up the fear of your feelings, you have let go of another piece of the tyranny of an abusive childhood. Knowing that it is OK to feel, and that you can decide what to do with your feelings, a world of possibilities opens to you. You are able to explore ranges of feelings, activities, and affectional choices (including sex) that are free of abuse.

Individual
Counseling

I want to put up a sign that says "closed for repairs." —A MALE SURVIVOR

Why Therapy? The idea of going into counseling or therapy can be very intimidating. You may have been raised with certain ideas about what therapy means. If, for example, you were brought up to believe that "people should be able to solve their own problems," asking for help feels like an admission of defeat. Further, you may have been taught that "only nut cases need shrinks." This leads to the idea that if you see a therapist, you are admitting to the world (and yourself) that you are crazy. Finally, you may think of therapy as an extreme measure, to be turned to only as a last resort.

Most movie and television portrayals of therapy and counseling don't help to ease your mind about the prospect. Therapists tend to be presented as severe, unresponsive, forbidding types who sit silently behind their patients—out of sight—taking notes and occasionally asking probing questions. The patient seems to lie on the therapist's couch for years, delving deeply into the obscurities of his infancy and childhood, spending small fortunes and endless hours to discover that the severity of his toilet-training has caused him to loathe his mother. Although there are some therapeutic situations that resemble this scenario, they are rare. The Hollywood image is parody—most counselors and therapists create a far more human and welcoming environment. But the old images persist. Even if you know that the movie version isn't real, it can be intimidating enough to make you want to stay away.

This chapter discusses some of the specific issues and problems that confront the incest survivor in individual counseling. It also offers guidelines for finding the right therapist. But before doing that, it may be useful to address some widely held myths about counseling and therapy.

There are many different types of psychological counseling and therapy. These are sometimes legal distinctions, which vary from state to state and among different professional groups. For our purposes I will not distinguish between counseling and therapy—or between counselor and therapist—but will use the terms interchangeably to refer to a one-way helping relationship with someone who possesses particular skills, training, and experience in dealing with the effects of various life experiences on emotions and behavior.

Let us look at some of the reasons people come up with to avoid seeking counseling:

1 / "I should be able to do it myself." The idea that we should be capable of thinking our way out of any psychological difficulty is a strange one. People who would readily consult experts to repair broken furnaces, fix their television sets, service their cars, or give them advice on major purchases are strangely reluctant to seek the help of someone with special training and practice in dealing with psychological issues. And that's really all a therapist is—a man or woman who, by virtue of having had specialized education and experience, has developed particular skills and insights into certain areas of human life. Not the least of the benefits of a counselor is that she or he sits outside the problem, providing a perspective that someone within your situation (you, your friends and family) can't. You go to a barber to cut your hair, to a mechanic to service your car, and a plumber to fix your sink. Why, then, would you leave your emotional well-being in the hands of amateurs? Are you any less important than a toaster oven?

2 / "If I go for psychological help, I'm admitting failure." This statement is very difficult to support by any kind of logic. If you had a broken leg you wouldn't expect it to heal itself; having it set by a doctor is no evidence of your personal shortcomings. On the contrary, it is the appropriate response to the situation. It makes sense to get the help you require.

3 / "It's not that bad." "It's not serious enough to require treatment." How bad does it have to be? How much pain is too much? How many years of isolation and unhappiness do you have to endure before going for help? Many people view therapy as a last resort.

Couples, for example, will often wait until separation or divorce is imminent before they seek professional counseling. Waiting until that point makes the job much harder. The couple (as well as the counselor) must wade through additional accumulated frustrations and resentments before getting to the underlying issues. To recognize problems early on—while they are still manageable—makes them a lot easier to deal with. Ultimately, by seeking assistance before things get "too bad," you are saving time, money, and energy. Perhaps the situation would be easier to accept if therapy were viewed as "maintenance" instead of as treatment. Something that is important to you deserves to be well taken care of. People who would never dream of waiting until their car broke down before changing the oil, who would be shocked at the idea of not cleaning their house until the Board of Health forces them to, see nothing illogical in waiting until they are in crisis before seeing to the care and maintenance of one of their most valuable possessions—their emotional well-being.

4 / "It's too expensive. I can't afford it." While it is true that psychotherapy can be an extremely costly and protracted procedure, it does not have to be that way. While some mental health professionals charge upwards of $125 for a 45-minute session, these are the great exceptions rather than the rule. And high cost does not mean that the care will be of higher quality. There is a wide range of services available to you, from private psychotherapy to organizationally, religiously and publicly funded agencies, hospital programs and clinics. Services may be offered by mental health counselors, social workers, psychologists, psychiatrists, pastoral counselors, and nurses as well as a range of nontraditionally trained (but often very able) professionals and nonprofessionals. These services range in price from very expensive to free, and many are covered in total or in part by health insurance. In an effort to make mental health services more widely available, many practitioners will adjust their fees to the financial situation of their clients. Don't be afraid to inquire, and don't feel that you will be looked down on or receive inferior treatment if you pay less for it. Don't deny yourself the attention you need. You are worth it, and there are high-quality professional services available at affordable prices.

5 / "I don't want people to know I'm in therapy. Everyone will think I'm whacko." No one has to know. Psychotherapists have a professional responsibility to protect the confidentiality of their clients. This means that therapists require permission from their clients before revealing their clients' identities or any information about them. It is necessary to face realities of life no matter how irrational they may be. One of these irrational realities is that prejudices still exist against people receiving psychological counseling. It makes no sense to punish someone who is dealing with his problems while rewarding someone who ignores or hides his difficulties. But prejudicial attitudes don't yield to reason. This is why active drunks can continue to find social acceptance while recovering alcoholics participate in programs that are "Anonymous." It is why professional sports figures who try to overcome their drug habits by entering treatment programs face the possibility of losing their careers. The message is clear: "Do whatever you want as long as no one is forced to notice it." This attitude—which assumes that there is something shameful about rebuilding a damaged life—is clearly wrong. But unfair as it is, we must recognize realities. Some jobs would be jeopardized if it were known that the jobholder is in therapy. People still gossip and engage in character assassination. It would be wonderful if all the survivors of all types of maltreatment could stand proudly— could openly proclaim their identities and their determination to put the abuse behind them. But this is not yet possible. When people finally recognize that *abuse, not recovery, is shameful*, they will encourage survivors to get the help they need. Then the subject will come out of the shadows. That time is coming, but it is not yet here, and responsible professionals recognize the need to protect the confidentiality of their clients.

There are also some parts of the country, types of careers, and other environments that are less open to psychological counseling. Not every city is like Los Angeles, New York, or Boston, where it is almost embarrassing to admit that you are *not* in therapy. One of my correspondents wrote, ". . . there is a 'midwest' mind set that begins somewhere west of Allentown, PA, and ends just east of Reno, NV, which says that talking directly about personal problems and asking for help from 'outsiders' is suspect." Although the writer may have more direct experience than I with that attitude, I don't think it is unknown on the east and west coasts. Nor is it found everywhere in the Midwest, as the excellent work done by counselors in Minnesota, Illinois, Wisconsin, Texas, and many other "heartland" locations will attest. Some of the best pioneering work on recovery from abuse is coming out of the Midwest. Narrow-mindedness is neither a midwestern nor a rural phenomenon.

Until psychotherapy is more widely accepted in all geographical areas, social classes, occupational and ethnic groups, it is important to insure that your confidentiality will be protected. You should have absolute control over who hears your story, when they hear it and under what circumstances. Ask your therapist to give you that guarantee. She or he is ethically committed to doing so.

6 / "I don't want some shrink telling me what to do." "I'm afraid it will completely change my personality." These kinds of concerns usually represent a fear of giving up control—a fear that is quite familiar to incest survivors. The reality is that you can always be in charge of the pace, direction, and intensity of your recovery program. And an experienced, able counselor will be able to help. You and your therapist should be working together toward your taking full charge of your life. You will still be yourself after therapy. And you will be able to take greater satisfaction in being who you are.

Beginning a program of counseling or therapy is, at best, somewhat intimidating. At worst, it can be a terrifying prospect. This is particularly so if it is your first encounter with a therapist, or if you have had negative previous experiences in therapy. You approach the situation with fears and questions. "Who is this person?" "Will I be able to trust him?" "Does she know what she's doing?" "Is he experienced in the areas I need help in?" "Will I be able to let down my guard enough to open up to her?" "Can therapy do any good at this point?" "Will he like me?" "Will she think I'm weird?" "What should I say? How much should I reveal?" "How will I know if it's doing any good?" These questions are legitimate. It is normal to have these fears, and reasonable to ask for information and reassurance. It is best to share your concerns with the therapist. The way he or she responds will give you information that will help you decide whether this is someone with whom you will be able to work. If your initial fears are dismissed as unimportant, it is less likely that the therapist will be able to adequately address your deeper concerns—or that you will be able to open up the way you need to. A later part of this chapter will offer some suggestions on what to look for in a therapist. But unless you can express your fears to your therapist—and feel that they are being listened to and taken seriously—it will be difficult to form a useful therapeutic alliance.

Important Concerns About Therapy

In addition to the anxieties faced by anyone embarking upon a counseling program, there are particular feelings that the therapeutic setting brings up for the incest survivor. It is important that the therapist and the survivor be aware of these feelings and discuss them. Not doing so can seriously hinder recovery. I will raise some of these issues, with suggestions as to why they are important and what can be done about them.

THE SETTING

Most counseling sessions take place in private, with only two people present. The door is closed and sometimes locked to eliminate the possibility of interruption. There is agreement that what goes on in the session is kept confidential. The client may even be expected to sit on a couch. For the incest survivor this may be frighteningly reminiscent of the original abusive environment. Most abuse takes place in secret. There are seldom other people present. And the perpetrator usually makes sure that secrecy is maintained. It is easy to understand how an incest survivor may feel uncomfortable in such a setting, without being consciously aware of why. How is it possible for you to be relaxed and trusting in a situation that restimulates the abuse memories? How can you face putting yourself into this situation week after week?

A counselor who has had experience with abuse issues is more likely to raise these questions. She may discuss with you possible ways of dealing with the problem. If the counselor fails to do so, you can initiate the discussion yourself. (Sometimes it's necessary to educate your therapist so that he can do the best job for you.) If the therapist shows respect for your concerns and is willing to explore ways of addressing them, you have taken the first steps toward forming a helpful therapeutic alliance. Unwillingness to do so may be evidence of a rigidity that will interfere with your progress. Recovery from the effects of incest is a recent area of therapeutic concern. Therapists must be open to putting aside preconceived notions, and be prepared to seek out solutions that work best for the survivor.

What, then, can be done about the problem of the therapeutic setting? It can be faced with flexibility and openness. Sometimes just opening awareness of the issue is enough. Recognition of a problem is the beginning of being able to solve it. If you know that you can talk about a problem whenever it arises—no matter how often it comes up—you're well on your way to getting over it. You may also want to make an agreement that if your counselor senses that you are shutting down emotionally (or appearing nervous) she will ask you what is going on. Remember that you may be unaware that it is happening. Asking your therapist to raise the issue is doubly helpful. It confronts the problem while inviting someone else to think about you.

Making some simple physical adjustments to the therapeutic setting can make a tremendous difference to the safety level. You may wish to keep the door unlocked. You might find that it feels safer to sit on a chair rather than a sofa. It can be helpful to increase the physical distance between you and the therapist until you feel comfortable. You may feel safe at particular times of the day and therefore seek to schedule your sessions during those hours.

You may want to discuss with your counselor what would allow you to feel most in charge of your sessions. You may feel safer walking around the room as you talk, instead of remaining in your seat. Or you may request reassurance (as often as you need it) that he will remain in his seat and will never touch you during a session. It is important that you and your therapist do whatever you can to allow you to get to the necessary work. Creating safety is a vital part of that process. Don't worry about your counselor taking offense at these precautions. They are no reflection on his trustworthiness; they represent an attempt to build trust.

If, after talking about the issues and making the physical changes, the one-on-one counseling setting still feels too threatening, you may want to discuss with your counselor the possibility of including another person in your sessions. You may wish to ask a trusted friend to come to one or more sessions. It may not even be necessary to actually follow through on this suggestion. It is sometimes enough just to know that you have your therapist's permission to do it. It reassures you that the therapy session doesn't *need* to be kept secret—that nothing abusive will go on. It is an option that you can exercise whenever you feel the need. If having another person actually in the room doesn't seem right for you, you can always bring someone along with you and have them remain in the waiting room or somewhere else "within shouting distance."

As you can see, there are many possibilities for altering the setting to better fit your needs. No doubt you and your therapist can come up with adjustments that work for you. (I would be happy to hear about any other creative solutions discovered by readers of this book.)

MONEY

The feeling that your counselor is "only doing it for the money, and doesn't really care" about you is a hard one to overcome. It touches on several issues for the incest survivor. It raises echoes of having had to pay for caring and affection. It doesn't matter that the current payment is monetary rather than sexual. The feeling remains that, in order to be cared about, you must pay. No one could love you for yourself alone. Doubting that your therapist genuinely cares about you leaves you open to questioning whether you can believe anything she says to you. Once again the issue becomes one of suspicion. "Can I trust caring that I have to pay for?" This creates a dilemma for both the therapist and the client, a dilemma that isn't solved by abolishing payment. Seeing therapy as "paying someone to love you" is a distortion. You aren't paying your therapist for love. You are paying for her to *think* about you. She has invested considerable time, effort, and expense in receiving training and developing the skills of a professional. It is correct that this professional commitment be compensated. The very fact that he has chosen to work in this emotionally demanding field can be seen as evidence of caring. Competent therapists display their caring by obtaining the very best training that is available, keeping abreast of current developments in their professional area, exchanging ideas and information with their colleagues, maintaining their own physical and psychological well-being, and bringing the results of their experience and their own very best thinking to bear on the issues raised by their clients.

The double-bind for the client looks this way: If the therapist charges for her services, then she doesn't really care about the client. If, on the other hand, she lowers or waives the fee, she won't provide the same quality of care that would be given to someone paying full fee. That is the old theory of "You get what you pay for." Once again, the survivor feels that he is in a no-win situation.

The solution to this problem is simple—communication. Cost of care is not the best gauge of its quality. Individual psychotherapy is offered on a "fee for service" basis. That is, you have a contract with your therapist that for an agreed upon fee she will provide you with psychological counseling. This fee should be negotiated at the onset of the course of treatment. It should be agreeable to both client and therapist. Therapy should not begin until both parties are comfortable with the financial arrangement. If you can't come to a mutually satisfactory agreement, it may be necessary to find another therapist. If either party proposes to change the financial arrangement, ample time should be given to discussion of the reasons for the change and exploration of alternatives. Once this financial situation has been agreed upon, it is best to accept it and adhere to it responsibly, so that you can devote your attention to the real business at hand—your recovery.

POWER

By definition, the therapist-client relationship is unequal. By entering into a course of therapy, you are putting yourself in the unusual situation of having to open up to a relative stranger. You are expected to share intimate details of your life, thoughts and feelings with someone who is *not* expected to share his personal life with you at all.

In other words, you are to *trust* your story to someone you barely know—someone in authority. This is not easy for anyone to do. For an incest survivor, it is tremendously difficult. You have had the experience of someone in authority abusing that trust in a damaging way. You were abused by someone who was known to you—someone who was supposed to love and protect you. If someone that close to you could violate a position of trust, what can you possibly expect of a virtual stranger? Power, control, and abuse have been powerfully linked by your incest experience. It is understandable that you would be wary of letting down your guard against those in power.

The way to handle the question of power is to *take your time*. Move very slowly, step by step, raising your fears and suspicions whenever they arise. Talk about it! If you feel that your therapist is being manipulative, tell him. If you think that he is pushing you in ways that don't make sense for you, let him know it. If you feel weak or childlike in his presence, it is important to talk about it. Your therapist isn't a mind reader. You can't expect him to guess what you are feeling. The more you talk about your feelings, the more you learn that it is OK to do so. A good therapist remains open to his client's interpretations of the therapeutic relationship. If your counselor isn't prepared to accept the possibility that he may have made a mistake, that he may be unconsciously manipulating or controlling the situation, that his ideas may not be appropriate for a particular client, then you probably don't have the right therapist for you. But before you decide that it isn't working, you must communicate your feelings.

Counseling is a relationship. There are two people involved. Don't assume at the first sign of disagreement that the relationship has fallen apart. Learning that two people, acting in good faith, can overcome disagreements and build trust is an important lesson. And it is a lesson that is learned slowly.

A good driver enters a superhighway cautiously, first checking for obvious dangers, then moving into the slow lane. As he becomes familiar with the road, he judges the flow of traffic before picking up speed. He signals before moving into a faster lane. Only the most reckless of drivers would charge full-throttle across three lanes of traffic without checking out the dangers. In the same way, the best way to build trust is to proceed carefully and patiently. Don't move any faster than makes sense for you. If you are not comfortable with the direction or speed of the therapy, slow down and read the signs or ask for directions. In that way, you learn the route. It becomes yours. You understand the components of trust and can create trusting relationships with other people.

Instead of looking at your counselor as someone who is telling you how to run your life (a sort of psychological back-seat driver), you can view him as an expert consultant: someone who may have traveled this route before, someone who knows how to read the road map, someone who is there for the times that you feel lost. No doubt you both will make mistakes, take some wrong turns. But it's good to have someone around to help you figure out how to get back onto the highway.

For a relationship to be mutually satisfying there has to be reciprocity. Both parties must feel that they are getting something from the interaction. But the exchange doesn't have to be exact. If each of us gives the other ten dollars, not much has happened. We might just as well have kept our own money. But if you give me a gift and I perform a service for you, we each have acquired something new. And we have each offered something to the other—that is reciprocity. By the same token, it is not appropriate for a counselor to use the therapy session to work on her own personal issues. The reciprocity is of a different order. It is a professional relationship, not an interaction of friends or lovers. If treated responsibly, with mutual respect for the nature of therapy (and its boundaries and limitations), your relationship with your counselor can be profoundly important and immensely helpful.

DIRECT EXPERIENCE

You may wonder whether somebody who hasn't been abused can really understand what you're going through. For a therapist to be helpful, does she have to be an incest survivor? Or, on the other hand, can someone who was sexually molested ever develop enough distance from the abuse to offer a realistic perspective on your problems? There isn't one absolutely correct answer to these questions. Advantages and disadvantages need to be weighted—and viewed in light of your particular situation.

I have heard people insist that it is necessary to be a survivor of abuse in order to work effectively with other survivors. I think that may be a somewhat misleading perspective. But, like most heartfelt opinions, it contains an element of truth. The accurate part, of course, is that the best way to *know* about anything is to experience it yourself. Only another survivor of abuse can truly claim to know what it is like to be in that situation. Even if the specifics of the abuse were different (and they do vary tremendously) the effects are remarkably similar. The importance of communication and interaction with other incest survivors cannot be stressed enough. But does this mean that your therapist needs to be an abuse survivor? I don't believe that it does. While it is true that no one who hasn't had a burst appendix can know what it feels like, few people would insist that their surgeon display his appendectomy scar before performing the operation. A therapist doesn't need to have experienced a problem in order to treat it. What she does need to do is *learn* about the issues involved. It is vital that she come to understand as much as possible about incest issues, including (and nothing is more important than this) the subjective effects of sexual abuse on the victim. (Incestuous sexual abuse is more than a physical assault. Therapy must explore the way you feel about yourself and what happened to you.) Some information about incest can be obtained from courses, workshops, and reading. The most important part, however, can only be learned from incest survivors. You are the expert. You must be listened to. You must be encouraged to talk—to tell your story over and over again. And the therapist must listen very carefully—with an open mind and with complete respect. Through this process, the counselor can learn how to best be helpful to you.

Feelings of hopelessness lurk behind assertions that only other survivors can provide adequate counseling. They sound very much like, "No one can really understand me." Implied in these statements is, "I'm so flawed that only someone else who is equally messed up can begin to understand what I'm going through." They reinforce the survivor's sense of isolation. Building an alliance with a therapist who is not a survivor can be a powerful contradiction to those feelings of hopelessness and isolation.

There are also both advantages and pitfalls to having a counselor who *is* an incest survivor. Empathy and understanding that grow out of direct experience are precious assets. You may feel that you are being understood for the first time in your life. Nothing is more valuable than that feeling; it is important that you experience it, either with your counselor or with other survivors. However, one of the potential problems of working with a therapist who is also an abuse survivor is the blurring of boundaries. Although there are similarities of experiences and effects, it cannot be assumed that all incest survivors are alike. People's life experiences vary greatly. Despite the similarities, there is great variety in the effects of and responses to childhood sexual abuse. There is a danger that a counselor who is also a survivor will identify too closely with your story, assuming that it is the same as her own—assuming that she knows what you are feeling without checking out those assumptions. This is a form of "mind reading" that is seldom helpful to the client. It is important that a therapist who is also a survivor has worked extensively on her own abuse history, so that she can bring perspective and objectivity to the therapy in addition to the empathy. If the therapist hasn't worked through enough of her own incest issues, it will be impossible for her to provide you with the help you need. She will bring her own issues into the therapy (whether or not they are *yours*), thus leading you in inappropriate directions. Or she will overidentify with your issues, creating a situation where there are two clients in the same room and no therapist. You will find yourself in the unhappy situation of needing to counsel your therapist. While this can be an interesting experience, it is not what you came there to do.

Whether or not your therapist is an incest survivor, she must be careful not to impose onto the therapy a pace or focus that is not right for you. The counselor must remain aware that you are not "just an incest victim." You are a human being, possessing a wide range of skills, attributes, feelings, and experiences. It would be a serious mistake to look at anything less than the whole person. There will be times when you will wish to work on topics that are unrelated to the abuse. This is not only appropriate, it is essential. Incest is not *who you are*. It is something that *happened to you*. Don't feel pushed to spend every minute of therapy working on the abuse. Your counselor must see you as a whole person, and encourage you to view yourself in the same way.

I believe that there are advantages and difficulties with any therapeutic situation; none is perfect. It is less important that you get a therapist who is (or isn't) an incest survivor than that you get the best available care. Be aware of the qualities that are important to you in a therapist, and keep searching until you find a satisfying counseling situation.

GENDER

"Should I see a male or female therapist?" There are no hard and fast rules here. When therapists first began to recognize issues of sexual abuse, it was assumed that all perpetrators were male and all victims, female. Because of this mistaken assumption, many counselors concluded that an incest survivor could only feel safe with a female therapist. Even when male survivors began to seek help, the counseling profession was slow to accept the reality of their situation. Recognition of the existence of female perpetrators was even longer in coming.

There are many factors which will influence the choice of whether to seek a male or female therapist. For some, the question of gender is simply not an issue. You may not care whether your counselor is male or female, but just want to find the best person for the job. On the other hand, you may "just feel more comfortable" with a woman or a man. There is nothing wrong with trusting your feelings on the matter. While it is possible to treat those feelings of discomfort as "clinical issues" to be worked out in therapy, you may not be ready to do that. Entering therapy is sufficiently anxiety provoking. If choosing either a male or female therapist makes you feel more comfortable, by all means do so. You can always work on your feelings about men or women in other ways—or choose to work with a different therapist at some other time.

Not everyone has the luxury of a wide choice. You may be in an area where there are very few therapists, or only one who has any experience in working with abuse survivors. You may have to go with the "only show in town." Or the best choice may be someone of the "wrong" gender. You may even find that there is no counselor with relevant experience in your area. Don't despair. A few years ago none of us knew anything about these issues. Our knowledge is increasing rapidly. Find yourself a smart, caring, dedicated professional and encourage him to learn what he needs to know in order to be effective as your therapist.

All other things being equal, you will feel safer choosing a therapist who does not remind you of the perpetrator. This would suggest that it might be better to begin with a therapist of a different gender than that of the person who abused you. But this is simply a suggested guideline, not a rule. And gender is not the only attribute or quality that might remind you of the perpetrator. Other aspects of appearance, such as voice quality, speech mannerisms, gesture, style of clothing, and age, can evoke powerful memories. If you feel comfortable with the individual—if he is intelligent, insightful, well-trained, responsive, and encouraging—gender doesn't matter. You have found yourself a valuable resource.

MODALITY

"What type of individual therapy would be best for me?" This is a complicated question. There are many models of counseling and psychotherapy, reflecting different ways of interpreting human behavior. Although some basic knowledge of counseling theory and methods can be helpful, it won't be possible for you to do a thorough exploration of all the schools of psychological thought.

Like recovery itself, psychotherapy is a house with many doors. How you enter the house tends to be less important than the fact of getting inside. Some doors may be more convenient than others, some may be more difficult to open; others may be too small to get through or too heavy to move. My general opinion is that although some types of therapy may be better suited to your purposes than others, it is the choice of therapist that is more important. If he is competent, insightful, flexible, and encouraging, you have found someone who will be effective in whatever modality he has chosen. A rigid, controlling, unimaginative person will be a bad therapist no matter what training he has received.

Find someone you feel good about and then ask him to tell you his theoretical orientation. You don't have to be an expert yourself. When you interview prospective counselors, just ask them what kind of therapy they practice. Ask them what they see as the main issues involved in working with survivors of sexual abuse. Ask them how they go about setting up a program of counseling. How would they work with you? Put the questions in your own words. If you don't understand the answers, ask for clarification. Therapy should lead to understanding, not further confusion. It isn't necessary to hide behind clinical jargon. If they try to do so, they either don't know what they are talking about or don't know how to communicate directly. Neither makes for good therapy. Ask as many questions as you have to. Keep on asking until you receive answers that are satisfactory. Don't be afraid that you are wasting their time. Few decisions are more important than this. Give your choice of a therapist at least the same care that you would give to selecting a new house or car.

MISUSE OF THERAPY

The fact that there are many different helpful therapeutic styles does *not* mean that all therapies are helpful. Not everything that is called therapy is therapeutic—some so-called therapeutic practices are, at best, counterproductive for the incest survivor. At worst, they can be abusive. Some of the most glaring examples of the misuse of therapy follow. Watch out for them and avoid them, no matter how anyone attempts to justify them:

1 / Sex. There is *never* a legitimate reason for a therapist to have sex with a client. It is always abusive. It is always harmful to the client. For a therapist to engage in sexual interaction with an incest survivor is an inexcusable violation of a position of trust. Unscrupulous individuals have attempted to justify sex between therapist and client. They have called it by various euphemisms, such as "body work." They have attempted to legitimize it by saying that it is a way to "get at feelings," to "open up" the client, or even to "teach" the client "how to achieve intimacy." None of that is true; it is lies or self-deception. Sex between therapist and client is predatory. It is a replaying of the original abuse, taking advantage of the survivor's vulnerability to serve the personal ends of the therapist. It is natural to want to please your therapist. It can be flattering to feel that your therapist finds you attractive. It is all right to have sexual feelings for your therapist. It's a normal part of the therapeutic process, often referred to as *transference*. *Acting* on these feelings destroys the safety of the therapeutic alliance. If a counselor suggests or condones engaging in any form of sexual activity with you, leave immediately. You are being abused, and this time you have the opportunity to do something about it.

2 / Re-creating the abuse. As an incest survivor, you must never be revictimized. It does not matter whether the victimization is actual or symbolic, it is harmful. You have already spent far too much time in that position. Any role-playing, psychodrama, guided fantasy, or other technique that simulates the original abusive situation *with you in the role of victim* will be frightening and destructive to your recovery. This does not mean that role-playing or psychodrama can't be extremely useful techniques. They are therapeutic tools. Like any tools, if they are used correctly and appropriately, by someone who knows how to employ them, they can do a good job. But their proper use requires training and awareness of the requirements of the task at hand. For example, it can be very helpful to role-play a situation where you stand up to the abuser and take charge of the situation. A psychodrama that portrays how things *should* have been for you as a child can bring up powerful emotions and insights. You may wish to rehearse confronting your perpetrator. You can usefully engage in fantasy and imagery of what it would be like to be fully powerful and self-confident. These, and any number of other techniques, can be extremely useful. What they have in common is that they move you into a position of taking charge. Rather than re-creating the weakness, they focus on your strengths. Instead of forcing you back into the role of victim, they show you a way out of it. You are correct to resist any attempt to rob yourself of power by re-creating the victimization.

3 / Inappropriate touch. When you were abused you were robbed of physical control. Part of your recovery process demands that you be in *complete* charge of your body. You have the absolute right to decide who can touch you, and to set limits on when and how you are touched. You can always say no. This right extends to hugs, pats on the shoulder, and even handshakes. Although hugs and other physical contact can be reassuring, comforting, and healing, they can also be extremely frightening to an abuse survivor. No one should be able to touch you without your permission, no matter how well-intentioned they are. Beware of any therapy that *requires* you to be touched. The key to appropriate touching is permission. Do not be coerced or manipulated into doing anything that isn't right for you. If you don't want to be touched, then it isn't right to touch you. If you're not sure you want to be touched, it is probably best to wait. You can always do it later; you can't *un*do it. You don't have to acquiesce to please anyone else. You don't even have to explain your reasons. Your body is yours. That is enough. If your therapist can't accept that, he shouldn't be working with incest survivors.

4 / Authoritarianism. You've had enough of people telling you what to do. A great deal of harm was done to you by people who insisted that they knew what was best for you. Recovery means being in ultimate charge of your life. A program that is imposed from outside, by someone who claims to have all the answers, may be very tempting. "How nice it would be to give up control and let someone else make all the decisions." But it doesn't work. Beware of any counselor who tries to take over your life. Even if he has the best intentions, it just isn't helpful. You need autonomy over your life. A good therapist will help you to explore options. After examining possibilities with you, she will encourage you to be in charge of making your own decisions.

5 / Unresponsiveness. There are some therapists who provide virtually no feedback to their clients. The client is left to imagine what the therapist is thinking, projecting his own ideas onto the counselor. Direct questions are turned back to the questioner unanswered. While this style of therapy may be useful for some people, it isn't very helpful for incest survivors. You have lived much of your life in that kind of isolation—thrown back on your own resources, guessing at reality. What you are looking for is contact: communication and understanding. When an incest survivor asks a question it should be respected as a legitimate question deserving of a response. To do less than that leaves the survivor feeling isolated and crazy. A therapist can't have all the answers, but he should be able to help you find some of them. You need to question and test reality with someone who is open to exploring the world *with* you, without doing it *for* you or leaving you to do it alone. When you interview therapists, make sure they respond like real people.

6 / Criticism and judgment. You are an expert at self-criticism and negative self-judgments. You don't need to pay someone else to do it for you. People who are committed to only one point of view can be critical of any perspective that differs from their own. Whether the perspective is religious, political, academic or therapeutic, it indicates single-mindedness and rigidity. It is impossible to relax and open up to someone prone to constant judgments and criticism. Look for a therapist who, regardless of his personal beliefs, is open to a range of possibilities. That will be invaluable in helping you to overcome your own rigidities and any tendencies you might have toward "black-or-white" thinking.

Finding a Therapist

Once you have decided to see a therapist, how do you go about finding one? How do you know whether the person you've found is competent, professional, and knowledgeable? And how do you determine whether this person is the right counselor for you? These are important questions. You will be entering into an intimate, trusting relationship with your therapist, and you want it to be a good one. This isn't something that can be decided by closing your eyes and picking a name out of the Yellow Pages. It's important to go into your search for a therapist with your eyes wide open, using your best judgment, and availing yourself of all possible resources. The following suggestions may be helpful.

1 / If you have been in therapy in the past, think about what that experience was like for you. What was difficult about your relationship with the therapist? What did you find useful? What were the problems? Was your counselor patient, caring, reassuring, open, flexible, and accepting? Is she someone to whom you would want to return? If so—and if she is still available—you might wish to reenter therapy with this counselor. The advantage of this option is that the two of you have already established a history and a working relationship. If you don't wish to return, it would be useful to figure out why you don't. If you know what you want in a therapeutic relationship, it is far more likely that you can find one that meets your needs. If you like and trust your old therapist, but he is unavailable for resuming therapy, you may be able to ask him for suggestions and advice on finding someone else. If your former counselor is inexperienced in treating the effects of sexual abuse, he may wish to refer you to someone who has that expertise. This is not rejection, but professional responsibility. You wouldn't bring your refrigerator to someone who had only worked on telephones, no matter how good he was at fixing your phone. Make sure you let your old counselor know what you are looking for—and why—and be sure to ask why he has recommended these particular people.

2 / Talk to trusted friends, family members, and business associates. Ask them about their experiences in counseling and therapy. This can be particularly helpful if you have never been in therapy. You may discover that more people you know have been in therapy than you would have thought. If you have friends who are therapists, ask them for recommendations—and ask them why they have suggested these particular people. Once you have gathered some suggestions, your search isn't over. Not all therapeutic settings are right for everyone. Neither are all therapists. A counselor who is just the right match for your best friend may be quite wrong for you. Ultimately, you will have to trust your own judgment.

3 / Contact local agencies and organizations that deal with sexual abuse issues. Ask for recommendations of counselors who have experience with incest survivors. Even if the agency is located at some distance from where you live, it may be aware of resources in your area.

Among these important resources are women's centers and rape crisis centers. Yes, these can even be resources for a man! Since women have been at the forefront of dealing with sexual abuse issues, a women's center will most likely be able to help steer you toward a compatible counselor. Don't worry about being refused assistance because you're male. The issue is abuse, not gender, and the staff of most women's centers know that.

In addition to women's centers, many district attorney's offices have victim witness assistance programs or sexual abuse units. The workers in these units can furnish information and referrals. There are also local government agencies—departments of social services, child protective units, and the like—that have referral sources. Some religious and educational organizations have resources for helping survivors of abuse. Finally, you may be able to obtain referrals from the local chapters of professional organizations, such as the National Association of Social Workers, American Psychological Association, American Psychiatric Association, and American Mental Health Counselors Association.

4 / Contact national, regional, and local organizations established to support and educate people about incest and other sexual abuse. Organizations—such as VOICES in Action, Inc.; PLEA; Incest Resources; and Incest Survivors' Information Exchange—will often have local chapters or contact persons in your area. They may also have referral lists of local counselors who have indicated experience or interest in working with survivors. At the end of this book there is a resource list of many of these organizations. Remember that inclusion on a referral list does not automatically guarantee quality of service.

5 / Think about what you need in a therapist. What expertise is important to you? What personality traits? Examine your wildest hopes as well as your rational expectations. Then make a list of requirements. Decide which items on your list are most important to you—which ones are essential and which would simply be nice to find. If you are aware of your expectations and preconceptions, you are less likely to be disappointed.

6 / Make up a list of questions to ask the therapist in your initial interview. Don't be afraid to show up with an extensive list. Write them down so you don't leave any out. The questions on your list can range from practical details (What are your fees? Do you accept medical insurance? Do you have evening or weekend hours? What is your policy on cancellation of sessions?), to information about the therapist (What is your theoretical orientation? How long have you been a counselor? What is your training? What is your experience with incest? Do you receive supervision in this area?), to details about your proposed therapy (How long do you anticipate that I will be in therapy with you? What form will that therapy take? Will you give me specific feedback about my progress?), to other crucial issues (Can you assure me of complete confidentiality? Do you think sex between therapist and client is ever beneficial? [If you get any answer other than no, this is not the right therapist for you.] How do you feel about crying, raging, etc.?).

A responsible therapist will be happy to answer any questions you have. If she does not wish to answer a question, the counselor should, without defensiveness, explain to you why she believes that the question is inappropriate. If the therapist is unwilling to provide you with the information you need, find one who will.

7 / Shop around. Selecting a therapist is an important decision. Don't settle on the first person you find. Talk on the telephone with several counselors, and set up interviews with those who sound best to you. If you need to schedule a second interview with one or more therapists in order to decide, do so. If none of those you've interviewed is satisfactory, keep looking. Although this may be more expensive initially, it is a wise investment in your recovery. Don't let embarrassment keep you from shopping around. A responsible therapist will want to help you find the best person for the job. Take the time to do it right.

8 / Trust your impressions. If something feels wrong about the "fit" between you and a counselor, that can be sufficient reason for hesitating to select that person. You may need more information. You may be picking up on something that requires further exploration. You don't have to be able to explain your reasons—they don't need to be rational. If you feel unsafe with this person, it may be that her voice quality reminds you of your mother's or he wears the same aftershave as your father. Whatever the reason—no matter how nice the person really is—if you feel unsafe, it will be harder for you to open up. Raise the issue. A good counselor will not feel threatened by your honesty, but will be willing to discuss your hesitations and reservations. Although not an insurmountable problem—it can even be an opportunity—it is not necessary for you to take on every challenge. You have the option of staying with this therapist and working out whatever is eliciting those negative feelings, or you can find another therapist—one who feels more compatible. However you ultimately resolve the question, it must be addressed openly.

9 / Come to a decision. Although shopping around is important, it is also important to get on with the business of recovery. Beware of getting so involved in the process of finding the "ideal therapist" that you never begin the work that you need to do. Don't let perfectionism get in your way. Just as you have to accept that it is OK for you to make mistakes, you will need to understand that your therapist is human. No doubt you will both make mistakes. What is important is not perfection, but a mutual commitment to figuring out what went wrong, and how to solve the problem. If you find someone who is smart and caring, patient and accepting, skilled and flexible, stop searching. You have found the "perfect" therapist.

17

The Group

I used to think that I had to talk all the time in order to be heard, but I can be quiet and hear my story from the other people in the group. —A MALE SURVIVOR

"It was hard enough to tell *you* about my father. I could never talk in front of a whole group!" The idea of sharing personal information with a bunch of strangers is intimidating to most people. This is especially true for incest survivors. You are not alone if you feel terrified at the prospect of joining an incest survivors' recovery group. You've lived for years under a burden of shame, guilt, and denial that has kept you silent about the abuse. You've been afraid of the consequences of admitting that you have suffered sexual molestation. You have felt that disclosure of your history would lead to humiliation, disapproval, punishment, and further isolation. You've avoided the subject because talking about it brings up pain and sadness. If it's this hard to deal with your own story, how on earth could you stand listening to a roomful of other men sharing similar histories? It would be too immediate—too painful—too real. And where will it end? It has taken great strength and courage to finally admit the incest to one person. Even promises of confidentiality aren't very reassuring. So it's understandable that you recoil at the thought of taking this process further—making it "public knowledge." You wonder how anyone who cares about you could even suggest the possibility of an incest survivors' group. You may wonder whether you're ready for such an emotionally charged experience—whether you'll ever be ready.

Group participation is not a substitute for one-to-one counseling, but another aspect of the recovery process. When used in conjunction with individual therapy, it can be a powerful means of moving you toward your goal of taking charge of your life.

In this chapter, I will discuss the different types of groups and will address questions of how to decide what kind of group is right for you, how to find a group, and how to know whether you're ready for the group.

As discussed in Chapter 13, the first step in recovery is to tell someone. Telling your story to a supportive, encouraging person establishes the basis of a trusting relationship. Beginning such an interaction, however tentatively, is an act of healing—in the best sense of the word it creates a therapeutic relationship. When you undertake this trusting relationship with a competent, caring professional counselor, it becomes the foundation for forming other relationships. When you learn that you can trust someone, and not have your vulnerability abused, it opens the possibility of establishing important ties with other people. As your relationship with your therapist deepens and strengthens, he should encourage you to widen your circle of trust and intimacy. And, as you feel stronger and more positive about yourself, you will be more willing and better able to do so. Each time you tell someone about the incest—and every time that information is respected—it becomes a bit easier to accept that you are welcome in the world. Participation in an adult incest survivors' recovery group is an important way to experience that welcome.

Why Join a Group?

It is impossible to overstress the benefits of being able to share your feelings and experiences with other incest survivors. There is no more powerful contradiction to isolation than telling your story to people who:

- Can listen to what you're saying (and are even *eager* to hear it)
- Believe you
- *Know* that you're telling the truth about the abuse and its effects, *because they have had similar experiences*

Their histories don't have to be exactly the same as yours. It isn't really important whether the perpetrator was male or female, blood relative or not, one or more persons. The age of the survivors at the time of the incidents, the frequency and the intensity of the abuse make little difference. I have found no clinical justification for ranking the severity of different types of sexual child abuse. The similarities of the effects and feelings are important, not the specific details of the abuse. I stress this point because I have found that survivors are able to grab onto any excuse for feeling like they don't belong in the group. They can feel isolated because of being the oldest/youngest, most/least successful, richest/poorest, best/least educated; having been older/younger at the time of the abuse; having no specific abuse memories/remembering it in great detail; having been molested by a close/ distant/nonrelative; having had no/little/much violence attached to the abuse; having experienced "only" a single incident/prolonged abuse; having been abused by a single/several perpetrators; having enjoyed/ hated the abuse. These are all minor distinctions. What is important is that you not let the differences cause you to lose sight of the enormous similarities. Assume that you belong; don't yield to the pull to isolate yourself from potential allies.

As you tell your story and listen to others sharing theirs, you begin to realize that you are not alone. The feelings you've carried with you for so many years—the numbing, the isolation, and the failures—are not evidence that you are a sick or evil person. They are the results of your having undergone a terribly traumatic experience—one which would deeply affect any normal person. If the survivor of a shipwreck can do nothing more than cling to a floating piece of debris, who would blame him for not swimming to shore? It is normal behavior to do whatever you can to survive. Meeting other worthwhile, lovable people who, like you, have spent a great deal of time clinging to flimsy supports, can give you significant perspective on your own situation. It can also provide glimpses of hope. "If they deserve better—if they are able to make changes and take better charge of their lives, maybe there is hope for me." It may be for these reasons that the men in my incest recovery groups so actively support one another. It becomes very important to each group member that the other men in the group successfully attain their goals. Each time someone takes more charge of his life, it underscores the reality of recovery for everyone. Therefore, it is no wonder that I have witnessed men in my groups actually standing up and cheering one another's successes.

The group also provides a safe haven. It is a place where you don't have to explain why you feel the way you do, or why you've done the things you have. The group setting allows you to experience feeling connnected to other people without opening yourself to the risk of being abused. It lets you explore your feelings together with others who are doing the same thing. It allows you to look at your similarities to and differences from the other people in the group in a nonjudgmental context. Group participation is an important means of finding out who you really are and what you can become.

Even though a group is a *safe* place to be, it is seldom *comfortable*. You've spent a good deal of time and energy trying to avoid reminders of the past. You have steered clear of anything that elicits memories of your incest experience because of the painful feelings that such recall evokes. "Why then," you may wonder, "would I ever want to look for more pain? I'd have to be nuts to join an incest survivors' group. Not only would I be feeling my own pain, I'd be forced to listen to other people's stories as well. I don't know if I can take that." No, the group is not a comfortable situation. And no reasonable person would choose to spend his time dredging up painful memories in a roomful of other people who are doing the same thing—unless there was a powerfully compelling reason to do so. There are lots of other, more pleasant ways to occupy your life. If this were all you had to look forward to, you would indeed be crazy to undertake a group. But there is lots more to the group than painful emotions. The purpose of bringing up the feelings is not to learn to live with them, it is *to get through them*. It doesn't do any good to avoid or ignore the feelings. You know that. You've tried it, and you continued to feel bad.

The group doesn't *cause* the distressing feelings; it creates a safety that *allows* them to be felt. Once the pain is felt in a nonabusive atmosphere, it can be examined, understood, put into perspective, and diminished. There will be times during the course of the group when you will feel anxiety, fear, confusion, and anger. There will also be periods of calm, elation, excitement, and even joy. Although any of these conditions may be helpful, none is the ultimate purpose of the group. The group uses the feelings, both positive and negative, to lead to greater awareness. This awareness, in turn, can lead to changes of thinking, responding, and behaving. The ultimate goal is to achieve a more satisfying life. To the extent that it leads toward realization of that goal, you are rewarded for the discomfort of group membership. Being a member of a recovery group for incest survivors can be of inestimable value. The connections made by group members frequently prove to be among the most meaningful of their lives. They may be intense, volatile, and disturbing. They will sometimes be confusing. At times you will want more and at other times you'll wish you have never taken this on. Some group members have said, "I have to force myself to show up every week." "I sometimes think I'll just run out the door and never come back. But I keep coming back week after week because I know that I need to be here." Group participation will always be important, but rarely comfortable. That is why it is necessary to make—and continually remind yourself of—the distinction between "comfort" and "safety." The safety of the group—*genuine, uncomfortable safety*—provides what you need to do the work of recovery. "Discomfort" is temporary. Like "survival," it is a stage in an ongoing process. Eventually, the recovery process leads you to relationships that are both safe *and* comfortable.

Kinds of Groups   There are many types of groups, ranging from loose, informal, "drop-in" type gatherings that are open to anyone, to highly structured therapy groups that require a long-term commitment. Groups can be led by a professional therapist or by an incest survivor without formal training, or they may be "leaderless." The stated purpose of a group may be therapy, support, education, or some combination of the three. They may be time-limited or ongoing. Group membership may be fixed at a certain number of people or open-ended. The population can remain relatively stable over time or change from week to week. A group may focus only on incest or address more general life issues. The form of the group can vary as much as the content. In other words, there are infinite possibilities for a group experience. The type that you choose will depend on your needs, preferences, and the availability of services in your area. Some localities have developed virtually no services for incest survivors. Others are relatively rich in resources. If there are no groups currently available near you, all is not lost. There is the possibility of meeting some of your needs within the context of a general issues group, or of getting an incest survivors' group started yourself. Before you attempt that you may be able to attend workshops and conferences for incest survivors somewhere else in the country.

A word of caution: I urge you to think seriously before starting a group of your own. Many incest survivors are chronic caretakers. They put everyone else's needs ahead of their own. The result of this behavior is that the only one of their needs that ever gets met is their need to take care of other people. If you are this kind of person, then starting your own group is a setup. Once again, you will find yourself giving what you hope to receive, and satisfying everyone but yourself. Make sure that you are not sacrificing yourself to a pattern of caretaking.

My general recommendation would be first to establish a solid relationship with an individual counselor. With her help, explore the resources in your area. If a group exists, make sure that the group leader spends enough time with you to answer your questions *fully* before you join the group. In addition, be certain that your individual therapist has spoken with the group leader. The more open their communication, the better it is for your recovery.

There are advantages and problems with any type of therapy, individual or group. In the following paragraphs, I'll discuss some types of groups—what to look for, and what to watch out for. (See

Focus later in the chapter for the rules established in my recovery groups.)

PEER OR SELF-HELP SUPPORT GROUPS

These are groups set up by and for adult incest survivors. Leadership of these groups is usually informal. There may be a designated leader or leadership may rotate among group members from meeting to meeting or at specific intervals. A group may even consider itself "leaderless." They can meet weekly, biweekly, monthly, or sporadically. The purposes of such groups can include personal support of their members, education of themselves and the larger community, and advocacy for social and political recognition of the needs of incest survivors. Format of the meetings also varies according to what the group wishes to accomplish. Meetings may involve discussion of specific topics (relationships, sexuality, violence, fear of success, disclosure, confrontation), or guest speakers might be invited to address the group. Group members may have the opportunity to share their own stories. The meetings can follow a specific format or be quite loose and open-ended. Some of these support groups may be part of a specific recovery program, such as Incest Survivors Anonymous. In many parts of the country there are peer support groups for survivors formed on the model recommended by VOICES in Action (see resource list at the end of the book). Some support groups limit their activities to group meetings; others sponsor social gatherings, educational and fund-raising events and encourage group members to form friendships that extend beyond the meetings.

Fees for group membership are usually quite nominal, and many are free of charge. Since rules for membership vary widely from group to group, it is important that you get the information you need before joining one. At the very least, make certain that your confidentiality and your personal boundaries (both physical and emotional) will be respected by the other group members.

Peer support groups can be tremendously helpful to incest survivors. In addition to cutting through the isolation felt by most survivors, these groups contradict a common self-image—that incest survivors are flawed, helpless people who can't function on their own. Thus, the self-help group provides a means for taking active charge of your own recovery. The peer support group can also be a valuable supplement to your individual (and even your group) therapy. There is great advantage to be derived from standing up to your ingrained feelings of powerlessness and inadequacy by joining with other incest survivors in forming peer support groups.

Although there are many advantages to self-help groups, there are also some problems that you should be aware of and try to avoid. I believe that it is very helpful for a group to have a designated leader, convener or facilitator. This is someone whose responsibility is to think about the group as a whole. This person should be aware of the "flow" of the meeting: whether people are getting enough group attention (so the meeting isn't dominated by more assertive individuals while less outgoing members get lost); whether anyone appears to be in crisis; that the rules of the group are adhered to; and that the meeting begins and ends at the agreed-upon time. Someone should also be thinking about the continuity of the group from meeting to meeting. These are very important functions, which can be invested in a single person for a period of time, or can be shared by group members on a rotating basis. However it is done, having someone think about the overall welfare of the group can be critical to its success.

Another potential pitfall for peer groups is the immediacy of the incest experience for all participants. When heavy emotions come up—and they often do—it is important to have someone who is not going to get hooked by them. If everyone in the group becomes overwhelmed and sinks into despair, you end up with a roomful of victims instead of a gathering of survivors. Someone with a different life experience may be able to recognize more quickly the signs of becoming overwhelmed and provide the group with a perspective that keeps it from getting stuck in feelings. In the absence of such perspective, the group must be aware of the possibility of "shutdown," and figure out strategies for dealing with it. If this is not done, the group will probably not survive. Dealing with this issue enables the members to build a truly solid and effective support group.

Another problem for self-help groups is the screening of new members. Not everyone is able or ready to function as a responsible group member. For some survivors, the effects of the abuse include acting in antisocial ways. A survivor may be violent, verbally abusive, hypercritical, or otherwise prone to inappropriate behavior. An individual's neediness may be so extreme that he or she monopolizes the meetings, not allowing anyone else to receive group attention. It is commendable to want to insure that no one is excluded from group membership. Incest survivors know what it is like to be isolated in their pain, kept from getting the help they need. They don't want to put anyone else in that position. However, the inclusion of a deeply troubled individual can destroy a group. The enormity of his neediness can so drain the resources of the other group members that they are unable to derive any benefit from the group. An individual who is that needy will not get enough from the group to be of any real help to him. He isn't ready to function as a group member. He will eventually move on, feeling that this is another example of people failing to meet his needs. In the process, he may destroy or severely damage the group. He needs extensive individual therapy before he has enough available attention to enable him to be responsive to the needs of others.

Since few peer support groups have adequate resources for pre-screening potential members, it is helpful to be aware of the ever-present possibility that the group will be faced with such a situation. Although this problem is certainly not unknown in more structured therapy groups, an experienced counselor will have evolved a pre-screening procedure that will help to lessen the possibility of including inappropriate individuals in a group. He will also have experience in handling individuals who behave inappropriately in group settings.

Finally, we must look at the issue of control. We have mentioned that control is an important theme for incest survivors. A leaderless, unstructured situation can be terribly frightening to them. Some may deal with the fear by shutting down, numbing out, or leaving. Others will attempt to diminish their anxiety by taking control of the meeting. Taking control in this manner reduces their anxiety level, but it also prevents them from getting much real benefit from the group. It keeps the other group members at a distance. By taking over the group, members aren't forced to confront the very issues and feelings that brought them to join. This behavior can lead to power struggles and resentments within the group. Although not insurmountable, power struggles can be devastating to the survival of peer support groups that have no mechanism for dealing with them.

Some of these problems can be solved by good planning. Others are simply risks that are inherent in the nature of self-help groups. Awareness of these potential problems can help you respond more effectively should they arise. No situation is risk-free, and the problems I have raised are certainly not sufficient reason to keep you from participating in this type of group. Instead, keeping these cautions in mind, I encourage you to explore peer support groups as an important resource for your recovery.

GENERAL ISSUES GROUPS

This type of therapy group is usually long-term and ongoing. Membership may be all male, all female, or a mix of both sexes. Upon joining, group members are usually asked to make a commitment to remaining in the group for a significant period of time. As you might

expect, a general issues group can address any subject that is of interest to its members, including the dynamics of interaction within the
group. Depending on the group leader's philosophy, he will either
make sure that the group members keep their interaction focused on
relevant issues and that each person receives his or her share of attention; or he will not interfere, allowing the group members to establish
their own rules and problem-solving strategies.

One strong advantage to general issues groups is that they are
widely available. There are few cities and towns of any size that don't
have a therapist who leads groups. Many hospitals and clinics have
general issues groups. So do some schools, religious organizations,
and community centers. Some of these are quite inexpensive. In the
absence of specific incest survivor groups, you may wish to take advantage of existing resources and see whether you can tailor them to
meet your needs.

Another advantage is that, in a general issues group, you are not
forced to limit yourself to working on incest-related issues. This can
keep you from feeling as though all you are is an incest victim. It can
allow you a wider perspective on your life, and give you a broader
context in which to explore the abuse. The negative side is that the
topic of abuse may never be raised. You may find yourself reluctant
to talk about incest with people who aren't survivors themselves.
People who want to avoid a subject can always find reasons to do so.
You can spend months waiting for "the right time" to bring it up.
And, unlike an incest survivors' group, it is unlikely that the topic
will be discussed here unless you raise it. You will probably discover
that the other group members have issues that are "far more pressing"
than yours. And, if you do raise the topic, you might indeed encounter a reluctance on the part of the other group members (or even the
therapist) to talk about abuse. There may not be the encouragement,
safety, and understanding that you need to work on your recovery
program. You may feel as isolated in this group as you do in the
outside world. This can be a useful situation, enabling you to work
on those feelings of isolation—but only if they are recognized and
confronted directly.

At the very least, before joining a general issues group, discuss
incest with the group leader. Make sure that she knows that this is a
major part of your reason for joining the group. Be certain that her
responses to you are what you need. Ask the leader to help you talk
about your incest history in the group. Let her know how she can be
most helpful to you. Don't proceed until you are fairly certain that
you will be welcome in the group without having to conceal any part
of your life, least of all your incest recovery.

I think that, ideally, you should join a general issues group *after* you have been through a group that is specifically for incest survivors. Once you have worked on the incest in a specific group context, the general issues group becomes a logical next step. You are able to take what you have accomplished in the small laboratory of the incest group and test it in the general issues group, as you move toward greater participation in the larger outside world.

In summary, although not ideal for dealing with recovery from incest, a general issues group may be the best group resource that is available to you right now. If perfection is not available (it rarely is) that doesn't mean that you have to settle for nothing. Even though it may not be just the right thing for you, a general issues group can be very helpful.

SPECIAL ISSUES GROUPS (NONINCEST)

If there are no groups specifically for incest survivors in your area, you may want to join an existing group for survivors of other kinds of dysfunctional families. Even if there was no drinking, addiction, or battering in your family, you will very likely find that you have a great deal in common with people who were raised in alcoholic, drug-abusive, or violent households. Many of the ongoing effects are quite similar, and it can be encouraging to see that you are not alone in your feelings of isolation and low self-esteem due to a traumatic childhood.

The largest, best-known, and best-organized of these organizations sponsor "Twelve-Step Approach" groups throughout the nation. These include Alcoholics Anonymous (AA) for recovering alcoholics, Al-Anon and Alateen for those who are (or were) in relationships of any kind with an alcoholic, and Adult Child groups (ACOA or ACA) for people who were raised in alcoholic families. Following this model, many communities have developed related groups, including Narcotics Anonymous (NA), Narc-Anon, and Overeaters Anonymous (OA), Sex and Love Addicts Anonymous (SLAA) for people with sexual compulsions, Debtors Anonymous (DA), and Spenders Anonymous (SA). There are even Incest Survivors Anonymous (ISA) groups being formed in some parts of the country. What all these groups have in common is the recognition that their members were exposed to destructive family patterns they were helpless to overcome. By acknowledging the hurts of the past, joining with people who have had similar experiences, and undertaking a program that has a proven track record, they move toward taking charge of their lives.

It isn't necessary to embrace these programs entirely. You needn't become a "convert" or overwhelm your life with meetings. Proceed at your own pace. No doubt you will have some reservations. There will be some aspects of the program that you will find less useful than others, but don't make the mistake of discounting a program entirely because it isn't perfect. Stick with it for a while and use the parts that are useful. Tailor the programs to meet your needs. Use them as supplements to your therapy. It is extremely helpful to recognize that you have a range of available resources. Many incest survivors find that the meetings and literature of the "Twelve-Step" programs enable them to start on their own roads to recovery. You can usually find AA and Al-Anon groups listed in your phone directory (see resource list).

Another type of experience that several incest survivors have told me they find helpful is with the groups, classes, and workshops run by an international organization called reevaluation counseling (also called co-counseling). This is a nonprofessional, peer counseling method that attempts to heal past hurts through a process of encouraging emotional discharge (crying, shaking, raging, laughing) in a safe, accepting, encouraging environment. The co-counseling "community" has established some support groups for survivors of sexual abuse. They have worked hard to develop theory about the nature of oppression and liberation, approaching the issue of abuse from a societal as well as a personal perspective. As with any other modality, there will be some aspects of reevaluation counseling that can be helpful to you, and others that are less so. If you approach it (or any other group) with a combination of openness and questioning, you are most likely to find useful answers.

There are many other types of nonincest groups that are helpful to incest survivors. Resources vary widely. You will need to explore both national organizations and local groups to locate ones that are best for you.

Be wary of any program, group, or meeting that discourages you from expressing your feelings. Even if they are more comfortable, they will be less helpful.

SPECIAL ISSUES GROUPS (SEXUAL ABUSE)

There is a wide variety of groups that address the needs of survivors of sexual abuse. At this time, most are for women only, others are mixed, and a few are just for men. They may be specifically for rape victims, adults molested as children, or limited in other ways. There is also a wide range of philosophy, focus, procedure, rules, and *qual-*

ity. Group leaders have all sorts of reasons for starting groups; group members have many reasons for joining. At worst, a group leader may be abusive himself. The leader may not have worked out her own sexual abuse history, and may be using the group for these purposes. Don't assume that just because someone is leading a group he is competent to do so. Investigate carefully. Ask all the questions you need to, and if you aren't satisfied with the answers, don't join the group. Or check out the responses you received with another professional whose judgment you trust. Be particularly wary of hidden agendas. There are, for example, organizations whose philosophies include keeping the family together at any price. All too often, in an incestuous family, that cost is the physical and emotional well-being of one or more of its members. It is too high a price to pay. Not all families *should* remain together—forgiveness and reconciliation may or may not be appropriate goals for you—at this time in your recovery process or ever. Don't be pushed to accept any program that doesn't make sense to you.

"SHORT-TERM" OR "ONGOING" GROUPS

The question of whether to join a time-limited (8-, 10-, 12-, 16-week) or long-term group is a matter of the availability of services and your personal needs and preferences. There are advantages and difficulties with any option. For many survivors, a commitment of even a few weeks feels too frightening. If this is the case for you, you may want to consider starting with a single workshop, or a group that has a "drop-in" format, with no need to commit to more than one meeting at a time. A disadvantage to such an arrangement is that the population of these groups can be very unstable, shifting from meeting to meeting. In a situation like that it is harder to establish safety and intimacy. You never know whether people will be there or not, and it's difficult to get on with the work that needs to be done if you have to start over again each time someone new shows up. Sometimes, however, the drop-in group provides you with the right degree of freedom, enabling you to make a long-term commitment "one day at a time."

A long-term or ongoing group is one where the participants are expected to commit themselves to group membership for a significant period of time, often years. Advantages to such a group include the depth of trust and intimacy that can be established over time. Rather than only exploring incest issues, a long-term group has the time to deal with group dynamics. Interaction among the group members becomes the basis for understanding and changing your relationships

Focus

RULES AND AGREEMENTS FOR GROUP MEMBERS

The rules for my incest recovery groups are few in number, but very important. I'll list them briefly, along with my reasons for them.

Before joining the group, all participants are expected to:

1 / Have established an appropriate (nonabusive) relationship with an individual therapist, preferably of at least six months duration, and have been actively working on the abuse issues. They sign releases allowing me to exchange information with their therapists, so that we are working together toward recovery. The reason for this requirement is that what comes up in group is so powerful and intense that one and a half hours once a week, divided among eight men, isn't enough. Friends and family can't (and shouldn't be expected to) deal with it all. Individual therapy is the proper setting.

2 / Be dealing effectively with substance abuse problems. This means that, if they are alcoholics or addicts, they have been sober/drug-free for at least six months to one year and are actively working in a recovery program. The reason for this rule is that it is important that the intensity of the group experience not jeopardize their sobriety.

3 / Not have had a psychiatric hospitalization for a year before joining the

with people in the outside world. When handled properly, membership in an ongoing group provides perspective on the past, a solid base for present activity, and a jumping-off point for future changes. When a new person joins an ongoing group, he is able to benefit from the collective experience of those who have been there longer. The older group members receive from the newcomers fresh perspectives, as well as a sense of how far they have moved since joining the group.

Clearly, not everyone is ready or willing to make a long-term commitment to a group. If you are, it can be an invaluable experience. For many, it represents the first stable "family" they have known.

Most incest survivors' groups have a time-limited contract. This means that the group members agree to attend a fixed number of sessions over a specific time period. The length of these contracts varies, but they average 10–16 meetings. Barring an emergency, participants agree to attend every session, and the population of the

group. This gives them the opportunity to reestablish an everyday routine before they take on the intensity of a group experience. There is always time to join a group after one's life has stabilized.

4 / Not be in the midst of a *major* life crisis. I consider the group experience to be the major crisis in their lives. Any more would constitute overload.

5 / Not be currently living in an abusive environment or abusing another person. (I make the distinction between *feeling* like an abuser and actually being one.)

As group members, participants agree to the following rules:

1 / Complete confidentiality. Group members may share their own experiences with anyone they choose, but agree to do so in a way that completely protects the identity of all other participants.

2 / No touching one another without permission. Even so much as a handshake must be agreed to by both parties. Incestuous abuse violates personal boundaries in the most destructive way. A survivor's right to control over his own body must be respected absolutely.

3 / No sex between group members.

4 / No physical violence.

5 / Any contact with other group members outside the group, even a phone call, must be mentioned in the group. Within the limits of these rules, I encourage group members to socialize and support one another in exploring nonabusive friendships. But it must be done with complete respect of one another's limits and pace. Everyone has the right to decline to extend his participation beyond the group meeting time.

6 / Attend each session on time, sober and drug-free. Give ample notice of necessary absences and call in case of emergency.

Honoring these rules helps to establish a safe environment for recovery.

group remains stable from the first or second session to the last. Short-term groups usually have more structure than ongoing groups, sometimes focusing on specific topic areas or goals. Because they are time-limited, there is little time for exploration of group dynamics. The ongoing group can evolve gradually according to the wishes and paces of its members; the short-term group is more likely to feel a sense of urgency to "get down to business." The group will end on a specified date, whether or not it has accomplished what it set out to do. This can be strong motivation for getting on with it. Time-limited groups tend to be intense and powerful, and often are a logical bridge between drop-in meetings and long-term groups. It is amazing to see what can be accomplished in twelve weeks of hour and a half sessions divided among eight men. Short-term groups make up in intensity what they lack in duration. For some men, a twelve-week commitment can feel like a lifetime. Others feel that they "won't even be able to begin to get to the stuff in twelve weeks." The information is there for you to examine; see what is available in your area and make your own decision.

ALL MALE OR MIXED GROUPS

This, too, will depend in part on what resources exist in your area. I have known male clients who had the experience of being the only man in an incest survivors' group. For some, this felt like a safe environment; others found it isolating and uncomfortable. Where there are few resources for male survivors (and that is more the rule than the exception), any available groups are likely to be for women only. If a group is open to men, it is probable that you will be part of a very small minority. Even if you don't find this situation to be perfect, it may be better than nothing. Ideally, there should be more than one man in a mixed group, and the group leader must take care that the male participants do not become the repository of everyone's rage against male perpetrators. No matter how much you *feel* like a perpetrator, it is important that you not be treated like one by your group.

On the other hand, an all-male environment (especially if you were abused by a man) may be more than you are willing or able to take on right now. Ultimately, you must weigh the potential benefit against the terror and decide what kind of group is right for you. An all-male group, although frightening to contemplate, can make for a special kind of unity and understanding. In addition to some commonality of experience, its members can explore their feelings about sexuality and about women without having to worry about being oppressive or exploitive. The rules of the group, along with the mutual support that develops, become the basis for forming nonabusive relationships with men—a major step in the recovery process.

SEXUAL ORIENTATION

The clearest way that I can discuss the question of separate or mixed recovery groups for heterosexual and gay male survivors is to share my own experience. I hadn't originally intended to separate the groups by sexual orientation. My intention was to screen prospective members for active "homophobia" and "heterophobia," and include both gay and heterosexual men in my first group. When it turned out that I had about equal numbers of self-identified gay and "straight" men who wanted a group—and that I had enough people to form two groups (and over the objections of a few prospective group members who felt unwilling or unable to make that choice)—I decided to start a heterosexual and a gay group. My thinking about doing it this way was that sexuality and sexual orientation are highly charged issues for most incest survivors. These issues need to be explored in a safe, supportive environment. I felt that the heterosexual men needed the safety to explore their own fears about being gay—or being *labeled* as gay—including voicing their own antigay feelings without worrying about offending other group members. But I think that it isn't helpful for gay men to have to listen to expressions of homophobia. I also thought that the gay men needed to talk about their sexuality—including their sexual *practices*—without having to censor the information for fear of being judged or criticized. I was curious to see whether there would be any major differences between the groups.

My thinking was that, even though there were far more similarities than differences between the two groups—and there is no reason to *insist* that heterosexual and gay men be in separate groups—it would be helpful to make the separation. The two groups were quite similar in the nature of the issues that they dealt with, and the way in which members supported one another on all issues, including questions of sexual confusion.

If you don't have an all-heterosexual or all-gay group available to you, by all means consider joining an integrated group. (For an update, see the Preface to the Paperback Edition, page xiii.) Although it isn't ideal to be the only gay man in an all-heterosexual group or the only straight man in an all-gay group, even these situations can be worked out so you can have a worthwhile group experience. Discuss your concerns with the group leader before joining the group. Be honest; don't sabotage yourself. Offer as much information as you can, and ask for all the information that you need. This provides the best foundation for beginning any group.

AGE RANGE

Because it is necessary to attain some distance from the abuse before working on recovery, it is unusual to find men working on incest issues until they are in their thirties, forties, and fifties. For men in their teens and early twenties, the abuse is too close—they feel as though their survival is still in doubt—and a group of adult men can be very threatening. For this reason, it is far better to put teenagers in a group of their peers, whether all male or of both sexes. When teenagers, in the company of their peers, take charge of their own recovery, the results are impressive. The same consideration is useful, though not quite as important, for men in their twenties. Although I have seen men in their early twenties make great strides in groups where they were significantly younger than the other members, it is more difficult than in peer groups. The power differential usually feels too great.

Age doesn't appear to be a significant factor for men in their thirties, forties, and fifties. Perhaps this is because they either feel like scared children all the time or have taken on adult roles since they were quite young.

As with the other factors, you may have little choice of whether to be in a group of age-mates; don't let concerns about age keep you from getting what you need.

OTHER FACTORS

If you have the uncommon luxury of a wide range of choice, you can consider whether to join a group that is led by an incest survivor or a nonincest survivor (or whether you even want to have that information about the leader). You may consider groups with a single leader or two co-leaders—male, female, or one leader of each sex. These are options to consider; none is a major stumbling block. If you are in the happy situation of having a range of available services, by all means exercise your freedom of choice. But, when you have explored the options, *choose*. Don't grow old waiting for the perfect group to appear; join an adequate group and make it right for you. Doing so will give you a tremendous sense of your own power.

Finding a Group

Just as you did to find an individual counselor, just as you would before making any major investment, shop around. Ask friends and colleagues. Ask your individual therapist and other mental health professionals. Consult with organizations for survivors, rape crisis centers, women's centers, hotlines, social service departments, and other community resources. Contact the national and local offices of various advocacy organizations. Finally, in the absence of existing groups, consider becoming a contact person for other survivors who want a group, and then go out and hire yourselves an experienced group leader. If there is sufficient demand, there are ways of meeting it.

Are You Ready for a Group?

This is a tricky question. The answer depends on what you mean by "ready." If you're wondering whether you are able to deal with the demands of group membership, or if you need to just focus on yourself for a while, talk about it with your individual therapist. Explore the question together and come to a decision not based on some "absolute" criteria, but on what is best for you. My general recommendation is that people join a group only after they have been working on the incest in individual therapy for a significant period of time, at least six months to a year. But this is simply a suggestion, not a rule. Let your own best thinking, in consultation with the best information you can get, and the advice of your individual therapist, determine your course of action. (If the group leader does not think you're ready to join this group, try not to take it as personal rejection. Ask him why he thinks so, and attempt to listen without defensiveness to his reasons. You don't have to agree with the leader's decision, but you may benefit from knowing what considerations went into making it. You can then decide to wait a while before joining a group, or to look for another one.)

On the other hand, you may be ready but not *prepared* to join a group. If being ready for a group means that you can sail through it without feeling a thing, you'll never be there. Groups raise powerful emotions in their members. Sitting numbly through a dozen meetings won't do you much good. If you alternate between loving and hating the other group members, if you sometimes feel totally bewildered and out of control during the sessions, if you leave some of the meetings in turmoil, then chances are that the group is doing its job. As we said before, the goal is recovery, not comfort. You can't completely prepare yourself for giving up control. Like standing at the edge of a diving board, at some point you have to *trust* that you're ready—all your training has led to this moment; now is the time, go for it! The anticipation is usually a lot worse than the reality. Trying something new is never completely risk-free, but once you have done it, it will never again be quite as frightening.

My feeling must be obvious by now. I strongly believe that a group experience constitutes an extremely important component of recovery for male incest survivors. The recovery group provides a laboratory for investigating and testing life changes before you put them into operation in the outside world. Once you have been a group member, it will be extremely difficult to return to the same degree of isolation and confusion that you experienced before. Your direction is now forward, and the group provides much-needed fuel. Remember that you are taking this on *for yourself*, and that *everyone* benefits from your progress.

Confrontation

I needed to love my mother and father. . . . I could not afford to address them directly about the felonies committed against all of us. I could not hold them accountable.
—PAT CONROY, *Prince of Tides*

Confronting the perpetrator is a difficult and complex issue. You must give a great deal of thought to the question of why you would want to do it—and whether confrontation is in your best interest. If you choose to confront, it is important to consider when (and under what circumstances) you want confrontation to take place. There is no general rule about confrontation. It is a highly individual, personal decision. For some people it is a logical next step in recovery; for others it could be a dangerous and self-destructive act. To be helpful, your confrontation must come from a position of strength. It is unlikely that you will be feeling powerful when you first undertake your recovery work. But as your healing continues, you will come to recognize that you have great power, certainly far more than the perpetrator—a dysfunctional individual who abuses children. By the time you are prepared to confront the perpetrator, you will have much strength on your side. You will possess a sense of certainty—a readiness to insist that the abuser be *held accountable* for his or her acts. There are ways of bringing yourself to this point of self-confidence. If you take the time to do this, your confrontation—whatever specific form it takes—will be a powerful and positive event.

Survivors have all types of relationships with the people who abused them. Some have had no contact whatever for a significant period of time—through their own choice or due to external circumstances. Others remain financially, physically, or emotionally dependent on the perpetrator. Feelings toward the abuser run the gamut: love, hate, anger, fear, confusion, shame, guilt, embarrassment, tenderness, and protectiveness are often intertwined in a confusing jumble. Because of this complexity the decision to confront cannot be taken lightly. While I can't tell you whether confrontation is the right course of action for you (that is for you to decide), I hope that this chapter provides information that will help you make your decision.

When I speak of confrontation, I'm not necessarily referring to a direct encounter with the abuser. The real meaning of confrontation is *standing up to the abuse*. It indicates that you are giving voice to the reality that you are no longer willing to submit to victimization in any form. It is a statement of self-respect and self-determination. Confrontation, in this sense, is a major aspect of recovery. It represents the recognition that:

• What happened to you was abusive.
• Sexual child abuse is wrong.
• You did not deserve to be abused.
• You were not responsible for the abuse.
• People must be accountable for their actions.

Confrontation, then, proceeds from a position of growing strength which states that every human being deserves respect. Each person has the right to control his or her body. This includes *you!!* Whatever form it takes, and regardless of the outcome, confrontation should be an act of self-respect. When it is approached assertively (instead of passively or aggressively), you will be left feeling better about yourself, more able to move ahead with your life.

Sometimes, when incest survivors first recover abuse memories— or decide to do something about them—their first impulse is to rush to confront the abuser. There are many reasons for wanting to do this, but it is rarely a good idea. Like recovery, confrontation is a process that takes time. It calls for careful, thoughtful preparation. To rush headlong into confrontation without adequate planning would be foolhardy, reducing it to the level of acting out a male revenge fantasy (a John Wayne gunfight or a Rambo-like search-and-destroy mission). Although this might feel satisfying at the moment, it will serve to reinforce the stereotype that problems can be solved by aggression and violence—the very attitude that allows for the existence of child sexual abuse. Confronting the perpetrator on his or her own terms makes it harder and scarier than it needs to be. You will be far better off setting up the situation in the way that is best for you—making certain that you are ready, feeling strong and self-confident.

With proper preparation and planning, confrontation can be a healthy, important step in your recovery process. It makes good sense to keep confrontation in perspective. There is a great deal of work to be done first.

LAYING THE GROUNDWORK

Your most important groundwork involves examining your own experience with abuse. This examination consists of everything that has been discussed in previous chapters: telling your story to someone, repeating it in as much detail as you remember, adding details as they appear, attaching whatever feelings are accessible to you, finding people who will listen and believe you, sharing feelings and histories with other survivors, establishing an appropriate therapeutic relationship, entering a group for incest survivors if one is available, and building a solid support network. These preparations take time, but they are necessary if you are to be clear about confrontation.

Before you undertake confrontation, you want to be as clear as possible about how you feel about the abuse, the perpetrator, and yourself. Confrontation is not going to be a magic wand that will make everything all right. Although you have survived scarier and more difficult challenges, it is likely to be an exhausting, highly charged emotional experience—one that will bring up lots of material to be dealt with afterward. The perpetrator will not become your therapist. She or he is not going to suddenly become the loving, protective parent figure that you always longed for. If you begin with an expectation that confrontation will magically solve all your problems, you are certain to be disappointed. You owe it to yourself to be prepared. It is essential to understand your motivations and expectations. The way to do this is to become as clear as possible about incest in general and your abuse history in particular. The more secure you are about who you are—the more you believe that you are truly a good person who was in no way responsible for the abuse—the less likely you will fall victim to defensiveness, fears, and self-doubts. Work on your own understanding of your situation until you think that the time for confrontation is approaching. Don't depend on anyone else's time schedule; it will surely be arbitrary. You are the primary expert in deciding what is right for you. Learning to make these decisions for yourself will help you take charge of your life. The fact that it is your decision doesn't mean that you have to prepare for it in isolation. There is a good deal of information, support, and encouragement available to you, and it is always a good idea to remember that you are not alone.

Many other survivors have confronted their abusers—with a wide range of results. Although their situations aren't the same as yours, you can benefit from hearing about their experiences with confrontation. Other survivors have chosen not to confront. You may want to learn their reasons for that decision. It might be helpful to read the pamphlet called "How to Confront Your Perpetrator: Dead or Alive," by Lynne Lamb Bryant and Pat Dickman. It is available from VOICES in Action, Inc., P.O. Box 148309, Chicago, IL 60614.

In addition to learning about the confrontation experiences of other survivors, you can talk over your ideas and feelings with friends, sympathetic family members, and your therapist. These discussions don't have to be limited to realistic planning. (Remember, you haven't yet definitely decided whether or not to do it.) Allow yourself to express your wildest, most irrational fantasies of how it will be. You aren't committing yourself to anything; indulging in fantasies can help you to get a picture of expectations that you may not have been consciously aware of. Whether or not you ultimately decide to go ahead with the actual confrontation, this preliminary process can be very enlightening. Sometimes it even proves to be enough.

Remember: Confrontation is not the goal of recovery, it is a *tool* for recovery. Its value lies in how it is used. You deserve to take enough time to make the best decision for yourself. You can change your mind about the confrontation at *any* time during this process. You can decide to put it off because you aren't ready, or do it sooner than you had planned. You can decide that it just isn't something that makes sense for you to do at all. You can change your mind from minute to minute. The choice is always yours. Don't worry about disappointing anyone else; you're doing this *for yourself.*

PRACTICE

There are a number of ways to rehearse your confrontation, just as there are many ways to confront the perpetrator.

1 / Letter-writing. You may want to commit to paper your thoughts about the abuse and your feelings toward the perpetrator. This can be in the form of a letter to him/her, to a friend, a family member, the authorities, or even a newspaper. You can write several different letters, polishing them as you explore your feelings. You may or may not ever mail any of them. For now, the point in writing them is to learn more about yourself. You will be able to structure your thoughts and ideas and have a concrete document that you can refer to. Letter-writing provides a useful perspective. If you choose to proceed with face-to-face confrontation, your letter can help you to stay on track. When you have written your letter, take the opportunity to read it to some friends. Ask them for their reactions—how did it sound to them? The more feedback you get, the better. You can accept what is useful to you and ignore the rest. Even if you never use the letters directly, you may want to keep them. It can be helpful to reread them from time to time in order to see how your ideas and feelings have developed.

2 / Guided fantasy. Your therapist may be able to assist you in creating a fantasy picture of the confrontation. Ideally, this will be a symbolic creation of a situation *where you are in complete control*. It doesn't have to mirror reality, it can be pure fantasy. You can imagine yourself twelve feet tall with the strength of Hercules. You can be bigger, older, smarter, and stronger than the perpetrator. You can bring reinforcements in with you, real or fictitious. (Often children will employ make-believe protectors like Mighty Mouse, Superman, Wonder Woman, or Big Bird. They might select a pet dog, a family member, sports figure, or movie star. You can use one or more of them, or choose your own hero. This hero can even be *your adult self*, going back in time to befriend and protect yourself as a child.)

Whatever form your guided fantasy takes, it is important that it not include re-creating the original victimization. If your fantasy includes the perpetrator trying to abuse you, envision yourself clearly and powerfully thwarting the attempt. The picture should be one of moving away from the helplessness of the abused child into your full adult power. Take time afterward to discuss your feelings about the guided fantasy. What was helpful? What would you change? You can, if you wish, go back and do it again until it feels exactly right.

You may be surprised by the changes that this kind of exercise can bring about. For some, it is all the confrontation they need. Others can use it as a confidence-building step leading toward actual confrontation.

3 / Role-play. You can rehearse any number of confrontation scenarios, using friends, other group members, even dolls or clay figures to represent the perpetrator(s) and other relevant people from your childhood. Through role-play (or "psychodrama") you can try out various means of confrontation, and experience your responses to them. You are able to look at "ideal" situations as well as confrontations that don't turn out as well as you'd like.

GETTING SUPPORT

One of the most important aspects of preparation for actual confrontation is making certain that you have provided for support *at all stages of the process.* You will need to know that there are people you can call on for company, understanding, feedback, reality testing, and even physical protection before, during and after the confrontation. You deserve to have support, encouragement and protection *whether or not* you are in any physical danger from the perpetrator. Remember that there is a possibility that you will be *feeling* very small and vulnerable. Good allies can reflect a more powerful reality to you in the face of intimidating feelings.

Remember to plan for logistical as well as emotional support. You might want someone to drive you to and from the confrontation. Even if you choose to confront the perpetrator alone, it may make sense to have someone within sight or earshot. This is essential if you might be at some physical risk from the perpetrator, but may be desirable in any case. If the confrontation is to take place at some distance from your support network, you can arrange to have people waiting at telephones for your call, and meeting you upon your return. You can find out whether there are members of VOICES in Action or other support/advocacy organizations in the area where the confrontation is to take place. You may also ask for help in arranging transportation, meals, and lodging.

Even though you are capable of doing this all yourself, you should consider letting other people help you. It will probably be a new and challenging experience for you. *Just because you* can *do something doesn't mean that you* need to—*or even that you* should. (Survivors carry around so many "shoulds." Accepting support and assistance helps you to remove some of them.) There is true power and strength in community. Set yourself the challenge of availing yourself of that support. Finally, make sure that you have set up a session with your therapist, counselor or closest support person *as soon as possible* after the confrontation. And you will probably want to schedule extra follow-up sessions to deal with the results of the confrontation.

Implementing a Face-to-Face Confrontation

Once you have decided to go ahead with in-person confrontation of the perpetrator, you will want to set it up in the way that is most useful to you. (I have tried to avoid using the phrase "*your* perpetrator" in favor of "*the* perpetrator." Using the possessive pronoun gives a sense of alliance between abuser and victim. This can inhibit the work you are doing in breaking your connection to the abuse. Words are important; they can be binding or liberating. Try to practice using words that will enhance your sense of yourself as a strong, smart, capable adult.) Although you cannot have complete control over the situation, there are things you can do to increase the likelihood of getting what you need out of it. Confrontation won't be easy for you, but you don't have to make it any harder.

ARRANGING THE MEETING

Think about the advantages and disadvantages of letting the perpetrator know that this meeting is about to take place. If you choose to provide advance notice, you will need to consider how much information you are going to supply about the subject of the meeting. Remember, this confrontation is *for your benefit alone*. You don't have to protect the person who abused you; he didn't protect you. Giving some advance notice is, of course, necessary if you have no other way to insure that the perpetrator will be there, or if you have to travel to the meeting. It can also increase the perpetrator's anxiety level, making him more vulnerable to confrontation. On the other hand, it can allow him time to prepare coverups, denials, and even counterattacks. (These are likely to occur anyway; you will need to be prepared for them.) Think carefully about *what you need* in this situation before making your decision. If you choose to, you can make arrangements without going into detail about the content of the meeting. Arrangements can be made by letter or telephone; consider the advantages of each. Make setting up the meeting part of a process that increases your strength and self-confidence.

THE PLACE

Although no setting for a confrontation is likely to feel comfortable, it can (and must) be physically safe. You will want to choose a meeting place that will provide you with a maximum degree of security. It is hard enough to think clearly when you are nervous, without worrying about needing to protect yourself from violence or further sexual assault. I strongly urge that you avoid setting up the confrontation at the place where the original abuse occurred—or anywhere that reminds you of that place. Just being with the perpetrator will bring up old fears; being together in the place where he abused you is likely to be overwhelming. You will feel a greater pull to regress to a more juvenile, helpless condition, robbing you of strength that you need to keep on course. Therefore, choose a place where you are most comfortable, and feel adult—whether it is your home, that of a trusted third party, or neutral territory. It may also be a good idea to select a place that is familiar to you. You may choose to meet in a public place, such as a park or restaurant, where you can be aware of other people. In such settings it is more likely that the intensity of reactions to the confrontation will be kept to a manageable level.

You can see that you are no longer forced to be alone with the perpetrator, and you can leave anytime you want. You can have trusted allies within sight but out of hearing range, ready to be summoned if needed. On the other hand, a public place may make you feel too exposed. If the meeting takes place in private, you may choose to have someone, a friend or family member, present as a witness to the confrontation. This person can also become an important part of processing the experience afterward, validating your memories and providing another perspective on what occurred. If you prefer to meet the perpetrator alone, try to have supportive people waiting nearby, preferably where you can summon them easily. It is essential that you *realistically* assess the potential threat of physical danger presented by the abuser when confronted. Take precautions that will insure your safety *and* provide an extra degree of comfort. There's no such thing as being "too safe."

YOUR PRESENTATION

Once again, remember that you are doing this *for yourself*. How do you want it to be? This isn't a debate or a jury trial. There is no need to argue. Nor do you have to present "both sides" or protect the perpetrator from painful feelings. You have prepared for this moment carefully. You have thought about what you want to say and what you hope to achieve. You have decided whether you are seeking to express your anger, make accusations, or set the groundwork for reconciliation. You have played out your "ideal" as well as your "worst case" scenarios. You have considered possible reactions, as well as the possibility that his response will surprise you. Now is the time for you to present what you have to say.

You can state what you *know* to be true (and, perhaps, what you think happened and which parts are unclear). You can tell the perpetrator what the effects of the abuse have been for you. You don't have to go through this experience calmly or numbly. If the feelings come up, give yourself permission to *feel* them. You have a right to feel sad, afraid or angry. Crying will not weaken or invalidate what you are saying. On the contrary, it may help clear your mind so that you can present your thoughts more coherently. If there is something specific that you want or need to hear from the perpetrator, you may wish to ask for it at this point.

If you find yourself becoming increasingly anxious or panicky, slow down the pace—take some slow, deep breaths; take a few minutes to cry, shake, or giggle; think about something calm and beautiful; think about someone who cares about you; imagine a friend, hero, or the members of your survivors' group standing by your side. Take all the time you need; you've been waiting for this moment for a long time. Don't proceed until you're ready—then continue until you are finished. Don't allow yourself to be interrupted or distracted. There is always time for response, afterward. When you have finished, take the time you need to pull yourself together. Don't rush to soften the impact of what you have said; resist the temptation to protect the perpetrator from the impact of what you're saying. Be clear about when you are ready to listen to a response. You are in charge of what you do in this situation. Take good care of yourself—you deserve it.

POSSIBLE REACTIONS

There are any number of ways that a perpetrator might respond to confrontation. As much as you think you know a person, you cannot be one hundred percent certain that he will react in the ways that you have predicted. For this reason, you must prepare yourself for the possibility that the confrontation will not proceed precisely according to plan. As much as you have thought out what will happen—as much thinking, planning, fantasizing, and role-playing as you have done—be ready for some surprises. Remember that the fact that the proceedings don't follow your script to the letter doesn't mean that everything has fallen apart. When you have made all the reasonable preparations that you can, try to relax and remain open to what happens. This will feel like loss of control and may be frightening, but you are likely to learn far more by doing it this way. You may discover that flexibility—the ability to adjust to the requirements of a situation—makes you feel more powerful than rigid attempts to maintain control. Try to remember that the perpetrator will be at a psychological disadvantage, and you are proceeding from a position of strength. In most cases, when you are adequately prepared for confrontation, you really need not be afraid. Here are some of the more common responses by perpetrators when they are confronted:

1 / Denial. Probably the most commonly reported response to confrontation is that the perpetrator denies that the abuse took place. The denial can be total ("That never happened"), or coupled with an attempt to explain away the memory ("You are probably remembering a bad dream"; "You always had a vivid imagination"), to disprove it ("We didn't live in that house when you were five"; "There was no sofa in the attic"), or to deflect it ("There was a neighbor who used to hang around the park. I always thought there was something funny about him."). Other forms of denial include outrage, bluster and "guilt-tripping" ("How dare you accuse me of such a monstrous thing?" "How could you even think that I would do something like that?" "You are sick! You've always had it in for me!" "After all I've done for you!"). Denial may be accompanied by an offer to assist the survivor in "getting help" in dealing with his delusions. One male survivor even reported that, when confronted, his uncle responded, "That never happened . . . and, besides, you can't prove it." Be prepared to encounter denial. Don't let the situation turn into an argument or a debate. Don't allow a perpetrator to talk you out of your memories. Remember that she has lied to you before. Stick to your guns and don't get involved in an exercise in frustration. You don't have to convince the perpetrator that something happened. He knows that it did. Saying that something didn't happen doesn't erase the reality. For many survivors, the purpose of confrontation is to tell the perpetrator clearly, "I know what happened, and I'm telling you that I know it." This can be particularly important if you think that the perpetrator is (or will be) molesting someone else. You don't need acknowledgment of the abuse or permission from the perpetrator in order to proceed with your recovery. Your memories aren't invalidated by denial; you have confronted the perpetrator. You have stood up to the abuse.

2 / Ambiguous responses. These are likely to be the most difficult to deal with, since they can leave you feeling as though nothing happened. After putting all this time, energy, planning, and emotion into the confrontation, it appears that you are left with no more than you started with. Ambiguous responses are a form of denial, without actually stating that nothing happened. They include variations of "I don't remember." One client reported this response by the perpetrator, "I don't remember, but I can't imagine that I would do something like that." Also in this category are attempts to evade the question, change the subject, or distract you from the confrontation. Some perpetrators are very adept at these techniques. Don't be fooled by them. When you replay the situation afterward, removed from the immediacy of the feelings, you can see that evasion, confusion, distraction, and claims of lack of memory are simply more subtle forms of acknowledgment. If they truly believed that nothing happened, they would say so, simply and unequivocally. As you look beyond the surface, you can see that what had seemed ambiguous may be giving you a clear message.

3 / Acknowledgment. There are many possible forms of acknowledgment of abuse, ranging from reassuring to terrifying, from supportive to abusive. I'll mention some of the more common responses here, so that you can think about ways you might deal with them.

One of the more difficult situations arises when the incest is acknowledged without any acceptance of responsibility or expression of remorse. This situation occurs all too frequently; perpetrators are masterful at avoiding responsibility for their actions. Rarely do they seek help unless they are forced to. Even the most blatant and vicious forms of assault can leave some perpetrators unmoved. The form that this type of response takes is some variation of "Yeah, it happened, so what?" It may even carry with it a challenge (or thinly veiled threat), as in ". . . and what are you going to do about it?" Your decision about what to do next should include the understanding that a sociopathic personality is not going to feel remorse. Although you may be able to obtain legal redress of damages, you will probably never receive a heartfelt apology from such an individual. If you wait for that to happen, you will be disappointed. Consider the source of the response and move ahead with your recovery.

A perpetrator may acknowledge that the abuse did in fact take place, but try to minimize it. ("It happened so long ago." "It only happened once/a few times." "Nobody was really hurt by it." "It wasn't *that* bad, was it?" "Alright, it happened, now can't we just

FOCUS

AM I MAKING THE FAMILY CRAZY?

I know that some part of telling is wanting to heal the family. —A MALE INCEST SURVIVOR

If there's a fire and I call the engines—so who am I double-crossing? The fire?
—JUDY HOLLIDAY in the film *Born Yesterday*

Some time ago, during an appearance on a television show, I received a phone call from a young incest survivor. She said that she was afraid to talk about the abuse because it would "make everybody in the family crazy." She was probably correct in thinking that dealing openly with the abuse would send her family into an uproar. But it is a mistake to believe that she would be responsible for anything other than focusing attention on a serious problem. The family is already "crazy."

It is crazy to sexually abuse children. Calling attention to the abuse is an act of sanity. Members of a dysfunctional family cooperate in maintaining the dysfunction. It is necessary to destroy a system of denial so ingrained that it can sacrifice a child in order to keep things running smoothly.

Putting things right is more important than looking good to the outside world. The person who blows the whistle on abuse is rarely appreciated for it. Nevertheless he is performing a valuable and courageous act by beginning the healing process for the entire family. It is the abusive situation, not the healing process, that is "crazy."

Don't let concerns about upsetting the family's stability stand in your way; stability is no substitute for health. Neither is an image of respectability. Don't allow other people's fears or pathology interfere with your recovery. Don't be "guilt-tripped" or intimidated into silence; you know their ploys by now. Keep talking; you have a right to be heard. Continue to insist that what is *right* takes precedence over what is comfortable. It is the only way to free yourself from the abusive family patterns. If you can't get the support you need within your family, find it elsewhere. But keep insisting on your right to be heard—your right to recover.

forget about it?" "Let's just put it behind us." "I didn't mean any harm, I thought you liked it.") These minimizing responses are simply attempts to evade responsibility for the abusive behavior. You know what the effects have been for you. Don't allow your memories and your feelings to be so easily dismissed. You deserved better treatment then; you deserve better treatment now. And remember that the question of forgiveness may not be one that you are prepared to deal with at this time. Don't let yourself be pushed into anything that you're not ready for.

Acknowledgment can also be turned around into an accusation, with the perpetrator attempting to blame you for the abuse. In this case, the perpetrator acknowledges the incest, but attempts to shift the responsibility because "You liked it." "You wanted it." "You looked for it." It is hard to avoid being trapped by this twisting of the facts, particularly if you found any part of the abuse pleasurable. But this response is simply another form of denial—blaming the victim. Remember that, no matter how "attractive," "seductive," or "sexy" you were, he had a responsibility to protect and nurture you. Any other interpretation is a self-serving distortion of the facts. You never deserved to be abused—no matter what.

Another category of response involves acknowledging the incest and then, in one way or another, attempting to perpetuate it. The most overt forms include seduction, fondling, and even rape. (One survivor decided to respond to overtures of reconciliation initiated by his father many years after the original prolonged, violent, and vicious abuse. He chose a public parking lot in broad daylight as the location of their meeting. The survivor was sitting in the car with his father, who was by then an old man. The perpetrator took his son's hand and attempted to force it onto his crotch. The public nature of the setting, while providing some protection, did not lessen the traumatic effects of this encounter. See Philip's Statement, on page 78.) If there is a possibility of further victimization, it is essential that you protect yourself. There is nothing rational about child abuse; rationalizations don't make it permissible. Abusers do not protect their victims; it is up to you to make sure that you are in no danger of assault.

There may be dangers of nonsexual assault. Know whether the perpetrator has a history of (or potential for) violence. If confrontation carries the possibility of triggering a physical attack, you may wish to rethink your decision to confront. If you decide to go ahead with it, make certain that you are adequately protected. At the very least, you should tell someone else about the confrontation and *let the perpetrator know* that you have done so. Sometimes the presence of witnesses will be enough to prevent the possibility of violent behavior; in other situations, further precautions will be necessary. The perpetrator may also resort to *threats* of violence, particularly if she fears disclosure. Threats may be empty attempts to keep you silent, or can represent genuine danger. To avoid intimidation, take some time beforehand to think about whether the danger is real and how you would respond to such threats to yourself or to others.

Violence operates both ways. If you think that you might be in danger of losing control and physically attacking the perpetrator during confrontation, stop and think. Will the satisfaction of hitting, injuring, or killing your abuser undo the pain and suffering that he has caused you? Do you want to risk losing all that you have accomplished so far? Isn't prison too high a price to pay for momentary satisfaction? Will you feel guilty afterward? Do you really want to perpetuate a pattern of responding to other human beings in an assaultive manner? You know what maltreatment has done to you; do you want to be the kind of person who inflicts pain on others? I urge you to consider these questions very carefully, and to focus your energy on your own recovery instead of on the fleeting satisfaction of revenge.

Other, more subtle ways to continue the abuse include attempts by the perpetrator to engage you in some sort of alliance. The rationale might be keeping silent in order to protect others ("If this came out it would really hurt your mother." "Your father has a heart condition; finding out about this would kill him."). It could be an appeal to loyalty or sentiment ("Can't we keep this our secret?" "You know that there's always been a special bond between us." "Even though I've made mistakes, I'm still your uncle." "I love you and I know you love me."). Or it might simply be a plea for "understanding" or protection. See these ploys for what they are—desperate attempts by perpetrators to protect themselves from the consequences of their abusive behavior. By allying yourself with the perpetrator, you run the risk of accepting some of the responsibility for the abuse. Doing that would be a mistake which would interfere with your recovery. You did *nothing* to deserve what happened to you. Don't confuse acceptance of abuse with forgiveness. True forgiveness does not arise from denial. It can only occur when there has been a complete understanding of what has happened, including the nature of the wrongs and where the responsibility lies. For the perpetrator there can be no rehabilitation without admission of responsibility and feelings of remorse. Your recovery cannot be complete until you fully accept that your responsibility is to yourself. What is in your best interest is also what is best for those who truly care about you.

Finally, when confronted, the perpetrator may acknowledge *and apologize* for the abuse. This may, on the surface, seem to be the ideal response. But, although you have longed for this moment, it raises its own questions. What does the apology mean? Can it be trusted? You have been lied to before. Are you able to believe it this time, no matter how much you want to? Unfortunately, there are no easy answers. You must consider the response in the context of everything you know about this person—and everything you know about yourself. What does an apology mean to you if it is real? What if it is false? Remember to take all the time you need to consider your feelings.

Whether it is genuine or not, you are under no obligation to respond to an apology. An apology should not be an expectation that you will forget the abuse. It is only a step toward forgiveness if you choose to make it so. Don't do it a minute before you are ready to. Pretense is never a useful tool in recovery. If, after careful thought and exploration of your feelings, you decide to accept the apology, you still have the right to determine the nature of any future interaction with the perpetrator. You may decide never to see the person again. That is your right. What do you want? What are realistic expectations? The decision is yours. If you choose to have a relationship, it will have to be a brand new one, built slowly and with awareness. Apologies don't create instant trust. Think carefully about what you need in order to begin to establish a relationship that will be healthy for you.

Remember that even an unsatisfactory response can be useful validation of your thinking about the situation. Sexual child abuse is the act of a disturbed person. Don't expect that confrontation will produce a sane, predictable reaction. A crazy response can have the effect of affirming that what *happened to you* was in fact abusive. This affirmation can allow you to move on with your recovery.

FOLLOW-UP

Don't try to return to life as usual directly after the confrontation. You will need time to react, relax and process what happened. If you can, schedule a day or two off from work. Spend it in ways that you find pleasant and life-affirming. Visit with friends, whether or not you talk about what happened. Schedule extra sessions with your therapist and/or arrange to meet with other survivors. But also take time to play. Take a walk in the country; go for a bike ride; see a film—treat yourself well. Put yourself into situations that remind you that there is a world outside the abuse, and that you have a place in that world. It will be some time before you understand the full import of the confrontation; being kind to yourself serves to remind you of why you are going through all this.

Implementing Other Types of Confrontation

Not all confrontations can *or should* involve face-to-face interaction. The perpetrator may have died or otherwise be unavailable for direct confrontation. Even if she is physically accessible, there are any number of reasons why it might not make sense for you—now or ever—to face the person who abused you. Consider all the options, and remember that the choice is always yours. What follows is a brief discussion of some alternative means of confrontation.

1 / Symbolic confrontation. Earlier in this chapter, I wrote of some symbolic ways of confronting the perpetrator. These included letter-writing, guided fantasy, and role-playing. For some people it is sufficient to engage in symbolic standing up to the abuse. Doing so provides them with enough release and perspective that they no longer feel it necessary to confront the perpetrator directly. They are able to move on with their lives. Examine your own thoughts and feelings after you have confronted the abuse symbolically. Decide whether your need to confront has been satisfied or if further action is required.

2 / Mailing a letter. If you want to confront the abuse without facing the perpetrator directly, you can send a letter. Letter-writing has many advantages. You can take your time, preparing as many drafts as you wish, polishing and editing what you want to say, pausing to feel, rest, and consult with others before deciding on a final version. You can take as long as you like, and change your mind any time you want. In addition, you don't have to worry that interruption or intimidation might keep you from finishing what you want to say. Since this form of confrontation takes place at a distance from the abuser, you don't need to deal with his immediate reaction; you can resist any pulls to protect her feelings. You should keep copies of your letter, so that you can refer to it if there is any attempt to distort what you said. And, regardless of the response, you have more control over whether you wish to follow up the letter in any way. Confrontation by mail can be a good way to "just get things off your chest," or to put the perpetrator on notice that you will no longer stand for his abusing you or anyone else. (See Ivan's Statement, page 247.)

3 / Legal action. In some places, survivors have confronted perpetrators by pressing criminal charges or pursuing civil suits for redress of damages. This is a tricky business, not to be undertaken lightly. For some survivors, a lawsuit is a public statement of their intention to force the perpetrator to make amends for her actions; for others, it becomes another form of abuse. Think about it carefully; get all the information you need. Recognize that legal proceedings are likely to be costly, protracted *public* proceedings. There is no guarantee of success. Cases are tried on the basis of what is "legal," not what is "fair." Opposing lawyers will attempt to break down your story, sometimes by attempting to portray you as a liar, promiscuous, or crazy. Judges and juries may not be sympathetic. Should it come to trial, you will have to face the person who abused you, in public, under stressful conditions. Despite these limitations, some survivors have proceeded with legal action. Before you decide to do so, consult with your therapist about how the experience may affect you. But you will need more than therapeutic advice. Meet with one or more attorneys who have experience with sexual abuse cases. Learn what the laws are. (They vary from state to state.) Find out the statute of limitations for sexual abuse cases. Ask whether there have been any legal precedents, and what their outcomes were. Ask your attorney to give you a realistic idea of what you will be going through and to estimate your chance of success. Weigh the possible gains against the stresses and sacrifices. Think of who else will be affected by this course of action. Think about what you stand to gain and what you might lose. Then make the decision that is right for you.

4 / If the perpetrator is dead. The fact that the person who abused you is no longer alive doesn't mean that you no longer have a need for confrontation. Nor does it mean that confrontation is impossible. Although you cannot effect a direct, face-to-face confrontation, there are other ways to do what you need to. Many survivors have visited the cemetery where a perpetrator is buried and have talked to him at the grave. This can be just as powerful and emotional an event as confronting a living person, so be prepared for an outpouring of emotions. You may wish to prepare what you are going to say, or just let yourself go, trusting that the right words and feelings will present themselves. You can speak directly to the perpetrator, to God, or you can just speak for yourself. If you feel that talking to a dead person would be too embarrassing to do in front of someone, do it alone. Otherwise, you may choose to have someone accompany you to the cemetery. You may need a hug, a shoulder or a sympathetic listener afterward. Or you may need to be alone for a while. Set up the situation so that you can get what you need.

There is much to be gained by this type of confrontation. If (and when) it is right for you, go ahead and do it. One of my clients said that, after visiting his uncle's grave in the Midwest, everything in his hometown took on a new perspective. He was apprehensive because he had to visit his parents' home immediately afterward for a family gathering. These events had, in the past, been scenes of great discomfort for him. He was concerned that he would be too upset or too drained to participate in family interaction. But there seemed to be no way around it—he went. To his surprise he discovered that, by having gone to his uncle's grave, crying and telling him how badly it had hurt, expressing his grief, fear, anger—and love, he was able to let go of what had kept him from being a part of his family. He could understand how he had been resenting his parents for not protecting him from the abuse. He felt freed of the need to live with the abuse. He had returned the responsibility for the abuse to his uncle. A weight had been lifted from his shoulders, and he could begin to move ahead with his life. Upon his return to Boston, he immediately began to effect major changes in his life.

If you don't know where the grave is, or don't wish to do a graveside confrontation, you can use other representations of the perpetrator. Possibilities include speaking to an old photograph. Looking at her image can stir up the emotions that you need to take you through this procedure. You can also imagine talking to a deceased perpetrator by using some of the role-playing techniques that have been mentioned earlier. Or you may wish to write your own obituary or eulogy for the perpetrator, incorporating whatever you feel needs to be said. There are many ways to evoke the image of an abuser. Ask your therapist, other survivors, or friends to support you in discovering what works best for you. And, as with any other confrontation, make sure that you take sufficient time afterward to process the experience and appreciate yourself for having done it.

5 / Confronting "nonperpetrators." Confrontation does not have to be limited to the individual(s) who directly abused you. Remember that confrontation is a process of standing up to the *abuse*, not just to the abuser. In doing so you are standing up for yourself. You may have a need to confront other family members who failed to protect you. Did they know what was going on? If they knew, why didn't they put an end to the abuse? If they didn't know, why didn't they? The person or persons who acquiesced in (or encouraged) the abuse also reinforced your isolation. You have a right to feel betrayed; you don't have to protect anyone from your feelings—or theirs. Say what you need to say. Don't continue to sacrifice yourself to the pain of silence and pretense. When you decide to stand up to the abuse, everyone benefits. The people who care about you will want to help you heal the wounds of incest.

As you can see, the question of confrontation is not an easy one.

Whatever you choose to do about it, know that you have a right to be respected for your decision. Take the time you require, get the information and support you need, and proceed in the way that makes the most sense for you.

FOCUS

WHY DIDN'T THEY DO SOMETHING?

A question that plagues incest survivors is, "Why didn't somebody do something to stop the abuse?" When the adult survivor examines his childhood, he begins to question the role of the nonabusive parent and/or other adults in his life. Did they know what was going on? If they knew, why didn't they do something about it? If they didn't know, why not?

These questions speak to the power of denial. People will often ignore what they don't want to deal with. It is clear that nonprotective parents often know that something is wrong, whether or not they recognize the true nature of the situation.

There are many reasons why people fail to take action against child abuse. A dysfunctional family can create an "everyone for himself" atmosphere. Family members may be too concerned with their own survival to pay attention to any one else's. They may feel that they have to escape alone, without encumbrances. They may be in competition for scarce emotional resources and not want to tip the balance against themselves. Other family members may even feel jealous of the abused child for receiving special attention. They may fear

for their own safety, be confused about what to do, or simply not care.

But while ignorance, fear, confusion, and apathy are explanations for inaction, they are not excuses. Adults have a responsibility to protect children from harm.

An adult survivor may feel a greater sense of betrayal by nonprotective parent figures than by the actual perpetrator. His feelings of anger at this form of abandonment are appropriate. To allow abusive behavior through inaction is to condone it. It constitutes neglect, another form of child abuse.

Nonprotective parents can be most helpful to the survivor's recovery by accepting their role in the abuse. Attempting to make excuses, deflect the anger, or minimize the problem only serves to inflict more guilt and shame. It is a continuation of the abuse. Accepting the anger as justified may be more painful—and may deepen the rift between the survivor and the nonprotective adult—but it is better than a false closeness based on denial and pretense. Ultimately, it contributes to the healing process. There is no way to undo the past, but some genuine help can be offered in the present.

IVAN'S STATEMENT

There are many ways of confronting abusers
that don't involve face-to-face interaction.
In this letter to his mother (which he edited
for confidentiality), "Ivan" confronts the abuse
clearly and powerfully. He invites her to
participate in the healing process, but will
move on with his recovery whether or not
she is willing or able to do so.

June 30, 198—

Dear Mom,

I'm sure you've noticed that I haven't been in touch with
you lately. To be honest, the reason is that I've been avoiding
you. I've just needed that space, and have enjoyed it. I want
to keep not having contact with you for a while, maybe a long
while, but I don't want to feel like I'm avoiding you. So I
want to tell you why.

At last, I have the strength and safety in my life to begin to
face the facts about what it was like to grow up with you.
Some of the facts are good. Yes, we did go on vacation a lot,
and Jim and I did get a lot of encouragement from you, and I
know it wasn't all bad. But dammit, that wasn't all. It is very
hard to face the fact that it wasn't *all* good, that some of our
past is downright ugly and terrifying to go back to. But I have
to go back, because these ugly things have long-reaching,
powerful effects on my feelings and behavior and ability to
trust today. I am in the business of making myself grow, of
developing an ability to trust, to crawl out of the mindless
terror of my life, that all began with you. So here I am,
writing to you.

What is he talking about? I hear you ask. I am talking about
child abuse, and nothing minor at that. I realize that you may
find some of this hard to remember. Often you were drunk
when this kind of thing happened. Usually you were in a state
of intense rage at my father, or me, or somebody else. And all

of it is so very scary that I found it easier to "forget" about it for decades. So you may have done the same. Whatever you've chosen to do with your memories, I can't stand mine anymore. This really happened. To me. So, if you draw a blank, reach back and try to see it.

Let's get down to specifics. Most of this, the worst, happened before we moved south, from my birth to age four-and-a-half. From there it continued, but in less intensity. By then I had developed some survival mechanisms, and Jim's birth meant that you and I weren't alone as much.

In these early years I thought you were two people: "Mommy," and "Scary Lady." "Mommy" was nice and fed me and hugged me and put me to bed, and loved me. "Scary Lady" was violent and erratic. She would attack me sexually and physically, and I was so scared of her that I would literally freeze in terror.

I will give you a description of one specific incident, one that is particularly clear to me. It is also the one that has been the very hardest for me to accept, that someone who was supposed to love me, my mother, could ever do such an ugly thing to me. This is what happened:

1966, Anytown, USA. I saw you yelling at Daddy, really mad at him for something. You pushed him out of the door, hitting him. He tried briefly to stay, but left. Still confused and angry, you came to me, and picked me up. I believe this was in one of the upstairs rooms, one that faced toward the lake. I remember the morning sun coming in the window, warm. You had a knife or razor blade in your right hand. You were mad, yelling and moving your head around a lot. Your hair was all tousled, and your eyes were wide open but jerking around in a funny way. This was "Scary Lady." With a quick jerky movement, you cut my left hand between my first finger and my thumb with the knife. It was a good-sized cut, nothing minor, and it bled a lot. It hurt. You were surprised, and scared, and you dropped or put me down on the hardwood floor. You had blood all over your white or rose-colored blouse, and blood on your hands. You reached back down to me, I don't know why, but all I saw was your blood-stained hands coming at me again. I screamed and curled up. You ran out of the room, closing the door behind you.

I was very, very alone. I saw a small puddle of my blood on the wooden floor, next to where I lay. I saw blood coming out of my hand, warm and horrifying, like it would never stop. I didn't know how to apply pressure, I was only four; on the contrary, it hurt and I didn't want to touch it. I flailed around yelling and crazily moving my arms around. This lasted forever. Slowly, I felt my strength ebb, and my shock gave way to faintness. I passed out, still bleeding, lying in my own blood. You were long gone.

So I don't know how long I was passed out before you came back to clean up your mess. What strikes me all the more is my luck. As incoherent and angry as you were, you cut me wherever you could. If you had cut me an inch lower, on one of the veins on my wrist, you would have come back to find me DEAD. I'm sure that's what your first thought was when you came back into that hellish room. You really nearly killed me.

Do you remember this? I used to think that it was just a coincidence that I fainted often, especially at the sight of blood, and that I was afraid of knives. But, no. This is why. And the crappy thing is, that this isn't all I remember about what you did to me. I remember much more, and there are half-uncovered memories that I'm still too afraid to face.

Furthermore, this early stripping of my self-esteem and power led to a childhood in which four other people sexually abused me, including a very violent episode which resulted in my hospitalization for a urethra/bladder infection, my head-banging frustration in school, and my years of therapy with Dr. C———. These four are responsible for what they've done, but I never would have been as vulnerable to them had you not attacked me before they did. You really set me up for them, and I hate you for it. And I hate you for what you did yourself.

I wonder how you're feeling as you read this, but I really don't care now. I keep not wanting to tell, to force a weak "I love you," to do anything to protect you from your responsibility. I do hope you have the sense to seek help, to talk to a friend about this. But help or no help, sooner or later, you must face up to the reality of your violence against me.

What do I want from you? I mainly want you to know that I know, and that I am not remaining silent about this anymore. I want you to understand that I don't want to see you because I am angry at you. I want you to know that this was not just "in the past." There are long-term struggles that I face every day which make my life far more painful, difficult, lonely, and impoverished than it would have been without your abuse. I want you to know that therapy, which has saved my life, is expensive. It is my single largest expense next to rent. But I'm worth it, even if I'm the one who has to pay.

I would like some acknowledgment from you, even an apology. Ideally, I would like you to pay for my recovery expenses. Unfortunately, I don't expect any of this, I don't expect anything more from you than minimalization and denial. Keep these to yourself, if you can stand them. I challenge you to exceed my expectations, to take some responsibility for your past actions. If you can do this, write me. Otherwise, I don't want to hear from you. And don't expect me to reach out to you anymore, not now. I like this space, and intend to keep it.

So, this is why I'm not in touch with you. I know that deep down inside, you know what I'm talking about.

Very much alive,

Ivan

Copies sent to:

| Minister | Brother | Father |
| Uncle | My therapist | Selected friends |

About Forgiving and Forgetting

There are no verdicts to childhood, only consequences, and the bright freight of memory.
—PAT CONROY, *Prince of Tides*

Even the best-intentioned people may not know what to do when they see or hear about traumatic events. As caring individuals they want to be supportive and encouraging, but have no idea of what constitutes a helpful response. It is hard to witness someone who is in physical or emotional pain. It is natural to try to do everything they can to make the hurt go away. People want to help because they truly care but also because the situation restimulates painful memories of times when they were hurt. In the midst of this painful emotion, they are less able to think clearly, and may resort to cliches and other patterned responses. These unthinking reactions, while motivated by love and caring, often serve to increase pain by telling the sufferer that he must stop feeling bad. Unfortunately, in order to accomplish that, it would be necessary to stop feeling altogether. When bad things happen, it is appropriate to feel bad—and to express those emotions. This is an essential part of the healing process. However, because these emotions are a response to trauma, they tend to get confused with the hurt itself. The mistaken idea is that, if the person would only stop expressing the pain, he would stop feeling it—and it would go away. Well, it just doesn't happen that way. Crying is not grief; it is a way to get over the grief. Trembling is not an expression of cowardice; it is a way of moving out of the paralysis engendered by fear. But our culture tells us otherwise. We are uncomfortable with our emotions, and that discomfort is reflected in our behavior.

Whether the individual is an adult who is undergoing the loss of a loved one, or a child who has skinned his knee in the playground, the most frequent reactions he encounters are attempts to distract or "comfort" him—by getting him to turn off the expression of his feelings. A hurt child needs loving attention while crying, shaking, and talking his way through the feelings that come from having been injured. When he is able to receive that kind of attention, recovery is quite rapid. Having discharged the feelings and processed the event, he can return to playing—clearheaded and happy. But most adults are disturbed by a child's tears and attempt to stop them. They may do it with bribes and pacifiers. ("Here, don't you want an ice cream cone?" "If you stop crying, I'll buy you a toy.") This technique not only informs the child that it isn't OK to feel, it lets him know that adults are so upset by tears that he can manipulate them by crying. Adults may attempt other distraction techniques. ("Let me kiss it and make it better." "There, there, stop crying . . . look at that big doggie over there.") Or they may attempt to shame, ridicule or criticize the child into calm. ("Big boys don't cry." "You're acting like a little crybaby." "You weren't really hurt *that* badly." "You made a big crack in the sidewalk.") Finally, the adult may attempt to turn off the child's uncomfortable expression of feelings by threats of punishment ("If you don't stop crying I'll give you something to cry about.") or actual violence. All of these responses serve to aggravate the hurt. At best, a child who has been bribed, distracted, ridiculed, or punished remains cranky and irritable. He feels misunderstood, rejected, and isolated. Having had his difficulties belittled, he feels that help is unavailable. In the future, believing that he has no right to his feelings, he may avoid seeking help—retreating instead into "self-sufficient" isolation. Or he may become increasingly needy, seeking comfort and understanding in inappropriate ways. In either case, feelings of inadequacy and shame have been reinforced, further shaking the child's confidence that it is possible to take charge of his life.

We have all experienced these responses to childhood traumas. When we encounter them as adults, they have a familiar ring. We are likely to stop thinking about what we need, and react in ways that we learned when young. Although not the most helpful approach to pain, this kind of regressive behavior is a self-protective response. When we are undergoing upsetting experiences in adult life, we are less likely to be able to say, "I need you to just be there and allow me to cry" or "Just hold me." We have been taught to be "good soldiers" and not show our feelings. We know how to keep our own counsel and protect other people from our feelings. Incest survivors are particularly well trained in keeping people calm. Male survivors, carrying the additional cultural disapproval of men who cry, are extremely unlikely to express their feelings in the presence of others.

It is natural to want to create distance from painful emotions, whether one's own or someone else's. When the experience that generated the pain occurred in the past—as is the case with childhood sexual abuse—people will attempt to relegate it to the past. In the grip of their own painful feelings about sexual abuse and emotional expression, they are unable to think clearly; they cannot respond appropriately to the incest survivor's needs. Instead, they resort to giving advice that only serves to further isolate the incest survivor.

The most frequent form of advice is some variation of "You need to learn to forgive" or "It happened so long ago, why can't you just put it behind you?" Although they truly believe that they have the best interests of the survivor at heart, what they are in fact doing is the emotional equivalent of telling a person who was bitten by a rabid dog, "If you just ignore it, it will go away." Not only does this response reflect a total lack of understanding of the ongoing effects of sexual abuse, it delivers a clear message to the survivor. Aware of the listener's discomfort, he receives confirmation that what happened to him was so horrible and disgusting that he had better keep his mouth shut about it or he will drive everyone away. As a child he learned to pretend and protect the feelings of others; as an adult he is certain that he must continue the pretense. No one, he feels, could stand knowing who he really is. The inability of his listeners to tolerate his story and his feelings is seen as evidence that *he* is intolerable.

Nor is the inherent criticism in statements like "You should learn to forgive" lost on the survivor. If he were a "better" person (stronger, more forgiving, kinder, more mature), he reasons, then he would be able to put all this behind him and embrace the perpetrator. That he is unable to do so becomes yet another corroboration of his personal failings. This sort of guidance is harmful, and it is easy to buy into—since it reinforces the survivor's existing feelings of shame, self-blame, and responsibility for the abuse. This advice buttresses the wall of secrecy and silence—the very wall that needs to be torn down.

There are effective ways of helping someone who is having a rough time. One is simply to listen to him. Although our programming tells us, "Don't just sit there, *do* something!" the reverse is likely to be far more helpful. Instead of rushing headlong into inappropriate advice or action, *"Don't just do something, sit there!"* Sitting and listening to an incest survivor *is* doing something. It is doing something important. Showing that you care—that what he has to say deserves to be listened to, and that he has a right to have feelings about the abuse—is an important contradiction of the internalized negative messages. How many times have any of us had the wonderful experience of someone listening to us without offering judgment, criticism, advice, or blame? How often have we seen someone looking at us with love and approval while we talked about what it has been like for us? When has someone just held us as we shook, taken our hands as we cried, without trying to stem the flow of feelings? Those of us who have experienced this type of caring know how therapeutic it is. For an incest survivor, it is vital to receive aware, loving attention. No, listening to someone is not "doing nothing." Active, aware attention is a special skill. To develop that skill and offer it to another human being is a valuable gift. To the incest survivor, it can make a world of difference.

As an incest survivor, you may have to let people know how to be more effective allies in your recovery. You may need to teach them how to listen, giving them feedback about what isn't helpful—*as well as appreciation and encouragement for what is*. It isn't enough to criticize what they haven't done. If you only do that, they will eventually give up out of frustration. And you can't expect them to guess. ("If you really cared about me you'd know how I feel.") They are friends, not mind readers. Talk to them, show them, consult with them. If you don't know what's best for you, admit your confusion and try out a number of possibilities. One of them might work. The caring is what is most important; work out the details together.

Forgiving

In the preceding paragraphs I have written about how the concept of forgiveness can be used in unhelpful, avoidant, and punitive ways. Having done that, we can look at what remains. Is forgiveness ever appropriate? If so, under what circumstances? Do you, in fact, need to "learn to forgive" the perpetrator? Again, I won't make you wait for an answer. I will tell you, clearly and emphatically, that *it is not necessary for you to forgive the person who abused you!* Do what makes sense for you. Forgiveness may never be the right course of action for you. The choice to forgive or not to forgive is entirely yours.

Forgiveness—like any other aspect of recovery—is an individual matter. There isn't one answer that fits all survivors. The issue is complex. It requires time and careful thinking before even deciding whether the concept of forgiveness is relevant to your situation. Some survivors feel that forgiving the person who abused them allowed them to let go of ties to the past and move forward with their recovery. For others, forgiveness seems like acceptance of the abusive behavior. Many survivors are simply not ready to even consider the possibility. You are the only one who can determine what is right and what is possible for you. Once again, it is important that you not proceed according to someone else's values and agenda. The concept of "forgiveness" is open to a wide range of interpretation. You must examine the idea within the context of your own moral, ethical and cultural values if you are to make the decision that is right for you. And, even if you accept the *idea* of forgiveness, you must be the one to decide whether or not the time is right. Don't be pushed. If it is to be right, it must be genuine. While I can't tell you what to do, I have some suggestions that might help you feel better about your decisions:

1 / Take your time. Don't rush to forgive. Whether or not forgiveness will ever be relevant, it is not appropriate in the early stages of recovery. There is too much work that you need to do first. Part of that work involves identifying your feelings about the abuse *and the abuser*, and allowing yourself permission to feel the hurt, fear, and humiliation. As you begin to recognize the unfairness of your childhood—in the course of regaining your power—you will probably need to express your outrage at what happened and at the individuals *who were responsible*. These initial steps cannot be taken in an atmosphere of forgiveness. If forgiveness is to come, there is time for it . . . later. For now, you have other priorities.

2 / Protect yourself. Beware of getting trapped by pity. Be careful not to yield to the inclination to protect or take care of the perpetrator. Even though you may care deeply for him, he is not in need of your protection—you are! All too often premature forgiveness serves to revictimize the survivor. It takes the form of minimizing the abuse or sharing the responsibility for it. Remember that everybody benefits when abuse is stopped (including the perpetrator; acting abusively is never a healthy mode of human behavior). Your recovery is in everyone's best interest. Don't sacrifice it to misguided feelings of pity, protectiveness or responsibility.

3 / Explore your real feelings. Consider forgiveness. What feelings arise when you do? You may be surprised to discover that you already have some feelings on the subject. Pay some attention to those feelings; they came from somewhere. No one has more information about your situation than you. Planning to forgive is usually less effective than figuring out how you really feel about it. Examine your heart—you'll know if and when you're ready to forgive.

4 / You can change your mind. Recovery is a dynamic process. Things change. What is appropriate at one point in your recovery may be counterindicated or irrelevant at another. Right now you may feel that you will never forgive the perpetrator, and later on find that your feelings are quite different. Or you may attempt forgiveness only to discover that you are unable to do so. It is all right to change your mind; what you are doing is finding out what is right for you. You are trying on alternatives so that you can select the one that is best for you.

5 / Forgiveness takes different forms. If you choose to forgive the perpetrator, there are a number of ways to do so. You can say so directly. This will allow you to get an immediate response. As with confrontation, be aware that the response you receive may be quite different than you anticipated. There will be no Hollywood-style reconciliation scene with music and flowers. Declaring forgiveness may be a beginning step in building a viable relationship. Or your forgiveness may be rejected or misinterpreted.

Remember to prepare yourself for the possibility of disappointment. As discussed above, it is essential that you take steps to protect yourself.

If direct contact is not what you want, you can declare forgiveness on the telephone or by letter. The latter, of course, allows you to state what you wish without the possibility of interruption. You can also forgive someone without telling him directly, manifesting it through a change in your behavior. Finally, it is possible to forgive in your heart, without doing anything about it directly. It is your decision, to be shared only if you want to—with only those you choose to.

6 / It isn't "all or nothing." Forgiveness doesn't have to be total. A little can go a long way. You can experiment with a little bit of forgiveness, just to see whether it's right for you. You can move closer gradually or dance back and forth according to your needs. Remember, once again, your primary responsibility is to your own well-being.

7 / Think about what you mean by forgiveness. It is important that, in the process of forgiving a person, we do not condone the abuse. What happened to you was wrong. Child abuse is always bad. If you forgive the perpetrator, it must be with the understanding that you have decided to bear no malice toward someone who has committed a grievous offense against you. It is an act of pardon, not of exoneration.

Revenge

Revenge has been a forbidden topic. Although all children have fantasized about "getting even" with their parents, expression of these fantasies is usually greeted with reactions of shock and dismay. As an adult incest survivor you may be frightened by images of revenge. You may feel that your fantasies are wrong—that you should be above such base desires. But there is nothing wrong with feeling like avenging the hurts that you have suffered. You are correctly feeling outrage at an outrageous act. And you need the freedom to express your desire to punish the people who abused you. An incest survivors' recovery group or workshop is a particularly appropriate place for you to do so. One of the most exciting aspects of the group experience occurs when a participant begins to share his thoughts about taking revenge against the perpetrator. These can range from lurid fantasies of torture and physical violence to elaborately thought out plans for confrontation, public exposure, and/or legal action. Whatever their form, revenge themes are evidence that the survivor has stopped blaming himself for the abuse and is demanding that the perpetrator be held accountable for his or her actions. It is a powerful stance—the anger is that of righteous indignation. When a male survivor voices revenge fantasies to the group, he usually is surprised at the energy with which the other members support, encourage, and even build upon his ideas. A genuine bonding occurs as group members cheer one another on to more powerful behavior. You will also find yourself encouraging the revenge fantasies of the other group members.

Considering putting these revenge fantasies into effect is another matter. Although the saying tells us "revenge is sweet," it has a way of turning bitter. Remember that some forms of retribution carry severe penalties. You have been hurt enough; be careful not to do anything that will result in further pain. Revenge is not necessarily a bad idea, *if* it can take a form that will further your recovery rather than set it back. As delicious as the prospect of killing, injuring or even abusing the perpetrator may be, acting on those feelings is almost certain to be harmful to your well-being. You have been punished enough; don't risk further pain for the momentary satisfaction of getting even. There are other sayings about revenge: one is that it is "a dish best eaten cold." If you choose to pursue revenge, it may ultimately be more satisfying to seek redress through such indirect means as public exposure or litigation. It will certainly be safer. Perhaps the most realistic saying is "living well is the best revenge." Moving toward the creation of a satisfying life is certainly the sweetest aspect of overcoming the abuse. Enjoying your own recovery, helping others to effect theirs, and then working together to put an end to sexual abuse will provide profound and lasting rewards.

Self-Forgiveness Without question, this is the most important need of all. As long as you continue to accept blame for what happened to you—as long as you buy any part of the lies that you have been told—the abuse is continuing. Although having been abused does not call for forgiveness of others, it *is* necessary for you to "forgive yourself." You need to excuse yourself for all the wasted time, withdrawal, depression, and failures of your life. You need to "pardon" yourself for having behaved in ways that brought pain to others. You must forgive yourself for self-inflicted pain. It is often helpful to do this in the company of other survivors. They can make sure that you don't turn the process into another form of self-punishment. Self-forgiveness must not be a further assigning of blame. Instead, it is an acknowledgment of your basic goodness and a celebration of your survival. It represents a decision to include yourself in the kindness and respect that you extend to the rest of the world. As you continue to let go of blaming yourself, you are standing up to the abuse. Self-forgiveness is an important aspect of recovering your self-respect. When you begin to take delight in who you are—as you grow to respect your own perception, judgment, values and timing—you are well along in your recovery.

Moving On

And this morning I thought of the Resistance surfacing after the War, (the tyrant's body hanging in the public square) restoring the rightful names of the capital's streets, renaming the places where the old names now mean little.
   —RICHARD HOFFMAN, from his poem "Yesterday. Last Night. This Morning."

There is no specific moment when the incest recovery process ends —no instantly recognizable goal. As you undertake healing the wounds of childhood sexual abuse, you begin a journey of exploration and education. In the course of this odyssey you gain insight into yourself, your experience, and the world. You come to the realization that you are not alone. In sharing your story with others, you find that there are people who can listen to you, understand what you are saying, and believe that you are telling the truth. You discover that there are many other people who have undergone similar experiences. In encouraging one another to share your stories, you begin to forge a support network, made up of fellow survivors and other caring individuals (VOICES in Action refers to them as "prosurvivors"). Individual counseling and group therapy become laboratories that let you experiment with trusting other people—practicing in a safe environment until you are ready to take further risks in the wider world.

Breaking out of your isolation and developing support systems enable you to move ahead with the establishment of healthy social interactions. You begin to make new acquaintances, develop friendships, and even form nonabusive loving relationships. In the course of your recovery you continue to discover strengths, capabilities, and resources that you hadn't realized you possess. You learn more about the benign aspects of the world—where you can turn for help, information, and protection. And you begin to realize that the world isn't a completely dangerous place. You learn to distinguish between real and imaginary dangers—how to protect yourself from the genuine risks without needing to protect yourself from life. You give up the defensive stance that had forced you to see the world in all-or-nothing

Temporary Setbacks, Ongoing Recovery

terms; you accept that the world is neither completely safe nor totally dangerous. And you find that an imperfect world can be quite wonderful.

Over time, you build self-esteem, realizing that you have a right to a full, rich life. As you treat yourself with respect, you start to expect respectful treatment. And you notice that the world seems to be treating you better. Feeling that you deserve more of the good things in life, you find yourself taking steps in your education, career, community, and personal life that didn't seem possible before. (In fact, they weren't available to you while you were trapped by the effects of the abuse.) When you look back at where you were, you are amazed at the extent of the change. Life hasn't become perfect, but it is livable—and sometimes even satisfying.

Be gentle with yourself and keep the following issues in mind:

1 / Discouragement. These changes don't come easily. Recovery takes time. It's an ongoing process that requires courage and determination. You will feel pain and confusion. There will be times when nothing seems to be happening; at other times you'll be discouraged and want to give up. Sometimes you'll wonder if the rewards are worth the pain, and you'll doubt that you're up to the struggle. Even when good things happen, old feelings of fear and mistrust will arise to undermine your gains. If you are feeling vulnerable, any setback can cause you to believe that you haven't really made any progress. A relatively small disappointment appears to undo all your accomplishments. Expect that there will be times when you feel exhausted, overwhelmed, and hopeless. The hurts of incestuous abuse are deep; recovery takes time. For every fast, exhilarating period of forward movement, there are times of slow, difficult growth, and plateaus of apparent inactivity. All of these are necessary parts of your recovery. If you understand their importance, you can anticipate them—not with relish, but with acceptance of the fact that they are temporary.

2 / Perspective. The road to recovery is rarely direct, and it is never a superhighway. (It usually feels more like an obstacle course.) Although you are experiencing general forward movement, a temporary setback can cause you to lose perspective. Feeling that all your work has been negated, you are tempted just to give up. It is for this reason that you must stop periodically and take stock of the situation. Times of inactivity are perfect for this endeavor. You can stop, rest, and take a look around you. Think about where you were at this time last year, two years ago, three. Think about the changes that you have made and the people who care about you. Despite your current bad feelings, does the present disappointment really negate all the progress you've made? You may want to take time to chronicle your recovery; a diary or journal provides you with visible evidence of how your thinking and feelings have changed. When you're feeling discouraged, take time to test reality. Talk to friends and other survivors. Share your feelings with them, and ask them for feedback. They may remind you of things that you've forgotten. Go to a meeting or social activity, and get back in touch with your support network. It is also helpful to talk with someone who has just recently begun to deal with his own incest experience. Seeing him going through the initial agonies of discovery, sharing your experience and insight, will help him out, while providing you with some useful perspective on your own progress.

3 / Relaxation. Feeling discouraged and overwhelmed provides you with another message. This business of recovery isn't easy. You've been working too hard. As much as you want to get through this all at once, it doesn't happen that way. You need time for rest, relaxation, and play. Vacations aren't charity. They were invented for a reason. They are given to employees because they are good for business. Taking time to recuperate from the rigors of everyday life allows you to return to the struggle with renewed energy. When I suggest to an incest survivor that he take some time to play, he will often reply that he doesn't know how to relax. If I encourage him further—saying that learning to enjoy life is part of recovery—he is likely to say, "OK, I'll work on it." My response is, "Play on it." You don't have to wait until it's all over before taking enjoyment from life. Allow yourself pleasure along the way. It will remind you of why you are doing all this in the first place. Relaxation is not a distraction from the task at hand; it is an important part of that task. A well-rounded, satisfying life includes play as well as work; leisure as well as activity. If you don't know how to enjoy yourself, it's time that you learned. Enlist the help of people who know how to play—what more pleasant favor could you ask of someone? Do some things you've thought about, but never did because they were too silly/frivolous/juvenile/foolish/wasteful. Even though recovery is serious, it doesn't always have to be heavy. You've always guessed that there should be more to life than pain and struggle. And you were right. Accept that you deserve to take part in the pleasures of life, not just the pain. Accept my assurance that rewarding yourself is an essential aspect of your recovery.

4 / Acceptance of progress. There will be times when you question whether the rewards of recovery are worth all the effort. You will wonder whether you have the stamina to sustain a project that promises to go on forever. (Even though you know that there really isn't any other choice. You have tried withdrawing, numbing, and a host of other strategies—and the pain remained. You're doing this because you have to. It's the only course of action that makes sense. And once you've begun to recover, difficult as it is, there's really no turning back. You know, deep down, that you're on the right track. But the knowledge doesn't keep you from sometimes feeling uncertainty, discouragement, and doubt.) When you start to feel this kind of self-doubt, it is helpful to get a good, healthy dose of appreciation. It can come from friends, other incest survivors, or *yourself*. You need acknowledgment that what you are doing is very difficult. You need reassurance that it is understandable that you are feeling discouraged and overwhelmed. And you deserve admiration for having decided to put an end to the way abuse has ruled your life. Accept the fact that the progress you have achieved is genuine. Bask in the appreciation, admiration, and encouragement of those who know what you've accomplished. If you're ready for it, ask for a hug or two. Look in the mirror and see how you have changed. Admire what you have done and what you are going to do.

What We're Up Against

Earlier chapters addressed the need for joining together with other incest survivors (and prosurvivors) for mutual support, understanding, and affirmation. Beyond this personal aspect of the recovery process, there is another important reason for survivors to interact with one another. The ideas and attitudes of the overall culture toward incest must be reshaped. This can only be done actively and cooperatively. Laws must be changed, books and articles must be written, and the outcry must be heard in all quarters. It must be shown that we are no longer willing to put up with a society that ignores or romanticizes abuse and thereby sacrifices its children.

The only way that these fundamental changes can be accomplished is through strength of numbers. Moral outrage doesn't seem to be enough if only a few people express it. There are powerful forces operating to hold the abusive attitudes firmly in place; to dislodge them will take further strength and concerted action. Even if you don't think of yourself as "political" or as an "activist," it is easy to see why you must work to help bring about these changes. As long as incest continues to be ignored or condoned—as long as children continue to be abused—you will be faced with an ongoing reminder of what happened to you.

It has been said that no one can truly be free as long as anyone is enslaved. Sadly, entrenched attitudes don't change easily. Change must be fought for and won—often at great cost. Blacks, women, Jews, and trade unionists had to struggle for recognition of their rights (and must continue to fight to consolidate their gains and keep moving forward). Gay men and lesbians, people with physical disabilities, mental patients, some ethnic, religious and racial minorities, and other groups are actively engaged in trying to bring about widespread recognition that there is a problem, and that it is up to all of us to do something about it. It is to everyone's advantage to bring about these changes for our children, our loved ones—and ourselves.

Who, then, stands in the way of these changes? Wouldn't everyone agree that child abuse is a serious problem that needs to be remedied? Unfortunately, the answer to these questions is that there are many forces at work to oppose change (some are conscious and active; others support child sexual abuse through denial, minimizing, and apathy):

1 / There are those who fear to deal with the issue at all. It is too ugly, too frightening, or an otherwise too distasteful "can of worms," and they don't want to touch it. If pressed, they resort to excuses like "It isn't really *that* widespread a problem." The response to that bit of nonsense is that incestuous abuse is epidemic, affecting millions of people. Even if only one child were being abused, it would be wrong, hurtful, and cause for outrage. But the fact is that sexual abuse of children is widespread, and for centuries we have accepted a system that allows these kinds of harmful attitudes and behaviors to be perpetuated. Now is the time to stop it. Ignoring or denying a problem has never been known to make it go away. The world turned its attention away from Nazism, allowing millions of Jews, Catholics, gays, mentally ill, Poles, Gypsies, physically handicapped, political opponents, and others to be slaughtered. To deny reality is to condone the abuse. It is everyone's responsibility to put an end to sexual abuse.

2 / There are powerful economic forces working to keep us from putting an end to child abuse. There is a multimillion dollar industry in this country that depends upon the sexual exploitation of children. One need only look at mass media advertising to see children being portrayed as seductive objects of adult sexual desire. To show it condones it. We are allowing ourselves to be titillated by the outrageous and repulsive. In addition to the "acceptable" forms of exploitation, fortunes are being made in child pornography (which has been dubbed "kiddie porn" by the media—a cute diminutive that serves to soften the reality in the same way as calling a weapon of mass destruction a "nuke"). Runaway and "throwaway" children, boys and girls, in increasing numbers are to be found as prostitutes. Rather than seeking to protect these children, society's institutions tend to ignore them. This allows them to be exploited by unscrupulous people for personal economic gain. What has been called the "pro-incest lobby" stands in the way of implementation of child protective legislation. We cannot continue to allow people to profit at the expense of our children and our collective well-being.

3 / There are individuals and groups that seek to justify gratification of their own sexual desires. There are people who argue that sex with children is acceptable, consensual, or even beneficial. When their activities are criticized, they throw up smoke screens, crying about freedom of association and individual rights. They fool many well-meaning people into seeing this as a "civil rights" issue, rather than what it is—a sexual abuse of power, exploiting children who are unable to advocate for themselves. They join with the economic exploiters of child abuse in railing against the "erotophobia" of a society that tries to deny that "children are sexual beings." They stridently attempt to obscure the distinction between sex and sexual abuse. This perversion of the concept of civil liberties limits protection to the perpetrators, ignoring the rights and needs of children for nonabusive nurturing. Thus pedophilia becomes acceptable and children become sexual playthings. We can no longer afford to sacrifice children to gratify adult sexual desires.

4 / There are people who attempt to justify incestuous abuse by cloaking it under the concept of the privacy and sanctity of the family. This is a tricky and touchy area. It is within their family context that children are first exposed to cultural, religious, moral and social values. Because of the inarguable primary importance of family, we have developed a social system that supports it with laws, protective agencies, tradition, economic support, cultural mythology, and community feelings.

The family has become a quasi-sacred concept, and people are extremely reluctant to interfere with it on any level. Any attempt to do so is greeted with outrage at the infringement of human rights by an unfeeling government, press, or other outside agency. Unfortunately, this well-meaning defense of the right of a family to determine its own beliefs and activities is based on the concept of a healthy family—one that is dedicated to the well-being of all its members. In that instance, while one might disagree with some of the family's values and ideas, they can be respected as evidence of the diversity that exists in a large, pluralistic society. Interference would constitute a major violation of the right to freedom of belief. Assistance would come in the form of establishing a system of excellent, affordable child care. But when abuse enters the picture, the need for protection of children supercedes the right of parental control. It is a time for direct, decisive action in the child's best interest. This does not mean that the rights of the family can be ignored. On the contrary, great pains must be taken to ensure that the situation is indeed abusive, and that we are not simply facing a disagreement about child-rearing philosophies. We must understand all we can about child sexual abuse and its effects. We must develop clear and reasonable definitions of abuse and procedures for dealing with it. But the child must be protected throughout this process.

People who maintain the value of "family unity" at all costs are misguided. All too often, that cost is the welfare of one or more children sacrificed to an image that doesn't reflect reality. A dysfunctional (alcoholic, violent, neglectful, sexually, or emotionally abusive) family is harmful to children. All children have the right to the protection of a healthy, loving family. Where such a family does not exist, it is up to society to protect the child from harm. We can begin by seeing to it that we interrupt existing cases of abuse as completely as possible. Wherever feasible, we should work to help families to recover from their dysfunctional patterns so that they can become whole. When this isn't possible, we must establish healing environments for the victims—as soon as the abuse is discovered. (The state of our current foster care and child protective systems is woefully inadequate. Removal of a child from a destructive family without placing him in an environment that is substantially healthier does not insure that his situation will improve.)

On a larger scale, we must all cooperate in changing some of our ideas about family, moving from acceptance of an authoritarian, patriarchal model to one that is based on a cooperative encouragement of all its members toward competence, confidence, and self-esteem. The unity of such a family doesn't need to be legislated; its harmony is a natural outgrowth of mutual respect.

How, then, can we accomplish the monumental task of changing our society to one where child sexual abuse is nonexistent? If the idea feels overwhelming, chances are you're feeling as though you have to do it all yourself—yesterday. Although the task is large, our resources are extensive. You don't have to do it all, and you aren't alone. If each of us undertakes what we do best, we'll make it. For some, this will be a matter of public action: lobbying for child protective legislation, picketing, running for public office. For others, the best course of action will be changing public attitudes through education: speaking and/or writing in classrooms, the media, and to community, educational, religious and professional organizations. For all of us, it is a matter of reexamining our own ideas, priorities, and behaviors, changing those that need to be changed, and helping those around us to do the same. This could mean resolving to spend more time with children, attending more meetings, talking about incest and other abuse whenever you can, perhaps sharing some of your own experience, or simply determining to treat all children and adults (including yourself) with respect.

Yes, changing the world is a tall order, but I believe that it can (and must) be done. And just think of how empowering it will be when we accomplish it. If you have any doubt of the importance of this undertaking, take a few minutes to stop, close your eyes, and imagine a world that is free of child abuse. Picture the results of treating *all* adults and children with respect and consideration. Think of how all aspects of society would be affected—family, community, education, religion, business, the military, art and literature, politics, entertainment. Can a world that really nurtures its children have room for nuclear war, murder, violence, rape, homelessness, poverty, famine, or bigotry? Can we really cherish our children, hoping that they will face the future safely and confidently, while building larger and more frightening weapons of destruction? (Dr. Leslie Fenn, a Boston-area physician who works with incest survivors, has been encouraging people to recognize the direct link between the way we treat our children and the ever-present threat of nuclear devastation.) Would it be possible for people to starve while food goes rotting in silos? Would we keep on poisoning our environment, knowing that succeeding generations could perish for lack of healthy air and clean water? Would it even be conceivable that someone would be kept from a decent life because of race, gender, religion, nationality, sexual orientation, social class, language, physical appearance, age, state of health, or level of intelligence? Obviously, the answer is "No, of course not." If your image of a world that is free of abuse looks better than the one we have now, then the choice is clear. Ultimately, the business of learning to love ourselves —to treat ourselves with exquisite respect and caring—requires that people join together to make things right. By making a commitment to world survival, we move to another level of recovery.

Once you have moved through the various stages of recovery, you will find that your feelings about yourself and the world have changed. You will feel (and actually be) more in charge of your life. You'll find that you have more confidence about daily activities and greater energy with which to carry them out. All sorts of new possibilities are now open to you.

For some survivors, this is the point at which they are able to put the victimization behind them and move on with their lives. Although their incestuous childhood will never be forgotten, it has been put into perspective. Abuse no longer dominates their every waking moment, draining joy and satisfaction from all their activities. They are able to enjoy a normal, satisfying life—one which contains the full range of pleasures, frustrations, joys, sorrows, and upsets that comprises a healthy human existence.

For most incest survivors, there remains one important piece of recovery. It involves engaging in activities which allow some positive meaning to emerge from the pain. The essence of this very important bit of closure is finding that they can use what they have learned (in the course of enduring and surviving abuse *as well as* in the process of recovery) to help other incest survivors. This type of activity (Dr. Judith Herman refers to it as "altruism") provides many incest survivors with the last piece of understanding that they need. Having accomplished it, they are free to go on with their lives.

The exact form taken by this last piece of activity depends upon the needs, skills, and personality of the individual survivor. You might find that what has worked for others will be useful to you, or you may need to create your own particular solution. The self-esteem that you have regained and developed during your recovery process will enable you to design a method that works for you. The following list includes some activities that other incest survivors have found helpful:

1 / Education. As you well know, there is very little reliable information about incest available to the general public. What does exist is often incomplete—or simply incorrect. There are millions of people who need to know the facts about childhood sexual abuse. (Some of them even *want* to hear the information.) More important, the information that is available usually concerns the details of abuse, along with some examples of the ongoing effects. There is virtually nothing about recovery. There is no one better able to educate both the public *and mental health professionals* about recovery than someone who has undergone the process. In a word—*you!*

You don't need to be a professional educator; you can find the outlet that fits your style. If you are comfortable with public speaking, you can talk at schools, churches, community groups, and other public forums. You can talk to parents, children, and/or other survivors. You may be surprised to find that there are groups of mental health, human service, and medical professionals that are eager to hear what you have to say. The media may be receptive to your message, and you are likely to find yourself being interviewed in newspapers or magazines—or appearing on radio or television public affairs shows. (Remember that you are under no obligation to do any of these things—or to do them in any way that isn't right for you. Don't allow yourself to be pressured, bullied, or coerced. That would be a form of revictimization. And it would do no one any good.) If you find it easier to put yourself out less visibly, consider writing about your experiences in articles, books, or letters to the editor. Your writing can be nonfiction or take the form of novels, short stories, plays, or poetry. You can express yourself (and spread the information) through song, dance, painting, or sculpture.

Don't be stopped by the feeling that nobody would be interested in what you have to say—or that you are too inarticulate or untalented. That's all nonsense, coming from the old misinformation that you received about yourself. You are the expert here. No one knows better than you what happened, how it felt, what the effects were—and what you did about it. And that's the information that can be so very helpful to other people. Just say it in your own words, at your own pace. Take charge. You will be amazed at how powerful you feel when you stand up to the abuse in this way.

2 / Lobbying and legislation. Very few states have enacted laws that adequately deal with the realities of child abuse or the needs of adult survivors. In many localities there are groups working to promote legislation that will protect children from having to suffer sexual abuse, and to extend or eliminate the statute of limitations on criminal and civil prosecution of perpetrators. You can find out what the existing laws are in your state and join (or start) a group which seeks to influence legislation in this area. There is tremendous satisfaction to be derived from knowing that you have had a hand in insuring that our society recognizes and adequately responds to the needs of incest survivors.

3 / Advocacy. Although it is important that our laws address the needs of survivors, the legal process is often painfully slow. In the meantime, it is important that incest survivors know what resources are presently available to them, and how to make the best use of existing services. You can join with any number of citizens' rights organizations to advocate for wider dissemination of information and greater availability of support for survivors. You can join with other survivors in forming a group that will pressure government, social service, educational, religious, and other organizations to be more responsive to the needs of survivors. A community that is committed to ending the abuse of any of its members is improving the quality of life of all its citizens. You have a special expertise that makes you a valuable part of that process.

4 / Direct action. Another form of advocacy is taking direct action to protect someone else who is being abused and seeing that she or he gets the right kind of help. This could mean standing up to the abuse of another member of your family; it may involve forcing other family members to face the facts of incest. You may also work toward the establishment of a visible, vocal incest survivors advocacy organization in your community—on the order of rape crisis hotlines, battered women's shelters, "safe houses." You can advocate that existing agencies take a more active role in incest-related issues, or start an organization whose sole purpose is protection and advocacy for survivors of childhood sexual abuse. It isn't as intimidating as it may appear. You can take on as much *or as little* of this task as makes sense for you. Many large and powerful organizations began with one or two people recognizing a need—and filling it. Maybe it's time for you to do some intimidating of your own—taking a stand that employs your newly recognized power.

5 / Direct service. Just as many drug and alcohol counselors are themselves former addicts and alcoholics, some of the most effective counselors and therapists for incest survivors were sexually abused as children. It may make sense for you to use what you have learned about incest recovery to help other survivors. You can do this as a volunteer (working on a hotline or in a peer counseling setting) or obtain the training required to take a professional role in addressing the needs of incest survivors. Whether it involves law, medicine, psychotherapy, social work, teaching, politics, the arts, religious or charitable work, there are many ways to add a professional focus to what you have learned during your recovery process. The time that you have spent in recovery hasn't been wasted. *It was not time taken* *out of your life—it has been (and continues to be) an important part of your life.* All thinking people, in one way or another, must undertake a journey of self-discovery. Don't devalue your process, make use of it. You have developed an important body of knowledge and experience. It is yours to employ in the ways that best serve you. To do so provides a positive example for other survivors, while consolidating the gains that you have made. Everyone wins.

6 / Combined activities. Any of the foregoing activities can be undertaken in combination. The newsletter of the Incest Survivors Information Exchange of New Haven, Connecticut (see resource list), for example, offers articles, poetry, drawings, and personal statements by incest survivors as well as information about resources, research, legislation and other matters of concern. Your work can be as general or as specific as you wish. It can be yours alone, or you can work with others, formally or informally. You can spend as much or as little time at it as is right for you. You can fit into existing structures or create your own. And you can always change the focus of what you do so that it continues to meet your own needs. Figuring out how to keep track of what is best for you while you are helping others is a vital bit of learning. Remember that when you are truly doing what is best for you, it is also in the best interest of those around you.

A word of caution about this aspect of recovery. *It doesn't work if you attempt it prematurely.* Many incest survivors rush to help others before they have done enough work on their own recovery. They do it for a number of reasons. They may be avoiding the pain of dealing with their own abuse. If that is the motivating reason, then it isn't part of moving on—helping others has then become another form of numbing. The survivor is attempting to provide what he needs for himself—with little chance of getting it back. It may be a continuation of a caretaking pattern that is deeply ingrained in his image of himself. It can be evidence of his feeling that he doesn't deserve the attention—that the only justification for his existence is what he can do for others. This is a reflection of what the abuse has done to destroy his self-esteem. It should not be respected. If you recognize that tendency in yourself, do your best to resist it. There will be plenty of time to assist others in their recovery, once you have taken care of your own. Taking the time to ensure that you have established a solid foundation for yourself will allow you to be far more effective in helping other survivors. Resist the feelings of urgency. Not only is there no need to hurry this process, attempting to do so doesn't work. Furthermore, there is no requirement that you undertake this type of altruism at all. It is not obligatory, and only works well if it is a logical outgrowth of your own individual path of recovery. Be patient with yourself. You will be providing other survivors (and the world) with a healthy example of positive growth. Instead of hiding or running, you will be "moving on" with your life, helping others as you help yourself.

PART FIVE

Other People, Other Resources

21

For (and About) Partners, Family, and Friends

This chapter is written for people who are in relationships with men who experienced sexual child abuse. I have two reasons for including it in a book that is directed to incest survivors. First, it is a recognition that there is virutally no information available for spouses, lovers, family, friends—and counselors—of survivors. Until such time as I am able to expand this chapter into a book for prosurvivors (or until someone else writes such a book), I hope that I can provide some helpful information for those of you who are in caring relationships with male survivors of sexual child abuse.

This chapter will examine some of the issues faced by people who care about men in recovery. It will attempt to provide perspective on the possibilities *and limitations* of supportive relationships. Unfortunately, one chapter cannot begin to deal adequately with so complex a situation. I want this to be a starting point for an enormous outpouring of information that needs to be provided for (and *by*) people who are involved with incest survivors. In addition to the paucity of information, there is a tremendous lack of *services* for partners and friends of survivors. It is hard enough to find adequate services for survivors—there is virtually nothing available for those who are involved with them.

My hope is that this chapter will encourage those who care about incest survivors—professionally and personally—to start thinking about supporting the supporters. There is great need for literature, workshops, and support groups for partners and friends of incest survivors. (I'll use the term "friend" generically, to include spouse, lover, significant other, as well as nonromantic involvements.) Al-Anon evolved in response to the needs of people who are involved with alcoholics. In the same way, we must look to how we can help people who are experiencing the secondary effects of incest—the friends and partners of the survivors.

There is a second reason for including this chapter. It is important that the male incest survivor understand that he is not the only person being affected by the abuse—and by the recovery process. I want the survivor to be able to gain some perspective on how his feelings and behavior may be perceived by those around him. This chapter suggests what the survivor can and can't realistically expect from people who care about him. It may allow him to give up unrealistic, "frozen" needs and let in the genuine acceptance and love that are available to him. His partners and friends have a stake in his recovery, and they are inevitably undergoing their own changes in accommodation to his. Realizing that this is so enables the survivor to see recovery as a cooperative, interactive process—one that involves allies working to bring about changes that benefit everyone involved.

As the consequences of incest affect the male survivor, they influence the lives of all the people with whom he interacts. The closer and more intimate the relationship, the more deeply felt are the effects. This is true whether or not the friend is aware that the abuse took place. We know that abuse affects the life of a survivor whether or not he has clear memories of the incidents. It causes him to play out aspects of his childhood unconsciously in his adult relationships. In the same way, his friends may not be aware of the cause of the behavior, but they will be experiencing the results on a daily basis. Just as it is difficult for a survivor to maintain emotional (and physical) intimacy in relationships, it isn't easy to sustain a relationship with a survivor.

Even if the friend has worked out a relatively comfortable mode of interaction, when the survivor begins his recovery process all bets are off. The feelings that are stirred up are intense, powerful, and confusing. As the survivor questions every aspect of his life, his relationships cannot fail to feel the pressure. In fact, his interactions with those closest to him are likely to mirror the changes that he is going through; relationships will undergo strain and hard times. In addition to the elation that comes with progress and change, there will be times of great emotional upheaval, confusion, frustration, and misunderstanding. It's quite a ride, and not every relationship is up to it. Despite all the caring and good intentions in the world, recovery is a risky time for relationships. The chances of surviving this process with friendships intact (though perhaps bloodied) are increased immeasurably if both parties have some idea of what they are getting into.

FOCUS

IF YOU SUSPECT ABUSE

Even though an incest survivor may not have told you anything, you may suspect that he was abused as a child. He may not have shared the information because of fears of not being believed, being scorned or ridiculed, or being seen as undesirable or unmanly. It may be that he hasn't accepted it as abuse, or that he hasn't been able to admit it to himself. If you suspect that your friend is an incest survivor, you can raise the issue of sexual abuse on a general level, showing your openness to talking about it; you can let him know that you are willing to listen to anything he wants to share with you, or you can wait until he is ready for disclosure. Don't be impatient or overly protective. Avoid "leaping into action." Remember that we are talking about *his* recovery, not yours. Respect his pace. You can't—nor should you—do it for him.

If you know (or even have suspicions) that child abuse is currently taking place, be sure to do everything that you can to see that it is stopped. You don't have to wait until you have concrete evidence—there isn't enough time. The hurts compound daily. If you have no direct control over the situation, report it to the proper authorities. In most localities the child protective/social service agencies will investigate even anonymous reports of child sexual abuse. Insist that appropriate action be taken. Threaten public exposure if necessary. It is important to your friend, to you, and to the world that we create the kind of society where sexual abuse of a child is literally unthinkable. This is everyone's responsibility. Most incest survivors have known nonprotective adults who ignored the abuse or did nothing to interfere with it. Their logical conclusion is that no one cares—that there is no safety or protection anywhere in the world. Imagine the difference it would have made to their lives if even one adult had believed them and stood up to the abuse.

Among the participants at a recent workshop for both male and female survivors were a sister and brother. She had been sexually abused by their father. Her brother was the one who had stood up to the perpetrator and put a stop to the abuse. He had come to the workshop to continue to support his sister in her healing. In the process, he was working toward his own recovery from the effects of having been raised in a dysfunctional family. His presence at the workshop was important for everyone there. It was deeply moving to all of us to see visible evidence of someone standing up to abuse. It contradicted feelings of isolation and lack of safety in the world. In the brother's own words, "I'm not such a wonderful person . . . It had to be done and I did it." To the rest of us, he is a Hero.

It is always the right time to stand up to abuse. We all need to be heroes.

Note to the Survivor: It is important to be as clear as you can in letting people in your life know what is going on. They cannot mind read. Even if they see that something is up, they can only guess at the complexity of what you're going through. The more openly you share with them, the better they will understand how to be there for you in a useful way. If you learn to state your needs specifically, you have a better chance of having them met. At the same time, you must recognize that this recovery process is *yours*. Your expectations and demands must be realistic. As close and caring as the relationships are, you are separate people. They can't be expected to feel what you are feeling. They have lives of their own, and can't give them up to facilitate your recovery. The more realistic your expectations are of the people who care about you, the less you will feel abandoned when they cannot be there for you all the time.

Weather forecasting is an inexact science. We know that hurricanes cause upheaval, but it is impossible to know the extent of the devastation until afterward. Some storms produce high winds and driving rain. Others cause flooding and damage to life and property. Still others pass harmlessly off shore, dissipating their energies virtually unnoticed. In the same way, we cannot accurately predict the exact course of anyone's recovery. As each person's personality is unique, as his life experiences are his alone, his recovery will follow a path that differs from anyone else's. But, whatever its form, a hurricane is still a hurricane. And there are some things that we know about the nature of this phenomenon. In the same way—although you cannot know exactly what to expect of any individual recovery process—there are some common manifestations for which you can prepare yourself. If they don't occur, you are no worse off. If they do, your preparations can help you ride out the storm.

The fact that you are in a caring relationship with an incest survivor means that you have already accomplished something significant. If you have read the preceding chapters of this book, you know that trust is an overriding issue for any survivor of abuse. To the extent that you have managed to establish some level of trust with him, you have created a degree of safety. You may be the first (and only) person that the survivor feels he can trust. If this is true, you have probably already experienced some of the negative aspects of the situation.

Since the incest involved abuse of a position of trust, the very fact that he is trusting you brings up his fears of further abuse. The times that you are the closest and most loving (physically or emotionally) are likely to be the most difficult for the survivor. On the other hand, if he accepts that you are trustworthy and truly care about him, he is likely to view you as his "only" chance for a caring relationship, and cling tightly to you. You may feel smothered, crowded, and overwhelmed. There may be jealous demands placed on your time and energy. And there may be a tendency for him to want you to withdraw with him from the rest of society, creating your own "safe" and isolated little world. If this is the case, demands on you can increase to the point of occupying every moment of your life. Any attention to your own needs—or interest in other people—will be seen as abandonment. You may be accused of not caring enough, or even of behaving abusively.

If you find that you enjoy this type of jealous, demanding relationship, it may be because it speaks to a frozen childhood need of your own. Healthy relationships exist in the open; healthy lives require variety and interaction. No one can (or should be expected to) meet all of another person's needs. If you are involved in a relationship that is draining you of all energy, free time, and independence, you would be well advised to think about what you are getting out of it. This would certainly be a time to explore therapy or counseling for yourself. There are several good books on the topic of co-dependency in relationships. Reading them may help you to understand your situation. Another resource (whether or not you were raised in an alcoholic family) is Al-Anon or ACOA meetings. These programs teach people how to detach themselves from the unhealthy aspects of caretaking relationships.

Co-dependent relationships are ultimately unhealthy because they inhibit the growth of both parties. People in healthy relationships respect one another's individuality and support each other from a position of self-respect. Only by beginning with the premise that *you deserve and demand to be treated with respect* can you hope to help someone else achieve the same goal. What is true for the incest survivor is also true for you: *To get your real needs met is always in the best interest of those who care about you.* Resist becoming a caretaker. It isn't good for him or for you. By taking charge of your own life (no matter how selfish it feels), you are providing a model of recovery for your friend. If the relationship survives the changes, it will be stronger and healthier. So will both of you.

As difficult as it is to sustain a relationship when the ability to trust has been weakened, many incest survivors do manage to engage in long-lasting friendships, marriages, and other intimate relationships. Some of these are strong and loving; others are needy and huddling, immature and shallow, or lonely and isolated; still others depend on actually or symbolically reliving the abuse. (**Note:** It is never helpful to allow yourself to be abused in a relationship, no matter what the rationale. If you cannot stop the abuse yourself, leave. Furthermore, it is never healthy to abuse another person, no matter how great the provocation. Anyone who invites abuse is reliving past hurts; be careful not to reinforce this behavior.)

Whatever the dynamics of these relationships are, they can remain stable over relatively long periods of time as long as there is no serious threat to the mutually accepted (often unstated) rules. But a stable relationship is not necessarily a healthy one. There are dysfunctional and abusive relationships that endure for many years. Each party to the relationship knows his or her role and plays it well. There is a certain comfort in knowing that there will be no surprises. But, in order to last, these associations must remain stagnant. Any growth or positive change on the part of either partner threatens the delicate balance that keeps the union intact.

When the incest survivor begins to work actively on his recovery, all of the rules are up for reevaluation. And the ripples are felt in every corner of his life. As his insights, feelings, and behaviors change, it is inevitable that all his relationships will need to adjust to the transition. As part of this process you may find that the person you thought you knew so well is behaving like a total stranger. Familiar traits and actions will alter their focus. Feelings and reactions will be magnified and intensified. And there will be times when you will feel confused or lonely. This is a difficult time. But it is also a necessary time of healing. When things are the roughest, try to remember that it won't last forever. *Recovery is a time of crisis; the crisis is temporary.* But be prepared. As I said to the incest survivors in another part of this book, it will feel worse before it gets better. This is equally true for those around them. And you are under no obligation to stick it out through the hard times. Staying or leaving is your choice. Not all relationships can stand the strain of the recovery process. Those that manage it are irrevocably altered. We don't know what the precise outcome will be, only that it will be healthier (though not necessarily much easier). It will therefore have to be reassessed as a brand-new relationship, and both partners will have to decide whether it makes sense to continue with it. If you choose to be there through the recovery process, be assured that there will be rewards —the real pleasures of forging a mutually nourishing relationship with another adult. There may still be hard times, but the daily interactions will no longer be in service to past abuses. There will also be room for joy and celebration.

As much as I'd like to be able to prepare you for what will happen, it is sure to be a surprise to you when the changes begin to take place. I can only give you notice of some reactions that you might encounter:

1 / Withdrawal. Overwhelmed by the enormity of the feelings he is experiencing, the survivor may retreat physically or emotionally. He may engage in long periods of silence, be generally uncommunicative, or require more time alone. At these times he might disappear for long periods or show disinterest in his usual pursuits. When this happens, it is likely that friends of the survivor will feel that they have been shut out or rejected. You are likely to feel confused and resentful. It can be very isolating to have someone close to you "check out." In the absence of communication it is hard to know what is going on, whether you had anything to do with it, and if there is anything you can do to help. And it's easy to jump to the worst conclusions. But there are many possible explanations for the withdrawal.

The survivor is experiencing a confusing welter of emotions. He may simply need the time and space to sort some of them out. Or he may not know what to say to anyone. He might be attempting to protect you from his pain or to avoid letting his angry feelings explode in your direction. He may also be having some negative thoughts and feelings about you that he doesn't want to express until he can make some sense out of them. He could be reacting to feelings of hopelessness and self-doubt that have nothing to do with you.

Unless you think that there is danger that he will harm himself (or others), the best course of action is to do little or nothing. Reassure him that you care about him, and that you are here to listen if he wants to talk—and then allow him the time he needs. You can always do more later if necessary. For now, try to resist intrusion into his solitude by caretaking or expressing resentment at being excluded. It is likely that what is going on inside him has nothing to do with you. Even if it does, nagging him about it will shut him down even further. He may be working through these issues elsewhere—in individual therapy or a recovery group. If so, it is an appropriate way to deal with these issues. It is to your advantage to support that process. An active, welcoming patience can pay dividends for both of you. As he learns to open up communication in therapy and group, you will probably find that your communication improves as well. In the meantime, consider getting similar support for yourself—whether that involves therapy, individual counseling, or participation in a support group. Problems in relationships are rarely one-sided. It will be helpful for you and your friend to discover your part in the unhealthy aspects of the interaction.

2 / Mood swings. The course of recovery is never smooth and steady. There are times of rapid, visible progress, periods of apparent inactivity, and occasional lapses into old patterns of behavior and feelings of hopelessness. These changes of focus can evoke powerful emotional reactions. The survivor can be flying high one day, full of confidence in his progress, only to sink into despair the next. A moment's tenderness can quickly explode into anger. Needless to say, these mood swings are difficult and confusing to friends of the survivor. This is particularly true if you have taken on the caretaking role of insuring that he is protected from his "bad" feelings. Difficult as it may be, you must train yourself to step out of the caretaking role. The survivor's feelings are *his*. You did not cause them, nor are you responsible for alleviating them. Furthermore, they are necessary to the healing process. As hard as it is to see someone you care about in pain, you must allow him room for having—and getting through—his feelings. Celebrate the good times with him. Be there for the hard times if you can (and if you are allowed to), but recognize that he must do his own recovery work. Your support will help to make his recovery easier.

3 / Crying jags. You may find that your survivor friend, once so completely in control of his emotions, seems to be crying all the time. Don't be dismayed. Welcome and celebrate the tears when they come. They are an important facet of the process—"the lubricant that allows recovery to move forward." If he cries in your presence, try not to be embarrassed or to distract him from the tears. Don't try to "make him feel better." The crying itself will accomplish that. You can occasionally share an encouraging word or two, but stop talking if it seems to distract him from the tears. You will see that, if the safety is present and the encouragement is there, he will cry as long as he needs to. When he is finished, he will be calmer, clear-headed, and a little tired. And both of you will be less worried that crying means being "out of control."

4 / Irrational anger. As the survivor begins to accept the unfairness of what happened to him, feelings of anger will begin to surface. Expression of anger may be an unfamiliar experience for him. He may come from a family where any angry word or feeling inevitably led to physical violence or other abuse. If this is the case, he will have learned to keep his emotions—particularly angry feelings—rigidly in check. Starting to express anger can be a terrifying experience for him and for those around him. The tiniest angry expression feels like he is raging out of control. Inexperienced as he is in expressing anger, he is likely to vent it inappropriately. The first target for his angry feelings can be the person that he feels safest with—you. This isn't a comfortable position in which to find yourself. The slightest area of disagreement can trigger an excessively angry response, and you end up feeling like a target. There doesn't seem to be anything that you can say or do that will prevent these outbursts. This is a tricky area to deal with. It is important to remember that if the angry response is completely out of proportion to what is going on, it probably has nothing to do with the present situation. Something in the present is restimulating old memories and feelings. The safety of the current situation allows these feelings to be expressed.

Whereas this knowledge can help you understand what is going on, it doesn't do much to help you feel good when someone you care about is yelling at you. Nor should you accept the situation passively. Verbal abuse doesn't benefit anyone. It is perfectly acceptable to validate someone's right to feel angry *without accepting that you have caused his anger*. You never have to be the target of abusive behavior. (It should go without saying that you never need to expose yourself to violence or other physical harm. If you even suspect that an encounter might become violent, leave the situation immediately. You can always straighten it out later.) You can assure your friend that you understand that he is angry. You can let him know that if the anger has anything to do with something you have done, that you are willing to work it out with him. But tell him that if he continues to rail at you, you will leave until he is able to discuss it with you more calmly. Then, if he continues, do just that.

When someone is in the midst of an angry outburst, it is unlikely that he will be amenable to reason. Neither will yelling back at him solve anything. Neither of you will really be hearing what the other one is saying—you'll be too busy feeling attacked. Later, during a calmer time, the two of you (perhaps with a third party present) can discuss what was going on. You can let him know that you care about him, but are not willing to allow yourself to be the target of misdirected anger. You can ask him for suggestions about how you can respond in a helpful manner without becoming a target. By not accepting anger that doesn't belong to you, you are helping your friend to focus it where it belongs. He is then able to learn to use his anger to facilitate his own recovery. It changes from weak, frightened, defensive posturing to the power of righteous indignation—standing up to the abuse.

5 / Blaming. Similar to the irrational anger is the tendency to cast blame. When the survivor begins to accept that he was not to blame for what happened to him—and that he is not to blame for everything that is wrong in the world—he is apt to search for who *is*. He hasn't been exposed to the idea that not everything that happens is somebody's fault. It is difficult to understand the concept of responsibility without blame. His feeling is that if it isn't his fault, then it must be yours. And you find yourself in a situation where you can't do anything right. The correct response to irrational blame is the same as to irrational anger. Don't accept it if it isn't yours. Let your friend know (at the time, if he can hear it; later, if he can't) that you understand that he is upset. Enlist his aid in thinking about the situation. Assure him of your good intentions to work with him to solve whatever problem exists, *without needing to find a villain*. In doing this you are both refusing to fall victim to further effects of the abuse, while allowing any blame to be placed where it belongs.

6 / Unreasonable demands. It isn't easy to say no to someone you care about. It becomes even more difficult when the person is obviously having a hard time. You want to step in and make it all better. You want to solve the problems, salve the wounds, relieve the pain and resolve the confusion. As the incest survivor puts increasing attention and effort into his recovery, he may also place greater demands on the time and energy of those around him. If this is allowed to continue unchecked, it can fill all the available space, leaving you little room to lead your own life. Even though you might want to, you can't do it all for him. This is his recovery process and he has to go through it. The most helpful thing for you to do is to decide on how much time is reasonable for you to offer your friend, and limit yourself to that. Don't buy into protestations that you are abandoning him. This is not selfish or uncaring behavior. It is important that you reserve what you need in order to keep your own life on an even keel. If you burn yourself out, you are of no use to your friend or yourself. Continue to reassure your friend about the importance of his recovery, and that you are in full support of the process, but don't be put upon. He doesn't really need another model of martyrdom or self-sacrifice. The best image to offer him is of someone who cares for others without giving up looking after her- or himself. This image of self-respect can only help both of you.

7 / Sexual behavior. Since the incestuous abuse was acted out sexually, it is inevitable that recovery will involve feelings about sex and intimacy. If your relationship with the survivor has a sexual component (or even if it doesn't), you can expect that you will be encountering difficulties in these areas. Among the unreasonable demands may be insistence on more frequent sexual activity than you find comfortable. You may feel pressure to engage in sexual practices that are not acceptable to you. On the other hand, the incest survivor may lose interest in any form of closeness or touching, including sexual intimacies. You may even find yourself in the position of being with someone who wants sex one minute and is repulsed by the thought of it the next. He may demand sex, but recoil from being touched. He may be unable to achieve an erection, or might seem to be sexually aroused all the time.

This is certainly a confusing situation to be in. The reason that you're having such a hard time making sense out of it is that it doesn't make any logical sense. It is pure feeling, reacting to powerful changes in the survivor's perception of his experience. He is trying to sort out the meanings of abuse, sex, love, caring, and intimacy. He is testing the world and trying to learn about reasonable, nonabusive boundaries between people. The most helpful thing that you can do in this instance is to be scrupulous about maintaining your own boundaries.

This sexual testing may occur whether or not your relationship was sexual previously. Whether you are friend, therapist, or family member, it is possible that you will be dealing with it. He may have learned that the way to get close to someone is to relate sexually, and this behavior reappears during times of crisis. This is not the time to begin a sexual relationship. He is too vulnerable. You would both be allowing yourselves to be seduced by an old pattern of distress. Yielding to a sexual pull at this point will severely damage the trust and intimacy that you have established.

If you are already sexually involved, do nothing that doesn't make sense to you. Remember that the essence of incest is taking sexual advantage of a trusting relationship. The incest survivor needs to know that it is all right to say no and to have that refusal respected. At the same time, difficult as it is, you must respect the survivor's need to refrain from sexual activity. Don't take it as evidence of lack of love and caring. It probably has nothing to do with you. He is asserting his right not to be sexual unless it makes sense for him. If both of you understand and accept this basic right to control over your bodies, it will ultimately lead to more fulfilling intimacies, sexual and otherwise.

8 / Regression. As the memories of childhood return, there can be a pull to behave in a more juvenile (or infantile) manner. Sometimes this takes the form of healthy playfulness. At other times, the survivor may get unusually clingy, needy, silly, whiny, self-centered, inarticulate, incompetent, irresponsible, or childish. He may resort to comforts (or obsessions, compulsions, and addictions) that he employed when the abuse was taking place. There's really nothing that you need to do about these regressive behaviors (some of them may even be enjoyable) unless they are actually dangerous. As people used to say about you when you were a child, "This is just a stage he is going through." In this case it isn't a flippant comment. The incestuous abuse robbed the survivor of a normal childhood. Regression may be an attempt to reclaim some portion of what was lost. It is OK to seek comfort from a teddy bear, a pet, or a newly discovered capacity for silliness. You as a trusted friend may be able to provide a safe context for expression of the regressive behavior.

9 / Physical abuse. A genuine recovery process never requires that the survivor behave abusively or be abused further. There is never anything positive to be gained by allowing yourself to be the victim of physical abuse. Neither is abusing an incest survivor (or any other person) ever helpful in any way. If the feelings of anger and resentment require a release, it is OK to bring them up by hitting a punching bag with a baseball bat, pounding a pillow, or screaming into a friend's shoulder (it effectively muffles the sound so that neighbors don't call the police). You can engage in wild revenge fantasies with the survivor, sharing what you would like to do to the perpetrator. He can beat up a doll or other representation of the abuser. He can buy a cheap set of dishes and smash them. But the anger must be focused in the right direction—toward the hurts of the past. It is not helpful to create another victim. You are not the perpetrator; don't let yourself be treated as one. It is unlikely that someone who was not abusive in the past will suddenly become brutal, but if he does, get protection. If you feel physically threatened or even intimidated, leave immediately. You can talk about it later when things are calmer. Make it clear that people who love each other do not hurt each other. People who have a healthy level of self-respect don't permit themselves to be harmed. Any attempt at physical abuse should be seen for what it is—a capitulation to the original abusive behavior. Protecting yourself from harm is consistent with recovery. If your friend becomes abusive (or suggests that you abuse him), let him know that you care about him (and yourself) enough to reject the abuse.

10 / Resentment. As the survivor becomes aware of what he has lost to the abuse—and as he begins to accept that he deserved (and deserves) better treatment—he may feel and express resentment. The resentment may be general and focused on lost time and opportunities. He may resent the loss of childhood or the time, money, and anguish involved in the recovery process. These are understandable resentments, and it is fairly easy to empathize with them. It becomes more difficult when the resentment is focused on a specific person (you) because you didn't have to be subjected to the same kind of pain. "It was easy for you, your father didn't . . ." It isn't helpful to argue that you didn't have it that good, or that your having been abused wouldn't have made life any better for him. It will be easier on you if you see this expression of resentment for what it is—a longing for a normal life. It really has nothing to do with you. Try to ignore the direction of the attack and respond to the underlying message. *It wasn't fair. It never should have happened. You have a right to feel resentful.* Don't waste your time taking on blame or responsibility that clearly isn't yours. Validate his feelings and move on.

11 / Confusion and preoccupation. Putting the past into perspective and establishing strategies for the present and future require a tremendous outlay of thought and feeling. Recovery becomes the central focus of the survivor's energy and the task can seem all-encompassing. This means that he has less attention for other matters, and may appear bewildered and remote. Even a normally well-organized, efficient individual can become "spacey" and careless. You might have to speak to him a couple of times before he hears you. Routine chores can be left undone, bills unpaid and phone messages unanswered. Try not to get too upset about this, even if it means that you have to take up some of the slack for a time. This state of mind is usually temporary, lessening as the recovery process becomes incorporated into the survivor's life. If this situation is intolerable to you, you are welcome to insist that he pull himself together enough to carry his load—but don't be surprised if he is unable to comply fully. Try to remember that he isn't doing this to upset you. If you can have the patience to ride out this storm, he will eventually return to a normal level of responsiveness and responsibility.

12 / Fear. As the powerful feelings generated by past hurts are dealt with openly in the present, the survivor will experience frightening emotions. The fear may intimidate him to the extent that he will avoid even those people and activities he normally enjoys.

This is also a temporary state, and should resolve itself once the most difficult part of this process is past. While it is going on, you can validate the survivor's feelings, reassuring him that what happened to him was, indeed, frightening. You may offer to sit with him or hold him gently while he shakes, shivers, and/or sobs the fear away. If the avoidance continues for a long period of time, you might suggest that you accompany him in visiting some friends or engaging in some pleasurable activities that aren't too threatening. They can provide a healthy focus of attention away from the pain and fear. Although recovery is a long-term, ongoing process, it doesn't have to occupy his every waking moment. Relaxation restores energy. Laughter is healing. If he is unwilling to participate in these excursions, go yourself. Don't become a prisoner of someone else's fear; avoid burn-out yourself. You can be a better, more effective friend if you pay attention to your own needs.

13 / Mistrust. The survivor in recovery is actively questioning all of his previous assumptions. Recognizing that much of what he learned was misinformation and outright lies, he is reevaluating his entire world. He must learn (perhaps for the first time) who and what can be trusted. It is hard to be mistrusted by someone you care about. If the survivor indicates that he doesn't trust you, try not to personalize it. Most likely it is a statement about himself ("I have trouble trusting people") and has very little to do with you. He is relearning how to trust and the first step is recognition that he doesn't trust people. The fact that he can tell you about it is evidence that he feels relatively safe with you. If *you* are certain that you are a trustworthy friend, you needn't be upset by the survivor's trust difficulties. In time, as the recovery continues, his trust of you will grow.

14 / Inconsistency of response. Just as a survivor can experience mood swings, the powerful changes he is going through can translate into unpredictable behavior. Whereas you once knew what range of responses you could expect from him, it now seems that nothing is guaranteed. You are left feeling confused, bewildered, and even abandoned. Is this the same person you knew and cared about? Once again, these rapid, unpredictable changes of behavior are reactions to confusing internal dynamics. Don't be alarmed. In time, things will become more stable and consistent. In the meantime, you can explore the inconsistencies with the survivor. Avoid taking a critical or censuring tone; seek to open communication with your friend in order to understand what is going on.

The early stages of active recovery are highly intense, trying times. Unusual strains are put on relationships. You may experience all, some, or none of the foregoing responses. In any case, the configuration will be unique to your relationship. The only reassurance that I can offer is that *it does get easier*. You won't be riding the whirlwind forever, and the rewards of recovery are great. In the meantime, keep remembering that you are not the perpetrator, and it does no good for you to allow yourself to be a target of hostility, ill will, or abuse. Be clear about that. Be alert to any tendency on your part to engage in "survivor's guilt." (The term *survivor's guilt* most commonly refers to a phenomenon that was identified among men who served in the U.S. armed forces in Vietnam. Upon their return to their homeland, they found themselves unable to explain why they had survived the war while their buddies had died. The inexplicable unfairness of their situation produced a reaction of self-blame for not having been able to save their friends, and shame at having survived. This torment is a common component of the form of Post-Traumatic Stress Disorder that is known as *Post-Vietnam Syndrome*.)

You were not to blame for the childhood abuse of your friend. You were not there and could have done nothing to stop it. Don't let your own misguided guilty feelings freeze you into helplessness. Not having been abused as a child is nothing to be ashamed of. In fact, because the hurts that you experienced were different than the incest survivor's, you may be in a better position to provide him with support, encouragement, perspective, and alternatives to dysfunctional relationships. (See Chapter 11 for a discussion of relationships where both partners are survivors.) Don't try to join him in his pain—doing that would create two victims. Instead, provide him with a picture of life beyond the abuse. Insist on your right to respectful treatment as you provide a healthy model of self-respect. Trust your caring and include yourself under its umbrella. Good luck.

FRANK'S STATEMENT

Frank's statement shares some of the supports and
resources he has discovered and developed in his journey
of recovery. He is thirty-four years old.

Since I learned to read I have loved fantasy and science
fiction literature. I could escape into a character, travel in
strange worlds, find truth, justice, life, and love. I think I
understand why now.

Until two years ago I denied my family had any serious
problems. When Nancy, the woman I love, started going to Al-
Anon adult child meetings, she told me about the program. I
was amazed at what it was doing for her and for our
relationship. I read the literature, thought about my father's
drinking, and called some relatives to check memories. I figured
out that my father had a drinking problem. In the next couple
of months it became clear to me that while I did not even
drink, I had a problem. My parents and I live five hundred
miles apart. We interacted only a few times a year. In spite of
this I had a large and constant problem in my life, a mark left
from my childhood. This was a new way of thinking for me.

I went to my first Twelve Step meeting. The speaker talked
about how he had become very sick over his wife's drinking. I
clung to my chair as he described their relationship and his
life. It fit like a glove. It was not that either of us drank. We
had an alcoholic relationship. What other type of relationship
could we have learned in our families? We tried to change,
regulate, and control each other instead of ourselves. We did
not trust. We avoided intimacy. Seeing this hurt so much I
thought my heart would break and at the same time it felt like
the relief of having a splinter pulled.

My life took on a new character. I found myself quite
magically dealing with one appropriate issue after another. An
issue would start with pain and confusion and resolve into just
what I needed to learn next. I was being given what I needed
to learn, helped step by step toward health. The first Al-Anon

meeting I went to is a good example of this. At that meeting I first admitted to myself that the drinking in my family of origin had been very harmful to me. Looking back on it, I can see that I worked up to the moment of insight at the meeting by gathering and puzzling over information about my family and odd bits of my life. Then at the meeting while hearing the man's story, the pieces came together in an extremely painful moment. It was very hard to admit what I saw now in myself. After the realization there was a readjustment period, during which my new understandings made changes in a surprising number of places in my life. It was wonderful to make sense of things that never did before.

I was surprised to find this process repeat itself again and again. The next thing I had to admit to myself was that the driving force behind my wanting to save the world came from these very problems in my own family and myself that I would not heal or even admit. I had used a sense of mission to hide my own need. My own pain had driven me to more and more frantic acts of trying to help others. After years of "sacrificing myself" at home and at work, admitting that was a tough pill to swallow.

Now I admitted I had pain. Now I would simply try to see what was going on when I hurt; before, I tried to hide it. I had hidden my feelings from even myself for most of my life. Each admission seemed worse than the last. I had to admit that I was a people pleaser and that I had a terrible self-image. With each tearful victory came wonderful insights. As I adjusted to my new understanding, I would make wonderful gains in areas like self-confidence, fear of people, and embarrassment about memories from my childhood. I could know with certainty things about my life I did not understand before. I found myself becoming much better at acting on my feelings and integrating them into my decisions and plans. I could know whether I liked someone or not. Before, I would have tried to reason out whether I should like them or not.

I did not discover these issues in a book or from other people. These issues rose inside me out of my own pain. I found that this is the journey of my life. The one I had looked for in fantasy. I have a life and it is mine. I know what it means to me and why. It is exciting. I am going places. It means something in the sweep of history if the abuse and obsession in my family that have been passed on for so many generations stops here with this generation. That goal has more of what is real in it than the goal I had before of trying to feed the hungry and clothe the poor. Not because one goal is better than the other, but because one is the task that is in front of me now. I truly want my freedom. When I did not know myself, I did not know I was not free. My working for someone else's benefit, when I was in terrible need and could not admit it, was denying myself and just acting out. This may explain why my efforts worked out the way they did. I did not achieve the goals I stated, and in fact, when I look back over my actions, I can see they were quite confused and erratic. I am freer now. I am able to understand so many feelings for the first time—like in a fairy tale when a magic door opens and a new world and adventures unfold, allowing the character to grow and learn. My life became like that for me. Instead of hiding my confusion and raging emotions inside and trying to fix others, I am feeling what it is like to be me and I am trying to help myself.

I have enjoyed a great deepening in my ability to be close with people. I learned to see more in other people as I became friends with my own pain. Nancy and I were able to marry. When I look on the communication I had then, it seems so little and shallow compared to now. Making the room in my life to be close with people has had many parts. Finding my feelings is one of them. Some others are: Admitting my family of origin was not there for me allowed me the space and the reason to let others in. Admitting that what had passed for love and closeness before in my life was not adequate allowed me to look for something else. Admitting I needed understanding allowed me to look for it. Being able to understand someone else's story and comment on it draws me into people's lives. I still have trouble organizing my time, so how I spend it reflects what is most important to me. While I no longer work sixty hours a week, I do not yet plan in regular, ongoing time with friends, but see them catch as catch can. I think what is in front of me now has a lot to do with how I organize my time. I need to admit how hard it is for me to schedule what I really choose in a clear plan without becoming overcome with the fear of disappointment or being exposed as a failure. I have a terror of finding out just how much of the time I am involved in obsessive behavior and how often I cannot control. That keeps me from clear planning.

If you work hard on yourself and give yourself a safe space with relaxed time to really look at yourself, the rewards are amazing. On my honeymoon I had such a space. My wife and I had this very special time to look at ourselves, so we read together, as was by now our habit, literature to help us explore ourselves. While reading *On the Way to the Wedding* by Linda Leonard, I came across a part about a woman who had been deeply hurt by the incest between her father and her sister. I had known about the incest between my father and my sister before I moved out of my parents' house. In spite of this, I had never allowed myself to feel what it was like to have my sister abused by my father sexually and in so many other ways. For the first time I named as pain this upswelling of feelings I felt every time I tried to have sex. I saw why I usually came so soon, running from intimacy I was trying to find. The original examples of what maleness was to me were: drunkenness, violence, and sexual abuse. Every time I made love I had to face feeling myself the abuser and the abused. Every time I tried to be intimate, a pain was triggered. I wept for my sister and myself. As I looked at my pain to see what it would tell me, I found something hard to admit to. The first memories I had were only the physical pain and from that an intuition of what happened. Someone had raped me as a child and I knew who, but was so afraid of it my throat closed so I could not speak it. My father.

That was in the beginning of the summer. The weight of what I worked on was heavy. When I was dealing with the pain of being raised in an alcoholic household with the help of Al-Anon, things had moved faster. I would come to a new realization sometimes by having to sink into pain for an hour or two. Afterwards I would bounce back deeper and stronger. With incest I would sink into the pain and keep sinking for hours, crying and thrashing till I sought relief in an activity like eating or computer games. These quickly became obsessive. I can remember playing a computer game all night. As the sun came up, tears ran down my cheeks from staring at the screen for so many hours. I then left for work. Going to sleep is particularly hard for me when I am avoiding the pain I am in. Before the incest surfaced, when I was dealing with alcoholic family issues, the time between the beginning of a realization and the feeling of renewed vigor could take up to a week, with something big enough to take a week coming up about monthly. The incest was harder for me. The weight of these dark realizations went on longer. Renewed vigor came later, less often, and for shorter periods. Also I was having trouble

finding help. Al-Anon was not for me the forum I needed for
my incest work. It helped a lot—I found other survivors at
meetings, but it was hard to talk about incest. I had no clear
memories; I had grave doubts and questions about how I would
face my parents, sisters, and friends with the truth. Sometimes
I would pretend there was some other explanation for these
memories and feelings. A turning point came when I found
such denials depressed me and knew I had only one way I
could go.

I looked for groups on incest. It is hard for a man to find
services that help with having been sexually abused. There is
not a lot out there. In January I started with a group for male
survivors of sexual abuse. The night before the group started, I
began getting clear memories of what had happened to me. Just
having a place, a forum, allowed them to start coming out. I
heard other people's stories in the group. I found it easier to
believe or feel for someone else. I could believe them and I
could see how they were not to blame, but I could not see it
with myself. We were all that way at times. What a relief to
find people like me. Many things people explained about
themselves were the same in me and I had not seen or
understood them before. This was a way of learning about
myself that was faster, easier, and a lot less lonely. It is so
clear to see that if a child is abused certain ways, certain
problems happen. They happened to each differently, but the
ways we were so much the same allowed me to see myself,
believe myself, and not be ashamed of myself.

Listening to each other's stories and talking about them was
how we started. We have covered a lot of ground together. We
have struggled painfully through one person after another's
description of trouble at work, with their boss or with their
customers, till I could tell the parts where incest/dysfunctional
family issues were active in those situations. Our work lives
were confused by issues like fear of authority, inability to trust,
lack of boundaries, the need to buy love or respect, and fear of
being found out. As I could see how many of my reactions
come from these issues, I changed. Sharing with other people
allowed me to see ways I was very strange. How could I have
seen them before. I had only known this way of life. I denied
I had pain, fear, or anger as a matter of course. My parents
had denied their pain, fear, and anger. I had learned from
them that if you pretended something was not happening, it
was not happening. It is so hard to see that I am living in

fear, spending great amounts of energy pretending not to be in pain, never trusting anyone, and expecting always to be betrayed. As we struggled through many topics—work, money, sex, relationships, children, food, friendships, clothing, possessions, and more—I came to see how completely affected my life has been. It is a package deal. It is not likely one's parent would be a child molester and at the same time a very good role model from whom to learn how to balance work and personal life—to relate to a boss or customers, to budget money, to enjoy friendships or sexual relationships, or to eat a well-balanced diet. Our parents had many compulsive behaviors and addictions. These are the people we learned how to live from.

I found a lot of help in I.S.A. (Incest Survivors Anonymous), a twelve-step program. At the meetings we hear and tell about how incest has affected us and how we are overcoming what happened, and we find a way to trust again. I need to ask for spiritual help. It is hard to trust God after what happened. That may be the greatest damage of all. Without that trust I would not be able to accept this amazing process of healing that has been given to me.

I have gained in my understanding of my compulsive behaviors around money by visiting Debtors Anonymous. I have also been helped in my understanding around my sexual compulsions from Sex and Love Addicts Anonymous.

I have gained a lot from individual therapy. An interesting point is that I am often blocked by my inability to trust my therapist when we are alone together. Because of the nature of my abuse, one-on-one work in an unequal relationship is harder than in a small intimate group.

I used to work full time and more. I now work twenty to thirty hours a week. I go to a meeting or individual therapy three or four times a week. I want to get back to work. I want to have less pain and upheaval in my life. I try to be patient with my progress. I want this to end. An important part of my recovery is learning not to wait for my recovery to end so I can go back to my life. Sometimes I still think, soon this will all be over and I can forget it and live like before. But I have grown too much to go back to many of my old ways. Many of those old ways were terrible. I lived in fear, hiding from myself and everyone. I forget that when I am tired. I just did not have the type of problems where I could simply take a break from the rut, fix a few things, and go back. I will have a different life. I told my parents, sisters, and friends. I have changed so much. Deep stuff like the way I think, feel, work and how I act around people. I do not know what my new life will be like. When I am feeling strong I believe what Nancy says, we will be embarrassingly happy. I wait for things to settle out. The realizations about myself are still painful and still come about the same pace. They are still hard to admit, figure out and integrate into my life. I still say to myself after I come to understand something, "What else could I have to deal with? It must be over." Then I slam up against the next behavior of mine or remember something horrible or both. I believe God is giving me the pieces I need as I can deal with them. It is my journey and I pray for the strength to hang on to it.

Other Resources

There are many resources available to assist you in your recovery from the effects of incest. Because of my particular experience and training, I have focused this book on what to look for in the area of counseling and psychotherapy. (See Chapters 16 and 17.) I have tried to expand a traditional definition of therapy to include what I have found to be of use to survivors in their recovery. In this chapter I shall mention a variety of other techniques and resources that incest survivors have told me were helpful to them. These do not fall in my primary areas of expertise and some have not been explored in a systematic way. I shall mention them here only briefly, in the hope that those of you who wish to do further investigation for yourselves will do so. I welcome your comments about what you have found helpful in your own recovery.

Important: I want to stress that my mentioning other resources does not constitute a recommendation. As with psychotherapy, these are tools which can be used or abused. It is always important to examine resources, accepting only those that make sense to you. Anyone who has overeaten knows that even the best food can cause distress when you consume too much of it —so think about how much is right for you. By the same token, good ingredients that are badly prepared can produce terrible results. What works in one situation—or for one individual—may not be helpful in another. The quality of the practitioner can be even more important than the quality of the practice. So be aware. Take the time to find the right person for the job. If you aren't comfortable with the situation, back off. Get all the information you need, and proceed at your own pace. Don't allow yourself to be pressured or steamrollered. This is your recovery, and you have every right to know what you're getting. Finally, remember that there are no "magic cures." Recovery from abuse is a long-term process. Beware of shortcuts or "miracle" programs. Any of the approaches listed in this chapter can be valuable as *part* of an overall recovery program.

Body Work

Many survivors have initially recovered memories of abuse while engaging in some sort of physical activity that involved being touched. For some it was while engaging in sexual activity or other interpersonal intimacy. For others, it may have been casual touch that in some way triggered memories of the original abuse. And a great number of survivors have found that incest memories have come up while they were undergoing some sort of physical treatment that is designed to relax, heal, or otherwise treat the body. When you think about it, it makes perfect sense that memories of physical abuse are triggered by physical contact. It also makes sense, since the hurts were inflicted in a physical way, that the healing process should include a physical component. (**Important:** This does *not* mean that sex should be considered a therapeutic technique. Beware of any so-called healer or therapist who attempts to convince you that she or he can help you to recovery by teaching you to be "less uptight" about sex. This is not recovery; it is sexual exploitation and only adds to the abuse.)

There is tremendous healing power in loving, nonabusive touch. It can be a very important aspect of incest recovery, but once again, only if *and when* it is right for you. For some people receiving a massage is a delightful, relaxing experience. For others (especially for many survivors) it can so closely replicate their abuse histories that it becomes an occasion of abject terror. In any case, what the various types of body work have in common is that they involve being touched by another person. This will inevitably bring up feelings. You will have the choice of letting yourself feel (even the uncomfortable feelings) or shutting down your emotions. I recommend that you choose the former option, once you have established the safety to do so. It may be more comfortable (and more familiar) to lie there feeling nothing, but it isn't going to help you recover.

If you choose to explore some sort of body work, I encourage you to consider the following guidelines:

1 / Talk to other people who have tried it—preferably other survivors. Get an idea of what you can expect. Ask whether any pain is involved. Ask how you will be touched. Are you clothed during the treatment? Can another person be present if you choose? Get recommendations of competent and sensitive experts.

2 / Interview the practitioner. If he is reluctant or unwilling to answer all your questions to your satisfaction, he is not being responsive to your needs. Ask about what will be done to you, and what the benefits of these treatments are. Ask about the frequency and duration of treatment. Ask about any possible risks. Is there any reading that you can do about this practice? Ask about her professional training and other qualifications. If there is a professional organization which approves, licenses, or certifies this treatment, is the practitioner a member? The process of being touched is likely to bring up feelings. How comfortable is she with the expression of emotions? Will you be allowed to cry, shake, laugh, and show other emotions whenever you need to? Can you have someone else present if you choose to? (Sometimes just knowing that you have that option is enough to make you feel safer.) Can the procedure be terminated at any point that you want it stopped? Speak with more than one person. There may be a range of ideas and approaches. Select the one that you feel safest with.

3 / Ask yourself some questions. Why am I interested in doing this? Do I have enough information? If not, what more do I need and how can I get it? Do I feel that this person is trustworthy? Was I treated with consideration, respect, and professionalism? Did he ask enough questions to get the information he needs to do his job well? Did he avoid intrusive personal questions that have nothing to do with the treatment? Did he seem to really hear my concerns? Am I ignoring my own feelings and reservations in order to be a cooperative client? Do I feel safe and powerful enough to get what I need out of it? To cry, if I need to? To tell the practitioner to stop if I don't like what he is doing? What (if anything) do I need to tell this person about myself? About the abuse? Am I ready to go ahead with it?

4 / Provide information to the practitioner. If you have thought about why you are interested in this treatment and what you hope to get out of it, provide the practitioner with any information that you think will be useful to her. You must decide whether you want to disclose information about the abuse and, if so, how much. It might be difficult to ask questions about the practitioner's experience working with survivors without explaining why you are asking. But it is likely to be important to you to know how she feels about incest issues, and what information and experience she already has.

5 / Give yourself permission. Allow yourself to feel and express the feelings that are evoked by the body work. Talk about the memories, thoughts and feelings with friends and with your therapist. And assess the benefits. Give yourself permission to stop if you don't think it's helpful (no matter what the practitioner says). And give yourself permission to continue with it if it's helpful (or even just because it feels good—you deserve it).

6 / Trust your judgment. Please yourself. You don't need to have a "legitimate" reason not to do it. None of these treatments is a requirement for recovery. Not wanting to do it is reason enough. Don't "caretake" the practitioner. Give yourself practice in saying "no" to what isn't right for you, and "yes" to what is.

Types of body work that incest survivors have reported to me as helpful include the following:

CRANIO-SACRAL THERAPY

Not as well known as many other types of body work, cranio-sacral therapy is an outgrowth of osteopathy. It is an extremely gentle manipulation of the bones of the skull and of the spine as well as the body's system of connective tissue. It can be performed while the client is clothed. Despite (or perhaps because of) the gentleness of this approach, many survivors have found that it evokes extremely powerful memories and emotions. As with all the techniques I shall list, the quality of care will depend upon the skills and sensitivity of the practitioner. Without the right practitioner, even the finest technique will fail to accomplish your aims. Keep looking until you find the person who is right for you. One cranio-sacral practitioner I spoke with (who is himself an incest survivor) indicated that he asks clients about their abuse histories. He suggests to incest survivors that they do the work in conjunction with psychotherapy for dealing with their deep feelings and memories.

MASSAGE

There are, of course, many types of massage. They range from sensual/sexual practices performed by untrained individuals to therapeutic techniques carried out by licensed professionals under the auspices of medical personnel. Some are light and gentle, some active and vigorous, and others may be quite painful. Although they vary in style, intensity and goal, what they share is that you will be having parts of your body touched by another person. Surrendering sufficient control over your body to allow it to be touched doesn't mean allowing it to be abused. Make sure that you know what to expect. Question massage therapists about their training, certification/licensing and what type of massage they do. If their answers are vague or evasive, don't proceed with the treatment. They should know what they are doing and find the time and patience to explain it to you properly. Types of therapeutic massage that incest survivors have reported to me as helpful include Shiatsu and Swedish. Shiatsu (also called acupressure) is the stimulation of acupuncture points by finger pressure. Shiatsu does not employ needles. Swedish is what Westerners most commonly think of as massage. It uses long strokes over large areas of the body.

RELATED TECHNIQUES

Other manipulative healing techniques that don't define themselves as massage but have related components include Polarity Therapy and Reflexology. Polarity is a deep-relaxation therapy that uses massagelike techniques, working with the entire body. Reflexology (also known as zone therapy) is a system of treating the whole body by deeply massaging "reflex points" on the soles of the feet—or sometimes the hands.

DEEPER BODY WORK

Although I know very little about these practices, I have worked with clients who swear by the benefits of Rolfing, Soma, and Feldenkrais. Rolfing and Soma are systems for realigning the muscles and bones. They involve deep and occasionally painful muscle work. Feldenkrais is a very gentle, noninvasive system for "reeducating" the body through movement. Once again, I would suggest doing your homework before embarking on a course of treatment, both in terms of the technique and the individual practitioner.

ACUPUNCTURE

Acupuncture is a Chinese healing art that has been successfully practiced in the Orient for many centuries. It is now receiving recognition in Western medicine. An acupuncturist I questioned about his work with incest survivors told me that it can be useful in dealing with chronic physical manifestations of abuse in conjunction with psychotherapy. Remember that acupuncture, which involves the use of small needles, is an invasive procedure which, while virtually painless, can evoke powerful memories of having your body invaded.

(This, by the way, is true of any invasive medical examination or treatment procedure. Make certain that any suggested invasive procedure is necessary, and be prepared for heavy feelings.)

DANCE, MOVEMENT, EXERCISE, AEROBICS, SPORTS, AND WEIGHT TRAINING

Any of these activities can be quite helpful when you are ready for them. Their benefits include improving your physical well-being and increasing your strength, stamina and agility. You will enhance your self-esteem through improving your body image and deriving a sense of what you can accomplish. And regular exercise will simply make you feel better. (Expect that physical activity will also bring up emotions. If you have felt badly about your body, you will have feelings about using it and displaying it. Don't let that discourage you; feel the feelings and keep going. It is the same as other areas of recovery; it gives an opportunity to work through the sad and frightening emotions to the joy that is on the other side.) As with any other activity, these programs are most beneficial when they are done sensibly. Make certain that you choose one that is reasonable—don't allow yourself to take on too much (setting yourself up for injury and failure) or allow yourself to become an "exercise junkie" (engaging in the activity to numb out feelings or to keep you from living a full and varied life). Try to select an activity that is done in the company of others, rather than alone, so that you add another social dimension to your life. When they are well chosen and kept in perspective, physical activities are of tremendous value in recovery.

OTHER BODY WORK

This list is by no means exhaustive. There are many methods of healing and treating the body, some traditional and others new. I am an expert on none of them, and have only mentioned those I have because they have been recommended to me by incest survivors. Please investigate them (and any others) as carefully as you can. Share the information, both positive and negative, with others. Let me know what you find out.

Prayer, Meditation, and Spirituality

This is a tricky area. Americans consider religion, like family, to be a private and personal matter. We have institutionalized noninterference with religious beliefs and practices and have passed laws to insure freedom of religious expression. It is not my purpose here to champion or attack religious beliefs. Just as I am not an expert on body work, I don't pretend to offer expertise on the specifics of any religion or spiritual path. I have had some people tell me that their religious (or spiritual) beliefs and practices are all that enabled them to survive the abuse. Others have told stories of abusive religious institutions, beliefs, and attitudes that have added to their hurts and interfered with their recovery. I have no doubt that all of these experiences and perspectives are true. What I suggest is that you examine your spiritual needs with the same care that you use to approach other areas of your life. They are certainly as important.

Attitudes and practices vary widely among religious traditions and within specific religions. Religious doctrine is open to a wide range of interpretation. Scriptures can be found and quoted to support virtually any position. It will be important for you to examine the teachings of your faith (or of a belief system that you are considering for yourself). Find out whether they are protective of children or consider a child to be his or her parents' property. What are the attitudes toward sex and sexuality? Do the teachings encourage positive self-esteem or are they rooted in guilt and shame? Are they rigid or flexible? Are individuals required to submit unquestioningly to the will of one authoritarian leader, or is there room for individual choice and decision making? Is there a sense of warm, caring community? Does it encourage contact outside the group or try to limit your contacts to the group members? Is there room for you to be yourself—and to grow as an individual? In short, *be wary of any religion or community that resembles your abusive childhood*. Your faith can be a powerful healing force or a means of perpetuating your hurts. One man's salvation may be another's hell.

As difficult as it is to question your basic religious beliefs and practices, it is important to do so. While some of my clients have said that their religious or spiritual beliefs have been the most important aspect of their survival and recovery, others have found it necessary to abandon their childhood religion in order to leave the abuse behind. Some have adopted other religious traditions and spiritual practices (Eastern as well as Western), created their own belief systems, or chosen a purely secular lifestyle.

I don't advocate any specific religious or secular path. This is a profoundly personal decision. I do, however, strongly believe that no incest survivor (or anyone else) should spend another minute in an abusive or exploitive situation—including those which cloak themselves in the mantle of religion. There are good, caring people in all religions and good, caring people who hold no specific religious beliefs. And there are hurtful, destructive individuals in any environment—religious and secular. It isn't necessary to be "a religious person" in order to recover, but it *is* vital to be in a situation where you are treated with respect and consideration. If your religious system doesn't provide this, you should question what you are getting out of it. If it does, it can be a powerful aspect of your recovery.

PRAYER

There are probably as many forms and definitions of prayer as there are religions. Prayers can be highly structured formulas, involving requests, questions or giving thanks to a specific Supreme Being, or a nonspecific pouring out of thoughts and feelings into the Universe. Prayers can be expressed silently or aloud, alone or in the company of others. There are those who view artistic expression, music, or good deeds as forms of prayer. Some incest survivors report that prayer provides them with feelings of calm, comfort and connection with a strength that goes beyond themselves. It offers them a perspective beyond the abuse.

MEDITATION

Like prayer, there are many forms of meditation, ranging from the deeply religious to the purely secular. Some define it as communication with God or forces of the Universe; others see meditation as a pleasant means of relaxation or self-examination. Some people contend that prayer and meditation are simply different names for the same phenomenon. As is true of prayer, meditation can provide benefits on a physical and emotional level. When one meditates, there is a focusing of attention that results in a measurable "relaxation response." It is possible to slow the pulse and lower blood pressure through meditation. The practice of meditation can be a highly structured, formal undertaking, involving sitting in one position and/or chanting for hours on end—or it can be as simple as sitting on a river bank and watching the water flow. For those who practice it, meditation can be a way of slowing down, "getting in touch with" themselves, and treating themselves kindly.

ASCETIC PRACTICES

I would urge you to be extremely careful about entering into any program or practice that involves sensory deprivation, punishment, prolonged fasting, pain, shame, or humiliation. Whatever their rationale, they are likely to be based on distress, and by confirming all the negative self-image of the abused child will end up re-creating an abusive environment. You have had more than enough pain and deprivation in your life. It's time for celebration.

Hypnosis is a powerful tool which, like any tool, can be extremely useful when used correctly. Also like any tool, its misuse carries the potential of harm. In hypnosis, you are dealing with areas of the mind that are not usually accessible to direct communication. This part of what is commonly called the "unconscious" operates through imagery and metaphor. Like meditation, prayer, and guided imagery, hypnosis can be employed effectively for relaxation and stress reduction. It has been successfully used as an aid in habit control, dealing with fears and phobias, and control of pain. In my clinical practice I have used hypnosis to help women reduce pain and anxiety associated with childbirth and to help people deal with anxiety attacks, sexual dysfunction, and fear (of dentists, public speaking, interviews, airplanes, and lightning).

Hypnosis

The area where I am most hesitant to use hypnosis, however (particularly with incest survivors), is in attempting to recover memories of abuse. My thinking about it is twofold. First, memories are blocked for a reason. They are hidden in order to enable the individual to survive a traumatic situation. I have found that, when the proper degree of safety and distance from the abuse have been achieved, the memories tend to present themselves. I question the benefits of dragging out memories before you are ready to deal with them. Second, I don't think it makes sense to set recovery of specific abuse memories as the primary goal. Doing this gives the misleading impression that if you recover the memories everything will be all right. If you adopt this mistaken notion, you will be deeply disappointed when you discover that there is still much work to be done after the memories are in place. As I have stated earlier, you can do powerful recovery work in the absence of any specific childhood memories.

If, however, you choose to do hypnosis work around incest issues, make sure that you find the right person for the job. We are not talking about parlor games here. The hypnotist (or hypnotherapist) should be professionally trained in psychotherapy so that he is prepared to help you deal with whatever issues and feelings are brought up. She should, in addition, have had some direct experience in working with abuse issues. All of the considerations that I discussed about selecting an individual therapist apply to your choice of hypnotherapist. If you already have an individual therapist, make sure you discuss it with him fully, and if you go to someone else for hypnosis, insist that he speak with your therapist directly. Be clear about what you want to accomplish, and remain in charge of your program. If at any point you feel that you wish to end the process, feel free to do so. Remember that you don't have to answer to anyone for the way you structure your recovery. You are doing this for yourself.

Organizations

Each week I learn about more services for survivors in various parts of the country. I have had personal interaction with some; some have been recommended to me; and I have no direct knowledge of others. Inclusion in this list does not constitute my endorsement of a particular program or service. And no matter how wonderful a program or organization is, it may not be the right one for you at this particular point in your recovery. You can explore this list of resources (carefully, I hope) to determine what will be useful to you. I'd like to thank Dan Sexton of the Survivors of Childhood Abuse Program for his cooperation and assistance in putting this list together.

Adults Molested as Children United, P.O. Box 952, San Jose, CA 95108, (408) 280-5055. This program focuses on treatment that incorporates "guided self-help." AMACU is part of the **Parents United**, a nationwide support organization for incestuous families. There are wide differences among individual chapters, so be sure to investigate carefully to make sure that your needs are met. Some chapters stress forgiveness and family unity as primary goals, not providing survivors with sufficient support in expressing their anger or confronting perpetrators. Some survivors have reported that certain chapters fail to provide adequately trained leaders, maintain appropriate boundaries between counselors and clients, and/or show evidence of homophobia. Other survivors have found the program beneficial as it offers the opportunity to directly confront and work with the perpetrators.

Alcoholics Anonymous (AA), Al-Anon, Adult Children of Alcoholics (ACOA), Overeaters Anonymous (OA), Sex and Love Addicts Anonymous (SLAA), Gamblers Anonymous, Debtors Anonymous, Spenders Anonymous, and, of course, the relatively new **Incest Survivors Anonymous (ISA)**, P.O. Box 5613, Long Beach, CA 90805, (213) 428-5599. These are national organizations whose local chapters should be listed in your telephone directory. If you have trouble locating them, call your local newspaper, hospital social service department, library, community service agency, high school guidance counselor, or any mental health professional. These organizations provide local meetings, outreach and other community activities. As the names suggest, membership is confidential. There are no dues or membership fees. These self-help groups are self-supporting and have proven enormously helpful for many people. Free information pamphlets are available.

C. Henry Kempe National Center for the Prevention and Treatment of Child Abuse and Neglect, 1205 Oneida Street, Denver, CO 80220, (303) 321-3963. An agency that focuses on child abuse treatment, training, and research.

Forensic Mental Health Associates, A. Nicholas Groth, Ph.D., Director, RR#1, Box 404, Lakeside Beach, Webster, MA 01570, (617) 943-2381. A source of printed information and professional training.

Harborview Sexual Assault Center, 325 9th, Seattle, WA, (206) 223-3047.

Healing Hearts, P.O. Box 6274, Albany, CA 94706, (415) 465-3890. Established for the benefit of adult survivors of ritual abuse, this organization is committed to the development of healing-oriented information services.

Incest Recovery Association, 6200 North Central Expressway, Suite 209, Dallas, TX 75206, (214) 373-6607. Mental health professionals engaged in incest recovery and education. I.R.A. provides groups for male and female survivors, public education, and professional training. It offers some simple, helpful brochures and a newsletter.

Incest Resources, Inc., Cambridge Women's Center, 46 Pleasant Street, Cambridge, MA 02139, (617) 354-8807. A non-profit organization founded in 1980 which provides educational and resource material for female and male survivors and for professionals working with survivors.

Incest Survivors Resource Network International, P.O. Box 911, Hicksville, NY 11802, (516) 935-3031. ISRNI provides educational resources through participation in national and international conferences and committees.

International Society for the Study of Multiple Personality and Dissociation (ISSMP&D), 5700 Old Orchard Road, Skokie, IL 60077, (708) 966-4322. Books and literature are available upon written request.

Looking Up, P.O. Box K, Augusta, ME 04330, (207) 626-3402. For nonoffending survivors only, Looking Up provides movement workshops, conferences, wilderness trips and training designed to "promote independence, build trust and help in reclaiming of [the] body's energy and strength." Looking Up publishes a newsletter and does public education, lobbying, professional training, and consultation.

National Association for Children of Alcoholics (NACOA), 31706 Coast Highway #301, South Laguna, CA 92677, (714) 299-3889. Provides literature, referrals, and networking for children of alcoholics.

National Clearinghouse for Alcohol Information, 1776 East Jefferson Street, Rockville, MD 20852, (301) 468-2600. Publications providing information about alcohol, drug, and prescription drug abuse.

National Coalition Against Sexual Assault (NCASA), 8787 State Street, East St. Louis, IL 62203, (618) 398-7764. NCASA is a coalition of professionals who provide services for all victims of violence.

National Cocaine Hotline, (800) 638-8682. Referrals to resources in the caller's area.

National Council on Alcoholism, 12 West 21st Street, 7th Floor, New York, NY 10010, (212) 206-6770.

National Gay Task Force Crisis Line, (800) 221-7044. Victim assistance and incident reporting for acts of anti-gay and anti-lesbian violence. The Crisis Line offers counseling to gay and lesbian youth, their families and friends, referrals to support groups and AIDS information. (Hotline hours are 3:00–9:00 p.m., Eastern Standard Time.)

National Organization for Victims Assistance (NOVA), 717 D Street, N.W., Washington, DC, 20004, (202) 393-6682. This agency focuses on victims of violent crimes and offers a 24-hour information line.

National Self-Help Clearinghouse, Graduate School, City University of New York, 33 West 42nd Street, Room 1222, New York, NY 10036, (212) 840-1259. Provides listings of self-help groups throughout the country.

Parents Anonymous, 6733 S. Sepulveda Boulevard, #270, Los Angeles, CA 90045, (213) 419-9732. Has a national hotline and local self-help groups throughout the country for abusive and potentially abusive parents.

P.L.E.A., 356 West Zia Road, Santa Fe, NM 87505, (505) 982-9184. Hank Estrada, Director. An organization of professionals and non-professionals, P.L.E.A. (Prevention, Leadership, Education, Assistance) addresses itself specifically to the concerns of non–offending male incest survivors. P.L.E.A. publishes a quarterly newsletter of articles by survivors, recommended readings and resource lists; $20.00/4 issues.

The Safer Society Program, Shoreham Depot Road, RR1, Box 24-B, Orwell, VT 05760, (802) 897-7541. A national project of the New

York State Council of Churches, The Safer Society Program maintains national lists of agencies, institutions, and individuals providing specialized assessment and treatment for youthful and adult sexual victims and offenders. It publishes papers, surveys, and pamphlets on these programs as well as on prevention issues, and networks among professionals serving victim and offender populations.

Secular Sobriety Groups, P.O. Box 15781, North Hollywood, CA 91615, (818) 980-8851. These groups offer a secular alternative for those who do not wish to rely on a "higher power."

Sunny Von Bulow National Advocacy Center (NVAC), 307 W. 7th Street, #1001, Fort Worth, TX 76102, (817) 877-3355. For victims of violence.

Survivors of Childhood Abuse Program (S.C.A.P.), 1345 El Centro Avenue, P.O. Box 630, Hollywood, CA 90028. Begun in April, 1987, S.C.A.P. is concerned with research, treatment, training, consultation, public education, development of a national network of professional and technical resources, and advocacy on behalf of survivors of incestuous and other dysfunctional family systems. They provide crisis intervention, information and referrals through the National Child Abuse Hotline, 1-800-422-4453.

Survivors of Incest Anonymous, World Service Office, P.O. Box 21817, Baltimore, MD 21222, (301) 282-3400. Recently merged with **Sexual Abuse Anonymous (SAA)**, of St. Cloud, MN.

VOICES in Action, Inc., P.O. Box 148309, Chicago IL 60614, (312) 327-1500. (Long-distance calls are returned collect.) An acronym for Victims Of Incest Can Emerge Survivors. VOICES is a national network of male and female survivors and "prosurvivors" (people who support and encourage survivors in their recovery). It has local groups and contacts throughout the country, and offers a free referral service that provides listings of therapists, agencies, and self-help groups that have been recommended by other survivors. Membership benefits include a "survival packet" of resource material which includes information for male survivors. They also offer members a newsletter, an annual conference, and training for group leaders. VOICES offers over a hundred confidential special interest groups, allowing for correspondence among survivors who experienced particular kinds of abuse.

Newsletters

For Crying Out Loud, c/o Cambridge Women's Center, 46 Pleasant Street, Cambridge, MA 02139. Although this newsletter is written by and for women with histories of sexual abuse, the information that it contains is relevant and helpful for male survivors.

Incest Survivors Information Exchange (ISIE), P.O. Box 3399, New Haven, CT 06515. This newsletter provides a forum for female and male survivors of incest to share their thoughts, ideas, information, poetry, writings, and art work. Published by female survivors.

The "Looking Up" Times, RFD #1 Box 2620, Mt. Vernon, ME 04352, (207) 293-2750. A newsletter for survivors of sexual abuse.

The Newsletter. Published by VOICES in Action, this newsletter for adult male and female incest survivors is provided as part of the annual $35 membership fee. The Newsletter provides information, resources, book reviews, and writings by and for survivors. It is expanding to include more attention to issues of male survivors. (See VOICES listing for address.)

Parents United Newsletter, P.O. Box 952, San Jose, CA 95108, (408) 280-5055.

Survivors Network Newsletter, c/o Crawford, 18653 Ventura Boulevard #143, Tarzana, CA 91356. Information, resource location and education for adult survivors of childhood abuse and neglect.

Books, Articles, and Pamphlets

This bibliography includes writings that may be of interest and help to the adult male incest survivor. I have included works written specifically for male survivors (there are few such works in existence) and also for female survivors (these are seldom foreign to the concerns of male survivors). Also included are works that are not specifically concerned with incest, but have been helpful to survivors in their recovery. I have not included a great deal of research-oriented, academic, or professional material, as this book is aimed at the nonprofessional. Those readers who wish to pursue the professional literature might begin with the *Male Sexual Abuse Bibliography,* prepared by Peter T. Dimock, ACSW, 1656 Laurel Avenue, St. Paul, MN 55104, (612) 644-1521 or the *Journal of Interpersonal Violence,* Sage Publications, Inc., P.O. Box 5084, Newbury Park, CA 91359.

ON THE TOPIC OF INCEST

Adults Molested as Children: A Survivor's Manual for Women & Men, by Euan Bear with Peter T. Dimock, Safer Society Press, Orwell, VT, 1988. A simple, straightforward manual written by a survivor to help other survivors understand "what they are going through now as a result of what they went through then."

The Best Kept Secret: Sexual Abuse of Children, by Florence Rush, Prentice-Hall, Englewood Cliffs, NJ, 1980. A historical and feminist treatment of sexual child abuse.

Betrayal of Innocence: Incest and Its Devastation, by Susan Forward and Craig Buck, Penguin Books, New York, NY, 1978.

By Silence Betrayed: Sexual Abuse of Children in America, by John Crewdson, Boston, MA, Little, Brown, 1988.

Circle of Hope, by Perry Tilleras, Hazelden, 1990. Stories of AIDS, addiction, and recovery.

Conspiracy of Silence: The Trauma of Incest, by Sandra Butler, Volcano Press, San Francisco, CA, 1978, updated 1985. An excellent feminist analysis of sexual child abuse.

The Courage to Heal: A Guide for Women Survivors of Child Sexual Abuse, by Ellen Bass and Laura Davis, Harper & Row, New York, NY, 1988. (Audio version available from Caedmon, a subsidiary of Harper & Row, Publishers.) This is the big one! *The Courage to Heal* is an encyclopedic volume that lovingly explores all aspects of the healing process. Although directed toward female survivors, you will find that most of it speaks directly and profoundly to your experience. Just change the pronouns. This landmark work is destined to become a classic in the field.

The Courage to Heal Workbook: For Women and Men Survivors of Child Sexual Abuse, by Laura Davis, Harper & Row, New York, NY, 1990. Combining checklists and open-ended questions, this innovative and in-depth workbook is designed for use by women and men, individually or as the basis for working in therapy or in groups.

The Dark Side of Families: Current Family Violence Research, edited by David Finkelhor et al., Sage Publications, Newbury Park, CA 1983.

"Deadly Silence," by Rachel Adelson, *The Village Voice,* New York, December 22, 1987, pp. 33–35.

The Drama of the Gifted Child: The Search for the True Self, by Alice Miller, Basic Books, New York, NY, 1981. (Originally published as *Prisoners of Childhood.*)

Father-Daughter Incest, by Judith Lewis Herman, Harvard University Press, Cambridge, MA, 1981. Judith Herman, M.D., is a Boston-area psychiatrist. Her approach is both clinical and strongly political (feminist). The information can be generalized beyond the scope of father-daughter incest.

For Your Own Good: Hidden Cruelty in Child-Rearing and the Roots of Violence, by Alice Miller, Farrar, Straus, & Giroux, New York, NY, 1983.

"Group Treatment for Those Involved with Incest," by David G. Zimpfer, *Journal for Specialists in Group Work*, November, 1987, pp. 166–177.

I Know Why the Caged Bird Sings, by Maya Angelou, Random House, New York, NY, 1970. Moving and life-affirming autobiography by a brilliant writer who is also an incest survivor.

Incest: A Family Pattern, by Jean Renvoize, Routledge & Kegan Paul, London, 1982. Jean Renvoize was a member of the British Association for the Study and Prevention of Child Abuse and Neglect, Subcommittee on Child Sexual Abuse. The book is a thoughtful treatment of the subject of incest in a family context.

Incest and Sexuality: A Guide to Understanding and Healing, by Wendy Maltz and Beverly Holman, Lexington Books, Lexington, MA, 1987. Drawing examples from work with teenagers and adults, the authors provide an excellent resource for understanding and solving sexual difficulties. They offer a brief section about male survivors.

Incest: When Boys Are Victims (brochure). Available from Looking Up, P.O. Box K, Augusta, ME 04330.

I Never Told Anyone: Writings By Women Survivors of Child Sexual Abuse, edited by Ellen Bass and Louise Thornton, Harper & Row, New York, NY, 1983. This is a moving compilation of women's personal accounts of sexual child abuse.

Kiss Daddy Goodnight: A Speakout on Incest, by Louise Armstrong, Hawthorn, New York, NY, 1978; *Kiss Daddy Goodnight: Ten Years Later,* Pocket Books, New York, NY 1987.

"Male Child Sexual Abuse: The Best Kept Secret," by E. Tick, *Voices,* Fall 1984.

A Male Grief: Notes on Pornography and Addiction, by David Mura, Milkweed Editions, P.O. Box 3226, Minneapolis, MN 55403, 1987. An important, insightful, and moving essay connecting child abuse and adult addiction to pornography.

Men Surviving Incest, by T. Thomas, Launch Press, Walnut Creek, CA, 1989. A male survivor shares the process of recovery.

My Father's House: A Memoir of Incest and of Healing, by Sylvia Fraser, Ticknor & Fields, New York, NY, 1988. Paperback edition published by Harper & Row, New York, NY, 1989.

Outgrowing the Pain: A Book For and About Adults Abused as Children, by Eliana Gil, Launch Press, San Francisco, CA, 1983, or Dell, New York, NY, 1983. A simple, easy-to-read little book about recovery from all types of abuse.

"The Pro-Incest Lobby" by Benjamin Demott, *Psychology Today,* March, 1980.

Recovery, by Helen Benedict, Doubleday & Co., Garden City, NY, 1985.

Recovery for Male Victims of Child Abuse: An Interview with Hank Estrada, Incest Survivor. To purchase a copy, send $6.50 to Red Rabbit Press, 356 West Zia Road, Santa Fe, NM 87505.

The Secret Trauma: Incest in the Lives of Girls and Women, by Diana E. H. Russell, Basic Books, New York, NY, 1986. This academic work provides statistics on the incidence and effects of incestuous abuse of female children.

The Sexual Healing Journey, by Wendy Maltz, HarperCollins, New York, NY, 1991. This is an excellent work on healing the sexual hurts of sexual child abuse.

The Silent Children: A Parent's Guide to the Prevention of Child Sexual Abuse, by Linda T. Sanford, McGraw-Hill Paper Backs, New York, NY, 1980.

A Sourcebook on Child Sexual Abuse, edited by David Finkelhor, et. al., Sage Publications, Newbury Park, CA, 1986.

"Suffering in Silence: The Male Incest Victim," by M. Nasjleti, *Child Welfare,* 1980.

Survivor's Guide, Survivors of Childhood Abuse Program, Childhelp USA, 6463 Independence Avenue, Woodland Hills, CA 91367, (800) 422-4453. This 32-page pamphlet ($4.00) is chock full of information and resources for survivors. (Also available in Braille and cassette versions.)

Thou Shalt Not Be Aware: Society's Betrayal of the Child, by Alice Miller, New American Library, New York, NY, 1984. A reassessment of Freud's Oedipal Theory by a brilliant and humane psychoanalyst. *Thou Shalt Not Be Aware* emphasizes the reality of sexual child abuse.

Treatment of Adult Survivors of Childhood Abuse, by Eliana Gil, Launch Press, Walnut Creek, CA, 1988.

Treating the Young Male Victim of Sexual Assault, by Eugene Porter, Safer Society Press, Syracuse, NY, 1986. A short, straightforward book, primarily directed toward clinicians.

United We Stand: A Book for People with Multiple Personalities, by Eliana Gil, Launch Press, Walnut Creek, CA, 1990.

"What No One Wants to Know," by Celia Dwyer, *Matrix Women's News Magazine,* 108 Locust Street, Santa Cruz, CA 95060, 1991. Article on female perpetrated child sexual abuse.

Why Me? Help for Victims of Child Sexual Abuse, by Lynn B. Daugherty, Mother Courage Press, Racine, WI, 1984. A short, simply written book that contains useful information for survivors.

ON RELATED TOPICS OF INTEREST TO SURVIVORS

Adult Children of Alcoholics, by Janet Woititz, Health Communications, Inc., Pompano Beach, FL, 1983.

Childhood Comes First: A Crash Course in Childhood for Adults, by Ray E. Helfer, Kempe National Center, Denver, CO, 1978. For help in learning to communicate with your "child within."

Feeling Good, by David D. Burns, New American Library, New York, NY, 1980. In a practical, down-to-earth style, Dr. Burns provides a program for overcoming depression and other life problems.

Healing the Shame that Binds You, by John Bradshaw, Health Communications, Pompano Beach, FL, 1988.

"It Will Never Happen to Me!", by Claudia Black, Ballantine Books, New York, NY, 1981. For adult children of alcoholics and other dysfunctional families.

Learning to Live Without Violence: A Handbook for Men, by Daniel Jay Sonkin and Michael Durphy, Volcano Press, San Francisco, CA, 1985.

Love, Medicine and Miracles, by Bernie S. Siegel, Harper & Row, New York, NY, 1986. An important book about self-healing and recovery by an exceptional surgeon.

Struggle for Intimacy, by Janet Woititz, Health Communications, Inc., Pompano Beach, FL, 1985. Although written for adult children of alcoholics, many incest survivors have gained insight and help from this book.

Touching: The Human Significance of the Skin, by Ashley Montagu, New York, NY, 1971.

Unspeakable Acts: The True Story of One Community's Nightmare, by Jan Hollingsworth, Congdon & Weed, New York, NY, 1988. Ritual abuse.

When Bad Things Happen to Good People, by Harold S. Kushner, Avon Books, New York, NY, 1983. This book, by a rabbi, speaks to all who experience trauma and loss.

Breaking Silence, a 56-minute color documentary film (16mm and VHS) on incest and sexual abuse of children, available from Future Educational Films, 1628 Union Street, San Francisco, CA, 94123, or Film Distribution Center, 13500 NE 124th Street, Suite 2, Kirkland, WA 98034, (206) 820-2592.

Partners in Healing: Couples Overcoming the Sexual Repercussions of Incest, a 43-minute videotape made by Wendy Maltz, co-author of *Incest and Sexuality.* Available from Independent Video Services, 401 East 10th Avenue, Suite 160, Eugene, OR 97401, (503) 345-3455.

Surviving Sexual Abuse, a dramatic 27-minute videotape in which four people talk about their experiences of being sexually abused and surviving the trauma. Information available from Dialogs, Inc., 865 Conger Street, Suite 6, Eugene, OR 97402.

"I Will Stand Fast," poignant, supportive, wonderful music by Fred Small. Available from Flying Fish Records, 1304 West Schubert, Chicago, IL 60614.

"Survivor," a joyous and life-affirming audio cassette by Nancy Day. To purchase send $11.50 to Nancy Day, P.O. Box 8371, Pittsburgh, PA 15218, (412) 795-3375.

There are many techniques and resources available to aid you in your recovery. It is important that each of us explore possibilities and decide on the combination that works best. Any activity has the potential of being helpful or harmful, well-used or abusive, liberating or addictive. Nobody has all the answers; no method is perfect. A primary part of recovery is learning to trust your own judgment while respecting your ability (and your right) to seek out your own best allies and the most helpful solutions. Many others have walked this path before you. You don't have to go it alone, and you don't need to reinvent the wheel. But you do have to exercise judgment and care. Whether we are talking about therapy, religion, body work, sports, social activity, hobbies, career, community, family, friends, recovery programs, books, films, local or national organizations, tailor the available resources to meet your particular needs. It may be more difficult than accepting someone else's package, but the results will be far more satisfying.

A Final Word

This section is very brief and contains nothing new. I've said it all in other parts of the book—but some things bear repeating.

I want to send you a personal message. I want you to complete this book hearing reassurance, encouragement, admiration and love. You have embarked on a voyage across troubled waters to the other side of your hurt. Your pain will end and you will heal. Recovery is real.

You once had to do it alone, but things are different now. Every day more men and women join you as friends, helpers, and allies. Support, resources, and hope for the future are genuine—and they are available to you. Take full advantage of them. You, in the full richness of your humanity, deserve all the abundance that life has to offer. Continue to cherish yourself.

As you, and your brother and sister survivors, continue to heal the wounds of the past, as you maintain your progress toward full recovery of your power and humanity, and as you confront your own abuse history and stand up against abuse everywhere—you are changing the world.

My love to you.

Index

Abuse
    commonality of experience, 14–
        15, 38–39, 91
    as core of sexual child abuse, 60
    defining, 11–16
    as masculine attribute, 43–45
    patterns of, 20–24
    and power, 60–61
    reality and incidence of, 13
    sexual child, *see* Sexual child
        abuse
    by survivor, 72, 131, 280, 286
    variations in experience of, 14–
        15
    victim's enjoyment of, 132–133
Abusers, *see* Perpetrators
Abusive environment: avoiding in
        therapy, 195–196
Abusive family: definitional
        problems, 12–14
Abusive relationships: of
        survivors, 131, 280, 286
Acting out: by sexually abused
        children, 72
Acupuncture therapy, 301–302
Addictive behavior
    sexual compulsiveness, 111,
        129
    in victims, 109–111
Adolescents
    promiscuity/prostitution of,
        129, 264
    recovery groups for, 225–226
    sexual stereotypes taught to, 49
Adult survivor, *see* Survivors
Adults Molested as Children
        United, 306
Advertising: and stereotypes, 33–
        34
Advocacy, 269
Aerobics therapy, 302
Age
    to recall abuse safely, 102
    of recovery group members,
        225–226
AIDS: incest-related, xvi

Alcoholics
    counseling for, 193
    reality perception of children
        of, 128–129
    recovery by, 141
    recovery organizations for,
        306–310
    two-survivor relationships of
        children of, 133–134
    victims as, 109, 110
Alcoholics Anonymous (AA),
        219, 306–307
All-or-nothing thinking, 119
Altruistic activity, 267–271
Amnesia: as survival strategy, 69,
        98–104
Anger
    as expression of power, 50
    and recovery, 142, 282–284
    and revenge against
        perpetrator, 257–258
    survivor's fear of own, 152–153
    true vs. dramatized, 50
Anthropology: culture and
        personality schools of, 40
Ascetic practices: in recovery,
        304–305
Asexual victims and survivors,
        54–55, 56
Associations for survivors, 306–
        310
Assumed identities of survivors,
        92–93
Athletic compulsiveness: of
        survivors, 121, 122
Attractiveness: survivor's fear of
        own, 122

Bass, Ellen, xxii, 136, 139
Believe the Children, 307
Betrayal, sense of: in exposure of
        secrecy of sexual abuse,
        150, 156
Bisexual victims and survivors of
        sexual child abuse, 54–55
Black, Claudia, 128

Blame: survivor casting, 284
Blocking: memories of sexual
        child abuse, 100–101
Body building
    and perfectionism, 121, 122
    as therapy, 302
Body control
    loss of, in sexual child abuse
        victim, 70–71
    regaining, in recovery, 135–
        136, 204–205
    and touching in counseling,
        204–205
Body work
    evaluating, 298–300
    for recovery, 298–302
    types of, 300–302
Book resources: for survivors,
        310–314
Boston Associates to Stop
        Therapist Abuse
        (BASTA), 307
Boys, *see* Children; Sexual child
        abuse; Victims
Bryant, Lynne Lamb, 231
Bulimia, 121, 122

C. Henry Kempe National
        Center, 307
Caring: misequated with sex,
        127–128, 136, 185
Catalyst: for recalling sexual child
        abuse, 103–104
Chemical addictions: in victims,
        109
Child abuse
    defining, 11–16
    sexual, *see* Sexual child abuse
Child care programs, 265
Child pornography, 263–264
Child victims and survivors, *see*
        Survivors; Victims
Childhood
    loss of, in sexual abuse, 67–77
    loss of memory of, 69, 98–104
    myths about, 67–68

About
the Author

Mike Lew, M.Ed., a psychotherapist, trained cultural anthropologist, and group therapy leader, is co-director of The Next Step Counseling and Training Center in Newton Centre, Massachusetts. A leading expert on recovery from child sexual abuse, particularly issues surrounding adult male survivors, he gives public lectures, professional training, and workshops for survivors nationwide.